Talk-in-Interaction: Multilingual Perspectives

Pragmatics & Interaction

Editor
Gabriele Kasper

PRAGMATICS & INTERACTION, a refereed series sponsored by the University of Hawai‘i National Foreign Language Resource Center, publishes research on topics in pragmatics and discourse as social interaction from a wide variety of theoretical and methodological perspectives. P&I welcomes particularly studies on languages spoken in the Asian-Pacific region.

Talk-in-Interaction: Multilingual Perspectives

edited by
Hanh thi Nguyen
& Gabriele Kasper

NATIONAL FOREIGN LANGUAGE RESOURCE CENTER
University of Hawai'i at Mānoa

The contents of this publication were developed in part under a grant from the U.S. Department of Education (CFDA 84.229, P229A060002). However, the contents do not necessarily represent the policy of the Department of Education, and one should not assume endorsement by the Federal Government.

ISBN (10) 0–9800459–1–6
ISBN (13) 978–0–9800459–1–8
Library of Congress Control Number: 2009924739

The paper used in this publication meets the minimum requirements of the American National Standard for Information Sciences–Permanence of Paper for Printed Library Materials.
ANSI Z39.48–1984

book design by Deborah Masterson

distributed by
National Foreign Language Resource Center
University of Hawai'i
1859 East-West Road #106
Honolulu HI 96822–2322
nflrc.hawaii.edu

Contents

About the Authors

Jack Bilmes (PhD, Stanford University) is a professor of anthropology at the University of Hawai'i at Mānoa. He has done fieldwork in Northern Thailand and the U.S. Federal Trade Commission. He is the author of *Discourse and Behavior* and of articles on various subjects, including microanalysis of verbal interaction, narrative, formulation, public policy, social theory, and Thai interaction and social organization. bilmes@hawaii.edu

Marta González-Lloret (PhD, University of Hawai'i) is an assistant professor of Spanish at the University of Hawai'i at Mānoa. Her research interests include computer-assisted language learning, second language learning and teaching, conversation analysis, and intercultural communication. marta@hawaii.edu

Eric Hauser (PhD, University of Hawai'i) is an associate professor of English at the University of Electro-Communications in Tokyo, Japan. His research focuses on conversational interaction, in particular, interaction that occurs within English language classrooms and similar settings. This research has involved such matters as the organization of language correction from the perspective of participants, facework during conversations conducted for the purpose of language learning, and participant orientation to and construction of classroom context. hauser@bunka.uec.ac.jp

Christina Higgins (PhD, University of Wisconsin-Madison) is an assistant professor of Second Language Studies at the University of Hawai'i at Mānoa, where she teaches graduate courses in sociolinguistics, interpretive qualitative research, and global English. She researches language ideology and social identity in multilingual and multicultural discourse from a variety of qualitative and interpretive perspectives. In addition to her doctoral research on Swahili-English bilingualism among Tanzanian journalists, she has researched the use of language varieties in Tanzanian hip hop, the identities of L2 Swahili speakers living in Tanzania, and cross-cultural communication in HIV/AIDS education events sponsored by nongovernmental organizations. cmhiggin@hawaii.edu

Keiko Ikeda (PhD, University of Hawai'i) is an associate professor in the Division of International Affairs, Kansai University, Japan. Her primary research interests are sociolinguistics, pragmatics, and the L2 classroom from a conversation-analytic perspective. keikoike@ipcku.kansai-u.ac.jp

Midori Ishida is a PhD candidate in the Department of Second Language Studies at the University of Hawai'i at Mānoa. Her research interests include second language pragmatic development and the roles of interaction in second language acquisition. Her study on the effects of recasts on the acquisition of Japanese aspect was published in *Language Learning*. She is currently conducting research on the development of interactional competence in Japanese as a second language during study abroad from a conversation-analytic perspective. mfurukaw@hawaii.edu

Gabriele Kasper (Dr. phil., Ruhr-Universität Bochum, Germany) is a professor of Second Language Studies at the University of Hawai'i at Mānoa. She has published on various topics in second language pragmatics and research methodology. Her current research revisits some of these earlier themes from the perspectives of conversation analysis and related discursive approaches. gkasper@hawaii.edu

Younhee Kim is a PhD candidate in the Department of Second Language Studies at the University of Hawai'i at Mānoa. Her research interests include interlanguage pragmatics, conversation analysis as an approach to second language acquisition, and the marking of epistemic stance in second language conversation. She has published in *System* and coauthored a book chapter in *Language Learning and Teaching as Social Inter-action* (Palgrave Macmillan, 2007). younheek@gmail.com

Hanh thi Nguyen (PhD, University of Wisconsin-Madison) is an assistant professor at Hawai'i Pacific University. Her research interests include the development of interactional competence in a second or professional language, classroom discourse, and Vietnamese applied linguistics. htnguyen@hawaii.edu

John Rylander is an assistant professor at Kansai Gaidai University in Osaka, Japan. His research interests are in conversation analysis, the instruction and learner development of interlanguage pragmatics, and group dynamics in the language classroom. rylander@hawaii.edu

Scott Saft (PhD, University of Hawai'i) has taught linguistics, English, and Japanese at various institutions in Japan and the United States. He is currently working at the University of Hawai'i at Hilo. His research focuses on the analysis of Japanese conversation in institutional settings, including faculty meetings, media broadcasts, and medical institutions. His work has been published in journals such as *Language in Society*, *Research on Language* *and Social Interaction*, *Journal of Pragmatics*, and *Discourse & Society*. saft@hawaii.edu

Asuka Suzuki is a PhD candidate in Japanese Linguistics in the Department of East Asian Languages and Literatures at the University of Hawai'i at Mānoa. Her current research interests include conversation analysis, linguistic anthropology, and Japanese pedagogy. She is working on her dissertation on laughter in Japanese multiparty interaction by applying conversation analysis. asuzuki@hawaii.edu

Steven Talmy (PhD, University of Hawai'i) is an assistant professor in the Department of Language and Literacy Education at the University of British Columbia. His research interests include critical analyses of discourse, sociolinguistics, K–12 ESL, the sociology of ESL education, and qualitative research. steven.talmy@ubc.ca

Acknowledgements

We are grateful to the following external reviewers for their insightful comments on the chapters in this volume:

Donald Carroll, *Shikoku Gakuin University*

Dennis Day, *University of Southern Denmark*

Thanh-Ha thi Do, *Vietnam National University*

Nick Enfield, *Max Planck Institute for Psycholinguistics*

Chie Fukuda, *University of Hawai'i at Mānoa*

Joseph Gafaranga, *The University of Edinburgh*

Angela Cora Garcia, *Bentley College*

Andrea Golato, *University of Illinois at Urbana-Champaign*

Makoto Hayashi, *University of Illinois at Urbana-Champaign*

Yuri Hosoda, *Kanagawa University*

Kathryn Howard, *University of Pennsylvania*

Tomoko Ikeda, *University of Texas at Austin*

Shimako Iwasaki, *University of California at Los Angeles*

Salla Kurhila, *University of Helsinki*

Yo-An Lee, *Sogang University*

Li Wei, *Birkbeck College, University of London*

Elizabeth Miller, *University of Northern Carolina at Charlotte*

Emi Morita, *National University of Singapore*

Kristian Mortensen, *University of Luxembourg*

Sung-Ock Sohn, *University of California at Los Angeles*

Yumiko Ohara, *University of Hawai'i at Hilo*

David Olsher, *San Francisco State University*

Jae Eun Park, *University of California at Los Angeles*

Susan Strauss, *Pennsylvania State University*

Carmen Taleghani-Nikazm, *Ohio State University*

Hansun Zhang Waring, *Teachers College, Columbia University*

Samuel Vuchinich, *Oregon State University*

Transcription Conventions

Based on Jefferson (2004)

symbol	**meaning**
[	Point of overlap onset
]	Point of overlap ending
=	No break or gap in speech (latched speech), or continuation of the same turn by the same speaker even though the turn is broken up in the transcript
(number)	Silence measured by 0.1 s
(.)	Brief pause of about 0.1 s
:	Prolongation of the immediately prior sound; the longer the colon row, the longer the prolongation
↑	Shift into especially high pitch in the next sound
↓	Shift into especially low pitch in the next sound
.	Falling intonation
?	Rising intonation
,	Slightly rising intonation
WORD	Especially loud sounds compared to the surrounding talk
°word°	Especially quiet sounds compared to the surrounding talk
word	Emphasized speech
word	A focal linguistic item [in **boldface**]
(word)	Transcriber's best guess of the words or speaker
word-	Cut-off sound
xxxx or ( )	Unintelligible speech or unidentifiable speaker to transcriber
<word>	Slowed down sounds compared to the surrounding talk
>word<	Speeded up sounds compared to the surrounding talk
.hhh	Audible inbreath
hhh	Audible outbreath
(h)	Plosiveness, associated with laughter, crying, breathlessness, etc.
((description))	Transcriber's description
→	Focal line in analysis

Reference

Jefferson, G. (2004). Glossary of transcript symbols with an introduction. In G. H. Lerner (Ed.), *Conversation analysis: Studies from the first generation* (pp. 13–31). Amsterdam/Philadelphia: John Benjamins.

Abbreviations used in word-by-word glosses of Japanese transcripts

IP	interactional particle (e.g., *ne*, *sa*, *no*, *yo*, *na*)
SB	subject particle (-*ga*)
O	object marker (-*o*)
LK	linking particle
TP	topic marker (-*wa*)
PT	other particle
QT	quotation marker (-*to*, -*tte*)
Q	question marker (*ka* and its variants)
N	nominalizer (e.g., *no*, *n*, *mono*)
SF	sentence filler (e.g., *e::*, *ano*)
CP	copula
NG	negative morpheme

Verb inflections (indicating the form of a predicate, with a hyphen after the predicate, e.g., CP-POL)

PAS	passive
POL	polite
PLAIN	plain
HON	honorific

1 Categories, Context, and Comparison in Conversation Analysis

Gabriele Kasper
University of Hawai'i at Mānoa

Introduction

This volume examines language-mediated interaction across a range of social settings, activities, languages, and cultural contexts. It shows how participants in these diverse scenes accomplish the interactional tasks at hand; construct familial and institutional identities, social affiliations and disaffiliations; produce, attribute, claim, contest, or resist categorizations as members of ethnic, linguistic, or cultural groups; and develop interactional competencies in second or foreign languages. With varying emphasis in analytical focus, the chapters scrutinize how the interlocutors make these complex and often interlocking projects visible to each other through the organization of their talk. While some authors attend specifically to interactional organizations such as turn-taking, sequence organization, and repair, others to the use of social categories, and still others to particular linguistic resources such as personal pronouns, discourse markers, interactional particles, or language alternation, the chapters in this volume share a concern with the interrelations between sequential, categorial, and linguistic practices and resources.

Despite the diversity of analytical topics and, as we see below, epistemological interests, the contributors take a common stance on the foundational role of interaction in social life. Interaction, according to Schegloff (2006), furnishes "the infrastructure for

Talk-in-interaction: Multilingual perspectives, pp. 1–28, Hanh Nguyen & Gabriele Kasper (Eds.), 2009
Honolulu, HI: University of Hawai'i, National Foreign Language Resource Center

social institutions, the natural ecological niche for language, and the arena in which culture is enacted" (p. 70). As such, interaction also constitutes the main site for human development at ontogenetic and microgenetic levels, to borrow Vygotsky's terminology. Through participation in situated interactional practices, children and other novices develop the interactional competencies that enable them to participate in the life of their communities (Ochs & Schieffelin, 2008). Interaction has therefore taken the center stage in several approaches to second language learning that view language use and development as a social practice (L2 learning as a local social activity, Hauser, this volume; Rylander, this volume) and social process (more effective participation in a practice over time; Ishida, this volume; Kim, this volume). Irrespective of their particular investigative focus and consistent with the view of interaction as the "primordial site of sociality" (Schegloff, 1996), the chapters in this volume examine their material from the ethnomethodological perspectives of conversation analysis (CA) and membership categorization.

CA examines how coparticipants accomplish coordinated actions and maintain order in social activities through their verbal and nonverbal conduct. In its history of 40 years, CA has developed from its origins in sociology to a transdisciplinary approach to the study of talk and other conduct in interaction. The CA literature comprises a large and cumulative body of research findings and a robust analytical apparatus that is continually being expanded and fine-tuned. In addition to an extensive journal literature and numerous edited volumes, there are now several introductory monographs (Hutchby & Wooffitt, 2008; Liddicoat, 2007; ten Have, 2007), introductions to discourse analysis with a substantial treatment of CA (Rapley, 2008; Wooffitt, 2005), and monographs with a focus on CA as an approach to interaction and learning in second language classrooms (Hellermann, 2008; Markee, 2000; Seedhouse, 2004). Condensing the coverage offered in these texts is not possible or necessary in this introductory chapter. I therefore begin with a few brief remarks on CA's origin in ethnomethodology and some of its defining methodological principles and practices. Then I discuss in more detail two topics with particular relevance to this volume, CA's treatment of categories and context. Under the larger topic of context, I also consider how CA approaches the study of institutional interaction. Finally, I turn to the role of comparison in CA. Examples from the studies in this volume are given throughout.

CA and ethnomethodology

The foundation for conversation analysis as an autonomous and alternative approach to standard sociology was laid by Harvey Sacks, in collaboration with his colleagues Emanuel Schegloff and Gail Jefferson, in the 1960s and 1970s.

Although Sacks drew on a wide range of sources from philosophy and the social sciences, including linguistics (Schegloff, 1992; Silverman, 1998), the influence on Sacks's thinking by Erving Goffman and Harold Garfinkel, two iconoclastic figures in American 20th century sociology, was particularly prominent. From Goffman, Sacks took the proposal that the "interaction order," embodied in natural face-to-face conduct, is a topic worthy of, and in fact fundamental to, sociological inquiry. Goffman and Sacks's insight that interaction is organized in an orderly manner rather than being a matter of capricious "performance" contrasted with the sociological preoccupation with macrostructures and abstract theory building. Goffman's work, especially his studies of face-work (1967) and the later proposal of footing in the organization of participation frameworks (1981), continues to inform conversation-analytic research (e.g., Goodwin, 2007; Lerner, 1996). But Goffman's legacy did not result in a school or subdiscipline within sociology. The wealth of perceptive observations and analyses that characterizes his work did not transform into a coherent research program on the interaction order and a formal analytical apparatus that others could have taken up and further elaborated. Sacks's lectures (1995a, 1995b) and publications, by contrast, laid the groundwork for the large, cumulative, and diverse enterprise that CA is today.

Sacks's debt to Garfinkel and his brainchild, ethnomethodology (EM), is visible throughout Sacks's lecturing and writing. Although EM and CA have developed independent and internally diverse agendas and styles of inquiry (Clayman & Maynard, 1995; Maynard & Clayman, 1991), CA's "mentality" (Schenkein, 1978) and much of its methodology can only be properly understood against the backdrop of CA's ethnomethodological heritage. The usages of some central terms in ethnomethodology and CA also differ from their more familiar meanings in other theoretical contexts. I therefore introduce, in the briefest possible manner, some key ethnomethodological concepts that inform the studies reported in this collection.

Ethnomethodology investigates the "methods" (procedures, practices) by which social members make sense of the social world they hold in common and by which they accomplish their practical daily activities (Garfinkel, 1967; Heritage, 1984; Sharrock & Anderson, 1986). The notion of member is defined by Garfinkel (1967) as the "mastery of natural language," not to be understood as underlying grammatical competence in the generative-linguistic sense but as "conversational competence" (Garfinkel & Sacks, 1970, p. 354), that is, the interactional practices through which persons participate in social activities and that are evident in the organization of these activities. "Competence" is visible in persons' understanding and production of situated, concerted, orderly, local actions. No distinction is made between "competence" and "performance" because orderliness rests not only in the abstract organizations through which social actions are produced and understood but in the produced conduct itself.

Interactional conduct displays "order at all points" (Sacks, 1984, p. 22), and its meaningful orderliness is publicly available to coparticipants and analysts alike. Through mutually intelligible concerted actions, members produce their social world as an ongoing practical *accomplishment* (Garfinkel & Sacks, 1970). Rather than confronting members as pre-existing realities, social structures—institutions, identities, relations between persons, and organizations of activities—are methodically brought into being through actors' coordinated actions, on particular situated occasions. Building on the later Wittgenstein's theory of meaning (1953), language is seen as thoroughly *indexical*, or context-bound. The usage of *indexicality* is different from its common usage in linguistics; it is not limited to deictic expressions but extends to all linguistic and other semiotic resources as well as to the utterances for which such resources are selectively assembled. In other words, no linguistic elements or structures, no utterances or any kind of action for that matter, embody autonomous meanings in-and-of themselves. Instead, actions, categories, and the resources through which they are implemented get their meanings on each occasion locally, through the contextual understandings that coparticipants assign and display. More generally, the interpretation of any conduct depends on the circumstances in which it occurs. Social, historical, psychological, interpersonal, and other circumstances—proximate contexts such as the previous turn in ongoing interaction and distal contexts such as social structures—are not causally related or correlated to the production and understanding of an action, as in conventional social science.[1] Rather, context and action are reflexively linked, or mutually constitutive. *Reflexivity* figures as a central topic in a range of sociological theories and takes on different meanings depending on its theoretical context (Lynch, 2000; i.e., "reflexivity" as a social-scientific term is indexical). For ethnomethodology, reflexivity is "not an epistemological, moral or political virtue" but "an unavoidable feature of the way actions are performed" (Lynch, 2000, p. 26). Thus, every action-in-context carries with it the methods of its production; actions are understood through the same sense-making practices by which they are produced; descriptions, rather than "representing" a scene, constitute the scene, or a version of it, in the first place. Reflexivity is a defining property of *accountability*, "the detailed, collaborative ways in which members manage their conduct and their circumstances to achieve the observably ordered features of their activities" (Zimmerman & Boden, 1991, p. 7). Activities are not only recognizable through their constitutive temporal interactional organization, but their orderly arrangement is *normatively* expected, or accountable. Upon hearing a question addressed to him or her, the addressee is normatively expected to produce an answer. By producing an answer, the speaker orients to the normative sequential trajectory generated by the question. By not producing an answer, the speaker generates a noticeable absence for which he or she can be held accountable ("You did not answer my question."). Thus, the orderliness of social activities neither resides in statistical regularities nor mechanical rule-following. Instead, ethnomethodology treats social norms as socially shared presuppositions and expectancy frameworks that participants attend to, both by acting in accordance with them and in their breach. In this sense, normative accountability has a profoundly moral dimension because it generates category- and activity-bound expectations to social conduct and enables its evaluation. The procedure through which participants make sense of an ongoing activity is called the *documentary method of interpretation* (Garfinkel, 1967, p. 78), whereby actors treat encountered behavior as evidence, or the "document" of, an underlying template, schema, or pattern. The underlying patterns are themselves derived from actual particular occurrences, so that the "documents" and their abstract schemata stand in a mutually informing reflexive relationship similar to a hermeneutic circle. Taken together, through the sense-making practices that participants continuously engage, they establish, maintain, and restore *intersubjectivity* as a practical interactional achievement. The ethnomethodological concept of intersubjectivity—again, a notion with multiple and partly opposed meanings in sociological, philosophical, and psychological theories—extends Alfred Schütz's phenomenological solution to the problem of how intersubjectivity may be achieved. Schütz (1962) proposed that for social actors to make sense of a world in common despite actual experiential differences, they routinely adopt the *reciprocity of perspectives* as an interpretive principle and thereby enable a shared sense of social scenes for all practical purposes. CA substantially elaborates how reciprocal perspective-taking informs and is achieved through the organization of interaction, which in turn constitutes the "architecture of intersubjectivity" (Heritage, 1984).

Membership categorization

Sacks developed ethnomethodology's program into two directions, both of which are represented in this volume. By far the more visible and influential direction is the sequential analysis of interaction that is commonly associated with CA. The strand of Sacks's work that received less uptake, especially outside of sociology, is to explicate how members generate and use categories referring to persons, called membership categorization (Sacks, 1972, 1995a, 1995b; Schegloff, 2007a; Silverman, 1998). The study of membership categorization has come to be known as membership categorization analysis (MCA, Hester & Eglin, 1997). While CA research on L2 interaction and learning has almost exclusively drawn on sequential CA, several chapters in this volume apply MCA together with sequential analysis.

Sacks (1972) described MCA's research domain as "the methodology and relevance of Members' activities of categorizing Members" (1972), a definition captured in the ambiguous argument structure of the phrase "membership categorization." Sacks's treatment of categories is different from the more familiar approaches in the social sciences. The predominant view is that category membership is transparent and has no need of focused examination in its own right. In applied linguistics, for instance, paired categories such as native-nonnative speaker, L1 speaker-L2 speaker, student-teacher, women-men, child-adult are routinely used as analysts' *resources*, without attention to whether and how such categories (as descriptions and performed incumbencies) are treated in the 'data' by the persons so categorized. Sacks insists that membership categories be taken as a research *topic*. As such, this is not a new proposal because categories have been a traditional object of investigation in several social sciences, for instance, linguistics and cognitive anthropology. Lexical semantics and ethnosemantics describe categories in terms of taxonomic relations of hierarchy, contrast, and inclusiveness. A complete inventory of ordered categories was thought to represent the semantic structure of a language or the cultural organization of a social group (e.g., Goodenough, 1956). While taxonomic relations do play a role in Sacks's approach to categories as social objects, the ethnomethodological concern is how categories are discursively produced on particular occasions and what members accomplish by using or invoking them.[2] Key questions for analysis include how categories are selected in particular contexts; what categorial relations, actions, and (more generally) predicates they are associated with; what inferences they enable; and what participants locally accomplish through their use. The research goal is to describe the generic, context-free apparatus that participants observably instantiate in locally particular, context-sensitive ways. Hence the nominalized verb, categorization.[3]

The key insights in Sacks's analysis of membership categorization are that (a) persons participate in a wide range of different categories, one or more of which can be made relevant on particular occasions; (b) similar categories are grouped together in collections; and (c) collections and categories are associated with rules for their application. Therefore, if one person has been described by a category from a collection, then the next person may be described by the same or another category from the same collection (consistency rule, Sacks, 1995a, p. 246). To render a person uniquely identifiable, a single category may be a sufficient description (economy rule, Sacks, 1995a, p. 246; for the complete apparatus, see Sacks, 1972, 1995a, 1995b; Schegloff, 2007a; Silverman, 1998). The apparatus is called a *membership categorization device*. For example, the category 'child' can be treated as part of such collections as "life stage" and "family relations" (Sacks, 1995, pp. 247–249). Participants determine through their interpretive work which categories a device collects on any occasion.

People reference, claim, or assign membership categories in other ways than by using reference terms. A critical insight of Sacks's apparatus, and one that closely binds up membership categorization with the sequential organization of talk, is that category incumbents are recognizable through the actions and activities they engage in. A category-bound activity is an activity conventionally associated with a membership category, not only empirically but as a normative expectation. For instance, in teacher-fronted classroom interaction, assessing or correcting a student's answer is normatively bound to the category 'teacher' (Lee, 2007; Richards, 2006; Rylander, this volume).[4] Nguyen (this volume) examines a very different category-bound activity, the recommendation sequence (*dặn*) in intergenerational Vietnamese family interaction. In an international voice chat between family members, Nguyen observes several occasions in which the father in Vietnam offered advice to his adult son who was visiting the US. In these sequences, the standardized relational pair[5] father-son was interactionally evoked through the complementary discourse identities of advice giver and advice receiver, mediated through the asymmetry of authority in the father-son relationship in the Vietnamese context. As Nguyen demonstrates, the reflexive constitution of familial relationships and the participation structure of who gives and who receives advice are embodied in the interactional organization, although it may occasionally surface as an expressly formulated social norm.

In later works, Sacks's framework has been considerably expanded and elaborated (e.g., Cuff, 1994; Eglin & Hester, 1992; Hester & Eglin, 1997; Jayyusi, 1984; Lepper, 2000; Watson, 1978, 1983, 1997). Two additions that I want to highlight here (with more to be added in the next section) were proposed by Watson (1978). One is to extend the attributes associated with a category from activities to predicates more generally. The extension from activities to predicates makes for more complex membership categorization devices as it adds "rights, entitlements, obligations, knowledge, attributes, and competences" (Hester & Eglin, 1997, p. 5) to the apparatus. The rights and obligations of teachers and students become matters of dispute in the ESL classroom interaction studied by Talmy (this volume), where they reflexively partition the teacher and participating students into the contrast pairs "good teacher"-"bad student" and "bad teacher"-"good student" as subcategorial relations in the standardized relational pair of teacher-student. The category-boundedness of knowledge becomes salient for the participants in Suzuki's study (this volume), which shows how the conversationalists treat a particular kind of knowledge (knowing one's blood type) as a predicate tied to the category of "Japanese person."

Watson (1983) further suggested that when a category comes with multiple lexical designations, alternative selections of the reference terms enable speakers to upgrade or downgrade the person(s) referred to using those terms. An example is in the excerpt below.

TG, 6: 01-03 (Schegloff, p. 478, 2007, [simplified])

```
Bee: nYeeah, .hh This feller I have-(nn)/(iv-)
     "felluh"; this ma:n. (0.2) t! hhh He
     ha::(s)- uff-eh-who-who I have fer Linguistics
     is [is real]ly too much, hh[h=
```

In Benwell and Stokoe's analysis (2006), Bee's repetition of *feller* in a "quotation voice" and her subsequent self-repair to *ma:n* "treats her own choice of a category as problematic" (p. 74). However, what *categorial* differences between *feller* and *ma:n* may be invoked is not clear. Taking Watson's (1983) extension into account, one might say that as the generic term for persons of male gender, *ma:n* could be heard as the "unmarked," seen-but-unnoticed lexical choice. However, in its position in Bee's turn, as a replacement for *feller*, *ma:n* conveys a more respectful stance and so upgrades the main character in the world of Bee's forthcoming story.[6]

As one thinks further about how categories are lexically formulated and what inferences choices between alternate reference terms engender, one could ask what implications (if any) cross-linguistically different lexicalizations of categories may have for local categorization. Bilmes (this volume) observes that the lexical ambiguity of the English word *child* as potentially referring to life stage or family relation is not present in Kammuang, a language spoken by the Muang in Northern Thailand. When the relevant device is age, the Muang use the lexical item *laɔ̌ɔn*; when family relations are at issue, they use the word *lûuk*. In the narrative analyzed in his chapter, Bilmes notes several occasions on which the narrator referred to his son-in-law as his *lûuk*. By bringing into focus the familial relations between father and son as a standardized relational pair, the narrator sets up a moral framework of obligation and responsibility that serves as a participants' resource to explain why the narrator went to considerable effort and expense on his son-in-law's behalf.

It may seem plausible to assume that such collections as family, gender, cultural affiliation, occupation, and other "transportable identities" (Zimmerman, 1998) pre-exist their local application. Yet the fundamental ethnomethodological position that membership knowledge is only available in its use also applies to membership categorization devices. Hester and Eglin (1997) remind us that "all categorizations are indexical expressions and their sense is therefore *locally* and *temporally* contingent" (p. 16, italics in original). Although largely "seen but unnoticed" (Garfinkel, 1967), social members exert agency by ascribing, describing, or engaging in category-bound activities and other category-associated predicates.

Membership categorization becomes noticeable for participants when the local assembling of a device is somehow obstructed or gets no ratification, for instance, when a category incumbent rejects a proposed categorization or acts in a manner treated as "out of line" with situationally relevant category predicates. Several studies (Day, 1994, 1998, 2006; Fukuda, 2006; Higgins, 2007, this volume; Nishizaka, 1999; Suzuki, this volume; Talmy, 2004, 2008, this volume) have shown how participants in different kinds of 'intercultural' interaction contest, resist, or subvert being categorized into ethnic, linguistic, or religious identities (see Higgins, this volume, for review). These studies have also examined what else gets accomplished through problematic membership categorization. Higgins (this volume) shows how in the course of pretopical talk between two Tanzanian journalist colleagues, one of the participants asks the other (in Swahili) about his religious affiliation (*wewe ni: ni Hindu* [are you Hindu?]). This initiates a presentation-eliciting sequence in which the respondent repeatedly rejects the ascribed religious identity and various predicates associated with it, while the questioner draws firm boundaries between her own religious identity as a Christian and other religious groups. Subsequently, the questioner treats the separating religious affiliations as a stepping stone towards comembership in the category of "helping others not of one's own ethnicity," which in turn serves as a resource to make a request for financial support to her interlocutor. In Suzuki's study (this volume), a membership categorization device becomes problematic when some parties to a conversation invoke "knowing one's blood type" as a tool to partition *nihonjin* (Japanese people) and *gaijin* ([white] foreigners) into mutually exclusive categories in the collection "ethnicity." A participant in the conversation whose identity as *gaijin* is made relevant at some point redraws the boundaries somewhat by accepting her incumbency in the category of *gaijin* while claiming, and subsequently demonstrating, that she does know her blood type. However, rather than treating her own 'deviant case' as occasion for calling into question the entire membership categorization device, the participant confirms that *gaijin* "generally" (*hutsuu*) do not know their blood types. Thus, by discounting her own case as that of an 'outlier' that does not challenge the generality of the category-bound predicate, the same participant leaves the categorization device intact and thereby contributes to the local construction of *nihonjinron*, a 'theory of Japaneseness.'

Membership categorization, then, is deeply implicated in the production of social relations, affiliation, and disaffiliation. We have already noted that in the process of assembling membership categorization devices, linguistic resources play a critical role. This observation raises the question of how multilingual practices may figure in categorial work. From a conversation-analytic perspective, researchers have investigated how language alternation within and across turns constructs alignment and disalignment, epistemic stance, and authority (e.g., Auer, 1984, 1999; Gafaranga, 1999, 2000; Li Wei, 2005; Torras, 2005). The chapters by Higgins and Talmy in this volume extend this work by examining how participants engage codeswitching as a resource in membership categorization.

Higgins shows how the interlocutors switch from Swahili to English as a method of resisting the other person's proposal of religious affiliation and categorial comembership. In Talmy's study, the teacher briefly switches from Standard English to Hawai'i Creole in an effort to get a "bad" student to comply with his directives. With the switch to Hawai'i Creole, a predicate strongly bound to the category Local (a person born and raised in Hawai'i), the relevance of the institutional, positioned standardized relational pair of teacher and student is momentarily backgrounded against the standardized relational pair Local-Local, which brings along an altogether different set of mutual rights and obligations.

The chapters by Higgins and Talmy in this volume are not the first to bring MCA to bear on the study of multilingual interaction. In an earlier paper, Gafaranga (2001) draws on MCA to examine the local orderliness of language alternation in the interactions of bilingual Rwandese speakers of Kinyarwanda and French. In clarifying his approach to bilingual talk, Gafaranga notes that

> order in bilingual conversation...can be approached in two different ways. Ethnomethodological studies address the problem of order in talk-in-interaction either from a Conversation Analytic (CA) perspective or from a Membership Categorisation Analytic (MCA) perspective. Similarly, order in bilingual conversation can be addressed either from an organisational (sequential) perspective or from an identity-related perspective (Sebba and Wootton, 1998). (p. 1906)

Gafaranga takes CA and MCA as separate lines of ethnomethodological investigation, a stance consistent with such prominent work on MCA as that of Jayyusi (1984). Others have made the opposite case, arguing that the production and understanding of actions and action sequences are both categorial and sequential and that the separate analytical strands need to be brought together (e.g., Edwards, 1998; Hester & Eglin, 1997; Watson, 1997). The chapters by Bilmes, Nguyen, Suzuki, Higgins, and Talmy in this volume show how such a synthesis benefits the analysis of ordinary conversation and institutional talk across settings and languages, including multilingual interaction.

Context

As the discussion so far suggests, membership categorization provides one window to CA's perspective on context. Consistent with its ethnomethodological stance, CA treats context as an ongoing members' project, a resource and product of participants' sense-making practices. In their extensive discussion of theories of context in philosophy and the social sciences, Goodwin and Duranti (1992) proposed the following analytical strategy to the analysis of context.

> first, approaching context from the perspective of an actor actively operating on the world within which he or she finds him- or herself embedded; second, tying the analysis of context to study of the indigeneous (*sic*) activities that participants use to constitute the culturally and historically organized social worlds they inhabit; and third, recognizing that participants are situated within multiple contexts which are capable of rapid and dynamic change as the events they are engaged in unfold. (p. 5)

In ethnomethodological view, 'the actor perspective' should not be confused with such cognitivist constructs as individual actors' 'perceptions' and 'attitudes,' to which researchers can gain access through interviews and other forms of self-report. Social members' emic perspectives of context are found in their situated practical activities, including their understandings of any context dimensions that they make relevant for each other. Context and social action reflexively shape each other through in situ categorization and the sequential organization of interaction, as the examples in the previous section have shown. CA's notion of context as an ongoing discursive coproduction contrasts with the more familiar correlational or causal models, in which contextual (macrostructural, psychological) factors as the independent variables predict or explain features of the talk as the dependent variables. Likewise, CA does not sit well with appeals to "the usual macrosociological suspects" (McHoul, Rapley, & Antaki, 2008, p. 43) in much poststructuralist and critical research in applied linguistics.[7] Any version of the "bucket theory of context" (Drew & Heritage, 1992, p. 19) runs into compatibility problems with CA, irrespective of its paradigmatic allegiance with "positivist," poststructuralist, or other traditions (McHoul & Rapley, 2001; McHoul, Rapley, & Antaki, 2008).

CA's notion of context needs to be further unpacked into two kinds of context. Context in CA primarily[8] refers to *sequential context*, the immediate (proximal) interaction-internal (endogenous) sequential environment that participants produce and orient to through their talk (Schegloff & Sacks, 1973). Interactional organization is *doubly contextual* in that turns are both *context-shaped* and *context-renewing* (Heritage, e.g., 1984, 2004). A speaker's current turn is shaped by the preceding turn and at the same time projects possible actions for a subsequent turn. Through the current speaker's turn in response to a prior turn (mainly, but not always, the immediately preceding turn), the current speaker displays how he or she understood that prior turn. In this sense, the endogenous interactional context is a participant-generated, bidirectional sequential environment, with a retrospective and prospective orientation. As Heritage notes, by means of the turn-by-turn organization of social action, "a context of publicly displayed and continuously updated intersubjective understandings is systematically sustained" (1984, p. 259).

The second order of context is the distal, interaction-external (exogenous) context. As noted above, MCA affords a systematic link between talk and social structure as it examines how participants invoke and use their commonsense knowledge of social context through membership categorization. A possible objection is that because MCA is limited to personal categories, it offers a crucial but incomplete apparatus for studying how social context becomes a locally relevant participant concern. However, the types of categories originally proposed by Sacks have subsequently been expanded to a wide range of objects, including place and activity categories (Schegloff, 1972) and institutions of varying size, scope, and specificity (e.g., First Hawaiian Bank in the Mānoa Market Place, the education system, the economy) (Coulter, 1982; see discussion in Hester & Eglin, 1997). Social context, then, refers to "a reflexively constituted relationship between singular actions and the relevant specifications of identity, place, time, and meaning implicated by the intelligibility of those actions" (Lynch & Peyrot, 1992, p. 114). Rethinking context in this way de facto resolves the distinction between endogenous and exogenous contexts, or between micro- and macrolevels of social organization, *in concrete, locally specific instances.* The chapters in this book demonstrate on a wide range of cases how different properties and processes of macrosocial context are "talked [or typed, GK][9] into being" (Heritage, 1984, p. 290): family (Bilmes, Nguyen), religion and ethnicity (Higgins), nationalist ideology (Suzuki), social inequality (Talmy), television media (Ikeda), the university (Saft), language education (Talmy, Hauser, Rylander, González-Lloret), and language socialization and acquisition[10] (Kim, Ishida). In other words, these studies join a large body of research showing how social structure becomes structure-in-action (Zimmerman & Boden, 1991).

For analysts, the challenge is to *demonstrate* rather than postulate the reflexivity of action and category, proximal and distal context, in the specific details of the talk itself. According to Schegloff (1991), the problem of a warrantable analysis is twofold. The first task is to demonstrate that some aspect of social context—category incumbencies, setting, activity—is visibly relevant for the participants at a particular moment. The problem of *relevance* is to show that, and how, "social structure" in the traditional sense enters into the production and interpretation of determinate facets of conduct, and is thereby confirmed, reproduced, modulated, neutralized or incrementally transformed in that actual conduct to which it must finally be referred" (Schegloff, 1991, p. 51).

In this volume, for instance, Suzuki shows how during casual talk on the topic of blood types, incumbency in the categories of *nihonjin* (Japanese person) and *gaijin* ([white] foreigner) becomes relevant for the participants, whereas other categories that also 'correctly' describe the participants, such as being female, graduate students, and roommates, do not. The second problem is to show that the aspect of social-structural context in question (setting, participant categories, macrosocial processes) is demonstrably evident in the ways in which the interaction is conducted, including sequence organization and turn formats, linguistic resources, topics, and organization of participation frameworks. This is the problem of *procedural consequentiality.* One example from this volume that documents how social context is procedurally consequential for the interaction is the recommendation sequence analyzed in Nguyen's chapter, through which the standardized relational pair 'father-son' becomes procedurally consequential for the participants.

CA researchers' obligation to demonstrate rather than merely postulate the procedural consequentiality of social context imposes stricter requirements for assuring the validity (specifically, the construct validity and internal validity) of their analytical claims than usually required in qualitative research (Maynard, 2003; Peräkylä, 2004; Seedhouse, 2007; Silverman, 2006). This analytical prescription governs CA irrespective of the type of contextual property whose bearing on the talk the researcher wishes to demonstrate. One broad category of talk in which the issue becomes especially urgent is institutional interaction. In this volume, several chapters examine how talk bears the marks of institutional activities. This brings up the questions of how the defining properties of institutional interaction can be described and what implications such characterizations may have for analysis.

Talk as institution and institutional talk

Interaction can be described as "institutional" in two ways (Drew & Heritage, 1992; Heritage, 2004). First, as the "primordial site of sociality," talk-in-interaction itself can be studied *as* a social institution, in fact *the* social institution on which all other institutions in any society are built (Schegloff, 2006). CA's primary and uniquely specialized goal is to describe the "procedural infrastructure of interaction" (Schegloff, 1992, p. 1338) in "formal, that is, structural, organizational, logical, atopically contentless, consistent, and abstract, terms" (Psathas, 1995, p. 3). Studies of interaction among diverse participants in a vast array of mundane activities have shown that talk is organized in a systematic, orderly fashion through the technologies for turn-taking, turn design, actions, sequence organization, and repair (e.g., Drew, 2005; Hutchby & Wooffitt, 2008; Schegloff, 2006, 2007b). Moreover, participants display *normative* orientations to these organizations (cf. section on ethnomethodology), a further indication that the procedural apparatus for interaction provides the socially institutionalized foundation of actors' *interactional competencies.* In their situated talk, participants configure the *context-free* interactional apparatus in *context-sensitive* ways to fit their projects in the local activity. The apparatus of interactional organizations sustains any interaction, but *ordinary conversation* holds a special status among activities managed through talk-in-interaction (Drew, 2005; Schegloff, 2006). Ordinary talk is the medium through which children first experience the world and people conduct a wealth of activities in their daily lives, regardless of differences in the wider social and cultural settings (see Bilmes, Nguyen, Higgins, Suzuki, Ishida, and Kim, this volume, on different aspects of ordinary conversation). Conversation analysts therefore view ordinary conversation as the basic form of interaction as a social institution.

The second sense in which interaction can be characterized as institutional is that social institutions are largely constituted, maintained, and transformed *through* interaction (Drew & Heritage, 1992; Heritage, 2004). To get an institutional activity done—a medical consultation, a news interview, a language lesson, etc.—participants reconfigure the organization of ordinary conversation so that it orients to the specific "institutionality" of the event. What makes an interaction institutional, then, is not where it takes place (in a courtroom, classroom, dentist's office) or whether the parties occupy positions in an institutional structure, but whether the participants address themselves to an institution-specific agenda. Heritage identified three properties that define institutional interaction: (a) goal-orientations tied to institution-relevant identities (doctor and patient, teacher and student, etc.), (b) special constraints on allowable contributions, and (c) institution-specific inferential frameworks and procedures (Drew & Heritage, 1992; Heritage, 2004). Of these, the first feature is the most consequential because the remaining two derive from it. To take classroom interaction as an example, through teachers' evaluations and corrections of student contributions, participants orient to the purpose of classrooms as sites for knowledge installation (Macbeth, 2000, 2004). Seedhouse (2004) observed that the organization of student-teacher interaction in a language classroom is reflexively related to the teacher's pedagogical goals. While Rylander (this volume) finds support for the reflexive link between a pedagogical goal and the form of repair sequences, he cautions that the specific goals themselves cannot be assumed but have to be traced in the local sequential context.

In the study of institutional talk, then, CA observes the principles and procedures for analyzing ordinary conversation, but with the additional aim to demonstrate how participants orient to the specifically institutional properties of the interaction (Drew & Heritage, 1992). To establish how the work of the institutional event under study gets done, Heritage (2004) recommends that analysts inspect the following places for whether and how the participants organize their conduct in institution-specific ways.

- Turn-taking organization (Are the turns participant-managed or pre-allocated? Is the turn-allocation tied to institutional identities? Is the access to turns asymmetrical?)
- The overall structural organization of the interaction (Ordered interactional phases?)
- Sequence organization (Are there activity-specific sequences, such as initiation-response-follow-up in teacher-fronted classroom interaction?)

- Turn design (What actions are done through the talk? How are they implemented through linguistic and other resources?)
- Lexical choice (Do the participants use any special registers or address forms?)
- Epistemological and other forms of asymmetry (Is the distribution of relevant knowledge and participation opportunities tied to institutional identities?)

The CA literature on institutional talk is extensive and has developed into a research program of its own (e.g., the edited collections by Drew & Heritage, 1992; Heritage & Maynard, 2006; McHoul & Rapley, 2001; Zimmerman & Boden, 1991). Several chapters in this volume (Ikeda, Saft, Talmy, Hauser, Rylander) contribute to this body of research. Yet just what sorts of claims analysts can warrantably make about the institutionality of institutional interaction is a topic of debate. Some ethnomethodologists have taken different positions on the issue of whether the entire project of institutional CA is compatible with ethnomethodology's focus on social members' *local* sense-making practices (Hester & Francis, 2000a, 2000b, 2001; Watson, 2000). This debate has not yet reached CA in applied linguistics and second language studies and is well worth taking up. On the criterion of procedural consequentiality, questions about purportedly institution-specific sequence structures have been raised as well. For instance, Schegloff (1991) doubts whether claims to the specifically institutional character of extensive insert sequences between request and response in calls to the police (Zimmerman, 1984) can legitimately be made, arguing that long insert sequences are also found in ordinary conversation. This controversy suggests that two sorts of claims might be usefully distinguished. One is the strong claim that a particular organizational feature of talk is uniquely specialized for an institutional purpose. A case in point is the multiple question-answer sequence with its associated turn pre-allocation and turn-type pre-allocation, an institutional speech exchange system that even has a vernacular name, the interview. The weak claim would be that the interactional phenomenon is fundamentally the same as in ordinary conversation but serves an institution-specific purpose in the activity. One example is the multiple question structure often seen in interviews. Multiple questions (questions on the same or closely related referential point) are not unique to interviews (Gardner, 2004). However, they appear to be used more frequently by interviewers than ordinary conversationalists because they are an effective device to pursue the interview's institutional mandate (Linell, Hofvendahl, & Lindholm, 2003), for instance, to get candidates in an oral proficiency interview to produce ratable speech samples (Kasper, 2006; Kasper & Ross, 2007). Under the weak claim, one could also ask how participants use generic linguistic resources to accomplish institutional agendas. An illustration is the study by Saft (this volume), in which he shows how the participants in faculty meetings at a university in Japan deploy the marker *maa* to avoid and terminate arguments and thereby move the business of the meeting forward.

Applied CA

Because of the different projects of CA as the study of interaction as institution and institutional interaction, ten Have (2001, 2007) proposed referring to the first as "pure" CA and the second as "applied" CA. To avoid the evaluative connotations of "pure," and in keeping with the standard distinction between basic and applied science, I prefer to refer to the branch of CA that investigates the procedural infrastructure of interaction, comprising sequential and categorial analysis, as basic CA. While the largest portion of applied CA examines institutional interaction, ten Have (2007) suggests that applied CA can subsume a wider range of studies adopting CA for discipline-specific purposes and perspectives. An increasing number of studies motivated by critical and feminist agendas engage CA (e.g., the edited volume *Talking Gender and Sexuality*, McIlvenny, 2001). Ten Have (2007) offers an instructive summary of some prominent (and some undeservedly neglected) work on feminist CA. In this volume, Talmy's study adopts a critical perspective on second language education by examining how the category of ESL student gets reproduced and contested in classroom interaction. As he notes, a fundamental question that researchers motivated by a critical impetus have to confront and solve is how to reconcile their agenda with CA's ethnomethodological stricture to examine local coproduced interaction as the participants' sense-making practices from their (emic) perspective, that is, to make explicit the particiants' implicit membership knowledge rather than to interpret or replace it by sociological and other researcher-generated theory. Talmy shows—as do Higgins and Suzuki in their chapters, although they do not explicitly situate their studies within a critical research tradition—that CA policies do not only *not* get in the way of pulling into view the workings of educational, nationalistic, and ethnic ideologies and the resistance and acquiescence they meet, but that CA offers a methodology to ground these analytical outcomes in the observable realities of the participants. Together with feminist CA research, these studies give us an indication of CA's far-reaching potential to address issues of inequitable power relations, discrimination, hegemony, resistance, and social transformation, a seed already sown in Sacks's lecture on "'hotrodders' as a revolutionary category" (1995a, p. 396).[11]

Documenting social transformation and change in interaction requires that interactional activities be investigated over a longer time span. In analogy to longitudinal ethnography (Corsaro, 1996), Maynard (2003) recommended *longitudinal CA* to trace changes in interactional practices that may be linked to changes in the participants' life world. Using the example of news delivery sequences, Maynard reported studies showing how chronically ill persons or their families adjust their practices of giving and receiving news about the diagnosis and progression of the disease as the person's health changes. As a research design, longitudinal CA allows researchers to track changes in interactional organization over time and is therefore capable of addressing such topics as language socialization and acquisition and the development of professional competencies. Changes over time become visible by comparing instances of the focal object at different points on a temporal axis, as I discuss below.

Comparison in CA

Comparison is a fundamental analytical practice in CA, and in this regard, CA is in no way unique. Comparing and contrasting objects is a necessary empirical method to establish patterns, regularities, or rules, to find out in what ways patterns are stable and variable, and to account for variants or varieties. We noted that the project of CA as a basic science is to describe the procedural infrastructure of interaction. For this purpose, researchers start with an initial observation of some phenomenon in a data corpus and assemble provisional collections of that phenomenon (a sequence, an action, or a resource). Because the goal is to describe the context-free structure of the object, it strengthens the validity of the analytical claims if the corpus includes material from a wide variety of contexts (ordinary conversation; various institutional, face-to-face, telephone, and electronically mediated interactions). Through comparing individual instances, the structure of the object becomes increasingly sharper, so that it becomes possible to determine which cases are members of a more distinctly defined collection and which are not. It is also through comparison that subcategories of the phenomenon are formulated. Finally, deviant cases—instances that cannot be subsumed under the proposed regularity—are compared to the good exemplars of the provisional pattern to probe whether the tentative account can be confirmed or needs to be expanded or revised. The analytical strategy bears similarities to theoretical sampling and the constant comparison method in grounded theory analysis (see Charmaz, 2006, for a recent update; ten Have, 2007, chapter 8, for application to CA).

Comparison also figures centrally in applied CA. To establish the institution-specific arrangements of talk, analysts compare a particular type of institutional interaction to ordinary conversation. Drew and Heritage (1992) highlight the comparative focus in the study of institutional interaction, noting that "(t)he basic forms of mundane talk constitute a kind of benchmark against which other more formal or 'institutional' types of interaction are recognized and experienced" (p. 19). For instance, the distinctive pre-allocation of turns and turn-types in interviews and teacher-fronted classroom interaction becomes visible when compared to ordinary conversation, where turn-taking is participant-managed. Most commonly, the research goal is to characterize an object in one particular type of institutional interaction. To that end, analysts compare how the object is structured in institutional activity-sequences (e.g., the question-delivery structure in news interviews, Heritage & Roth, 1995; the news delivery sequence in clinical interaction, Maynard, 2003) and in ordinary conversation, although such comparison is often implicit rather than formal. But the comparison can go along other lines, too. Through longitudinal CA, institutional transformation can be made visible. In one study, Clayman and Heritage (2002) document historical changes in journalists' questioning style in U.S. presidential press conferences by comparing questions addressed to Presidents Eisenhower and Regan, finding that the portion of adversarial questions increased sharply over the 40-year period. In addition to within-type comparison on a historical axis, between-type comparison of an object in several different types of institutional activities brings out commonalities and distinctiveness. Drew (2003) illustrates this strategy by examining formulations[12] in four institutional settings: psychotherapeutic consultations, call-in radio programs, news interviews, and industrial negotiations. His preliminary findings support earlier proposals that formulating is a generic, context-free practice, whereas the different linguistic forms of the formulations are not interchangeable but enable participants to manage different institutional activities. Yet another relation among institutional activities that invites comparison is different subcategories of a superordinate activity. One example is the different types of language proficiency interviews analyzed by Lazaraton (2002). In this volume, Ikeda compares the focal activity, the triadic television interview in Japan, with dyadic interviews. She argues that the tripartite format is more common than the dyadic version because it affords the journalists better opportunities for challenging the interviewee while offering good entertainment value.

Moving beyond activities managed through one particular language, cross-cultural and cross-linguistic comparison allows researchers to establish to what extent interactional objects are stable or diverse across societies and languages. Zimmerman (1999) refers to this type of comparative research as *horizontal comparison*. An example is the sequence organization of telephone calls, especially their openings and closings. Two edited collections on telephone calls in diverse settings and languages attest both to remarkable commonalities and to crosscultural elaboration and historical change (Luke & Pavlidou, 2002; Thüne & Leonardi, 2003; see also Schegloff, 2002, for a cautionary note on the cross-cultural comparison of telephone openings). Although Zimmerman (1999) strongly encourages horizontal comparison, he also reminds us that CA does not share the premise of standard social science that interaction varies fundamentally according to sociostructural and cultural context, a key difference between cross-cultural pragmatics and horizontal comparison in CA. Thus far, the procedural infrastructure of interaction described in basic CA has proven to be a robust and sufficiently flexible support system to pursue any kind of interactional business in any language. The chapters in this volume, including interactions in Chinese, English, Japanese, Korean, Spanish, Thai, and Vietnamese, confirm the robustness of the interactional apparatus, but the studies by Bilmes, Nguyen, and Ikeda also show how participants orient to culture-specific priorities through categorization and sequence organization.

A further productive line for horizontal comparison is *cross-linguistic* studies at the intersection of grammar and interaction. Some examples are the interactional use of causal markers (Ford & Mori, 1994) and syntactic practices in same-turn self-repair (Fox, Hayashi, & Jasperson, 1996) in English and Japanese, "yes, but" prefaced utterances in dispreferred responses in Danish and German (Steensig & Asmuß, 2005), and contrastive connectives in the organization of dispreference in Korean, Japanese, and English (Park, 1998). Although the mutual organization of interaction and grammar has become a research focus in its own right (interactional linguistics), comparative studies in particular are still few and far between. Cross-linguistic comparison is not the central goal of this volume, but some of the chapters provide a springboard for such comparison. For example, the studies by Bilmes and Nguyen provide a glimpse into how personal pronouns are used in Thai and Vietnamese.

As a final area for horizontal comparison, cross-medial CA is used to see how participants adjust their interaction to fit the affordances and constraints of the medium. For instance, González-Lloret (this volume) observes that in synchronous computer-mediated chat, turns do not appear onscreen incrementally but as complete units, as finished products rather than as ongoing projects that allow the coparticipants to witness the process of turn production. Because turn-taking is mediated by such production conditions as the speed of typing and server speed, the postings appear "out of turn" compared with copresent interaction. However, the participants orient to the interaction in much the same way as in mundane face-to-face conversation, for instance, by providing second pair parts to first pair parts even when the serial adjacency is disrupted by unrelated turns (i.e., not by an insert sequence). For the participants, the apparatus of interactional organization appears to retain its normativity in computer-mediated communication as much as in talk.

Turning to the second category of comparison recommended by Zimmerman (1999), *vertical comparison* refers to "studies of the acquisition of conversational structures" (p. 198). For a theoretical rationale, Zimmerman contends that

> studies are needed that examine from a conversation analytic perspective the process and stages by which interactive talk emerges. Language and interaction go hand in hand: Acquiring a language is an irremediably *social* enterprise. (...) Talk is *doing*; speech, one kind of bodily movement..., is interwoven with objects and other people in the extensive and extended course of practice entailed by an emerging sociality. (p. 198; italics in original)

Zimmerman's view of L1 acquisition and socialization has a familiar ring to SLA researchers who study L2 learning as the development of interactional competencies. With reference to work by Ervin-Tripp (1979, 1982) and Wootton (1997), he calls for CA research to examine how "(c)hildren acquire competency in their native language over the course of development" (p. 198). For SLA researchers, this call should be welcome and alleviate the concern that CA is not cut out to investigate L2 development. In this volume, two chapters represent different versions of vertical L2 comparative research. Kim adopts a cross-sectional design to examine how the Korean discourse markers *-nuntey* and *kuntey* are used by L2 learners of Korean at different proficiency levels in ordinary conversations with Korean L1 speakers. Building on Park (1998), she compares the (non)occurrence of the discourse markers in the learners' utterances in turn-initial, turn-medial, and turn-final positions. Kim finds a developmental pattern that corresponds to the diachronic grammaticalization process shown for the discourse markers and that she theorizes as an instance of acquisitional grammaticalization.

Vertical comparison from a longitudinal perspective was adopted by Nguyen (2006, 2008), who examined how pharmacy interns developed their interactional competence in the professional activity of patient consultation over an 8-week period. The case studies document how over time, an intern became more apt at presenting expert information to patients while establishing affiliative relationships with them (Nguyen, 2006) and how the interns progressively organized the sequential ordering of tasks in the consultation more effectively (Nguyen, 2008). In this volume, an example of vertical comparison is Ishida's longitudinal study of how an L2 learner of Japanese develops his use of the interactional particle *ne* during study abroad in Japan. Over a 10-month period, the student expands his use of *ne* to different sequential contexts and so is able to engage more actively and effectively in developing the talk. His growing interactional competence is also evident in his use of the response formula *soo desu ne*, which has a poor fit to the prior turn at first but later becomes an effective resource for conversational alignment. In addition to its substantive findings, the study highlights the gains of CA's analytical methods, such as to inspect the sequential development of the talk prior and subsequent to the analytical object of interest. One topic to pursue in future research is the way in which L2 speakers' available interactional competences in other languages organize their participation in L2 talk and what developmental changes may be seen in that regard. This research strategy will combine horizontal and vertical comparative L2 CA research and open new horizons for the conversation-analytic study of second language development.

Notes

1 See section on 'context' for more discussion.

2 Eglin (1980) compares in detail an ethnosemantic and ethnomethodological approach to reference terms for Canadian doctors.

3 For Jayyusi (1984), 'categorization' is the outcome of the activity of 'categorizing.' 'Categorization' is used both in the product and process sense elsewhere in the MCA literature and the two do not need to be distinguished for the present purpose.

4 The three cited studies show how the students and teachers in the otherwise very different classroom scenes orient to the teachers' category-bound activities as situated practices. Although recognizable as common methods of organizing teaching as "knowledge installation" (Macbeth, 2000), whether participants treat assessments and corrections as category-bound to the category of teacher needs to remain a question for analysis rather than a foregone conclusion. The analytical task is to show whether and how the participants operate a membership categorization device, this time. For discussion of transsituational versus praxeological ethnomethodological versions of MCA, see Eglin (1980) and Hester and Eglin (1997).

5 Two categories from the same collection are associated to each other through mutual rights and obligations.

6 This analysis differs from that of Schegloff (2007), who proposes that Bee's use of reference terms shows description, not categorization. However, in my understanding of this story-preface, Bee's reference to the 'feller'/'ma:n' 'I have fer Linguistics' invokes the standardized relational pair (cf. note 4) "instructor-student," which does become procedurally consequential in the unfolding narrative.

7 Examples from influential poststructuralist social theories include Althusser's (1977) "interpellation," and Bourdieu's (1977) "habitus" and "dispositions." A recent example from applied linguistics is Block's (2007) approach to the identities of second language learners. He distinguishes ethnic, racial, national, migrant, gender, social class, and language identities, defined in transsituational macrostructural terms (p. 43).

8 "Primarily" is intentionally ambiguous here. It refers (a) to the strongly predominant sequential line of CA research, developed most prominently in the work of Emanuel Schegloff and the late Gail Jefferson and recently showcased in Lerner's (2004) collection of CA studies "from the first generation." (b) Within sequential CA, context is, first and foremost, sequential context.

9 An increasing volume of research on various types of computer-mediated interaction shows how participants orient to the specific affordances of these media (González-Lloret, this volume).

10 Socialization and acquisition are included here because social structure arguably incorporates the processes for its reproduction.

11 Sacks concludes this lecture by drawing implications of MCA for the study of social transformation: "It's in that regard, then, that the important problems of social

change, I would take it, anyway, would involve laying out such things as the sets of categories, how they're used, what's known about any member, etc., and beginning to play with shifts in the properties of a category, and shifts in the rules for use" (p. 402).

12 Formulations are actions in which a speaker explicitly states his or her understanding of what a previous speaker has said. They take such forms as "you mean x."

References

Auer, P. (1984). *Bilingual conversation.* Amsterdam: Benjamins.

Auer, P. (Ed.) (1999). *Codeswitching in conversation: Language, interaction, and identity.* London: Routledge.

Benwell, B., & Stokoe, E. (2006). *Discourse and identity.* Edinburgh, UK: Edinburgh University Press.

Block, D. (2007). *Second language identities.* London: Continuum.

Bourdieu, P. (1992). *Invitation to a reflexive sociology.* University of Chicago Press.

Charmaz, K. (2006). *Constructing grounded theory.* Los Angeles: Sage.

Clayman, S. E., & Heritage, J. (2002). *The news interview: Journalists and public figures on the air.* New York: Cambridge University Press.

Clayman, S. E., & Maynard, D. W. (1995). Ethnomethodology and conversation analysis. In P. ten Have & G. Psathas (Eds.), *Situated order* (pp. 1–30). Lanham, MD: University Press of America.

Corsaro, W. A. (1996). Transitions in early childhood: The promise of comparative, longitudinal ethnography. In R. Jessor, A. Colby, & R. A. Shweder (Eds.), *Ethnography and human development: Context and meaning in social inquiry* (pp. 419–456). Chicago: Chicago University Press.

Coulter, J. (1982). Remarks on the conceptualisation of social structure. *Philosophy of the Social Sciences, 12*, 33–46.

Cuff, E. C. (1994). *The problem of versions in everyday situations.* Boston, MA: International Institute for Ethnomethodology and Conversation Analysis/University Press of America.

Day, D. (1994). Tang's dilemma and other problems: Ethnification processes at some multilingual workplaces. *Pragmatics, 4*, 315–336.

Day, D. (1998). Being ascribed, and resisting, membership of an ethnic group. In C. Antaki & S. Widdicombe (Eds.), *Identities in talk* (pp. 151–170). London: Sage.

Day, D. (2006). Ethnic and social groups and their linguistic categorization. In K. Bührig and J. ten Thije (Eds.), *Beyond misunderstanding: Linguistic analyses of intercultural discourse* (pp. 217–244). The Hague, Netherlands: Benjamins.

Drew, P., & Heritage, J. (Eds.) (1992). *Talk at work.* Cambridge, UK: Cambridge University Press.

Drew, P. (2003). Comparative analysis of talk-in-interaction in different institutional settings: A sketch. In P. Glenn, C. D. LeBaron, & J. Mandelbaum (Eds.), *Studies in language and social interaction* (pp. 293–308). Mahwah, NJ: Erlbaum.

Drew, P. (2005). Conversation analysis. In K. L. Fitch & R. E. Sanders (Eds.), *Handbook of language and social interaction* (pp. 71–102). Mahwah, NJ: Erlbaum.

Edwards, D. (1998). The relevant thing about her: Social identity categories in use. In C. Antaki & S. Widdicombe (Eds.), *Identities in talk* (pp. 15–33). Thousand Oaks, CA: Sage.

Eglin, P. (1980). *Talk and taxonomy: A methodological comparison of ethnosemantics and ethnomethodology with reference to terms for Canadian doctors.* Amsterdam: Benjamins.

Eglin, P., & Hester, S. (1992). Category, predicate, and task: The pragmatics of practical action. *Semiotica, 88*, 243–268.

Ervin-Tripp, S. (1979). Children's verbal turn-taking. In E. Ochs & B. B. Schieffelin (Eds.), *Developmental pragmatics* (pp. 391–414). New York: Academic Press.

Ervin-Tripp, S. (1982). Ask and it shall be given to you: Children's requests. In H. Byrnes (Ed.), *Contemporary perceptions of language* (pp. 235–243). Washington, DC: Georgetown University Press.

Ford, C. E., & Mori, J. (1994). Causal markers in Japanese and English conversations: A cross-linguistic study of interactional grammar. *Pragmatics, 4*, 31–61.

Fox, B., Hayashi, M., & Jasperson, R. (1996). Resources and repair: A cross-linguistic study of syntax and repair. In E. Ochs, E. A. Schegloff, & S. A. Thompson (Eds.), *Interaction and grammar* (pp. 185–237). Cambridge, UK: Cambridge University Press.

Fukuda, C. (2006). Resistance against being formulated as cultural other: The case of a Chinese student in Japan. *Pragmatics, 16*, 429–456.

Gafaranga, J. (1999). Language choice as a significant aspect of talk organisation: The orderliness of language alternation. *Text, 19*, 201–225.

Gafaranga, J. (2000). Medium repair vs. other-language repair: Telling the medium of a bilingual conversation. *The International Journal of Bilingualism, 4*, 327–350.

Gafaranga, J. (2001). Linguistic identities in talk-in-interaction: Order in bilingual conversation. *Journal of Pragmatics, 33*, 1901–1925.

Gardner, R. (2004). On delaying the answer: Question sequences extended after the question. In R. Gardner & J. Wagner (Eds.), *Second language conversations (pp. 246-266).* London: Continuum.

Garfinkel, H. (1967). *Studies in ethnomethodology.* Englewood Cliffs, NJ: Prentice Hall.

Garfinkel, H., & Sacks, H. (1970). On formal structures of practical action. In J. C. McKinney & E. A. Tiryakian (Eds.). *Theoretical sociology: perspectives and developments* (pp. 338–366). New York: Appleton-Century-Crofts.

Goffman, E. (1967). *Interaction ritual.* New York: Anchor Books.

Goffman, E. (1981). *Forms of talk.* Oxford, UK: Blackwell.

Goodenough, W. (1956). Componential analysis and the study of meaning. *Language, 32*, 195–216.

Goodwin, C. (2007). Interactive footing. In E. Holt & R. Clift (Eds.), *Reporting talk: Reported speech in interaction* (pp. 16–46). Cambridge, UK: Cambridge University Press.

Goodwin, C., & Duranti, A. (1992). Rethinking context: An introduction. In A. Duranti & C. Goodwin (Eds.), *Rethinking context* (pp. 1–42). Cambridge, UK: Cambridge University Press.

Hellermann, J. (2008). *Social actions for classroom language learning.* Clevedon, UK: Multilingual Matters.

Heritage, J. (1984). *Garfinkel and ethnomethodology.* Cambridge, UK: Polity Press.

Heritage, J. (2004). Conversation analysis and institutional talk: Analysing data. In D. Silverman (Ed.), *Qualitative research* (pp. 161–182). London: Sage.

Heritage, J., & Roth, A. (1995). Grammar and institution: Questions and questioning in the broadcast news interview. *Research on Language and Social Interaction, 28*(1), 1–60.

Hester, S., & Eglin, P. (1997). Membership categorization analysis: An introduction. In S. Hester & P. Eglin (Eds.), *Culture in action* (pp. 1–23). Washington, DC: International Institute for Ethnomethodology and Conversation Analysis & University Press of America.

Hester, S., & Francis, D. (2000a). Analysing 'institutional talk': A reply to Watson. *Text, 20*, 373–376.

Hester, S., & Francis, D. (2000b). Ethnomethodology, conversation analysis and 'institutional talk'. *Text*, 20, 391–413.

Higgins, C. (2007). Constructing membership in the in-group: Affiliation and resistance among urban Tanzanians. *Pragmatics, 17*, 49–70.

Hutchby, I., & Wooffitt, R. (2008). *Conversation analysis: Principles, practices and applications.* Oxford, UK: Polity Press.

Jayyusi, L. (1984). *Categorisation and the moral order.* London: Routledge and Kegan Paul.

Kasper, G. (2006). When once is not enough: Politeness in multiple requests. *Multilingua, 25*, 323–349.

Kasper, G., & Ross, S. (2007). Multiple questions in oral proficiency interviews. *Journal of Pragmatics*, 2045–2070.

Lazaraton, A. (2002). *A qualitative approach to the validation of oral language tests.* Cambridge, UK: Cambridge University Press.

Lee, Y-A. (2007). Third turn position in teacher talk: Contingency and the work of teaching. *Journal of Pragmatics, 39*, 1204–1230.

Lepper, G. H. (2000). *Categories in text and talk: A practical introduction to categorization analysis.* London: Sage.

Lerner, G. H. (1996). Finding "face" in the preference structures of talk-in-interaction. *Social Psychology Quarterly, 59*, 303–321.

Lerner, G. H. (Ed.) (2004). *Conversation analysis: Studies from the first generation.* Amsterdam: Benjamins.

Li Wei (2005). "How can you tell?" Towards a common sense explanation of conversational code-switching. *Journal of Pragmatics, 37*, 375–389.

Liddicoat, A. J. (2007). *An introduction to conversation analysis.* London: Continuum.

Linell, P., Hofvendahl, J., & Lindholm, C. (2003). Multi-unit questions in institutional interactions: Sequential organization and communicative functions. *Text, 23*, 539–571.

Luke, K. K., & Pavlidou, T.-S. (Eds.) (2002). *Telephone calls.* Amsterdam: Benjamins.

Lynch, M. (2000). Against reflexivity as an academic virtue and source of privileged knowledge. *Theory, Culture & Society, 17*, 26–54.

Lynch, M., & Peyrot, M. (1992). Introduction: A reader's guide to ethnomethodology. *Qualitative Sociology, 15*, 113–122.

Macbeth, D. (2000). Classrooms as installations: Direct instruction in the early grades. In S. Hester & D. Francis (Eds.), *Local educational order* (pp. 21–71). Amsterdam: Benjamins.

Macbeth, D. (2004). The relevance of repair for classroom correction. *Language in Society, 33*, 703–736.

Markee, N. (2000). *Conversation analysis.* Mahwah, NJ: Erlbaum.

Maynard, D. W. (2003). *Bad news, good news: Conversational order in everyday talk and clinical settings.* Chicago: Chicago University Press.

Maynard, D. W., & Clayman, S. E. (1991). The diversity of ethnomethodology. *Annual Review of Sociology, 17*, 385–418.

McHoul, A., & Rapley, M. (Eds.) (2001). *How to analyse talk in institutional settings.* London: Continuum.

McHoul, A., Rapley, M., & Antaki, C. (2008). You gotta light? On the luxury of context for understanding talk in interaction. *Journal of Pragmatics, 40*, 42–54.

McIlvenny, P. (Ed.) (2001). *Talking gender and sexuality.* Amsterdam: Benjamins.

Nguyen, H. t. (2006). Constructing 'expertness': A novice pharmacist's development of interactional competence in patient consultations. *Communication and Medication, 3*(2), 147–160.

Nguyen, H. t. (2008). Sequential organization as local and longitudinal achievement. *Text and Talk, 28* (4), 501–528.

Nishizaka, A. (1999). Doing interpreting within interaction: The interactive accomplishment of a "*Henna Gaijin*" or "Strange Foreigner." *Human Studies, 22*, 235–251.

Ochs, E., & Schieffelin, B. (2008). Language socialization: An historical overview. In P. A. Duff & N. H. Hornberger (Eds.), *Encyclopedia of language and education, 2nd ed., Vol. 8: Language socialization* (pp. 3–15). New York: Springer Science+ Business Media, LLC.

Park, Y.-Y. (1998). A discourse analysis of contrastive connectives in English, Korean, and Japanese conversation. In A. Jucker & Y. Ziv (Eds.), *Discourse markers* (pp. 277–300). Amsterdam: Benjamins.

Peräkylä, A. (2004). Reliability and validity in research based on naturally occurring social interaction. In D. Silverman (Ed.), *Qualitative research* (pp. 283–304). London: Sage.

Psathas, G. (1995) *Conversation analysis: The study of talk-in-interaction.* Thousand Oaks, CA: Sage.

Rapley, T. (2008). *Doing conversation, discourse and document analysis.* London: Sage.

Richards, K. (2006). 'Being the teacher': Identity and classroom conversation. *Applied Linguistics, 27,* 51–77.

Sacks, H. (1972). An initial investigation of the usability of conversational data for doing sociology. In D. N. Sudnow (Ed.), *Studies in social interaction* (pp. 31–74). New York: Free Press.

Sacks, H. (1984). Notes on methodology. In J. M. Atkinson & J. Heritage (Eds.), *Structures of social action* (pp. 21–27). Cambridge, UK: Cambridge University Press.

Sacks, H. (1995a). *Lectures on conversation,* Vol. 1 (G. Jefferson, Ed., introduction by E. A. Schegloff). Cambridge, MA: Blackwell.

Sacks, H. (1995b). *Lectures on conversation,* Vol. 2 (G. Jefferson, Ed., introduction by E. A. Schegloff). Cambridge, MA: Blackwell.

Schegloff, E. A. (1972). Notes on a conversational practice: Formulating place. In D. Sudnow (Ed.), *Studies in social interaction* (pp. 75–119). New York: Free Press.

Schegloff, E. A. (1991). Reflections on talk and social structure. In D. Boden & D. H. Zimmerman (Eds.), *Talk and social structure* (pp. 44–70). Cambridge, UK: Polity Press.

Schegloff, E. A. (1992). Introduction. In H. Sacks (Ed.), *Lectures on conversation* (Vol. 1, pp. ix–lxii). Oxford, UK: Blackwell.

Schegloff, E. A. (1996). Turn organization: One intersection of grammar and interaction. In E. Ochs, E. A. Schegloff, & S. A. Thompson (Eds.), *Interaction and grammar* (pp. 52–133). Cambridge, UK: Cambridge University Press.

Schegloff, E. A. (2002). Reflections on research on telephone conversation: Issues of cross-cultural scope and scholarly exchange, interactional import and consequences. In K. K. Luke & T.-S. Pavlidou (Eds.), *Telephone calls* (pp. 249–281). Amsterdam: Benjamins.

Schegloff, E. A. (2006). Interaction: The infrastructure for social institutions, the natural ecological niche for language, and the arena in which culture is enacted. In N. J. Enfield & S. C. Levinson (Eds.), *Roots of human society* (pp. 70–96). Oxford, UK: Berg.

Schegloff, E. A. (2007a). A tutorial on membership categorization. *Journal of Pragmatics, 39,* 462–482.

Schegloff, E. A. (2007b). *Sequence organization in interaction.* Cambridge, UK: Cambridge University Press.

Schegloff, E. A., & Sacks, H. (1973). Opening up closings. *Semiotica,* 8, 289–327.

Schenkein, J. N. (1978). Sketch of an analytic mentality for the study of conversational interaction. In J. N. Schenkein (Ed.), *Studies in the organization of conversational interaction* (pp. 1–6.) New York: Academic Press.

Schütz, A. (1962). Commonsense and scientific interpretation of human actions. In A. Schütz, *Collected papers I: Studies in social theory.* The Hague, Netherlands: Martinus Nijhoff.

Seedhouse, P. (2004). *The interactional architecture of the language classroom: A conversation analysis perspective.* Oxford, UK: Blackwell.

Seedhouse, P. (2007) Interaction and constructs. In Zhu Hua, P. Seedhouse, Li Wei, & V. Cook (Eds.), *Language learning and teaching as social interaction* (pp. 9–21). Houndsmill, Basingstoke, UK: Palgrave Macmillan.

Sharrock, W. M., & Anderson, R. J. (1986). *The ethnomethodologists.* London: Tavistock.

Silverman, D. (1998). *Harvey Sacks. Social science and conversation analysis.* New York: Oxford University Press.

Silverman, D. (2006). *Interpreting qualitative data* (3rd ed.). London: Sage.

Steensig, J., & Asmuß, B. (2005). Notes on disaligning 'yes but' initiated utterances in German and Danish conversations: Two construction types for dispreferred responses. In A. Hakulinen & M. Selting (Eds.), *Syntax and lexis in conversation* (pp. 349–373). Amsterdam: Benjamins.

Talmy, S. (2004). Forever FOB: The cultural production of ESL in a high school. *Pragmatics, 14,* 149–172.

Talmy, S. (2008). The cultural productions of the ESL student at Tradewinds High: Contingency, multidirectionality, and identity in L2 socialization. *Applied Linguistics.* Advance Access published June 9, 2008. doi:10.1093/applin/amn011

ten Have, P. (2001). Applied conversation analysis. In A. McHoul & M. Rapley (Eds.), *How to analyse talk in institutional settings* (pp. 3–11). London: Continuum.

ten Have, P. (2007). *Doing conversation analysis* (2nd ed.). London: Sage.

Thüne, E.-M., & Leonardi, S. (Eds.) (2003). *Telefonare i diverse lingue* [Speaking on the telephone in different languages]. Milan: Francoangeli.

Torras, M.-C. (2005). Social identity and language choice in bilingual service talk. In K. Richards & P. Seedhouse (Eds.), *Applying conversation analysis* (pp. 107–123). Houndsmill, Basingstoke, UK: Palgrave Macmillan.

Watson, D. R. (1978). Categorisation, authorization and blame-negotiation in conversation. *Sociology, 12*, 105–113.

Watson, D. R. (1983). The presentation of 'victim' and 'motive' in discourse: The case of police interrogations and interviews. *Victimology, 8*, 31–52.

Watson, D. R. (1997). Some general reflections of 'categorization' and 'sequence' in the analysis of conversation. In S. Hester & P. Eglin (Eds.), *Culture in action* (pp. 49–75). Washington, DC: International Institute for Ethnomethodology and Conversation Analysis & University Press of America.

Watson, D. R. (2000). The character on 'institutional talk': A response to Hester and Francis. *Text, 20,* 377–391.

Wittgenstein, L. (1953). *Philosophical investigations.* Oxford, UK: Blackwell.

Wooffitt, R. (2005). *Conversation analysis and discourse analysis.* London: Sage.

Wootton, A. (1997). *Interaction and the development of mind.* Cambridge, UK: Cambridge University Press.

Zimmerman, D. H. (1984). Talk and its occasion: The case of calling the police. In D. Schiffrin (Ed.), *Meaning, form, and use in context* (pp. 210–228). Washington, DC: Georgetown University Press.

Zimmerman, D. H. (1998). Identity, context and interaction. In C. Antaki & S. Widdicombe (Eds.), *Identities in talk* (pp. 87–106). London: Sage.

Zimmerman, D. H. (1999). Horizontal and vertical comparative research in language and social interaction. *Research on Language and Social Interaction, 32*, 195–203.

Zimmerman, D. H., & Boden, D. (1991). Structure-in-action. In D. Boden & D. H. Zimmerman (Eds.), *Talk and social structure: Studies in ethnomethodology and conversation analysis* (pp. 3–21). Cambridge, UK: Polity Press.

2 Kinship Categories in a Northern Thai Narrative

Jack Bilmes
University of Hawai'i at Mānoa

Introduction and background

This is an analysis of a story told by Taa, a Northern Thai villager, in Kammuang, the language of the Muang, the major ethnic group in the region. A crucial element of the narrative is Taa's deployment of kinship categories, which are used in both literal and metaphorical senses. Through the use of these categories, the story is made motivationally and morally transparent. My analytical approach, with its emphasis on detailed examination of recorded speech and on the verbal context of particular speech items, derives from the early work of Harvey Sacks on "membership categorization" and formulation in general (Sacks, 1992).[1] I also draw on some older work in taxonomic analysis.[2] The most distinctive contribution of this paper to both these literatures is in its analysis of the structure and use of metaphor.

The interview with Taa that produced this story took place in 1990. Since my first fieldwork in the village of Sang Ton in 1971, dramatic changes had occurred in the village, especially in sharecropping arrangements. Although my major stints of fieldwork were in 1971–1972 and in 1988, I returned to the village every 2 or 3 years for short periods to visit with old friends and update my knowledge of village affairs. On this occasion, I had gone to Taa's house with three villagers (Cǎn, Sǒm, and Lǔang) and my wife (Pong) to talk to him. Taa was one of my favorite informants and a great raconteur. He laid out mats on the floor of the receiving area of his

Talk-in-interaction: Multilingual perspectives, pp. 29–56, Hanh Nguyen & Gabriele Kasper (Eds.), 2009
Honolulu, HI: University of Hawai'i, National Foreign Language Resource Center

house, and we sat in a circle, cross-legged (except for my wife, who sat in a more demure legs-tucked-under position), conversing on various matters of mutual interest. Finally, I broached the subject of sharecropping. I asked in particular about his service on the Land Rental Committee, an organization formed under a Thai government directive. Each *tambon* (a collection of neighboring villages) had such a committee, comprised of several appointed members. The committee had a number of functions, one of which was to mediate disputes between villagers concerning land tenure. He responded to my question by informing me that he had recently retired from the committee because the local government officials were "not following the law," motivated by "influence," in particular, by bribes. He proceeded to tell a series of stories illustrating his point.

The story told immediately before the one that is the subject of this paper was of the incident that was the proximate cause of Taa's quitting the committee. A wealthy, elderly woman in the village decided to sell some of her rice land. The buyer, who had sharecropped the land (and who happened to be Taa's brother-in-law), put down a deposit. According to Taa, the law stipulated that if the woman changed her mind, she would have to pay the buyer 10 times the amount of the deposit. The woman did change her mind and indicated that she was ready to pay the penalty. But, apparently, her son convinced her not to. Instead, he bribed various district officials, who then evaded their duty to enforce the law. Taa, in his capacity as a Land Rental Committee member, tried to intercede on behalf of the buyer but could not get anything done.

This narrative took a long time to tell, in part because it had many twists and turns and in part because those present participated a good deal, encouraging Taa to provide more detail. When he finally reached the end of his story, Taa said that it put him in mind of another incident, and he told the story which is analyzed below. I selected this story for analysis because it is relatively compact, with a clear beginning and end, and because I find it interesting and culturally revealing. The transcript, in phonemic symbols, with interlinear word-by-word and vernacular translation, can be found in Appendix A, together with an explanation of possibly unfamiliar symbols and translation conventions (Appendix B). A summary of the story follows. I have inserted into the summary (in parentheses) certain lines from the original transcript, which are central to the analysis.

Taa's narrative

Taa began, "I am reminded of something. I am reminded of the incident with Thawn." Thawn (who was Taa's son-in-law) had been a soldier and gone absent without leave. He did not have the proper discharge papers. Thawn's father (*pɔ̂ɔ man* [his father]) came to Taa and said that Thawn could get the papers, but it would cost 1,500 baht. His father, Kham, claimed that he did not have the money and asked for Taa's help. Taa asked Kham to help with the payment, but Kham pleaded poverty. So Taa went to the warden, who did in fact ask for 1,500 baht, which Taa paid. Then he had to go to the Provincial Office, where they asked for another 1,500 baht (and he paid). From there, he was sent to the City Hall, where they demanded 1,000 baht more (and he paid). Having done all that, he went to the army camp. "Oh," he exclaimed, "they have arrested my child" (*lûuk kuu*). "Oh, he is my son-in-law" (*lûukcaay*). They asked him for 3,000 baht. He said that he did not have it. The officer told him that, in that case, his child would remain in jail. So Taa tried a ruse, saying that Thawn would have to take his punishment. He then offered to take some of the officers to lunch. They went into the city (Chiang Mai) and ate and drank. It cost Taa 600 baht. At this point, Pong (my wife) asked him, jokingly, why he did not just flee (instead of paying), and he said, "I was worried about my child [*lûuk haw*]. I wanted to get my child [*lûuk haw*] out of there." Taa departed without paying any more on that day. He went back the next day and took two of the officers out for lunch. They asked him again for the 3,000 baht, but reduced it to 1,500, which he paid. He had told them that he would not pay, but when he saw the soldiers with chains on their legs, he changed his mind: "I don't want that to happen to Thawn." Then he returned to the subject of Kham, Thawn's father, who, he said, he knew to be a good-for-nothing. "He asked me to go to the city to get Thawn, but he wouldn't go. His own son [*lûuk man tέεtέε*]. He wouldn't go. He was afraid it would cost him money. So he came to bother the wife's father." (At this point, the subject changed to the case of another villager.)

Muang narrative

Taa's story followed in a transparent way from the other stories he had been telling in that it is yet another story about official corruption. Oddly, though, what Taa finally made of this story, his ultimate evaluation, was not about the behavior of the officials but about that of Kham, his son-in-law's father. This caused me to see the whole series of stories in a different way. They were not simply, or perhaps even primarily, about official corruption; rather, Taa was relating a picaresque series of adventures in which he was the honest and generous hero in a world of scoundrels, liars, and self-seekers. Perhaps this is why he missed a certain irony in his final story. After complaining that the government officials were not following the law and that they were being bribed, he proceeded to tell this story, in which he was trying to bribe government officials and get them to break the law.

Although Taa's story may be somewhat exotic in its subject matter, its structure is quite familiar to English speakers. It begins with "That reminds me," a preface (Sacks, 1974), relates a series of events in chronological order (Labov & Waletsky, 1967), and ends with an evaluation section (Labov & Waletsky, 1967). The story proper has a recognizable beginning (Kham asks Taa to obtain discharge papers for Thawn) and ending (Taa obtains the papers). Despite these generic characteristics, Muang narrative has at least one distinctive feature, the way that direct quotations are done. They are usually dropped into the story without being specifically marked as quotation. (Although Taa generally appended *ii nɔ́* [like that] to the ends of quotations, this was not an infallible marker because he also used the expression frequently with remarks that were not quotations.) This conversational practice, which was not limited to Taa, was a frequent source of confusion for me, especially during my first months in the village. Pronoun usage, it turns out, is an important resource in identifying direct quotations. Muang offers a rich variety of pronouns (including the "zero pronoun"—see Aroonmanakun, 1999; Campbell, 1969; Palakornkul, 1975) for first, second, and third person reference, and when the speaker uses a pronoun form that is not suited to his current audience, he or she may be surmised to be speaking in the voice of one of the characters in a story. A more careful study of these quotations may show that there are frequently other subtle markers, such as slight changes in voice quality, but I suspect that in some cases the hearer is left with no resource other than the context for identifying quotations of this sort.

Another feature of Muang stories (and of other kinds of Muang talk) that is worth mentioning is the very frequent use of what I call demonstratives, solicitors, and emphatic particles. This is not in evidence in the vernacular English translation, but one can see it in the interlinear translation in Appendix A. I use *D* for demonstratives, *S* for solicitors, and *E* for emphatic particles. (I also use *Im* for imperatives and *P* for polite particles (see Appendix B). Polite particles are rarely heard in talk among villagers, especially not in men's talk, and the male polite particle (*khap*) is, I believe, borrowed from the Central Thai "standard" dialect, which I refer to hereafter simply as "Thai.") The demonstratives might be translated in many contexts as "like that"; the solicitors, as "you know?" The emphatic particles, as the name implies, add emphasis but are difficult to translate. I might have attempted to include the demonstratives and solicitors in my vernacular translation, but they would have made the English seem clumsy in a way that the Kammuang is not. (Thai also uses such clause-final particles, but Kammuang has more of them, and speakers of Kammuang use them more liberally.)

"My child"

Taa refers to Thawn three times in the narrative as "my child" (lines 43, 81, 83). The first occurrence is of particular interest. Taa has just entered the army camp. Perhaps he realizes for the first time that Thawn has been arrested. At any rate, he exclaims "Oh! There it is! They have arrested my child [*lûuk kuu*]." The lexical item *lûuk* translates as "child"; *kuu* is a vulgar form of "I" or "me" (I address this later). The Muang possessive is formed by placing the pronoun (or other noun) after a noun. Although *lûuk* is translated as "child," the English and the Kammuang have an important difference. Sacks (1972), in his well-known analysis of "The baby cried. The mommy picked it up," notes that "baby" belongs to two "categorization devices." One is stage-of-life, the other, family. That is, "baby," in some contexts, refers to age; in others, to a kinship relation. The same may be said for "child." In Kammuang, the two devices are distinguished by different words: *lûuk* refers to the family relationship, and when age is at issue, the Muang use *la'ɔ̀ɔn*. Taa's use of the word *lûuk* is unambiguous as to age versus relation. In fact, because of the phraseology ("my child"), the English also makes clear that he is speaking of a family relation. However, some situations where *lûuk* is used without the possessive would present problems. For example, *lûuk pay nǎy* [child go where] can be translated (depending on the situation) as "Where are you going?" but with the further understanding that one is speaking to "child." However, an English speaker without the requisite knowledge of Kammuang would have no way of knowing whether *lûuk* indicated age or relationship.

After referring to Thawn as his child in line 43, Taa immediately clarifies: "Oh, he is my son-in-law" (he may have thought that my wife or I were not aware of this fact). I say "clarifies" rather than "corrects" because Taa goes on to refer to Thawn as his child twice more. Although Thawn is his son-in-law, he is also, in some sense, his child. To understand how this works, we might begin by considering a common semantic phenomenon in English, Thai, and many, if not all, other languages. Hamlet says, "man delights not me: no, nor woman neither, though by your smiling you seem to say so." The word "man" is here used at two levels of contrast. At one level, it refers to humankind in general. At the more specific level, it refers to man as contrasted with woman. The usage is diagrammed taxonomically in Figure 1:

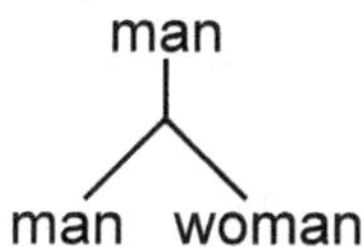

Figure 1. Two meanings of "man."

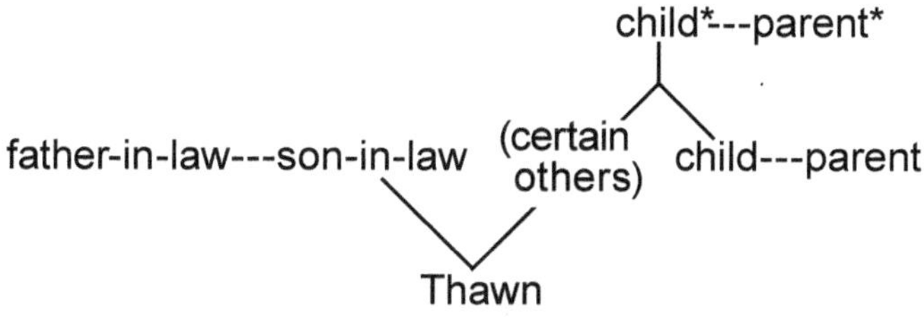

child*---parent*

father-in-law---son-in-law (certain others) child---parent

Thawn

Figure 2. "Child" as metaphor. *Note.* An asterisk refers to metaphoric usage.

The word "child," I argue, is likewise being used by Taa at two levels (see Figure 2). The difference from the previous example is that Taa, in calling Thawn his child, has created a metaphor for this specific occasion. (I use "child*" to indicate the metaphorical usage.)

Thawn is simultaneously Taa's child* and his son-in-law. "Certain others" is short for nondescendents, in one's child's generation, towards whom one feels the same sentiments as one feels towards one's own child. It is a nonlexicalized category—thus the parentheses. By diagramming the situation in this way, I am suggesting that "child*" is an extension of "child," in the sense that it has one or more of the attributes of "child," but not all of the attributes. This fits the common definition of *metaphor*. (The online Merriam-Webster dictionary defines metaphor as follows: "a figure of speech in which a word or phrase literally denoting one kind of object or idea is used in place of another to suggest a likeness or analogy between them." Thus, "Thawn is my child" is analogous to "John is a lion.") "Child*" is not a standard cultural category; it is metaphorical, constructed for this occasion. What I am proposing here, then, is an extension of taxonomic (Conklin, 1962; Frake, 1961, 1969) and membership categorization analysis (Sacks, 1992) to include special, nonconventionalized, metaphorical categories ("metagories"?).[3]

"Child" and "son-in-law" are members of what Sacks calls "standardized relational pairs" (indicated by horizontal dashed lines in Figure 2), being paired with "parent" and "father-in-law," respectively. (In Kammuang, "child" is part of a relational triad—*pɔ̂ɔ-mɛ̂ɛ-lûuk* [father-mother-child]. The equivalent of "parent" is simply *pɔ̂ɔ mɛ̂ɛ*). In casting Thawn as his child*, Taa is casting himself as Thawn's parent*. When we make a metaphor of one member of a standardized relational pair, we would seem to implicitly create a metaphorical counterpart. The metaphorical child* requires a metaphorical parent*.

Among the attributes of "child" is generation −1 and lineal descent. Further attributes of the standardized pair include mutual love and obligation.[4] These are what Watson (1978) calls "category bound predicates." Obligation is a socially ascribed attribute. A parent is expected to help and sacrifice for his or her child and vice-versa. The link between parent and child is perhaps the most significant relationship for Thais. The grown child is under permanent obligation to his or her parents and, in particular, should help to take care of them in their old age. Similarly, parents should be willing to, and indeed have an obligation to, make sacrifices for their children's well-being, even after the children are adults. Although a father-in-law may have some obligation toward his son-in-law, it is not of the same magnitude. Love, however, is personal; one may love a son-in-law like a son. Thus, in calling Thawn his child* but also pointing out that Thawn is his son-in-law, Taa is claiming love for Thawn while simultaneously denying the formal obligation to help that he would have in regard to his actual child (and, of course, denying lineality). He is making a considerable sacrifice for sentimental reasons rather than because he is obligated to do so.

The use of a metaphor requires some effort on the part of the hearer. The hearer must recognize the aspects of the source category that are preserved in the metaphorical usage. When we are told that John is a lion, what attributes of lions are we to understand John to possess? In deciding this, the hearer brings into play knowledge of topic, general context, and plausibility. Moreover, certain metaphors are partially conventionalized. When they become fully conventionalized, they appear in the dictionary and are therefore literal meanings. Thus, one meaning of "pig" (Merriam-Webster online) is "a dirty, gluttonous, or repulsive person."[5] Taa's usage of "child*," though, I take to be partially conventionalized. It is still metaphorical, but is ordinarily used, when it is used metaphorically, to suggest a sentimental attachment. Moreover, we need to ask what aspect of "child" fits the story Taa is telling. Sentimental attachment provides a motive for Taa's actions; at the same time, the need for a sensible motive leads us to understand his metaphor in a way that would provide that motive and thus to understand "child" as suggesting sentimental attachment.

Motivation

Taa presents his rather substantial sacrifice on Thawn's behalf as motivated by parental-like love. The invocation of a filial relationship between son-in-law and parent-in-law is, of course, not unknown to English speakers, where a son-in-law may address his wife's father as "Dad." But the father-in-law/son-in-law relationship may be more significant for Muang (and Thais in general), especially villagers, than it is in Western societies. This is not due to the kinship system as such. Muang kinship arrangements are, as are those of Western societies, characterized by the bilateral kindred. The important difference is in residential practices. Muang society (and Thai society in general) shows a strong normative and statistical preference for initial matrilocal residence after marriage, at least in rural areas (see Potter, 1976). When the new husband comes to live in his parents-in-law's house, he generally performs a form of bride service, working the household fields under the authority of the father-in-law. The couple may live with the wife's parents for a few years and then set up their own, independent household. One of the daughters and her husband generally stay permanently in her parents' house.

Note that Kammuang does not have a word that properly translates as "father-in-law." Rather, it has two expressions—*pɔ̂ɔmia* [wife's father] and *pɔ̂ɔphǔa* [husband's father]. The wife's father is, of course, the exact (male) reciprocal for son-in-law. In the case of matrilocal residence, the wife's father is the crucial in-law because the son-in-law generally works under the father-in-law's authority. In the less usual case of patrilocal residence, the crucial in-law is not the husband's father but rather the husband's mother. The transplanted wife, living with her in-laws, will have to deal primarily with her mother-in-law. Thus, the English expressions "father-in-law" and "mother-in-law" obscure what are, for the Muang, important distinctions.

Thawn had married Taa's daughter and left his home village to live in Taa's house. I do not know whether he was living there at the time of his induction into the army or whether he was expected to live there after his discharge. Nevertheless, largely because of residence arrangements, the relationship between Thawn and Taa was clearly close and familial. This was expressed in the narrative both by Taa's use of the word *lûuk* [child] and by his willingness to pay for Thawn's release.

Considering these arrangements augments the plausibility of Taa's implicit claim that his actions were motivated by love. However, the arrangements also provide for the plausibility of more selfish motives. Material considerations may also have influenced Taa's desire to help Thawn, especially if Thawn was still performing bride service. Even if he was not, Thawn, when released, would still resume responsibility for his wife, Taa's daughter. The motive that Taa actually invokes, perhaps with complete sincerity, puts him in the best possible light, acting selflessly on behalf of another, and stands in contrast to other plausible motives.[6]

The provision of a plausible motive—any plausible motive—has a more general narrative function. Sacks (1992, Vol. 1, pp. 121–125) notes that, when what actually occurred is somewhat ambiguous, we will give preference to an alternative that has an explanation. A related point is that the provision of a plausible motive makes a narrative more credible. If we could not see any good reason for Taa to act in the way that he claimed he did, we might doubt that the narrated events actually occurred. The demand for plausible motivation seems to be as salient for the Muang as it is for Westerners.[7]

Pronouns

In line 43, Taa refers to Thawn as *lûuk kuu*. As I have already noted, *kuu* is a vulgar form of "I/me," which may be used with inferiors, intimate friends, and those whom one wishes to insult.[8] This is the only point in the narrative where he uses *kuu*; elsewhere, he refers to himself primarily as *phǒm* (a Thai word that villagers use when speaking to high-status outsiders) or the more casual *haw*. The use of *kuu* suggests Taa's consternation at the situation, just as an English speaker might use vulgar language in similar circumstances.

However, this usage has more to it. There are few, if any, circumstances where Taa would use *kuu* in addressing me (perhaps if we got drunk together or he was in a rage), and, I think, none at all where he would use it in addressing my wife. By using the word in line 43, he is showing that this is what he was thinking at the time. That is, he was addressing, as well as referring to, himself with *kuu*. For him to address us using the word *kuu* would be unthinkable, and he knew that we knew that. He is able to put this mutual knowledge into play in creating a narrative effect. He did not have to say explicitly, "This is what I thought," or "This is what I said to myself." The word *kuu* does the work.[9]

Note that, in his other two usages of "my child" (lines 81 and 83), he says *lûuk haw* rather than *lûuk kuu.* The lexical item *haw* is a casual form of the first person singular (as well as being the standard first person plural), less formal than *phǒm* but not impolite. In these latter two cases, he is addressing Pong (who has just used the word *haw* in the sense of "you") directly, answering her question. These answers also make more or less explicit the relationship between *lûuk* and his motives for doing what he does.

One is reminded here of Dilthey's (2001) hermeneutic circle, Garfinkel's (1967, version of the) documentary method of interpretation, and Gidden's (1976) structuration. All these notions contrast with the assumptions of early sociolinguistics in that they point to the fact that linguistic expressions are not the straightforward product of contextual determination. Rather, they create and elaborate context even as they respond to it. In the narrative at hand, Taa draws on a subset of the extensive set of referentially equivalent forms of the first person singular available in Kammuang. On the one hand, he is constrained to produce situationally appropriate forms. On the other, he is able to manipulate his use of these terms to enrich his narrative, by influencing the hearer's understanding of what situation is constraining his selection of forms.

In particular, Taa is able to use pronouns to create "voices" in the narrative (Bakhtin, 1986; also Goffman, 1974, on "participation status"). In the narrative, we find Taa addressing Pong and me (the narrative was arguably for everyone present, but the level of politeness was adjusted to my wife and myself, who were also the primary audience in that we had asked the questions that precipitated his telling. Also, at certain points, he addressed us directly); Kham addressing Taa; Taa addressing Kham; Taa addressing himself; Taa addressing an officer; the officer addressing Taa; and Taa (when doing a word search) addressing everyone present. Much of the work of producing these voices is accomplished through variations in his use of first person singular pronouns.

We see here another implication of Taa's switch from his previous use of Thawn's name to "my child*." The expression "child*" allows him to use the first person singular pronoun (for "my"). In English, the implications of this are not evident, but given the wide selection of first-person singulars in Muang, Taa's choice of pronoun has expressive dimensions. As we have seen, it allows him to express his dismay at the situation and to create a distinctive "voice."

Father and father-in-law

Until line 43, Thawn is referred to by name. He is categorized immediately as "soldier," which is essential to the narrative. Taa does not even mention that he is Thawn's father-in-law. (Everyone present knew how he was related to Thawn, but he does not explicitly bring that relationship into play in the narrative until much later.) Kham is introduced as Thawn's father. Again, this is essential to the narrative because Kham is there in his capacity as Thawn's father. Ultimately, though, this category is found to have moral implications. Until the point in the story when he gets to the army compound, Taa presents himself as more or less mechanically acting in accordance with Kham's request. Only when Taa gets to the compound and presumably learns for the first time that Thawn has been arrested does he begin to refer to Thawn as his "child*." He mentions only briefly that Thawn is actually his son-in-law and then goes back to calling Thawn his child*. In the final, evaluation section of the story, Kham is reintroduced, once again as Thawn's father. Thawn is again referred to by his name. And Taa is no longer his father* but the father of Thawn's wife (line 124). That is, as in the beginning of the story, Kham's kinship relation to Thawn is presented as primary, Taa's as secondary. Whereas the kinship categorization of Kham is stable, those of Taa and Thawn are variable, and that variation seems to be fitted to the demands of the narrative and Taa's presentation of his own and Kham's moral character.

At the beginning of the story, Kham is presented neutrally and addressed by Taa as *pɔ̂ɔ kham*. When a Muang man reaches a certain age, around 50, people (especially younger ones) begin to add *pɔ̂ɔ* ("father] to his name. This is a relatively unmarked usage, conveying what might be termed "normal respect." In the evaluation section, Taa refers to Kham as *pùu kham* (line 117). In Thai, *pùu* means "grandfather" (on the father's side), but in Kammuang the word for "grandfather" is *pɔ̂ɔ úy*. The term *pùu* is a somewhat disrespectful usage: *pùu kham* can be translated as "old man Kham." This reflects Taa's negative judgment of Kham as a good-for-nothing, a man who refused to take responsibility for his own son and passed the job on to Taa, who was only the father-in-law. "If an incumbent of a given category...does not enact category-bound obligations... then these matters may be claimed as noticeably absent and as specifically accountable" (Watson, 1978, pp. 106–107).

In the final section, Thawn is referred to not merely as Kham's *lûuk*, but as his *lûuk tɛ́ɛtɛ́ɛ*, his "real child." This use of *lûuk tɛ́ɛtɛ́ɛ* is indexical in the sense that it is occasioned by Taa's previous usage of *lûuk* in referring to Thawn. Otherwise, saying that Thawn was Kham's *lûuk* would have been sufficient. In terms of kinship relations, the story progresses from Thawn (child) and Kham (father) to Thawn (metaphorical child*, actual son-in-law) and Taa (metaphorical father*) to Thawn (Kham's "real" child, Taa's son-in-law), Kham ("real" father), and Taa (father-in-law). Only in this final triad are the relationships juxtaposed in such a way as to bring out the moral point of the story. In pointing out the "real" relations, Taa has switched the emphasis from sentiment to obligation and from self-enhancement to blame.

At the beginning of the story, Taa is in a situation somewhat similar to his position in his previous stories. A poor villager has come to him for help, and he responds. As his investment in the situation increases, he provides himself with additional motivation—Thawn is his child*. This explains his actions within the narrative. In the evaluation section, however, Thawn is once more referred to by name. Kham is reinstated as Thawn's father, and Taa is merely Thawn's father-in-law. In each part of the story, Taa's references to and categorizations of Kham, Thawn, and himself seem designed to produce a specific "rhetorical" effect (Edwards, 1991, 1997). At each moment, Taa has a range of referentially adequate alternatives, and the choices he makes are constitutive of the coherence, credibility, and point of his narrative. Moreover, the meaning of the story is, to some extent, transformed at its conclusion, crucially through the deployment of kin terms. Given the previous context, we are prone to hear this narrative as a story of official corruption and of Taa's virtue. Finally, though, although it remains an illustration of Taa's virtue, it is also presented as an instance of Kham's selfishness and unwillingness to fulfill his kinship obligations.

Discussion

During the time of my initial fieldwork in the village, in 1971–1972, the villagers were discussing the possibility of electrifying the village. This would involve putting up posts and stringing a wire along the main road from the neighboring village, which bordered on the district center. In these discussions, I frequently heard the villagers mention "people who live near the main road" as contrasted with those who did not. This was an occasioned category. (In a 1983 article, Barsalou called such inventions "ad hoc categories.") Those who lived near the road would be able to easily access the electricity for their homes. This type of topically bounded category, despite its ubiquity, was ignored in the ethnosemantic literature. Categories were treated as established cultural objects. This is natural when one's interest is in culture, but it does not provide a very accurate representation of how people talk (or how they think). The metaphorical category is a special case of the occasioned category. To the degree that a category is metaphorical, it is occasioned—for this moment and for this purpose. In a word's context, it is to be understood in a special way, which is not the way the word would ordinarily be understood. Indeed, Taa more or less instructs us in his special usage by pointing out that Thawn is not literally his child but his son-in-law. Nevertheless, metaphors are built on a foundation of "normal," literal, culturally standard usages. Even if we take seriously (as I do) the observation that, as Edwards (1991) puts it, "categories are for talking," we cannot lose sight of talk's cultural/semantic setting.

Metaphors and literal usages are best thought of as extreme types, defining the ends of a scale. Consider the following examples:

1. Bacon comes from pigs.
2. It took a long time.
3 John is a pig.
4. My students are my children.
5. "Yonder all before us lie deserts of vast eternity."

In example 1, "pig" is used literally. "Long" in example 2 is a dead metaphor (Whorf, 1956); that is, although it seems to derive from an extension of the concept of physical length, we no longer recognize its metaphorical quality. "Pig" in example 3 is literal in the sense that its use in the meaning of slovenly person appears in the dictionary, but it still has the feeling of a metaphor. Example 4 is a semiconventional metaphor, while Andrew Marvell's use of "desert" in 5 is a novel, nonconventionalized metaphor. Taa's use of "child*" is probably best classed as type 4. It is not so unfamiliar a usage as to be startling or poetic, but perhaps not so standard as to warrant inclusion in a dictionary. The use of the word "child" will not be understood in its extended sense ("child*") without contextual cues. In the present case, the cues are in part sequential. First, Taa points out that Thawn is, in fact, his son-in-law. Subsequently, he eliminates the possible interpretation of his first use of "child" as a mistake by referring to Thawn twice more as his child.

Thawn's metaphorical use of "child" is for a particular moment and a particular narrative purpose only. He drops the usage in the evaluation section, where he points out that Thawn is Kham's "real child" and that he, Taa, is only the father of Thawn's wife. The contrast of metaphorical child with real child allows Taa to compare himself favorably with Kham. Taa, although he is not the real father, has behaved as a real father should. Kham, who is the real father, has not. The function of the metaphor, then, is not to offer a striking image or new connection; it is to create an intelligible narrative and ultimately, a moral contrast. A "child*," when all is said and done, is not a "child."

Acknowledgments

I thank Pongsuwan Bilmes and Pandit Chanrochanakit for their help with fine points of transcription and interpretation.

Notes

1 There is a fairly extensive subsequent literature on membership categorization analysis. Hester and Eglin (1997) offer a representative example. For an analysis of Thai narrative using a very different approach, see Burusphat (1991).

2 See, for example, Tyler (1969).

3 Watson (1978, p. 107) writes that "If an incumbent of some other category enacts obligations conventionally tied to another category, then we may see that person as 'borrowing' or 'usurping' incumbency of that other category, so that we have the recategorization of 'friends' as 'brothers' or 'sisters' and the like." This brief passage

is, as far as I know, the closest that membership categorization analysis has come to dealing with metaphorical extension of categories. The situation is similar in taxonomic analysis. Although, as my own analysis shows, taxonomic techniques are well suited to the analysis of metaphor, ethnosemantics (taxonomic and componential analysis) has been criticized for ignoring metaphorical usages (e.g., Keesing, 1972; Tyler, 1978).

4 Generation −1 and lineal descent are necessary, criterial, and "componential" attributes of the kin term "child" in its most literal sense. Sentiment is a prototypical attribute. Obligation is, perhaps, a bit of both.

5 In this connection, see Wegener (1885/1991, as cited in Langer, 1942) on "faded metaphors."

6 He reinforces his motive at lines 26 and 108, with the observation that he was already in deeply.

7 On this point, compare Sacks's (1992, Vol. 1, pp. 113–118) analysis of a conversational segment in which a man is recounting a domestic incident to a social worker. The incident resulted in the sister of the man's wife calling the police, but the story, as told, seems to contain insufficient reason for her to have done so. The social worker complains, "You're not telling me the story." Sacks points out that the credibility of the story is compromised by the lack of warrant for the events in the story.

8 The usual vulgar "I" in Kammuang is *haa* rather than *kuu*. In Thai, it is *kuu*. However, *kuu* is also a Kammuang word.

9 The effect here is very similar to flouting the conversational maxims (Grice, 1975). For example, here (in my words) is a Gricean analysis of a transparent falsehood (thus flouting the "quality" maxim): "I know that the speaker couldn't have meant me to take what he said literally (he knows very well that what he said is false, and he knows that I know it), so I must find an interpretation that brings his utterance back into line with my assumption that he is a proper conversationalist: therefore, he must have been speaking ironically." In the present case, I know that he could not have been addressing me with the word *kuu*, so he must have been addressing himself, an example, perhaps, of the flouting, and consequent implicature, of Leech's (1983) proposed politeness principle.

References

Aroonmanakun, W. (1999). *Extending focusing for zero pronoun resolution in Thai.* Doctoral dissertation, Georgetown University. Washington, DC.

Bakhtin, M. M. (1986). The problem of speech genres. In M. M. Bakhtin, *Speech genres and other late essays* (pp. 60–102). Austin, TX: University of Texas Press.

Barsalou, L. (1983). Ad hoc categories. *Memory and Cognition, 11*, 211–227.

Burusphat, S. (1991). *The structure of Thai narrative.* Summer Institute of Linguistics and the University of Texas at Arlington Publications in Linguistics.

Campbell, R. N. (1969). *Noun substitutes in Modern Thai: A study in pronominality. Janua Linguarum: Series Practica* (Vol. 65). The Hague, Netherlands: Mouton.

Conklin, H. C. (1962). The lexicographical treatment of folk taxonomies. *International Journal of American Linguistics, 28*, 119–141.

Dilthey, W. (2001). The rise of hermeneutics. In R. A. Makkreel & F. Rodi (Eds.), *Wilhelm Dilthey: Selected works, Vol. IV: Hermeneutics and the study of history* (pp. 235–260). ebook, Princeton University Press.

Edwards, D. (1991). Categories are for talking: On the cognitive and discursive bases of categorization. *Theory and Psychology, 1*, 515–42.

Edwards, D. (1997). *Discourse and cognition.* London: Sage.

Frake, C. O. (1961). The diagnosis of disease among the Subanun of Mindanao. *American Anthropologist, 63*, 113–132.

Frake, C. O. (1969). The ethnographic study of cognitive systems. In S. A. Tyler (Ed.), *Cognitive anthropology* (pp. 28–41). New York: Holt, Rinehart and Winston.

Garfinkel, H. (1967). *Studies in ethnomethodology.* Englewood Cliffs, NJ: Prentice Hall.

Giddens, A. (1976). *New rules of sociological method: A positive critique of interpretive sociologies.* New York: Basic Books.

Goffman, E. (1974). *Frame analysis: An essay on the organization of experience.* New York: Harper Colophon.

Grice, H. P. (1975). Logic and conversation. In P. Cole & J. L. Morgan (Eds.), *Syntax and semantics, Vol. 3: Speech acts* (pp. 41–58). New York: Academic Press.

Hester, S. & Eglin, P. (Eds.) (1997). *Culture in action: Studies in membership categorization analysis.* Washington, DC: International Institute for Ethnomethodology and Conversation Analysis and University Press of America.

Keesing, R. (1972). Paradigms lost: The new ethnography and the new linguistics. *Southwestern Journal of Anthropology, 28*, 299–332.

Labov, W., & Waletzky, J. (1967). Narrative analysis. In J. Helm (Ed.), *Essays on the verbal and visual arts* (pp. 12–44). Seattle, WA: University of Washington Press.

Langer, S. K. (1942). *Philosophy in a new key: A study in the symbolism of reason, rite, and art.* New York: Mentor.

Leech, G. N. (1983). *Principles of pragmatics.* New York: Longman.

Palakornkul, A. (1975). A sociolinguistic study of pronominal usage in spoken Bangkok Thai. *Linguistics, 165*, 11–41.

Potter, J. M. (1976). *Thai peasant social structure.* Chicago: University of Chicago Press.

Sacks, H. (1972). On the analyzability of stories by children. In J. J. Gumperz & D. Hymes (Eds.), *Directions in sociolinguistics: The ethnography of communication* (pp. 325–345). New York: Holt, Rinehart and Winston.

Sacks, H. (1974). An analysis of the course of a joke's telling in conversation. In R. Bauman & J. Sherzer (Eds.), *Explorations in the ethnography of speaking* (pp. 337–353). Cambridge, UK: Cambridge University Press.

Sacks, H. (1992). *Lectures on conversation: Volumes I and II.* (Edited by G. Jefferson). Oxford, UK: Blackwell.

Tyler, S. A. (1969). *Cognitive anthropology.* New York: Holt, Rinehart and Winston.

Tyler, S. A. (1978). *The said and the unsaid: Mind, meaning, and culture.* New York: Academic Press.

Watson, D. R. (1978). Categorization, authorization and blame-negotiation in conversation. *Sociology, 12*, 105–113.

Wegener, P. (1991). *Untersuchungen üüber die Grundfragen des Sprachlebens.* [Reissued by K. Koerner]. Philadelphia: Benjamins. (Original work published 1885)

Whorf, B. L. (1956). The relation of habitual thought and behavior to language. In *Language, thought, and reality: Selected writings of Benjamin Lee Whorf* (pp. 134–159). (Edited and with an introduction by J. B. Carroll; foreword by S. Chase.) Cambridge, MA: M.I.T. Press.

Appendix A: Transcript of "Taa's narrative"

001 Taa:
maa kɤ́ɤt hɔ̂ɔt hĭa
come think reach now
I am reminded of something.

002 lɛ́ɛw maa kɤ́ɤt hɔ̂ɔt mɤ̂a ãy thɔɔn hĭa
then come think reach when T Thawn now
I am reminded of the incident with Thawn.

003 mɤ̂a pen thahăan láknĭi ná aacaan
when is soldier flee S professor
When he was a soldier, he fled, professor ((addressing Pong, my wife)).

004 baythábian bɔ dãy ((laughs))
registration card not get ((laughs))
He didn't get his registration card ((laughs))

005 kɔɔŋnŭn bɔ dãy nɔ́
reserve status not get S
He didn't get reserve status ((i.e., he left the Army without proper discharge papers, making him a deserter.))

006 thɤ̆ɤŋ níi pɔ̂ɔ man wâa
so this father him say
So his father said,

007 ee pɔ̂n ca hɤ̃ɤ naa baykɔɔŋnŭn ná
eh they will give S reserve status card S
"Eh, they will give it, the reserve status card.

008 ca sĩaŋ pan hãa ná ĩi nɔ́
will spend thousand five S D S
It will cost one thousand five hundred ((baht))." Like that.

009 maa tittɔ̀ɔ phŏm
come communicate me
He came to me.

010 maa ũu phŏm wâa
come speak me say
He said to me

011 ee man bɔ mii ŋən naa ĩi nɔ́
ee he not have money S D S
Eh, he has no money, like that.

012 ee khɔ̌ɔ cûay man kam kãa ia
ee request help him time E D
Eh, please help him.

013 oo pɔ̂ɔ kham cûay tə́ ĩi nɔ́
oo father kham help E D S
((Taa quoting himself)) "Oh Kham, you help."

014 pɔ̂ɔ kham cûay tə́
father kham help E
"Kham, you help."

015 khãa bɔ mii panyaa ĩi nɔ́
I not have ability D S
((quoting Kham)) "I don't have the ability," like that.

016 ee man ca aw pan hãa ta naa ĩi nɔ́
ee they will take thousand five E S D S
((quoting Kham)) "Eh, they want a thousand five hundred."

017 thɤ̌ɤŋ pay hǎa satsadii ca aw pan hãa nɛ̂ɛnɔɔn kháp
reach go look for warden will take thousand five sure P
When I went to see the warden, he really asked for a thousand five.

018 pan hãa
thousand five
A thousand five.

019 lɛ́ɛw man bɔcây lɛ́ɛw tĩi satsadii kháp
then it not done at warden P
But it didn't finish with the warden.

020 pay hǎa satsadii
go look for warden
I went to see the warden

021 waaŋ ləəy pan hãa
put down done thousand five
and gave him a thousand five.

022 haw khiaw wâa ca lɛ́ɛw ĩi nɔ́
I think that will done D S
I thought that would be all.

023 uu aw nǎy dãy naay wâa
uu take which able you ((title)) say
Oh! No way! You see?

024 hɔ́ khãw wiaŋ pay hǎa tĩi'ãn sǎalaakǎaŋ
rush enter city go look for there provincial office
I rushed to the city, to there, the Provincial Office.

025 tĩi (pɔɔ) lúk sǎalaakǎaŋ hɔ́ɔŋ pan hãa
there (as soon as) reach provincial office call for thousand five
At the Provincial Office, they asked for one thousand five.

026 aw khǎa nãa lôm cɔ̂ɔŋ lɛ́ɛw nɔ́
take leg front immerse ditch already S
I was already in up to my waist,
027 càay pan hãa ĩi nɔ́
pay thousand five D S
so I paid the one thousand five.
028 Pong:
sǎam pan lɛ́ɛw nɔ́
three thousand already S
Three thousand already.
029 Taa:
sǎam pan lɛ́ɛw kháp sǎam pan
three thousand already P three thousand
Three thousand already Three thousand.
030 lɛ́ɛw pay tĩi annyǎŋ dǐawkɔ̀ɔn nɔ́
then go place what wait a minute S
Then I went to- what do you call it?
031 tĩi an haw pay cãaŋ haw pay cãaŋ haw pay cɛ̃ɛŋ
place uh we go inform we go inform we go inform
the place we go to inform- we go to inform- we go to inform-
032 tĩi an anyǎŋ á əə ná
place uh what Q hm S
The place uh what-
033 tĩi pɔ̂n cɛ̃ɛŋ kɔ̀ət cɛ̃ɛŋ taay
place they inform born inform die
the place that one goes to inform of births and deaths?
034 Som:
têetsabaan ná
city hall S
The city hall.
035 Taa:
têetsabaan tɛ̀ɛ têetsabaan sĩaŋ pan ía
city hall at city hall spend thousand D
City hall At the city hall, I paid a thousand.
036 Pong:
sìi pan
four thousand
Four thousand.
037 Taa:
sìi pan
four thousand
Four thousand.

038 aa têetsabaan thãa wâa bɔ nyaŋ án pɔ̂n kɔ̃ɔ bɔ láplúu tooy ĩi nɔ́
ah city hall if that not way that they then not handle with D S
Ah city hall, otherwise they wouldn't handle it.

039 sĩaŋ sìi pan ia
spend four thousand D
I was out four thousand.

040 Luang and Som:
hõo
hoo
Ho!

041 Taa:
aw khãw pay nay khâay
take enter go in (Army) camp
I went to the army camp.

042 oo aw lɛ́ɛw
oo take already
Oh! There it is!

043 aw lûuk kuu maa nyáp lɛ́ɛw ((laughs))
take child I come arrest already ((laughs))
They have arrested my child ((laughs))

044 oo annán lûukcaay nɔ́
oo that son-in-law S
Oh, he was my son-in-law

045 (**) ca aw sǎam pan nɔ́
(**) will take three thousand S
(**) They wanted three thousand.

046 Pong:
cèt pan
seven thousand
Seven thousand.

047 Taa:
((laughs)) cèt pan lɛ́ɛw nɔ́ ((laughs))
((laughs)) seven thousand already S ((laughs))
((laughs)) Seven thousand already ((laughs))

048 wâa hoo man khɤ̌ɤn tiktik
say hoo it rise continuously
I said "Ho! It keeps increasing.

049 phǒm kɔ̀ɔ bɔ mii nɔ́
I then not have S
I don't have it.

050 phɔ́wâa mŷa hŏn tii satsadii wâa ca aw pan hãa
because when first time warden say will take thousand five
Because at first the warden wanted one thousand five

051 kɔ̃ɔ sɣ̀ɣp maa hǎa tĩi
then continue come look for place
and then at the next place

052 annı́i kɔ̃ɔ sĩaŋ wáy hɛ̆ɛm pan hãa
this then spend keep again thousand five
I had to pay another one thousand five.

053 maa hǎa têetsabaan kɔ̀ɔ sĩaŋ pay hɛ̆ɛm pan nɣ̀ŋ ĩi nɔ́
come look for municipality then spend go again thousand one D S
At the city hall I paid one thousand more.

054 maa phée (*) cet pan
come here (*) seven thousand
I come here (*) seven thousand.

055 phŏm bɔ mii panyaa kháp ĩi nɔ́
I not have ability P D S
I don't have the ability." Like that.

056 kɔ̃ɔ khun bɔ mii panyaa kɔ̃ɔ thùuk khɔ̂ɔk nâakãa ĩi nɔ́ ((laughs))
then you not have ability then experience jail E D S ((laughs))
((quoting the officer)) "You don't have the ability, so your child will stay in jail."

057 lɛ́ kɔ̃ɔ man kɔ̃ɔ lɔ̀ɔk khǎw mɣ̆ankăn nɔ́
and then I then trick they also S
So, I also tricked them ((as they had tricked me)).

058 ɔ thùuk nǎy kɔ̃ɔ thùuk pay tə kháp ĩi nɔ́
ø experience whatever then experience go Im P D S
((quoting himself)) "Okay, he'll have to take his punishment.

059 man bɔ mii ŋən ĩi nɔ́
I not have money D S
I have no money.

060 ɔ́ ca aw sày khɔ̂ɔk kɔ̃ɔ aw sày tə́ ĩi nɔ́
Oh will take put jail then take put I D S
If you're going to put him in jail, go ahead."

061 dĭawnı́i kɔ̃ɔ kãy ca tĩaŋ lɛ́ɛw
now then close will noon already
"It is almost noon.

062 ca aw pay kin khãaw ĩi lɔ̂ɔ
will take go eat rice D E
I'll take you out to eat."

063 pay ĩi nɔ́
go D S
Go, like that.
064 pay láan nǎy kɔ̃ɔ
go shop which Q
"What restaurant shall we go to?
065 nam phǒmkhǎw pay tə́ ĩi nɔ́
lead we go Im D S
You lead us there." Like that.
066 phǒm kɔ̃ɔ khãw wiaŋ
I then enter city
So I went to the city.
067 phǒm kɔ̃ɔ tĩinǎy phǒm kɔ̃ɔ kin pay lɣ̂ay ii nɔ́
I then where I then eat go continuous D S
I just go wherever, I just eat whatever.
068 phǒmkhǎw níi kúaytǐaw thũay diaw
we this Chinese noodles bowl single
I had Chinese noodles, one bowl.
069 phǒm kɔ̃ɔ kin kɔ̃ɔ lɛ́ɛw pay lɛ́ɛw ĩi nɔ́
I then eat then done go done D S
I have one, that's enough.
070 lɛ́ɛw phǒm aw khǎw pay kin sĩaŋ hok lɔ́ɔy ((laughs))
then I take them go eat spend six hundred ((laughs))
So I took them to eat It cost six hundred ((laughs))
071 Pong:
phǎy ɔ̀ɔk
who pay
Who paid?
072 Taa:
phǒm la kháp
I E P
I did.
073 Luang:
nân thaaŋ phée kãa càay ((laughs))
that way here E pay ((laughs))
He paid ((laughs))
074 Taa:
phɔ́ haw pay líaŋ pə̂n lô
because I go treat them E
Because I treated them.

075 Jack:
kúaytǐaw peeŋ nɔ́
Chinese noodles expensive S
That was expensive Chinese noodles.
076 Taa:
kháp
yes
Yes.
077 Pong:
pə̂n kin nyăŋ hok lɔ́ɔy
they eat what six hundred
What did they eat for six hundred?
078 Taa:
óo anday mii khăw kɔ̃ɔ sàŋ maa kin khunnaay
oo which have they then order come eat maam
Oh, they ordered everything, maam.
079 man sìi hãa khon tɣŋ naaythahăan thahə̆ən nɔ́
it four five person all officer ((playword)) S
There were four or five, all officers.
080 Pong:
lέεw pennyăŋ haw bɔ lúk nĩi ((laughs))
then why we not rise flee ((laughs))
Why didn't you flee? ((laughs))
081 Taa:
oo kɔ̃ɔ haw kua wâa haw kua lûuk haw nĩi nɔ́
oo then I afraid that I afraid child my D S
Oh, I was afraid that- I was worried about my child ((l»uuk)).
082 haw kɔ̃ɔ khây dãy baykɔɔŋnŭn
I then want get reserve status card
I wanted to get his reserve status card.
083 haw khây dãy lûuk haw pón ĩi nɔ́
I want get child my escape D S
I wanted to get my child out of there.
084 haw ũu kăn pay ũu kăn maa
we speak together go speak together come
We conversed for some time.
085 kin lέεw kɔ̃ɔ sày bia sày lãw
eat done then put beer put whiskey
After eating, we had beer and whiskey.
086 pə̂n kin kɔ̃ɔ tua kin ((laughs))
they eat then I eat ((laughs))
They drank, so I drank too ((laughs))

087 ũu kǎn nua khây hǔa kǎn mûan nɔ́
speak together mixed want laugh together fun S
We talked enjoyably.

088 wan nán bɔ sǐa tɣ̂a ĩa
day that not lose time D
That day, I didn't pay.

089 nát thɛ̌ɛm wan nát thɛ̌ɛm wan
make-appointment again day make-appointment again day
We made another appointment, made another appointment.

090 Pong:
mot pay ìik lɛ́ɛw hok lɔ́ɔy
all gone go more already six hundred
It cost another six hundred.

091 Taa:
kháp
yes
Yes.

092 Som:
man ca kin lá kãa ((laughs))
they will eat E E ((laughs))
They're going to eat again ((laughs))

093 Pong:
pen sìi phan kap hok lɔ́ɔy lɛ́ɛw nɔ́
is four thousand with six hundred already S
It's four thousand and six hundred already.

094 Taa:
pik pay hɛ̌ɛm khâap
return go again time
I went back another time.

095 mùu nán bɔ tooy maa ná kháp
group that not accompany come S P
That group didn't come,

096 tɣŋ satsadii tɣŋ ãy wàaŋ níi
include warden include T Wang this
just the warden and Wang ((I do not know who this is)).

097 khâap nán sĩaŋ hɛ̌ɛm lɔ́ɔy hãasip ĩi nɔ́
time that spend again hundred fifty D S
That time cost another one hundred fifty.

098 Pong:
cet lɔ́ɔy hãasip
seven hundred fifty
Seven hundred fifty.

099 Taa:
cet lɔ́ɔy hãasip ĩi nɔ́
seven hundred fifty D S
Seven hundred fifty.

100 aw tok wanphûuk
so on tomorrow
The next day,

101 luŋ taa maa sĩaŋ sǎam pan
uncle taa come spend three thousand
((quoting officer)) "Uncle Taa, come and pay the three thousand.

102 luŋ taa kɔ̃ɔ maa sĩaŋ hɛ̌ɛm pan hãa ii nɔ́
uncle taa then come spend again thousand five D S
Uncle Taa, come and pay another thousand five.

103 sĩaŋ pan hãa
spend thousand five
Pay one thousand five."

104 sĩaŋ yùu hãa pan hãa hãa pan hãa
spend stay five thousand five five thousand five
I paid five thousand five hundred ((altogether)) Five thousand five.

105 tɤŋ kin tɤŋ wâa sĩaŋ hok pan pǎay ((laughs))
include eat include say spend six thousand more ((laughs))
With the food and all I spent more than six thousand ((laughs))

106 ?:
(**)
(**)
(**)

107 Taa:
((laughs)) əə ná lɛ́ɛw kɔ̃ɔ haw ləəy bɔ câaŋ wâa nyay
((laughs)) yeah S then then I so not able say anything
((laughs)) Yeah And I couldn't say anything.

108 man khǎa nãa lôm cɔ̂ɔŋ lɛ́ɛw nɔ́
it leg front overflow ditch already S
I was already in deeply.

109 man kántii wâa aw sày khɔ̂ɔk
they maybe say take put jail
Maybe they would put him in jail.

110 əə ca aw sày kɔ̃ɔ taam cǎy tə́ ĩi nɔ́
yeah will take put then follow heart Im D S
Yeah ((quoting himself)) "You put him there ((in jail)), it's up to you.

111 phǒm tɣŋ bɔ mii ŋən ĩi nɔ́
I definitely not have money D S
I have no money."
112 wâa ia nɔ́
say this S
That's what I said.
113 aw pay phɔ̀ɔ thahǎan nán sày sôo tooykǎn sɔ̌ɔŋ khɛ̃ɛŋ ((laughs))
take go look soldier that put chain together two leg ((laughs))
They took me to see the soldiers with chains on both legs ((laughs))
114 (**) óo aw lɛ́ɛw ((laughs))
(**) oo take already ((laughs))
(**) Oh, okay ((laughs))
115 hoo thɔɔn bɔ aw lɛ́ɛw nə́ ĩa
hoo Thawn not take already Im D
Ho, I don't want that to happen to Thawn.
((end of side one I may have lost a few seconds in turning the tape over.))
116 Taa:
maa khóp kǎn lɛ̀ɛw man bɔ aw nǎy ləəy
come associate together already he not take anything at all
Knowing him, I saw he was good for nothing.
117 pùu kham naa
grandfather Kham S
Old Kham
118 hɔ́ɔŋ phǒm pay wiaŋ tooy ãy thɔɔn
call I go city get T Thawn
He asked me to go to the city to get Thawn
119 man tɣŋ bɔ nyɔɔm pay naa
he definitely not willing go S
but he wouldn't go.
120 lûuk man tɛ́ɛtɛ́ɛ naa
child he real S
His own son.
121 man tɣŋ bɔ nyɔɔm pay naa
he definitely not willing go S
He wouldn't go.
122 man kǔa sĩaŋ ŋən
he afraid spend money
He was afraid it would cost him money.

123 Luang:
((laughs))
((laughs))
((laughs))
124 Taa:
lɛ́ɛw maa khâm pɔ̂ɔ mia ((laughs))
then come bother father wife ((laughs))
So he came to bother the wife's father
((At this point, they begin to discuss the case of another villager who was also in the army))

Appendix B: Kammuang phonemes and translation conventions

b b, as in “boy”

c voiceless palatal affricate, similar to j as in “John,” but without the voicing

d d, as in “dawn”

f f, as in “fun”

h h, as in “happy”

k voiceless, unaspirated, velar stop

kh k, as in “kiss,” frequently pronounced with affrication

l l, as in “lemon”

m m, as in “man”

n n, as in “none”

ŋ ng, as in “sing”

p voiceless, unaspirated, bilabial stop

ph p, as in “poem”

s s, as in “some”

t voiceless, unaspirated, postdental stop

th t, as in “top”

w w, as in “woman”

y y, as in “you”

a low, central, unrounded vowel, similar to o as in “not”

ɛ low, front, unrounded vowel, similar to a as in “mat”

e mid, front, unrounded vowel, similar to e as in “bet”

i high, front, unrounded vowel, similar to i as in “bit”

ɔ low, back, unrounded vowel, similar to ou as in “bought”

o mid, back, rounded vowel, similar to o as in “note”

u high, back, rounded vowel, similar to oo as in “boot”

ɤ high, central, unrounded vowel

ə mid, central, unrounded vowel

double vowel: indicates lengthening of vowel (vowel length is phonemic in Kammuang)

' glottal stop

x̀ low tone (x represents a vowel)

x̂ falling tone

x́ high tone

x̌ rising tone

x̃ high falling tone

x (with no tone marker) mid tone

Other transcription conventions

Double parentheses are used for author's comments. Asterisks in parentheses (*) are used for talk that the author was unable to transcribe. Each asterisk represents about 0.5 seconds of untranscribable talk. Pauses, overlaps, and other fine details are not indicated in the transcript because they were not necessary for the analysis.

E emphatic particle
S solicitor
D demonstrative
Im imperative particle
P polite particle

3 The Recommendation Sequence in Vietnamese Family Talk: Negotiation of Asymmetric Access to Authority and Knowledge

Hanh thi Nguyen
Hawai'i Pacific University

Cá không ăn muối cá ươn
Con cãi cha mẹ trăm đường con hư

"A fish (for cooking) that won't take salt will go stale"
"A child who resists the parents is rotten in
one hundred ways"

Con hơn cha là nhà có phúc

"When the son surpasses the father,
it is a fortunate family"

(Vietnamese folk sayings)

Introduction

A recent survey of families in Hanoi (Mai, 2005) revealed that parents frequently punish their young children and teenagers in the forms of scolding (64.9% of punishment occurrences), beating (25.6%), and others (9.5%). Interestingly, the survey also indicated that most children (45%) think that their parents' punishments are unfair, which suggests that children have their own independent judgment and that they may continue to disagree with their parents even after a punishment. Most importantly, the survey shows that as a child matures, talk is used more frequently by parents to deal with conflicts: when children are under 11 years old, they are scolded in 58.2% of punishment occurrences, when they

Talk-in-interaction: Multilingual perspectives, pp. 57–87, Hanh Nguyen & Gabriele Kasper (Eds.), 2009
Honolulu, HI: University of Hawai'i, National Foreign Language Resource Center

are 11–12 years old, 66.9%, and when they are 14–15 years old, up to 72.2%. The fact that Vietnamese family conflicts for older children are often managed through discourse compels researchers of discourse analysis and those who are interested in conflict management in family settings to look at family talk as a way to understand family tension and harmony.

Research on family conflict (mainly in English) has found that oppositional exchanges often occur in the forms of arguments, disputes, squabbles, and fights (Beaumont & Wagner, 2004; Vuchinich, 1990; Williams, 2005). However, intergenerational tension may also be felt in activities in which parents and children have asymmetric access to power and knowledge (see Williams, 2005). One such activity can be found frequently in Vietnamese family discourse, namely, *dặn*, roughly translated as "giving recommendations."

While the closest translation of the verb *dặn* may be "to give recommendations" (Dang, Le, & Pham, 1996), this does not do justice to the Vietnamese original, which can be more exactly translated as "to let somebody know what they need to remember to do" (Hoang, 1994). Further, the verb *dặn* has a caring connotation because it is an action normally performed by a responsible 'superior' person toward an 'inferior' person or by a responsible equal toward another equal, but usually not by an 'inferior' person toward a 'superior' person.[1] Typically, parents *dặn* children, or older siblings *dặn* younger ones; the reverse may occur, but it is rarer. Thus, quite similar to how picking up a crying baby may constitute a woman as the mother of that baby (Sacks, 1995), doing *dặn* can categorize the speaker as being responsible for the recipient. Perhaps because of this membership-category bound nature, *dặn* also entails a strong obligation for the recipient to agree with and to carry out the given recommendation. A good child listens to and follows a parent's words of *dặn* as implied in the first folk saying cited at the beginning of this paper. However, the dilemma of a recommendation sequence, like advice sequences in which one party suggests a "preferred course of future action" (Heritage & Sefi, 1992, p. 368) for another party, is that the giver needs to be familiar with the recipient's situation. Yet, parents do not always have the same level of access to knowledge and information as their children, something which is alluded to in the second folk saying above. *Dặn,* or a recommendation sequence, then, is a prime site to observe the management of a parent-child relationship, in which asymmetric access to authority and knowledge is displayed and negotiated. To the best of my knowledge, this important sequence in Vietnamese family discourse has not been studied,[2] and thus, this paper is intended to fill this gap.

This paper aims to examine the dynamics of parent-child tension and harmony in recommendation sequences from the ethnomethodological perspective (Garfinkel, 1967) that talk-in-interaction is the primary milieu for an understanding of social order. Through talk, members renew, resist, or create social relationships and identities as well as beliefs and values. An examination of abstract phenomena such as family conflicts and harmony then needs to be grounded in close analysis of talk-in-interaction. Taking this approach and using conversation analysis informed by ethnographic data (e.g., Goodwin & Goodwin, 1990), I aim to describe, in a bottom-up and data-driven fashion, how Vietnamese family members manage their asymmetric access to authority and knowledge while invoking their membership categories in the local organization of talk (Sacks, 1995) in the activity of producing and receiving *dặn*.

Among previous studies within this analytical approach, the most relevant insights as a background to understand Vietnamese *dặn* sequences come from research on English advice sequences in institutional settings. This is because a clear parallel can be drawn regarding the asymmetric access to knowledge and authority between the institutional agent and the layperson on the one hand and between a superior and an inferior in a family on the other. In institutional settings, Heritage and Sefi (1992) found that an advice-giving sequence occurs when a party (in this case, a health professional) "describes, recommends, or otherwise forwards a preferred course of future action" (p. 368). Also, advice sequences, such as those given by health visitors toward first-time mothers, are "explicitly future oriented" and "delivered in strongly prescriptive terms" (p. 368). In these expert-layperson advice sequences, this prescriptiveness was seen in the use of language that overtly marked the recommendation (i.e., the word *recommendation* or *recommend* was used), the imperative mood, and verbs of obligation (e.g., *ought to*). In this situation, in which parties had asymmetric access to knowledge and authority, Heritage and Sefi discovered that advice often needs to be licensed, either by the layperson's request, or by the expert's gaining a "ticket-of-entry" to advice-giving (cf. Sacks, 1995) such as by introducing a real or potential problem and then proceeding to give advice as a solution to that problem (see also Nguyen, 2003). Further, advice in this context might sometimes be resisted as the layperson asserts his or her own claim to knowledge.

Yet to be demonstrated empirically is whether the above features of advice-giving from experts to laypersons in English institutional settings are similar to or different from the structure and dynamics of *dặn* sequences in intergenerational interaction in a Vietnamese family. While findings from previous research may inform the analysis, no preconceived criteria for the identification of *dặn* sequences should be imposed upon the data other than that they need to be treated as such sequences by the participants themselves. Specifically, the participants may orient to a sequence of actions as being a *dặn* sequence by overtly mentioning the word *dặn* or by displaying to one another that a future course of action is being recommended by one party for another.

Methodology

The data for this paper are excerpted from a voice chat between two adult children in the US and their father in Vietnam. The father (Nam[3]) had never been to the US, and he participated in the chat from a city in Central Vietnam. The children were Hanh (Nam's oldest daughter, the researcher), who was in her early 30s, and Quốc, Nam's youngest son, who was in his late 20s. Quốc was staying with Hanh while he attended a short-term seminar at a university in the US. A webcam was used, but it focused on Hanh's 1-year-old son (Lim) instead of the chat speakers. The audio recorder was placed on Hanh and Quốc's side of the chat; thus, it recorded all live audio input in their room and Nam's voice as it was played on the loud speakers.[4] The recorded interaction was part of the participants' long-distance communication routines: Hanh had had voice chat sessions every other week with Nam and other family members for about 1 year prior to Quốc's visit. During Quốc's visit, they chatted every week, and this was the 3rd week of Quốc's stay. A detail that is crucial to understanding the conversation is that even though Quốc's seminar was only 1 month long, Hanh had arranged for him to stay with her family for a total of 2 months, with 2 additional weeks both before and after the seminar. The date of the chat was June 20, and the date of Quốc's return to Vietnam was July 14. Thus, Quốc had 24 more days in the US, including roughly 1 week of the seminar and 2 weeks after the seminar.

The chat conversation was transcribed and translated into English by the author. Conversation analysis informed by ethnographic information was performed on the data. The technology used for the voice chat was real-time audio streaming, with a minimal delay. The quality of the voice chat was nearly comparable to that of an international telephone call at the time of the data collection (June 2005). When delays and disturbances occurred, the participants' orientations to these can be seen in the transcript and, consistent with the conversation analytic approach, how the participants oriented to the constraints and affordances of the communication medium is addressed in the data analysis. The fact that participants in the conversation had to rely entirely on the audio medium for communication makes the voice chat data quite similar to the telephone data used extensively in conversation analytic research (e.g., Sacks, 1995; Sacks, Schegloff, & Jefferson, 1974; Schegloff, 1968, 1986).[5] The advantage of using this type of data, as Sacks et al. pointed out, is that the analyst has the access to what the participants used for communication, namely, the audio but not video medium.

A word needs to be said about my role as a participant and the analyst. As a participant, I had not begun any analysis of this type of data at the time of the conversation and data collection (besides the kind of analysis that social actors perform as they participate in social activities [Garfinkel, 1967]); thus, I was not biased by any preconceived analytical questions or hypotheses during my participation in the conversation. As the analyst, I had access to both the context surrounding the conversation and what was going on during the chat. This is valuable information to supplement the recorded audio data. More importantly, because this study involves family discourse, that is, discourse among a small group of people who share a long history of activities, concerns, and emotions, having the knowledge and competence of a member of this group enables me to use the participants' perspectives in the analysis.[6]

The chat lasted about 30 minutes, but this paper focuses on the first few minutes of the conversation, in which the father recommended that the son extend his stay in the US. Excerpt 1 begins a few seconds after the chat was initiated. At this point, both sides had established that the Internet connection was working for them (but the fragility of the connection can be seen in lines 03–07) and exchanged a few ritual inquiries about each other's health and general well-being, thus confirming mutual participation (Goffman, 1963). To capture the flow of the conversation, I present the segment in its entirety, in Excerpt 1.

Excerpt 1

01 N: thế a:: (0.7) học tập là có a
so uh study filler have uh
so uh your study uh have you

02 được cái: [gì: không,
PosM what no
got anything out of it

03 H: [°đâu rồi. mặt đâu rồi.°
where already face where already
where has it gone where has the face gone

04 (.)

05 N: a lô,
hello
hello

06 H: DẠ. DẠ.
yes yes
yes yes

07 (0.5)

08 N: học tập có a (.) được không,
study yes uh satisfying no
your study uh is it ok

09 H: °Ơ°.
oh
oh.

10 (0.2)

11 H: [nó-
he
he

12 Q: [học a:: gần xong rồi
study uh near finish already
study uh it's almost finished

13 tuần này nữa là xong.
week this more be finish
this one more week and it'll be finished

14 (1.0)

15 N: à. (.) tuần này là xong há?
oh week this be finish QuesM
oh this week and it'll be finished

16 (1.0)

17 N: à. thế a:
oh so uh
oh so uh

18 H: °thứ tư là xong [rồi.°
Wednesday be finish already
Wednesday and it'll be finished already

19 N: [thế nếu mà
so if
so if

20 học xong rồi mà họ cho phép ở lại
study finish already CondM they allow stay
you finish the study and they allow you to stay

21 thế thì à (0.3) con cứ ở (.)
so then uh child AffM stay
then uh you just stay

22 xxxx được là xxx không cần là (.)
xxxx PosM filler xxx no need filler
xxxx possible uh xxx no need to uh

23 tất nhiên là đi xa thì cũng sốt ruột,
of course be go far TopM admittedly fever intestine
of course when one is far away one is admittedly anxious

24 (0.7) nhưng mà (.) mấy xxx (khó).
but some xxx (difficult)
but some xxx (difficult)

25 (1.0)

26 H: ba mẹ sốt [ruột °cái gi°-
father mother fever intestine what
what are you two anxious about

27 N: [thời gian (làm bên ni).
time (work this side)
time (to do your work here)

28 H: sốt ruột cái gì ạ.
fever intestine what PolM
anxious about what

29 N: thời gian (làm bên ni).
time (work side this)
time (to do your work here)

30 N: à sốt ruột là ở nhà ấy mà:,
oh fever intestine be stay home StaM
oh it's just anxiety about home

31 kiểu đi xa ấy mà:,
manner go far StaM
it's like being far away don't you know

32 (1.0)

33 H: ((nói với L)) >°làm gì đấy°,<
((to L)) do what there
((to L)) what are you doing

34 N: ((trêu)) không biết hí:,
((teasing)) no know AlignM
((teasing)) you don't know do you

35 °chị Hạnh không biết hí:,° (0.3)
older sister Hanh no know AlignM
Hanh you don't know do you

36 H: ((cười L)) hì hì
((laughing at L)) he he
((laughing at L)) he he

37 N: [thế khi nào con-
so when child
so when you

38 L: [WA CHA WAI. ((babbling sounds))

39 H: ha ha ha.

40 N: ha, (.) a ha Lim đấy há?
ha ah ha Lim there QuesM
ha ah ha is that Lim

41 H: °dạ° CHÁU CHÀO ÔNG NGỌAI.
PolM child greet grandfather maternal
hello grandfather

42 L: wa cha cha chề. ((babbling sounds))

43 (0.2)

44 L: á a cha: ê ừ ừ hh ((babbling sounds))

45 (.)

46 N: thế a. (.) Quốc nghe ba dặn này.
so uh Quốc listen father recommend this
so uh Quốc listen to my recommendation now

47 (0.8)

48 Q: vâng.
yes
yes

49 N: là con hết- hết chương trình rồi. (1.0)
filler child end- end program already
so when your program has ended

50 thì con cũng cứ cố ở bên: kia, (.)
then child same AffM try stay side there
you still try to stay over there

51 càng à:: lâu càng tốt, (.)
more uh long more good
the longer uh the better

52 [để mình có điều kiện mà đi thăm qua:n.
so self have condition for go visit
so that you have the opportunity to go sightseeing

53 H: [((thì thào)) °càng lâu càng tốt,
((whisper)) more long more good
((whisper)) the longer the better

54 được hai tuần,°
PosM two week
((but)) we've got two weeks

55 (0.5)

56 N: để mình à đi xem xem
so self uh go look look
so that you uh can go and look around

57 [xxxx
xxx
xxx

58 Q: [vé thì đằng nào cũng mười bốn
ticket TopM either way same fourteen
the ticket says I'll return on the fourteenth

59 mới về rồi chứ a::: lâu tốt gì nữa,
new return already StaM uh long good what more
anyway what's the point of longer better

60 (1.0)

61 N: há? mười bốn tháng- (.) mười bốn tháng-
huh? fourteen month- fourteen month-
huh? the fourteenth of- the fourteenth of-

62 tháng bảy á há?=
month seven QuesM
of July is it

63 Q: =vâ:ng,
yes
yes

64 (0.7)

65 N: à. (.) thế là- thế lúc nó là
ah so be so time that be
ah so then so by that time

66 hết hạn rồi há?
expire already QuesM
your stay expires

67 (0.3)

68 H: vé rồi, mua vé rồi
ticket already buy ticket already
ticket already we bought the ticket already

69 thì [cứ thế mà-
so same that to
so we'll just go according to that and

70 Q: [thì mua vé rồi:?
EmM buy ticket already
but then we bought the ticket already

71 (1.0)

72 N: à à thế thì được.
ah ah so TopM good
oh oh then that's good

73 (1.0)

74 H: ((cười khúc khích)) hi hi hi
((giggles)) he he he
((giggles)) he he he

75 N: thế thì cũng còn à khỏang
so then same remain uh about
so then there're still about

76 à:::[::::::::::hai bốn ngày nữa,
uh two four day more
uh twenty four more days

77 Q: [hai tuần.
two week
two weeks

78 H: hai bốn ngày cả hết.
twenty four day all end
twenty four days all together.

79 N: thì mua vé rồi thì thôi,
EmM buy ticket already so no more
ok, you already bought the ticket

80 không có gì nữa.
no have what more
then there's no more to be said

81 (0.4)

82 N: nhưng mà nhớ là cố gắng là (0.3)
but remember that try filler
but remember that you've got to try uh

83 chỉ có là
only have filler
only uh

84 tập thể dục [cho nó khỏe, thật khỏe.
exercise for it healthy really healthy
to exercise to be healthy really healthy

85 L: [kiah, kiah ((babbling sounds))

86 (0.2)

87 H: °tập thể dục này. thấy chưa,°
exercise this see yet
exercise have you heard

88 N: rồi là cố gắng là
then filler try filler
then uh also try to uh

89 [thu thập thật nhiều (.) xxx đi tham quan
collect really much xxx go visit
collect a lot xxx go visit

90 L: [ku:wayt. (.) ku:wayt. (.) ku:way. kuwe. ((babbling sounds))

91 N: cho nó [xxx
for it xxx
so that xxxx

92 Q: [vâ:ng.
yes
yes

93 H: ((nói với L)) ô con nhìn này.
((to L)) oh child look this
((to L)) oh look here

94 N: thế từ hôm sang đến giờ
so from day cross to now
so from the day you arrived to now

95 thì mũi là tim thì răng,
then nose filler heart filler how
then how are your nose uh your heart

96 có bình thường không,
yes normal no
are they ok

This is a rich segment in terms of how *dặn* sequences are constructed and how the participants use interactional resources to achieve their social actions. In the analysis below, I provide a sequential analysis of how the participants manage tension and harmony in the *dặn* sequences.

Analysis

Context of the recommendation sequence: The opening of the conversation
Before I present an analysis of the *dặn* sequences, the conversation opening needs to be examined because it gives the reader a sense of how the participants renew their relationships in this mundane activity on this specific occasion. In lines 01–02, Nam asks about Quốc's studies. In the context of this being Quốc's

first time studying in the US, the question is potentially a genuine question and not a ritual inquiry, which marks it as the first topic of the conversation, and as such, it has the potential to shape the rest of the conversation (Schegloff, 1968; 1986). Quốc indeed treats Nam's question in lines 01–02 (repeated in line 08) as nonritualistic and gives an informative answer in lines 12–13. That Nam, not Hanh or Quốc, starts the first topic is immediately noticeable. Unlike in telephone conversations, where the party who initiates the call typically introduces the first topic as the reason for the call (Schegloff, 1968), in this online chat, both parties have agreed on a time to log in to talk, and thus, the responsibility to initiate the first topic is not on either side in particular. Nam's initiation of the first topic thus can be heard as indexing his role as the one in charge in the conversation, a role that he maintains despite his lack of knowledge compared to his more informed children, as we see later.

After Nam's question, no answer is provided because Hanh and Quốc are busy checking the webcam (line 03). Nam then reconfirms the connection with Hanh (lines 05–06) and repeats his question (line 08). Hanh and Quốc's continued preoccupation with the webcam (line 09) causes a bit of a delay, and finally, in line 12, Quốc starts to answer Nam's question (Hanh starts a turn in overlap with Quốc, then yields the floor in line 11). Interestingly, while Nam asks about the quality of Quốc's studies (*học tập có a (.) được không* [study-yes-filler-satisfying-no], line 08), Quốc talks about a logistic aspect of his studies: its progress in time and how much longer it will be. In other words, while Nam seeks an evaluative answer from Quốc about his studies, Quốc provides a description of his studies in neutral, nonevaluative terms. In so doing, Quốc avoids assessing his studies as good or bad, thus also avoiding categorizing *himself* to his father as a good or bad student and, as a consequence, blocking any opportunity for the father to assess Quốc's performance. This mismatch between the question and its answer is not too different from political news interviews in that it reflects the participants' differences in agendas and perspectives (Clayman, 2001). Indeed, this micromoment of interaction was reflexive of the history of Nam and Quốc's relationship, in which Nam had habitually criticized Quốc for his lack of physical strength, his inability to bring home a higher income, and his personal relationships, among other things (contrary to these criticisms, Quốc is a competent and successful architect and is socially well-adjusted). In this moment, Quốc's maneuver to focus on a slightly different aspect of his study cancels out any possible tension.

The harmony that Quốc manages to maintain in his answer to Nam's question is in fact ratified by Nam in his acknowledgement of Quốc's answer. In line 15, Nam says, *à* [Oh] which is similar to a change-of-state token in English (Heritage, 1984) and repeats the new information, marking Quốc's answer as newsworthy.

Thus, by not treating Quốc's evasion of his earlier question as problematic, Nam collaborates with Quốc to maintain the accord between them.

As this analysis shows, the participants' ongoing relationships and coshared history as family members were made relevant in the very first few moments of the conversation. In the context of these ties, the first recommendation sequence emerges, and it is the focus of the next section.

Establishing authority in the entry to the recommendation sequence

As mentioned above, Nam does not pursue his original question, and this may help maintain the harmony between him and Quốc. However, this may serve another purpose for Nam: to introduce a recommendation sequence. Couched within the context that Quốc's seminar is coming to an end, Nam initiates a recommendation sequence about Quốc's trip. This segment is reproduced as Excerpt 1.1.

Excerpt 1.1

17 N: à. thế a:
oh so uh
oh so uh

18 H: °thứ tư là xong [rồi.°
Wednesday be finish already
Wednesday and it'll be finished already

19 N: [thế nếu mà
so if
so if

20 học xong rồi mà họ cho phép ở lại
study finish already CondM they allow stay
you finish the study and they allow you to stay

21 thế thì à (0.3) con cứ ở (.)
so then uh child AffM stay
then uh you just stay

22 xxxx được là xxx không cần là (.)
xxxx PosM filler xxx no need filler
xxxx possible uh xxx no need to uh

23 tất nhiên là đi xa thì cũng sốt ruột,
of course be go far TopM admittedly fever intestine
of course when one is far away one is admittedly anxious

24 (0.7) nhưng mà (.) mấy xxx (khó).
but some xxx (difficult)
but some xxx (difficult)

After the sequence of question–answer–receipt is treated as completed (evidenced by the 1.0 s pause in line 16 [Excerpt 1] when no party continues to talk), in line 17, Nam produces a change-of-state token, *À* (cf. Heritage, 1984), and then says, *thế a:* [so-uh:], marking what is coming next as the upshot of the preceding turns. In line 19,[7] Nam continues his initiation of the new sequence by making the suggestion that Quốc continue to stay after his seminar has finished.

Thus, the initiation of the *dặn* sequence seems to be very similar to advice-giving sequences in professional settings in that it is occasioned by an inquiry from the recommender (in this case, Nam's inquiry about Quoc's studies); however, it is different in that it does not involve an allusion to a real or possible problem (Heritage & Sefi, 1992; Nguyen, 2003). The sequential organization of the *dặn* sequence can be summarized as follows:

father: initial inquiry about state of affairs
son: response
father: recommendation based on state of affairs

Thus, while a professional often makes an advice sequence relevant by introducing a problem, a father may not need to do so. This might index the higher degree of control that a father has over the recipient of the recommendation (his child) in the Vietnamese family compared to professionals in the English-speaking West.

Asymmetric access to authority and knowledge in recommendation delivery

Nam noticeably uses a conditional to begin his recommendation, *thế nếu mà học xong rồi mà họ cho phép ở lại thế thì à (0.3) con cứ ở (.)* ([So-if-study-finish-already-conditional marker-they-allow-stay-so-then-uh-child-affirmative marker-stay(.)]; lines 19–21). This use of the conditional on the one hand indicates Nam's lack of knowledge about the seminar that Quốc is attending; on the other, it effectively enables Nam to formulate a complete suggestion *without* having to interrupt it and ask for information from Quốc, thus maintaining his full control of the situation (i.e., he makes a suggestion without being interactionally contingent on Quốc's turn). Further, Nam's use of "child" to refer to Quốc here may serve to invoke the membership categorization and the relationship between Nam and Quốc. These features of the turn, I argue, index Nam's status as the father.

As Nam continues his turn, a technical difficulty occurs (line 22), which may have prevented Quốc and Hanh from recognizing the completion of the turn and giving a receipt. Perhaps because he did not receive any uptake on the suggestion, Nam continues his turn and mentions as a caveat to his suggestion that when one is far away, one is admittedly anxious (*tất nhiên là đi xa thì cũng sốt ruột* [of course-be-go-far-topical marker-admittedly-fever-intestine]; line 23). The word *cũng* [admittedly] in this case expresses concession, marking this utterance as a problematization of the recommendation. However, Nam then counters this problem with another statement which, due to technical problems, was not fully audible to Hanh and Quốc (*nhưng mà (.) mấy xxx (khó)* [but (.) some xxx difficult]; line 24). By bringing up a problem, Nam indicates his awareness of what the future action he suggests will entail, and then by countering it, Nam maintains the validity of his suggestion. Together, these functions seem to enable him to retain his authority.

After a repair sequence about the feeling of anxiety with Hanh (lines 26–35, Excerpt 1) and the interaction with Lim (lines 38–45, Excerpt 1), Nam re-initiates the recommendation sequence with Quốc in line 46. The next segment of the conversation is reproduced as Excerpt 1.2.

Excerpt 1.2

46 N: thế a. (.) Quốc nghe ba dặn này.
so uh Quốc listen father recommend this
so uh Quốc listen to my recommendation now

47 (0.8)

48 Q: vâng.
yes
yes

49 N: là con hết- hết chương trình rồi. (1.0)
filler child end- end program already
so when your program has ended

50 thì con cũng cứ cố ở bên: kia, (.)
then child same AffM try stay side there
you still try to stay over there

51 càng à:: lâu càng tốt, (.)
more uh long more good
the longer uh the better

52 [để mình có điều kiện mà đi thăm qua:n.
so self have condition for go visit
so that you have the opportunity to go sightseeing

53 H: [((thì thào)) °càng lâu càng tốt,
((whisper)) more long more good
((whisper)) the longer the better

54 được hai tuần,°
PosM two week
((but)) we've got two weeks

55 (0.5)

Nam marks the transition and claims the floor with *thế a* [so-uh] and this time addresses Quốc directly: *Quốc nghe ba dặn này* [Quốc-listen-father-recommend-this] (line 46). This pre-announcement of instructions effectively claims a multi-unit turn for Nam and singles Quốc out as the recipient of the upcoming instructions. Most significantly, it re-invokes Nam and Quốc's membership categorization in the father-son relationship (Sacks, 1995) via (a) the full reference to Quốc by his name and Nam's self-reference as *ba* [father] at a point where both of these address terms can be grammatically omitted, and (b) the use of the verb *dặn*, which is something parents normally do toward their children but usually not the other way around.[8] After this pre-announcement, Nam pauses (line 47), and only after Quốc has indicated his listenership and his orientation to the recommendation sequence with the acknowledgement token *vâng* [yes] (line 48) does Nam proceed with his recommendations. He repeats the suggestion that Quốc should stay longer after his study program (lines 46–54).

As before, the issuing of a recommendation indexes Nam's authority as the father. However, the dilemma of a recommendation is that the giver needs to know the situation of the recipient well, which is not the case here: Nam had not been to the US before, and he was not familiar with the details of Quốc's trip. Nam's lack of knowledge about Quốc's situation is reflected in his use of general descriptions in reference to Quốc's place and his activities there (see also Schegloff, 1972). For example, he refers to Quốc's physical place as *bên: kia* [side-there] (line 50), he does not specify a time period for the extension *càng à:: lâu càng tốt* [more-long-more-good] (line 51), he describes the activity that Quốc needs to remember to do as *đi thăm qua:n* [go-sightseeing] (line 52), and *đi xem xem* [go- look-look] (line 56, Excerpt 1) without mentioning any specific places.[9] Crucially, he does not know that Hanh and Quốc have arranged for Quốc to stay 2 extra weeks after the seminar and that a return date has already been determined on Quốc's ticket.

In line 53, Hanh points out the contradiction between Nam's recommendation and Quốc's actual situation, *°càng lâu càng tốt, được hai tuần°* [more-long-more-good, positive marker-two-week]. Her reproducing of Nam's exact phrase *càng lâu càng tốt* [more-long-more-good] serves to tie her comment back to that particular portion of Nam's turn to single it out as the problematic part. However, she says this in a quiet whisper, thus possibly marking it as intended for Quốc and not for Nam. On the one hand, by designing her turn as addressed to Quốc, she may be aligning herself with Quốc as cosharers of the information to which Nam does not have access. On the other, by producing the turn in a lower volume, Hanh marks her turn as a bystander's (Goffman, 1981) comment, and not a response to Nam's recommendation (this, of course, is also in line with her role so far in the interaction as the nonaddressee of Nam's recommendation). In that sense, Hanh is orienting to Nam's recommendation, which is still in progress. Thus, I argue that even though the content of Hanh's turn contradicts Nam's recommendation, she manages to display her respect for the father by using whispery speech quality and lower speech volume. By maintaining his listenership at this point, Quốc also displays his respect to Nam.

For ease of reference, the next segment of the conversation is reproduced as Excerpt 1.3.

Excerpt 1.3

56 N: để mình à đi xem xem
so self uh go look look
so that you uh can go and look around

57 [xxxx
xxx
xxx

58 Q: [vé thì đằng nào cũng mười bốn
ticket TopM either way same fourteen
the ticket says I'll return on the fourteenth

59 mới về rồi chứ a::: lâu tốt gì nữa,
new return already StaM uh long good what more
anyway what's the point of longer better

60 (1.0)

61 N: há? mười bốn tháng- (.) mười bốn tháng-
huh? fourteen month- fourteen month-
huh? the fourteenth of- the fourteenth of-

62 tháng bảy á há?=
month seven QuesM
of July is it

63 Q: =vâ:ng,
yes
yes

64 (0.7)

65 N: à. (.) thế là- thế lúc nớ là
ah so be so time that be
ah so then So by that time

66 hết hạn rồi há?
expire already QuesM
your stay expires

67 (0.3)

68 H: vé rồi, mua vé rồi
ticket already buy ticket already
ticket already we bought the ticket already

69 thì [cứ thế mà-
so same that to
so we'll just go according to that and

70 Q: [thì mua vé rồi:?
EmM buy ticket already
but then we bought the ticket already

71 (1.0)

72 N: à à thế thì được.
ah ah so TopM good
oh oh then that's good

73 (1.0)

74 H: ((cười khúc khích)) hi hi hi
((giggles)) he he he
((giggles)) he he he

As Nam continues with another turn construction unit (TCU) (line 56), Quốc interjects mid-TCU into Nam's turn space and contradicts Nam by introducing the return date on the ticket (lines 58, 59). By reproducing Nam's expression (*càng lâu càng tốt* [more-long-more-good]; line 53) Quốc ties his turn back to the problematic part of Nam's turn, a strategy used by Hanh earlier. However, unlike Hanh, he does not reproduce Nam's expression in full form but shortens it to *lâu tốt* [long-good] (line 59), which is hearable as a trivialization of Nam's recommendation. Further, he uses the expression *gì nữa*, which functions in Vietnamese to completely negate a previous point, thus marking his turn as a strong rejection of Nam's recommendation. A clash between the father's authority and the children's knowledge has emerged.

The ensuing gap of silence (line 60) signals a delay in Nam's response to Quốc's turn. When he speaks again, Nam shows surprise and confusion, evidenced in the rising intonation in *há?* [huh?], followed by several cutoffs, repetitions, and midturn pauses (lines 61, 62). With a question seeking Quốc's confirmation of the return date in line 62, Nam shifts his footing (Goffman, 1981) from being authoritative to being uninformed, and Quốc shifts from the recipient of a recommendation to an information provider. This participation framework continues in lines 65–70 when Nam asks another question about the reason for the return date. Note that he uses a statement (expressing an assumption) followed by a question marker: *à. (.) thế là- thế lúc nó là hết hạn rồi há?* [ah. (.) so-be- so-time-that-be-expire-already-question marker] (lines 65–66), rather than an open question such as *Sao lại phải về ngày đó?* [Why do you have to return on that day?]. Nam's use of this particular question format allows him to display *some* knowledge rather than a complete lack of knowledge (Pomerantz, 1988). I submit that this is evidence that even though Nam is seeking information, he still makes an effort to maintain his control of the situation.

However, the knowledge that Nam implicitly claims in his question in lines 65–66 is not validated by Hanh and Quốc because the reason for Quốc's return date does not have to do with the expiration of his trip but with the fact that the ticket has already been purchased. In line 68, Hanh introduces this information via a reduced and topicalized construction to mention the ticket first in her turn, *vé rồi* [ticket-already], thus highlighting the key information that explains why Quốc will need to return on the given date: the ticket. Only in the next TCU does she produce a fuller form of the same structure, *mua vé rồi* [buy-ticket-already] (line 68) and add that they will act accordingly *thì cứ thế mà-* [so-same-that-to] (line 69). However, she cuts her turn off in recognition of an overlap with Quốc (line 70). This is another sign that she constructs herself as a nonrecipient and Quốc as the recipient of Nam's recommendation.

Quốc's turn here is worth examining in further detail. First, he begins with an emphasis marker, *thì*, signaling the contrast between his turn and Nam's recommendation. Perhaps similarly to contrastive stress in Jewish arguments (in English), this emphasis marker functions to mark the turn as oppositional (Schiffrin, 1984). Quốc also formulates his turn as nonfinal by lengthening the final syllable and saying it with a rising intonation (this is noticeable especially in the context of the syllable's falling tone, *rồi*—see Figure 1 for a pitch comparison between Quốc's production of this word here and two other instances of this word in the conversation). The (1.0-s) pause after Quốc's turn also demonstrates that Quốc does not desire to continue his turn. By producing his turn as nonfinal and *not* providing an explanation for the consequence of the fact that the ticket has been bought, Quốc leaves it up to Nam, the only participant to whom this information is new, to draw the obvious conclusion. Possibly, this absence of explanation could imply Quốc's resistance to collaborate with Nam. This is further confirmed by a comparison of Quốc's turn here with Hanh's turn earlier in line 69, in which she attempted to give an explanation about the implication of the fact that the ticket had been purchased. This difference may reflect and construct their different relationships to the father: while Quốc was often criticized by Nam and thus had experienced some tension with Nam, Hanh had experienced this to a lesser degree.

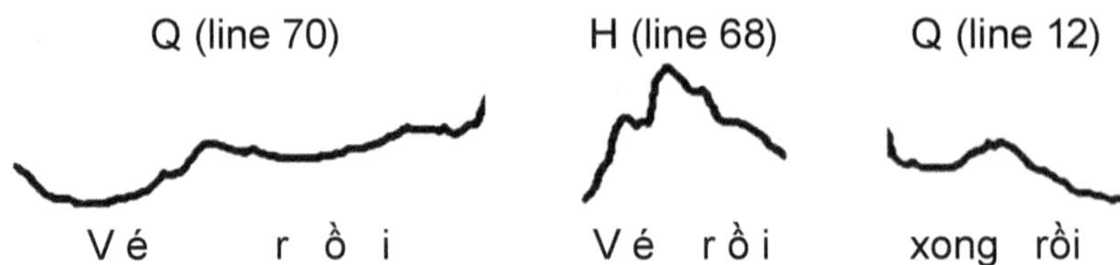

Figure 1. Comparison of Q's pronunciation of *rồi* in line 69 with H's pronunciation of the same word in an identical phrase and Q's pronunciation of the same word in another turn, showing that Q's pronunciation is distinctively rising.

At this point, Nam's recommendation has been nullified by the new information provided by Hanh and Quốc; thus, his authority as a father in this moment is also challenged. Indeed, Nam marks himself as undergoing a change of state in his understanding when, in line 72, he says *à à* [oh oh] (quite similarly to English *oh*, Heritage, 1984).

However, he begins to reassert his control by giving an upshot of the conversation via a positive assessment to show his approval of the situation: *thế thì được* [so-topic marker-good] (line 72). The tension between Nam and Quốc is reflected in Hanh's next action. After a pause following Nam's assessment, she giggles. Hanh's laughter tokens at this point seems to seek intimacy and affiliation (Jefferson, Sacks, & Schegloff, 1987) with Nam (and possibly Quốc as well) and to make light of the conflict at the moment (Vuchinich, 1990). I surmise that this laughter from Hanh at a point of heightened tension and when Nam's authority has been challenged serves to restore the harmony among the participants.

Continued asymmetric access to information in the uptake

The next few turns (lines 75–78), while not containing any oppositional exchange, continue to demonstrate the father's and son's distinctive perspectives and asymmetric access to information (Excerpt 1.4, reproduced from Excerpt 1).

Excerpt 1.4

75 N: thế thì cũng còn à khỏang
so then same remain uh about
so then there're still about

76 à:::[:::::::::::hai bốn ngày nữa,
uh two four day more
uh twenty four more days

77 Q: [hai tuần.
two week
two week

78 H: hai bốn ngày cả hết.
twenty four day all end
twenty four days all together.

79 N: thì mua vé rồi thì thôi,
EmM buy ticket already so no more
ok, you already bought the ticket

80 không có gì nữa.
no have what more
then there's no more to be said

In line 75, Nam gives an upshot of the new information with a turn-initial *thế thì* [so then] and mentions how many days remain until Quốc returns home (lines 75, 76). In the middle of his TCU, after he says *cũng còn à khoảng* [same-remain-uh-about], Nam uses an extremely prolonged hesitation marker as he seems to be doing the calculation for the number of days. Quốc seems to treat this hesitation marker as repairable and takes a turn (line 77) to mention the period of his extra stay after the end of the seminar, 2 weeks. Nam continues with his lengthened hesitation marker, then states the total number of days remaining until Quốc returns, 24 days. First, this shows that Nam did not design his hesitation marker in line 75 as a word search and that he still wanted to hold the floor while he did the mental math. Second and more importantly, the mismatch in Nam's and Quốc's turns reflects and displays their different access to information: while Quốc knows the specific schedule of his trip (seminar plus 2 extra weeks), Nam only knows the return date as it was just shared with him by Hanh and Quốc.

At this moment, Nam and Quốc have made different statements about the remaining amount of time for Quốc's trip, indexing their divergent perspectives. Precisely at this moment, Hanh takes a turn to reconcile their discrepancy. In line 78, she repeats the number given by Nam, *hai bốn ngày* [twenty four-day], and adds *cả hết* [all-end], thus implicitly explaining the difference between Nam's and Quốc's turns: while Quốc has 2 weeks left after the seminar, he has 24 days remaining from the day of the chat. In the broader context of the family, this moment renews Hanh's role as the mediator between Nam and Quốc: she is the older sister who is taking care of Quốc during his trip and the oldest daughter who relates very well to Nam.

Renewing authority in the closing and the opening up of a new recommendation

Nam closes the recommendation sequence with a turn-initial emphasis marker, *thì*, to make a consequential upshot of the preceding talk: *thì mua vé rồi thì thôi, không có gì nữa* [EmM-buy-ticket-already-so-no more, no-have-what-more] (lines 79–80, Excerpt 1.4). Nam's interactional work to close up the recommendation sequence even when the recommendation itself has been abandoned serves to index his control of the organization of the sequence and by extension, his authority as the father.

The next segment of the talk is reproduced as Excerpt 1.5.

Excerpt 1.5

81 (0.4)

82 N: nhưng mà nhớ là cố gắng là (0.3)
but remember that try filler
but remember that you've got to try uh

83 chỉ có là
only have filler
only uh

84 tập thể dục [cho nó khỏe, thật khỏe.
exercise for it healthy really healthy
to exercise to be healthy really healthy

85 L: [kiah, kiah ((babbling sounds))

86 (0.2)

87 H: °tập thể dục này. thấy chưa,°
exercise this see yet
exercise have you heard

88 N: rồi là cố gắng là
then filler try filler
then uh also try to uh

89 [thu thập thật nhiều (.) xxx đi tham quan
collect really much xxx go visit
collect a lot xxx go visit

90 L: [ku:wayt. (.) ku:wayt. (.) ku:way. kuwe. ((babbling sounds))

91 N: cho nó [xxx
for it xxx
so that xxxx

92 Q: [vâ:ng.
yes
yes

93 H: ((nói với L)) ô con nhìn này.
((to L)) oh child look this
((to L)) oh look here

94 N: thế từ hôm sang đến giờ
so from day cross to now
so from the day you arrived to now

95 thì mũi là tim thì răng,
then nose filler heart filler how
then how are your nose uh your heart

96 có bình thường không,
yes normal no
are they ok

After a brief pause (line 81) signaling the potential closing of the current recommendation, Nam opens up a new recommendation (line 82). He ties this new suggestion to the previously aborted one with a contrastive discourse marker, *nhưng mà* [but], thus implicitly establishing the relevance of his upcoming advice. Nam marks his new advice with the hallmark expression for recommendations in Vietnamese, *nhớ là cố gắng là* [remember-that-try-filler] (line 82), and tells Quốc to exercise to maintain good health. Before this conversation, the issue of Quốc's health and exercise had been a sensitive topic between Quốc and his family, especially with Nam. Nam had frequently nagged Quốc about exercising, and Quốc had not always followed up on Nam's suggestions. In this moment of interaction, the delicate nature of the issue seems to be displayed in Quốc's absence of an uptake to Nam's recommendation. Hanh provides a form of uptake: in line 87, she repeats Nam's advice to Quốc, thus aligning herself with Nam. In addition, she produces a question addressed to Quốc, *thấy chưa* [see-yet] (line 87), which orients to his absence of uptake and brings to the forefront Quốc's neglect of Nam's previous similar recommendations.

With Hanh's uptake, Nam moves on to make a third recommendation for Quốc regarding how he should take advantage of the extra time to enrich his experience as an architect (lines 88, 89). This time, perhaps because the topic does not have a negative history, Quốc responds with a receipt (line 92). After this, Nam introduces a different topic about Quốc's health (lines 94–96), and the recommendation sequence closes.

Summary and discussion

The above analysis uncovers both the shape of recommendation sequences in Vietnamese family discourse and the ways that the participants invoked different participation frameworks as they negotiated their different levels of access to authority and knowledge. First, the analysis shows that the three *dặn* sequences recorded in the data have the following general structure:

father: initial inquiry about state of affairs
child: response
father: recommendation about state of affairs
Option 1: child: receipt
Option 2: child: no receipt
another child: receipt
Option 3: child: challenge with new information
father: acknowledgement of new information/uptake/assessment
father: abandonment of recommendation and closing

Option 1 is exemplified by the third recommendation, Option 2 by the second, and Option 3 by the first (excluding the first attempt) in the data.

First, this general structure of *dặn* sequences differs from advice-giving in certain institutional settings (e.g., Heritage & Sefi, 1992; Nguyen, 2003) in that the giver does not need to invoke a problem as a "ticket of entry" (Sacks, 1995) for the recommendation, and the giver may abandon the recommendation in the face of new information presented by the recipient. More importantly, the analysis shows that a *dặn* sequence has recognizable patterns that participants can use as resources to manage and negotiate family relationships. This finding, together with the fact that there is a word in the Vietnamese language to refer to this type of sequence, suggests that *dặn* is a distinct social practice in Vietnamese families. Whether and how this practice also occurs in other participation frameworks (Goffman, 1981) among family members[10] and in other social groups needs to be explored in future research.

Methodologically, this study argues for the use of conversation analysis complemented by ethnographic information. The analysis presented here has been greatly enriched by the perspective of the analyst as a participant in the conversation under study. Thus, if an analyst were to interpret social interaction from the participants' perspectives, conversation analysis of talk needs to be informed by data about the participants' shared history. The analysis of family discourse, or any type of discourse in which participants have shared experiences prior to the talk, thus requires the incorporation of ethnographic information gained either through long-term observation or, in the case of this study, through participation as members of the same social group as the participants (see also Goodwin, Goodwin, & Olsher, 2002, and Moerman, 1992, for example).

This study's fine-grained analysis of talk in its local and larger context has also provided interesting insights about how certain linguistic features function in naturally occurring discourse, particularly, address terms in Vietnamese. Previous studies have suggested that address terms have static meanings and functions that are constrained by fixed social norms. For example, Vu (1998) claimed that

> if [the hearer] is a father to [the speaker], then according to their status relationships and the social norms of address for this case, [the speaker] has to use the term *ba* [father] to address [the hearer] and to call him/herself by *con* [offspring], and *this is normally required in all situations*, irrespective of whether or not [the speaker] is performing a face-threatening act. In other words, [the speaker] uses the pair *bố-con* [father–offspring] because s/he follows the rules of respectful politeness socially marked for the hierarchical relationship 'father-offspring.' (p. 90, emphasis added)

However, the analysis in the current study shows that address terms may be used selectively to invoke membership categories that have immediate interactional import to the action being accomplished (e.g., giving *dặn*) and that they may be omitted selectively to orient away from the invoked membership categories, as a way to resist an action (e.g., resisting *dặn*). The Vietnamese participants' dynamic use of address terms in the conversation analyzed thus supports the notion that identities are not fixed labels but are continuously *performed* and *constructed* in social interaction (see, e.g., Antaki & Widdicombe, 1998; Benwell & Stokoe, 2006), and that linguistic forms are never static entities, but they are dynamic interactional resources that can be used actively to accomplish social actions.

Importantly, the above sequential analysis of a few minutes of a chat conversation reveals in fine detail how asymmetric access to power and knowledge among family members can lead to tensions and how family members can deploy interactional practices such as the timely use of address terms and laughter to resolve these tensions and maintain harmony. In contrast to previous studies on family discourse, in which conflict was shown to take place in successive oppositional turns (Vuchinich, 1990; Williams, 2005), close examination of the data shows that the tension between the parent and children occurred transiently in single turns. Specifically, a conflict resulted within a recommendation sequence (in which the parent was claiming authority) when the child challenged the parent by introducing new information that undermined the parent's recommendation. The opposition thus stemmed from the clash between, on the one hand, the umbrella participation framework that the larger activity projected and on the other, the local participation framework that was invoked by a specific action.

The current study and previous research on intergenerational conflict are different in another way. In a study of a mother-daughter interaction in which the participants code-switched between Cantonese and English, Williams (2005) found that the daughter often took on an authoritative role, while the mother at times was seeking advice from her adult daughter, and one of the sources of conflict was the mother's resistance to this reversal of role expectations. In the present study, I found that tension occurred even when the participants' roles as parent and child were respected in the talk. Thus, it seems that in some cases, the cause of parent-child tension may lie in their respective asymmetric access to authority and knowledge rather than in resistance to role expectations. This is plausibly the reason for family tension even in a caring activity such as the Vietnamese *dặn* sequence.

The discursive practice examined here, the recommendation sequence, is deeply rooted in the hierarchical and family-oriented Vietnamese society in which, in certain domains and activities, parents have the authority and responsibility to give advice to their children, and the children are expected to follow this advice, as expressed in the two folk sayings that opened this chapter. While the type of conflict examined here is not as physically or emotionally brutal as other forms of parent-child conflicts (such as beatings or scoldings), it may help explain many forms of intergenerational disagreement: Parent-child tension may be brought about by asymmetric access to authority and knowledge among the participants.

Conflict, however, is not always something harmful that needs to be avoided. As Simmel (1908/1955) pointed out, social conflict serves to *organize* and *facilitate* personal relations. Indeed, through tension and its resolution, the family members in the conversation conveyed care and responsibility, shared new information, made collaborative decisions, and accomplished family tasks; in other words, they permeated one another's 'spaces' and extended their own 'space.' In the process of creating and resolving tension, the father acquired new knowledge from his children, and the children had the opportunity to see their father's care for them. In the same process, these family members recreated who they were vis-à-vis one another and who they were as a whole, thus strengthening the fabrics that bound them together as a social unit.

The topic of parent-child conflicts has repeatedly emerged in recent public discourse in Vietnam (e.g., VietNamNet, 2003, 2004, 2005). Participants in these discussions have put forth various explanations for these conflicts and how to resolve them. Sharing the same interest but taking a data-driven approach, I have tried to understand how tension and harmony is created and maintained in a conversation in an ordinary exchange in a Vietnamese family. This bottom-up way to examine 'big issues' in the local management of talk has proved to be fruitful and illuminating.

Notes

1 The concepts of 'superior' and 'inferior' need to be interpreted here as *performed* (Antaki & Widdicombe, 1998; Benwell & Stokoe, 2006) membership categories sensitive to activities and knowledge domains and not as fixed and stable roles. For example, an adult child with more medical knowledge may act as a 'superior'

toward an aging parent who does not have the knowledge or who is too weak to take care of him- or herself.

2 One instance of a *dặn* sequence was found as an example in Vu's (1998) study on politeness in Vietnamese; however, it was classified as a directive, and Vu made no distinction between directives involving immediate actions and those involving future actions (which is the case with *dặn*).

3 All personal names, except the researcher's, are pseudonyms.

4 A limitation of this is that no data indicates what Nam could and could not hear on his end.

5 Differences between voice chats and telephone conversions will be noted later in the data analysis.

6 Similar rationales for the role of the analyst as participant can be found in Tannen (1984).

7 In line 18, Hanh adds a detail about the exact end date of Quốc's study in a quieter voice, but it was not clear whether Nam heard it on his end.

8 See endnote 1 above.

9 I thank Jack Bilmes for bringing my attention to these features in Nam's turn.

10 See the example mentioned in endnote 1 above.

References

Antaki, C., & Widdicombe, S. (Eds.). (1998). *Identities in talk*. London: Sage Publications.

Beaumont, S. L., & Wagner, S. L. (2004). Adolescent-parent verbal conflict: The roles of conversational styles and disgust emotions. *Journal of Language and Social Psychology, 23*, 338–368.

Benwell, B., & Stokoe, E. (Eds.). (2006). *Discourse and identity*. Edinburgh, UK: Edinburgh University Press.

Clayman, S. (2001). Answers and evasions. *Language in Society, 30*, 403–442.

Đặng Chấn Liêu, Lê Khả Kế, & Phạm Duy Trọng (1996). *Từ Điển Việt-Anh* [Vietnamese-English Dictionary] (2nd ed.). Ho Chi Minh City, Vietnam: Ho Chi Minh City Publishing House.

Garfinkel, H. (1967). *Studies in ethnomethodology*. Englewood Cliffs, NJ: Prentice Hall.

Goffman, E. (1963). *Behavior in public places*. New York: Free Press.

Goffman, E. (1981). *Forms of talk*. Philadelphia, PA: University of Pennsylvania.

Goodwin, C., & Goodwin, M. H. (1990). Interstitial argument. In A. D. Grimshaw (Ed.), *Conflict talk: Sociolinguistic investigations of arguments in conversations* (pp. 95–113). Cambridge, UK: Cambridge University Press.

Goodwin, C., Goodwin, M. H., & Olsher, D. (2002). Producing sense with nonsense syllables: Turn and sequence in the conversations of a man with severe aphasia. In B. Fox, C. Ford & S. Thompson (Eds.), *The language of turn and sequence* (pp. 56–80). Oxford, UK: Oxford University Press.

Heritage, J. (1984). A change-of-state token and aspects of its sequential placement. In M. Atkinson & J. Heritage (Eds.), *Structures of social action: Studies in conversation analysis* (pp. 299–345). Cambridge, UK: Cambridge University Press.

Heritage, J., & Sefi, S. (1992). Dilemmas of advice: Aspects of the delivery and reception of advice in interactions between health visitors and first-time mothers. In P. Drew & J. Heritage (Eds.), *Talk at work* (pp. 359–417). Cambridge, UK: Cambridge University Press.

Hoàng, P. (1994). *Từ Điển Tiếng Việt* [Vietnamese Dictionary] (3rd ed.). Hanoi, Vietnam: Nhà Xuất Bản Khoa Học Xã Hội – Trung Tâm Từ Điển Học [Social Sciences Publisher—Vietnamese Lexicography Center].

Jefferson, G., Sacks, H., & Schegloff, E. A. (1987). Notes on laughter in the pursuit of intimacy. In G. Burton & J. R. E. Lee (Eds.), *Talk and social organization* (pp. 152–205). Clevedon, UK: Multilingual Matters.

Mai Thị Kim Thanh. (2005). *Chăm sóc sức khoẻ tâm thần cho trẻ em thông qua quan hệ ứng xử giữa các thành viên trong gia đình Hà Nội hiện nay* [Taking care of mental health for children through interaction and relationship among family members in Hanoi today]. Hanoi, Vietnam: Sociology Department, College of Social Sciences and Humanities, Hanoi National University.

Moerman, M. (1992). Life after C.A.: An ethnographer's autobiography. In G. Watson & R. Seiler (Eds.), *Text in context: Contributions to ethnomethodology* (pp. 20–34). London: Sage Publications.

Nguyen, H. T. (2003). The development of communication skills in the practice of patient consultation among pharmacy students. Unpublished doctoral dissertation, University of Wisconsin, Madison, WI.

Pomerantz, A. (1988). Offering a candidate answer: An information seeking strategy. *Communication Monographs, 55*, 360–373.

Sacks, H. (1995). *Lectures on conversation* (Vols. I & II, G. Jefferson, Ed.). Oxford, UK: Blackwell.

Sacks, H., Schegloff, E. A., & Jefferson, G. (1974). A simplest systematics for the organization of turn-taking for conversation. *Language, 50*, 696–735.

Schegloff, E. A. (1968). Sequencing in conversational openings. *American Anthropologist, 70*, 1075–1095.

Schegloff, E. A. (1986). The routine as achievement. *Human Studies, 9*, 111–152.

Schegloff, E. A. (1972). Notes on a conversational practice: Formulating place. In P. P. Giglioli (Ed.), *Language and social context* (pp. 95–135). London: Penguin.

Schiffrin, D. (1984). Jewish argument: The organization of diversity in talk. *Language in Society, 13*, 311–335.

Simmel, G. (1955). Conflict. In K. Wolf (Ed. and Trans.), *Conflict and the web of group affiliation* (pp. 11–123). New York: Free Press. (Original work published 1908).

Tannen, D. (1984). The pragmatics of cross-cultural communication. *Applied Linguistics, 5*, 189–195.

VietNamNet. (2003). *Làm sao lấp hố ngăn cách giữa các thế hệ?* [How to fill the gap between generations?]. Retrieved January 4, 2006, from http://www.vnn.vn/giaoluu/2003/10/31889/

VietnamNet. (2004). *Khi con cái ức chiếp cha mẹ* [When children bully their parents]. Retrieved January 4, 2006, from http://vietnamnet.vn/xahoi/doisong/2004/12/353850/

VietNamNet. (2005). *Vùng lên dưới ách thống trị của cha mẹ* [Rising up under the "dictatorship" of the parents]. Retrieved January 4, 2006, from http://vietnamnet.vn/xahoi/doisong/2005/07/464729/

Vũ Thị Thanh Hương. (1998). *Politeness in modern Vietnamese: A sociolinguistic study of a Hanoi speech community.* Unpublished doctoral dissertation, University of Toronto, Toronto.

Vuchinich, S. (1990). The sequential organization of closing in verbal family conflict. In A. D. Grimshaw (Ed.), *Conflict talk: Sociolinguistic investigations of arguments in conversations* (pp. 95–113). Cambridge, UK: Cambridge University Press.

Williams, A. (2005). Fighting words and challenging expectations: Language alternation and social roles in a family dispute. *Journal of Pragmatics, 37*, 317–328.

Appendix: Notes on Vietnamese particles and function words in the transcript (based on Hoang, 1994)

AffM (affirmative marker) *cứ*	particle to affirm an activity or state despite all conditions
AlignM (alignment marker) *hí:,*	(Central Vietnamese dialect) particle to express agreement (falling intonation) or to seek agreement (rising intonation); sentence-final
CondM (conditional marker) *mà*	function word to mark the next idea as a conditional statement
cũng (translated as "same")	function word to mean that a situation is the same as other situations, even though the mentioned situation is unusual; often used to add assertiveness to a statement
EmM (emphasis marker) *thì*	function word that, when used at the beginning of an utterance, expresses emphasis in the upcoming statement, often in contrast to a previous statement. This is not to be confused with the other functions of *thì* (see below)
PolM (politeness marker) *ạ*	particle to mark politeness and respect, always utterance-final
PolM (politeness marker) *dạ*	particle to mark politeness and respect, always utterance-initial
PosM (positive marker) *được*	function word to mark events as positive (good); this is in contrast to the negative marker *(bị)*
QuesM (question marker) *há* or *á*	particle placed after an affirmative statement to seek confirmation from the recipient
StaM (stance marker) *ấy mà:*	particle to mark the statement as something that should be of obvious knowledge, to affirm, persuade, or explain, with the implication that the recipient should be able to arrive at this knowledge on his or her own
StaM (stance marker) *chứ*	particle to assert the opposite to what the recipient has just said (e.g., a negation

	after an affirmation, or an affirmation after a negation)
thì (translated as "then")	time adverb to mark sequence of events, with the event introduced by *thì* being the later one
thì (translated as "so")	conjunction to show that the proposition to be mentioned is a certain or likely consequence of the proposition just mentioned
TopM (topical marker) *thì*	function word used after the topic in a topicalization construction

4 When *Gaijin* Matters: Theory-Building in Japanese Multiparty Interaction

Asuka Suzuki
University of Hawai'i at Mānoa

Construction of theories in social interaction

Studies in the sociology of scientific knowledge and ethnomethodology have emphasized the emergent and co-constructed nature of facts and theories (e.g., Gilbert & Mulkay, 1984; Lynch, 1985). Lynch, for instance, investigated neurobiological scientists' talk in the laboratory by applying an ethnomethodological approach. He demonstrated how scientists engage in vernacular arguments in which they propose, disagree with, and verify accounts of objects in pursuit of agreement. Based on these observations, he elucidated how mundane interaction is a constitutive part of scientific work. While Lynch maintained that such interaction does not necessarily lead to "monumental scientific discovery," he demonstrated how scientific 'facts' are contingently constructed and how 'theory' is interactionally developed by being built upon socially constructed facts. However, the collaborative construction of facts and theories through vernacular talk is not necessarily exclusive to interaction in the laboratory but is arguably found in nonspecialized, ordinary talk, such as family dinnertime conversations. For instance, Ochs, Taylor, Rudolph, and Smith (1992) examined dinnertime talk in English-speaking Caucasian American families and proposed that storytelling is a theory-building activity in which family members collaboratively construct, deconstruct, and reconstruct theories of

Talk-in-interaction: Multilingual perspectives, pp. 89–109, Hanh Nguyen & Gabriele Kasper (Eds.), 2009
Honolulu, HI: University of Hawai'i, National Foreign Language Resource Center

personal events. A theory-building activity, then, involves participants providing explanations that are then challenged and reworked by the coparticipants. Ochs et al. argued that these properties of storytelling in everyday interaction are similar to the scholarly processes of theory construction as shown by Lynch.

The type of theory-building activity that this paper focuses on is the activity of building *nihonjiron*, or folk "theories of the Japanese"[1] (Cook, 2006). Based on an analysis of dinnertime talk between students of Japanese as a second language (L2) in Japan and their host families, Cook argued that folk beliefs pertaining to *nihonjinron* are jointly constructed by participants and that her study is compatible with the notion of "storytelling as a theory-building activity" (Ochs et al., 1992) because it demonstrates how the participants offer explanations of generalizations that are then challenged by the coparticipants. Even though Ochs et al. and Cook were concerned with storytelling activities and how such activities may constitute a medium for fostering a novice's cognitive and linguistic development, Cook pointed out that the talk that she examined does not necessarily contain a temporal dimension, one of the characteristics of storytelling according to Ochs et al. What we may infer from these studies, then, is that the activity of theory-building is a phenomenon that is not only observed in storytelling per se but may also be understood as a recognizable activity in its own right. The methods by which *nihonjinron* is constituted in the interactions of native and nonnative speakers of Japanese have also been explored by other scholars (e.g., Cook, 2006; Iino, 1999; Nishizaka, 1999; Siegal, 1995, 1996), and this particular theory-building activity is discussed in the next section.

Construction of *nihonjinron* in talk

In her study on dinnertime talk between homestay students of L2 Japanese and their host families mentioned above, Cook (2006) investigated how particular vernacular theories pertaining to *nihonjinron* emerged through the talk and how they were often initiated by the host family, yet subject to be challenged or aligned with by the students and other members of the host family. In one excerpt, a host mother initiated the topic of the Japanese food *natto* [fermented soy beans], with the assumption that *gaijin* [foreigners] do not like *natto*, and therefore, the homestay student participant in the conversation would not like it either. In this way, the host mother made the student's identity as a *gaijin* relevant while simultaneously invoking her own identity as a *nihonjin* [Japanese person]. In fact, the student, who happened to like *natto,* subsequently oriented to the host mother's presumption by referring to herself as *henna gaijin* [strange foreigner].

Similarly, Nishizaka (1999) showed how a non-Japanese interviewee was constructed as a particular type of *gaijin* by an interviewer. Specifically, using conversation analysis (CA) and membership categorization analysis (MCA), Nishizaka demonstrated how the interviewee's claimed knowledge of Chinese compounds is oriented to by the interviewer as a feature not typically associated with incumbents of the category *gaijin*, for whom it is presumed that Chinese compounds would be difficult. At this point, the interviewer deploys a version (see Cuff, 1993; Lepper, 2000) of the category *gaijin*, i.e., *henna gaijin* [strange foreigner], which reflexively works to make such presumptions about *gaijin* visible in the interaction while simultaneously constructing the interviewee as being exceptional to the category *gaijin*. Similar to Cook's data, this categorization of the interviewee as an exception to the category *gaijin* invokes certain generalizations about *gaijin*, which in turn is built on certain theories of the Japanese, or *nihonjinron*.

Examining interactional contexts similar to Cook's (2006) study (i.e., interactions between Japanese host families and non-Japanese homestay students), Iino (1999) demonstrated the prevalent practices of the host families of comparing Japan to the United States with an emphasis on the uniqueness of Japanese culture and how such practices evoke *nihonjinron*. In his study, he discussed how such talk is closely tied with what he calls *gaijinization*, the process by which the students of Japanese are situated as *gaijin*.[2]

In short, the studies by Cook (2006), Nishizaka (1999), and Iino (1999) suggest that theories such as *nihonjinron* do not have an independent existence prior to interaction but are rather an occasioned notion brought into being in and through the interaction at hand. Moreover, these studies also indicate that the interactional constitution of *nihonjinron* is immediately related to the coparticipants' identities, such as the contrasting identities of *gaijin* and *nihonjin* as well as the hybrid *henna gaijin*. This chapter extends previous research by specifically examining the ways in which a participant's identity as a *gaijin* is intertwined with the construction of a particular kind of *nihonjinron* in a mundane conversation.

Taking an ethnomethodological approach, this study analyzes a dinner table conversation that involves four people from Japan and one person from North America. I aim to investigate how the identity of *gaijin* is made relevant and contested when the participants engage in theory-building activities, in particular, the construction of *nihonjinron*. Specifically, I analyze how the participants accomplish various social actions such as proposing, verifying, counterarguing, and defending *nihonjinron*. As Lynch (1985) demonstrated, these actions are constitutive elements in constructing a theory. This study also shows how, in accomplishing such social actions, the participants are simultaneously negotiating cultural membership with a coparticipant who is interactionally framed as a particular kind of *gaijin*. Such an investigation allows us to see how the construction of *nihonjinron* is a dynamic process in which the participants' identities of *nihonjin* and *gaijin* are closely tied in with the social actions constitutive of the theory-building activity.

One activity in which the notion of *gaijin* was made relevant in the examined conversations is a discussion of the relationship between blood types and personal attributes. In associating blood types with particular personalities, the participants accomplish the various social actions that arguably constitute another theory-building activity, which I call 'theories of blood types.' Because readers may not be familiar with how blood types are commonly understood in Japan and how they are often studied, some explanation is in order.

Japanese folk theories on blood types

By 'theories of blood types,' I refer to claims about an association between the so-called ABO blood types and personalities, which is widespread in Japan. The four ABO blood types are A, B, AB, and O. In Japan (as possibly elsewhere), people commonly associate each blood type with specific temperaments. For example, blood type A is often associated with being 'delicate,' while blood type O is said to be 'carefree' (Hasegawa, 2005). One such association became influential as nationalistic propaganda in the 1930s, when a eugenic theorist postulated it to advocate the superiority of the Japanese nation. The ideology of ethnic superiority was built on the claim of a unique distribution ratio of blood types among the Japanese population among other ethnic groups; hence, blood type could arguably be related to *nihonjinron* (Oguma, 2002). In Japan today, debates on the association between the ABO blood types and temperaments are still ongoing in books and mundane conversation, on television and the Internet (e.g., Hasegawa, 2005; Matsuda, 1991; Sato & Watanabe, 1992).[3]

In vernacular and scientific discourse alike blood types and temperaments are treated as tangible entities, and blood types are often presumed to cause particular temperaments. However, as Lynch (1985) showed, scientific 'facts' do not exist 'out there' to be discovered but are rather interactional outcomes, from which a scientific theory may be developed. This stance is also taken by discursive psychologists, who investigate how claims and versions are produced through talk and what people accomplish through them (Edwards, 1997; Potter, 1996). Hence, examining how notions such as blood types and personality are made relevant through social interaction is one way to approach the social dynamics of theory construction, such as the construction of a theory of blood types. This study examines how the participants associate notions of blood type and personality interactionally through the various social actions they accomplish (e.g., proposing and verifying) that are arguably constitutive elements of theory construction (Lynch, 1985). However, the participants are not concerned with the biological blood types of a person. The analysis shows how the participants treat blood types as assignable based on their judgment of a person's personality. Instead of attempting to consider the veracity of debates concerning theories of blood types, I suggest an alternative perspective on *a* theory of blood types by demonstrating how social actions during mundane blood type talk may constitute the social activity of building a theory of blood types.

A further aim of this chapter is to examine how the participants' social identities as *nihonjin* and *gaijin* are not only made relevant but are reflexively intertwined with the activity of constructing *nihonjinron,* itself embedded in the activity of building a theory of blood types. The analysis specifically focuses on the process by which a participant's identity as a *gaijin* is tied to the constitution of a particular kind of *nihonjinron* and how the participant who is interactionally framed as a *gaijin* negotiates cultural membership with the coparticipants. To this end, this chapter examines a conversation in which *nihonjinron* emerges together with theories on blood types as the identity of the participant from North America as a *gaijin* is negotiated in talk.

Note that while I discuss two theory-building activities concerned with *nihonjinron* and theories on blood types, these activities do not stand as separate events in the examined conversation. Rather, they are intertwined with each other. Treating *nihonjinron*-building activity as the central concern, I first focus on how the participants make Japanese and *gaijin* identities relevant and embed these categories in their activity of building theories of blood types. In the last part of the analysis, I examine how theories of blood type are co-constructed by the participants and how the present *gaijin* is complicit in their construction.

This study

Data

The data for this study are derived from an approximately 2-hour video-recorded dinner conversation in an apartment shared by five graduate students at an American university. Four of the participants (Chika, Kaori, Rina, and Sachi) are from Japan and one (Lisa) is from North America.

Methodology

Adopting a CA approach, this chapter examines how the participants accomplish social actions that constitute the activities of building *nihonjinron* and theories on blood types by analyzing the turn-by-turn development of talk. The study also uses MCA to investigate how the participants do categorizing when engaging in the activities of building theories; that is, how the participants are put into categories that are associated with category-bound predicates and how they contest and negotiate this categorization. I am concerned with how this negotiation of categories is closely tied to the activities at hand; that is, the activities of building *nihonjinron* and theories on blood types. In the analysis, I do not assume the relevance of the participants' social identities prior to the analysis and instead demonstrate how particular social identities are visibly made relevant through the interaction. Consequently, instead of presuming the relevance of national or ethnic identities such as Japanese and non-Japanese or any other transportable identities (Zimmerman, 1998) for that matter, this study examines how particular identities may become relevant through interaction. Specifically, by focusing on the way in which the term *gaijin* is used, I show how the term not only invokes identities (i.e., *nihonjin* and *gaijin*) that have local relevance for the participants at specific interactional moments but is closely tied to the activity at hand; that is, the construction of a particular kind of *nihonjinron*.

Analysis

Relevance of gaijin *to the construction of* nihonjinron

This section examines how *nihonjinron,* in the form of generalizations, emerges in conjunction with the topic of blood types. It also shows how the construction of *nihonjinron* involves the process of *gaijinization,* a process in which a coparticipant's identity as a *gaijin* is made relevant when another speaker attempts to receive verification of the generalization. In Excerpt 1, we find what was reported by Cook (2006) and Iino (1999); that is, the construction of *nihonjinron* sometimes takes the form of generalizing about *gaijin* in contrast with *nihonjin.* Such generalizations, as Cook showed, and as is also evident in the present data, are often initiated by Japanese participants who emphasize the uniqueness of Japanese cultural practices. Specifically, in the segment, the speaker initiates the generalization that *gaijin* do not know their blood types. This generalization stands in contrast with the Japanese practice of knowing one's own blood type. This evokes *nihonjinron* in the sense that the practice is treated as exclusive to Japanese. In this section, therefore, the term *nihonjinron* is used interchangeably with 'generalizations about *gaijin.*'[4] Prior to the beginning of Excerpt 1, Sachi and Kaori are talking about the appearance and character of a Spanish woman whom they went out with, a topic which is subsequently developed into talk about this woman's blood type.

Excerpt 1

```
01 Chika: sugoi kawaii hito   nan desho
          very  cute   person N   CP
          "she's a very cute person isn't she"

02        (.5)
```

```
03 Kaori: kawaii yo.
          cute   IP
          "yeah she's cute"

04        (.5)

 5 Chika: chotto  (ma    ga warukatta ne)
          a little pause SB bad-Past  IP
          "there was a little pause wasn't there"

06 Sachi: hh so[o  soo
          hh Right right IP
          "right right"

07 Kaori:      [tottemo: (.) majime: da yone.
                very          serious CP IP
                "she's very serious isn't she"

08 Sachi: un.
          yeah
          "yeah"

09        (.7)

10 Chika: (      )

11 Kaori: zettai     eegata da yo.
          absolutely A-type CP IP
          "she's got to be ((blood)) type A"

12 Sachi: eegata da ne::? are  wa[::,
          A-type CP IP    that TP
          "yeah that is ((blood)) type A isn't it"

13 Chika:                         [.hh heh

14 Sachi: doo           kangaetemo [ne.
          no-matter-how think-if    IP
          "no matter how you think of it"

15 (   ):                          [°un°
                                     yeah
                                     "yeah"

16        (.3)

17 Rina:  shiranai no, jibun no: ketsuekigata.
          know-Neg IP  self  N   blood-type
          "doesn't she know her own blood type"
          ((gazes at Sachi))

18        (.)
```

19 Sachi: shiranai n janai?
know-Neg N CP-Neg
"I don't think she knows does she"
((gazes at Rina))

20→ **gaijin** tte °anmari shiranai yone°.
foreigners TP very-much not-know IP
*"***gaijin** *don't know do they"*
((gazes at Rina))

21 (.)

22 Sachi: shitteru?
know
"do you know"
((gazes at Lisa))

23 Lisa: nani?
what
"what"

24 Sachi: [ketsuekigata.
blood-type
"your blood type"

25 Kaori: [Sachi-chan, supein-jin o **gaijin**
address Spanish O foreigner
26 [tte yuu nomo bimyoona::
TP say N delicate
"Sachi-chan calling a Spanish person **gaijin,**
I don't know about that"

27 Lisa: [a:: watashi wa shitteru kedo:
oh I TP know but
"oh I know my blood type but"

28 Sachi: hutsuu wa shiranai
generally TP know-Neg
29 yone:[:
IP
"generally they don't know do they"

30 Lisa: [hutsuu wa shiranai.
generally TP know-Neg
"generally they don't know"

31 (.8)

The generalization emerges in line 20, *gaijin tte °anmari shiranai yo ne°* [*gaijin* don't know, do they?], which is used as an account for why the speaker, Sachi, thinks a friend of Spanish origin does not know her own blood type. The talk between Kaori and Sachi triggers a question from Rina, *shiranai no, jibun no: ketsuekigata* [doesn't she know? her own blood type] in line 17. The generalization about *gaijin* emerges as a response to this question. Specifically, Sachi produces *shiranai n janai?* [I don't think she knows, does she?] in line 19, and further provides an account for her epistemological stance with *gaijin tte °anmari shiranai yone°* [*gaijin* don't know, do they?]. This generalization by Sachi, however, takes the form of an assertion ending with the tag-question marker *yone*, which makes it relevant for a coparticipant to provide verification to establish the *nihonjinron* as a joint project. Yet Sachi is unable to receive any uptake of her utterance. This is when she subsequently produces *shitteru?* [do you know?] in line 22, while shifting her gaze from Rina to Lisa. This gaze shift becomes consequential to the way in which Lisa's identity as a *gaijin* is made relevant to the construction of the generalization.

Sachi's shift of her gaze in producing the question in line 22 demonstrates that she selects Lisa as the primary recipient of the question (Goodwin, 1981). This embodied action is critical because without the gaze, the absence of an address term would make it ambiguous as to who the recipient of the turn is. However, the direction of Sachi's gaze is not the only means by which she accomplishes the selection of a respondent. The participants' assumptions as to who would be the appropriate person to respond to the question may also play a role (Lerner, 1993, 2003; Mori, 2003). By shifting her gaze from Rina to Lisa, Sachi displays that not Rina but Lisa is the more appropriate person to respond to the confirmation question and thereby verify the generalization.

To verify that *gaijin* do not know their own blood types, an obvious course of action is to directly ask the copresent incumbent of *gaijin.* Sachi displays this reasoning in reformatting her question from *gaijin tte °anmari shiranai yone°* [*gaijin* don't know, do they?] (line 20) to *shitteru?* [do you know?] (ine 22). The question "Do you know?" specifically asks the recipient about a personal matter (i.e., whether or not she knows her own blood type), in contrast to "*Gaijin* don't know, do they?" which asks her about incumbent *gaijin* in general. In fact, when Lisa subsequently initiates a clarification question, *nani*? [what?] in line 23, Sachi specifies the absent object of the sentence *ketsuekigata* [blood type] in line 24, instead of repeating the prior utterance *shitteru?* [do you know?]. In so doing, Sachi is constructing an identity for Lisa as a *gaijin*—that is, someone with the epistemic authority requisite to verify her generalization that "*gaijin* do not know their own blood types." Hence, by asking Lisa to confirm the generalization, Sachi makes Lisa's identity as a *gaijin* relevant.

In her response (line 27), Lisa presents herself as an exception to the proposed generalization. Her utterance *watashi wa shitteru kedo:* [I know (my blood type), but] contains the contrastive markers *wa* and *kedo,* which project an upcoming contrastive remark; that is, even though *Lisa* knows her blood type, *gaijin* do not *generally* know their blood types. Note that Lisa could simply have produced *shitteru* [I know] as an appropriate response in Japanese rather than what she actually produces in line 27, *watashi wa* [I] with a contrastive marker, *wa*, in responding to Sachi's question. However, by adding a contrastive marker and a modifier (*kedo* [but]), Lisa presents herself as an exception to the proposed generalization; that is, she is presenting herself as a nontypical *gaijin*. Subsequently, Sachi completes Lisa's utterance by producing *hutsuu wa shiranai yone:* [generally they don't know] in lines 28–29, an utterance that is consistent with Lisa's projected upcoming remark as well as with Sachi's previous generalization. *Yone* is attached to Sachi's assertion of the generalization, such that the assertion is provided contingently; this contingency lies in the projected acceptance of the account by Lisa. In line 30, Lisa verifies Sachi's statement as she partially repeats Sachi's utterance *hutsuu wa shiranai* [generally they don't know], thereby agreeing with Sachi's generalization. In short, a type of *nihonjinron*, in the form of a generalization about *gaijin,* emerges around the topic of blood types. The *nihonjinron* is, moreover, not constructed at an abstract level but as an interactional achievement through which a participant's identity as a *gaijin* is made relevant in accomplishing the social action of verifying the emerging theory about Japaneseness.

We have seen that while Lisa agreed with Sachi by verifying Sachi's generalization about *gaijin*, she presented herself as an exception to this generalization. The next section examines how Lisa further contests being labeled as a typical *gaijin*, a label that was made relevant in the establishment of *nihonjinron.*

Contesting the label gaijin *in defense against a counter-assertion*

In Excerpt 2, the verification of the generalization that *gaijin* do not know their own blood types is called into question. This section examines the way in which this challenge is subsequently treated by Lisa, which turns out to be a complex procedure that seems to involve not only defending her prior verification but also simultaneously contesting being categorized as a typical *gaijin*. Excerpt 2 begins when Rina utters, *datte iiaaru toka itteru yo:, ketsuekigata:* [but in ER people are talking about, blood ty:pes] in lines 32–33[5] while gazing at Lisa. ("ER" is a popular U.S. TV show about the dramas in an emergency room context).

Excerpt 2

```
32 Rina:  datte iiaaru toka itte[ru  yo:,
          but   ER      QT   say-Prog IP
33        ketsuekigata: (.) (     )=
          blood type
          "but in ER ((television series)) people are
          talking about ((gazes at Lisa)) blood types"

34 Sachi: =.hh heh [heh iiaaru. .hh
                        ER
                        ER
```

35 Lisa: [demo watashi mo
but I also
36 oo shika shiranai no.
O-type only know-Neg N
37 purasu ka mainasu ka shiranai.
plus or minus if know-Neg
"but I only know that I'm ((blood type)) O too.
I don't know whether I'm plus or minus"

Rina produces her turn in lines 32–33 as a counterargument to challenge Lisa's verification of Sachi's generalization; in other words, Rina is presenting a statement contradictory to Sachi's and Lisa's view that foreigners do not know their blood types. First, we see that Sachi rejects this counterargument. In line 34, she repeats the name ER with laughter, which makes the turn hearable as, "well, ER—that's different/doesn't count." Sachi may be rejecting Rina's reference to the people on ER as an example of *gaijin* because they are medical professionals (and thus, either having knowledge about blood types is one of their category-bound predicates or they talk about blood types only from technical perspectives, unlike what is going on in this conversation). For Lisa, Rina's counterargument not only can challenge the verification about *nihonjinron* that has just been established (i.e., *gaijin* generally do not know their own blood types), but it can also question Lisa's stance as an atypical *gaijin*: If it is common for *gaijin* to know their blood types (as in ER), Lisa's knowing her own blood type does not necessarily qualify her to be an atypical *gaijin*. Hence, Lisa's next turn can relevantly involve two kinds of defense: one is against Rina's challenge towards her verification of Sachi's generalization about *gaijin*, and the other is against Rina's questioning Lisa's social identity as an atypical *gaijin*.

In response to Rina's statement counter to her previous verification of Sachi's generalization, Lisa produces a turn (in partial overlap with Sachi's) beginning with *demo* [but] in line 35. This contrastive marker projects her next statements, *watashi mo oo shika shiranai no* [I only know that I am blood type O, too] (lines 35–36), as a defense against Rina's turn. By naming her specific blood type in this sequential context, Lisa reasserts her alignment with the generalization that generally *gaijin* do not know their blood types and marks herself as an exception to this generalization. What Lisa is doing is very similar to what the *natto*-loving homestay student in Cook's (2006) study did, that is, constructing her identity as an atypical exemplar of the category *gaijin*, a *henna gaijin* [strange foreigner], rather than challenging the integrity of the category, namely, that *gaijin* do not know their blood types. In this light, Lisa's next utterance in line 37, *purasu ka mainasu ka shiranai* [I don't know whether I'm plus or minus] may serve to construct herself not as an extreme *henna gaijin* who knows more than the average Japanese about blood types (evidence for this average Japanese knowledge about blood type can be seen in Sachi's turn in line 39 in Excerpt 3). These two utterances serve to affiliate Lisa with the other participants as members of the same cultural group.

***The resurfacing of the label* gaijin**

Despite Lisa's effort to construct herself as an atypical *gaijin*, or a 'strange' *gaijin*, however, she is again assembled into the category *gaijin* in the subsequent interaction. In this section, I examine (a) how Lisa's alignment with her coparticipants (as members of a cultural group) was taken up by another speaker, yet it failed to accomplish an affiliation with another speaker, and (b) how this failure led to Lisa's being (re)framed as a (typical) *gaijin*.

Excerpt 3

```
35 Lisa:           [demo watashi mo
                    but   I       also
36        oo      shika shiranai no.
          O-type  only  know-Neg N
37        purasu ka mainasu ka shiranai.
          plus   or minus   if know-Neg
          "but I only know that I'm ((blood type)) O too.
          I don't know whether I'm plus or minus"

38        (.)

39 Sachi: a [watashi mo   shiranai yo.
          oh I        also know-Neg IP
          "oh I don't know that either"

40 Kaori:   [oo?
             O-type
             "are you ((blood type)) O"

41 Lisa:  watashi shiranai.
          I       know-Neg
          "I don't know"

42 Kaori: a  shiranai n da. buraddo taipu.=
          oh know-Neg N CP  blood   type
          "oh you don't know your blood type"

43 Lisa:  =oo     oo     wa shitte-=
           O-type O-type TP know
          "I know I'm ((blood type)) O ((blood type)) O"

44 Kaori: =oo     na no?
           O-type N  IP
          "are you ((blood type)) O"
```

```
45 Lisa:  oo      na no.
          O-type N  IP
          "yeah I'm ((blood type)) O"
```

Prior to this segment, we saw that Lisa's knowledge of a specific blood type (O) is made relevant in her affiliation with the other speakers as members of a cultural group (lines 35–37). This display of affiliation with the coparticipants is subsequently taken up by Sachi in line 39, *a watashi mo shiranai yo* [oh I don't know that, either], in which she demonstrates a similar lack of knowledge about the blood subtypes, "plus or minus." This turn is significant because it takes up Lisa's display of her affiliation with the other participants in lines 35–37. Indeed, Lisa appears to confirm her alignment with Sachi by repeating *watashi shiranai* [I don't know] in the subsequent turn (line 41).[6] However, at the point of Sachi's production in line 39, Kaori overlaps with Sachi, asking a confirmation question on Lisa's blood type. As a result, when Lisa takes her turn in line 41, Kaori takes it as a response to her (Kaori's) question. This is evidenced by Kaori's next turn, *a shiranai n da. buraddo taipu* [oh you don't know your blood type] (line 42). Consequently, the sequence goes back to whether Lisa knows her blood type, a topic in which Lisa's identity *gaijin* has been made relevant as seen in Excerpts 1 and 2. Note that when Kaori produces "oh you don't know your blood type," she uses an English word, *buraddo taipu* [blood type], with the Japanese pronunciation instead of the Japanese word *ketsuekigata* [blood type], which has been used by the coparticipants up to this point. *Buraddo taipu* is not part of the Japanese lexicon, and thus, it is specifically created and designed for Lisa. Thus, it seems that Kaori's use of this term works together with the content of her turn to re-assemble Lisa into the category (typical) *gaijin*.

The resurfacing of Lisa's identity as a *gaijin* may also be observed in the way that Kaori's turn in line 42 (when Kaori says *a shiranai n da. buraddo taipu* [oh you don't know your blood type]) erases Lisa's developing identity display up to this point. Recall that through this display, Lisa has been showing an affiliation with the other speakers as comembers of a cultural group. Kaori's action may be seen as 'disattending' to this accomplishment. Such disattending may be arguably related to the (re)construction of Lisa's identity as a *gaijin* (see Paoletti, 1998 for a related discussion on how disattending can construct a participant's identity as, for example, a "senile old person").[7]

The irrelevance of the label gaijin

The recorded conversation continues with Lisa retelling her blood type to the coparticipants in response to Kaori's confirmation request (line 44). This section focuses on how the issue of the relevance or irrelevance of Japaneseness and *gaijin*-ness resurfaces during the activity of building theories on blood types and how this is dealt with by the participants.

Excerpt 4

```
45 Lisa:  oo     na no.
          O-type N  IP
          "yeah I'm O"

46 Kaori: oe:::?
          O
          "O"

47 Rina:  (pojitibu) ga ooi  n da yone?
          (positive) SB many N CP IP
          "there are (positive types) aren't there"

48 Lisa:  un.
          yeah
          "yeah"

49 Sachi: ee      ppoi        kedo ne?
          A-type  seems-like but  IP
          "she seems like a type A ((person)) doesn't she"

50        (.3)

51 Lisa:  hh. heh heh heh [(soo)?
                            right
                            "is that so"

52 Kaori:                 [ee     ka
                           A-type or
53        eebii ka dotchika da yone?=
          AB-type or either CP IP
          "yeah she's either A or AB isn't she"

54 Rina:  =demo sore tte doko made apurai
          but that QT where till apply
55        dekiru n daroo  ne? eegata no seekaku=
          can    N wonder IP  A-type N  personality
56        tte nipponjin dake? janakute?=
          QT  Japanese  only  CP-Neg
          "but I wonder how much we can apply
          can A personality be applied only to Japanese?
          isn't it the case?"

57 Kaori: =[koko to  koko de   oo     da yo:::
            here and here with O-type CP IP
          "here and here are O"
          ((points at Lisa and herself back and forth))

58 Lisa:  n:
          yeah
          "yeah"
```

```
59 Kaori: chigau yo:::
          wrong  IP
          "that can't be the case"
```

I comment on the participant's discussion about blood types in the next section, but here, I focus on how Rina questions the applicability of the theory of blood types to Lisa, when she (Rina) says *demo sore tte doko made apurai dekiru n daroo ne? eegata no seekaku tte nipponjin dake? janakute?* [But I wonder how much we can apply? Can A personality be applied only to Japanese? Isn't it the case?] in lines 54–56. Rina's remark with a tag question, *janakute*? [isn't it the case], displays her presumption that the category "blood type A personality" is applicable only to the category "Japanese." In other words, this suggests the inapplicability of "blood type A personality" to *gaijin*. Because this question is raised when Kaori and Sachi are applying blood type A personality to Lisa, Lisa is again assembled into the category *gaijin* or non-Japanese. The relevance of the category *gaijin* may also implicate a type of *nihonjinron* as we have observed in Excerpts 1 and 2. What is different about the emergence of the *nihonjinron* this time is that, despite Rina's use of the turn-final *janakute?* [Isn't it the case?] (line 56) to make it relevant for the other participants to agree with her statement, they do not orient to her point in subsequent turns. In lines 57–60, for example, Kaori continues to associate the specific blood type (namely, O) with a particular personality by applying them to Lisa and herself without responding to Rina's turn. Thus, Kaori is treating the emerging theories on blood types as applicable to Lisa by showing disorientation to Rina's proposal for the generalization and instead continuing with the ongoing activity of building theories on blood types without excluding Lisa.[8] Consequently, the label *gaijin* or non-Japanese is made irrelevant to Lisa by the participants.

The activity of building theories on blood types

Throughout the conversation, we have seen that the participants make knowledge about particular blood types (i.e., whether or not one knows one's own blood types, and what kind of blood types one knows) relevant to the activity of building *nihonjinron*. For instance, we have observed how Lisa's knowledge about her own blood type is made relevant to construct her identity as a *gaijin* or, contrastingly, an atypical *gaijin* or a *henna gaijin*. We also see the emergence of a theory about blood types oriented to by all participants in Excerpt 4, and this deserves closer examination.

In Excerpt 4, note that Lisa's response concerning her blood type is received with disbelief (line 46). The recipients, Sachi and Kaori, then surmise the blood types that seem to 'fit' Lisa, and subsequently assert their conclusion about what her blood type should be, despite the fact that Lisa has repeatedly stated her biological blood type (lines 36, 43, 45 in Excerpt 3, and line 45 in Excerpt 4).[9] In line 49, Sachi produces *ee ppoi kedo ne*? [she seems like a type

A (person), doesn't she?], by which she asserts that Lisa's personality is like that of a person with blood type A instead of her biological blood type, O. Kaori aligns with Sachi as she provides alternatives that are similar to Sachi's judgment: *ee ka eebii ka dotchika da yone*? [she's either A or AB, isn't she?] (lines 52–53). Thus, by assigning different blood types to Lisa, the participants are not treating blood types as fixed, but rather as something that is *assignable* to a person, *irrespective of actual biological blood types,* based on that person's personality as judged by the assigners.[10]

In the previous sections, we have seen how Lisa's display of knowledge about her own blood type was treated as a way of negotiating her identity in relation to the membership categories (typical) *gaijin*, atypical *gaijin*, or *henna gaijin*. In this section, however, we see that Lisa's biological blood type was treated as irrelevant, as the participants assigned different blood types that seemed to fit Lisa's personal attributes better. In associating Lisa's personality traits with specific blood types, the participants accomplished social actions such as asserting their assessments of the other group members' personality types and verifying their assessments by eliciting and performing alignments. I suggest, therefore, that such social actions (i.e., proposing and verifying) constitute an activity of building theories on blood types, which intertwines with another theory-building activity, *nihonjinron*.

Conclusion

This study builds on previous studies that have demonstrated the constructive nature of theory in interaction by examining the ways in which participants engage in activities to build certain theories, including *nihonjinron* (theories on Japanese) and theories on blood types. In both activities, participants accomplish various social actions such as proposing, verifying, and arguing over their accounts in relation to topics such as *gaijin* and blood types. These social actions are in a sense similar to those in Lynch's (1985) findings, in which he demonstrated, through a detailed analysis of talk among scientists in a laboratory, how scientific facts are proposed, argued over, and verified in pursuit of agreement. The data in the current study suggest that theory-building activities may be recognizable activities that can also be observed in noninstitutional or mundane talk.

This study first demonstrates how *nihonjinron* is constructed through the way in which participants propose, verify, and argue over generalizations concerning *gaijin* and how this construction is a complex process that involves the process of *gaijinization*, that is, the way in which a participant's identity as a *gaijin* is made relevant. The *gaijinization* process is, for instance, observed when verification is pursued to establish a proposed generalization about *gaijin* (Excerpt 1). However, a participant's incumbency in the category *gaijin* was also modified in defending against a counterassertion to the verification of the generalization (Excerpt 1). Despite this contestation, the relevance of *gaijin* was made to resurface though the nonaccomplishment of an alignment sequence where a confirmation of alignment was crucial to establish comembership with the other speakers as well as to verify certain theories (Excerpt 3).

With respect to the other, related activity examined in this study (building theories on blood types), I demonstrated how the participants associated their coparticipants' personalities with specific blood types and how in so doing they accomplished various social actions such as proposing and verifying their judgments about one another's personalities. I propose that such social actions (i.e., proposing and verifying) also constitute part of the theory-building activity. This approach to understanding theories on blood types in social interaction has several implications for psychological studies that investigate the correlation between blood types and personality. For instance, such studies seem to presume that notions such as blood types and personality are relevant, tangible, and clear-cut prior to the analysis. However, the participants in this study did not treat biological blood types as relevant; instead they treated them as something assignable to others depending on their own perceptions of the others' personal attributes. Further, they did not treat blood types as fixed categories: they showed agreement that one participant's personality did not clearly fit one specific blood type and could be "either A or AB." Thus the participants were shown to treat blood types as a qualities rather than as fixed categories.

During both of the theory-building activities, the issue of the relevance (or irrelevance) of a participant's identity as a *gaijin* emerged. While the participants collaboratively made one participant's identity as a *gaijin* relevant at one moment, they also treated it as irrelevant at another moment. The irrelevance of the participant's identity as a *gaijin* was observed when none of the members took up the proposition of a new *nihonjinron* by continuing with the ongoing theory-building activity on blood types (Excerpt 4). This finding may bear implications for second language learning. Based on the findings reported here and based on Cook's (2006) quantitative analysis, which suggested that Japanese host family members frequently bring up topics related to cultural beliefs or *nihonjinron* when communicating with nonnative speakers of Japanese, an important implication is that nonnative speakers or language learners may often be faced with the important task of learning to negotiate their cultural membership in addition to acquiring linguistic skills. What is noteworthy is that the nonnative speaker of Japanese in this study is highly proficient, compared to most of the participants (who are novice or intermediate level speakers) in Cook's study. This suggests, therefore, that the task of negotiating cultural membership may occur irrespective of the learner's proficiency in the language. How frequently and in what contexts nonnative speakers may be faced with the task of negotiating cultural membership are questions that future research can address.

This study demonstrates that the ways in which the identity *gaijin* may be made relevant or modified in the activities of building *nihonjinron* and theories on blood types are contingent on the turn-by-turn development of talk. Hence, this study further supports the conversation analytic stance that the relevance of identities such as *gaijin*, or the relevance of interculturality, should not be presumed prior to social interactions (Mori, 2003; Nishizaka, 1995, 1999; Omori, 2007; cf., Antaki & Widdicombe, 1998; Schegloff, 1997; Wagner & Gardner, 2004). This study also shows that in activities such as the construction of *nihonjinron*, identity may not simply be invoked; rather, it becomes central in accomplishing the activity. For instance, this study shows how a participant (Lisa) managed to maintain the integrity of *nihonjinron* (by defending prior verifications) while simultaneously categorizing herself as an exception, a 'strange' *gaijin*. The activity of building *nihonjinron* in this study was thus closely tied with the *gaijinization* process, which directly and centrally involves participants' identities such as Japanese, *gaijin,* atypical *gaijin,* and *henna gaijin* [strange *gaijin*] that are made relevant in talk-in-interaction. A detailed analysis of the sequential development of talk allows us to see the intricate ways in which theories such as *nihonjinron* and theories on blood types may be constructed in vernacular talk. I argue, therefore, that a conversation analytic and ethnomethodological approach is crucial in approaching the social constructions of theories to fully appreciate the social dynamics of theory construction in talk-in-interaction.

Acknowledgements

I am very thankful to the editors of this volume, Gabriele Kasper and Hanh Nguyen, the anonymous reviewers, Jack Bilmes, Dina Yoshimi, and Cade Bushnell for their highly constructive comments on the earlier versions of this paper. Responsibility for any remaining errors remains with me.

Notes

1 *Nihonjinron* refers to 'theories on Japanese,' the ideology that emphasizes the uniqueness of Japanese in contrast with non-Japanese groups in explaining particular behaviors and characteristics of Japanese people (Yoshino, 1992). While *nihonjinron* may be identifiable when participants are specifically talking about the uniqueness and exclusiveness of the Japanese in terms of specific behaviors and/or characteristics in contrast with non-Japanese groups, it may also become evident when Japanese participants are discussing the absence of specific characteristics in non-Japanese groups, invoking the uniqueness and exclusiveness of the Japanese. The word *nihonjinron* in this study refers to the latter.

2 The term *gaijin* refers to 'non-Japanese' or person(s) from countries other than Japan, typically from Europe or North America. This term is considered politically

incorrect (the politically correct term is *gaikokujin*, which also refers to the same group of people). In this study, the term *gaijin* is used by the participants; hence, I use this term throughout the chapter.

3 In psychology, a number of correlational studies have been conducted to probe into an association of the ABO blood types with personality (e.g., Costa & McCrae, 1992; Cramer & Imaike, 2002; Digman, 1990; Goldberg, 1990; Gupta, 1990; Jang, Liversley, & Vernon, 1996; Rogers & Glendon, 2003; Wu, Lindsted, & Lee, 2005).

4 This study thus deals with two different levels of analysis in association with *nihonjinron* that need to be distinguished: what participants talk about (i.e., generalizations about *gaijin*) and what social actions they accomplish in talking about such generalizations. The analysis focuses on the latter: how the social actions that the participants accomplish in talking about these generalizations constitute a theory-building activity, *nihonjinron* in particular.

5 Due to the syntactic ambiguity of the subject in Rina's statement, *datte iiaaru toka itteru yo:, ketsuekigata:*, her utterance can also be translated as, "But *gaijin* talk about ER or something, blood ty:pes."

6 The absence of *mo* in Lisa's utterance seems odd if she is showing her alignment with Sachi. This may have to do with the absence of gaze from Sachi because she turns her gaze towards Kaori during the overlap with Kaori's utterance. As a result, Lisa seems to fail to accomplish mutual alignment with Sachi concerning not knowing plus or minus.

7 I am very thankful to Cade Bushnell for pointing out the relevance of discussing how the action of disattending constructs a participant's identity here.

8 The participants' different treatments of Lisa's status (i.e., as an outsider at one point and a part of the same cultural group at another point) show how flexible a person's status is. That is, the relevance or irrelevance of such a status is squarely contingent on the particular sequential placement of talk (e.g., Mori, 2003).

9 The participants seem to exclude Lisa from the blood type "O" group because their perception is that her personality is inconsistent with the kind of personality possessed by "O people."

10 What is also interesting besides assigning different blood types is the way in which particular attributes are assigned to Lisa's personality. For instance, her personality is treated as known and shared knowledge among the participants. In other words, her personality is oriented to as something that requires no need for explications. Such participants' orientations are also observed when Kaori makes a comparison between Lisa and herself (lines 57 and 59). In producing "*koko to koko de oo da yo:::* [here and here are blood types O] and then *chigau yo:::* [that cannot be the case] while pointing to both Lisa and herself, for instance, Kaori again does not provide explications of their personalities. This shows that their personalities and the differences between their personalities are treated as shared knowledge by the coparticipants.

References

Antaki, C., & Widdicombe, S. (1998). Identity as an achievement and as a tool. In C. Antaki & S. Widdicombe (Eds.), *Identities in talk* (pp. 151–170). London: Sage.

Cook, H. M. (2006). Joint construction of folk beliefs by JFL learners and Japanese host families. In M. A. DuFon & E. Churchill (Eds.), *Language learners in study abroad contexts* (pp. 120–150). Clevedon, UK: Multilingual Matters.

Costa, P. T., & McCrae, R. R. (1992). Four ways five factors are basic. *Personality and Individual Differences*, *13*, 653–665.

Cramer, K. M., & Imaike, E. (2002). Personality, blood type, and the five-factor model. *Personality and Individual Differences*, *32*, 621–626.

Cuff, E. C. (1993). *Problems of versions in everyday situations.* Washington, D.C.: International Institute for Ethnomethodology and Conversation Analysis & University Press of America.

Digman, J. M. (1990). Personality structure: Emergence of the five-factor model. *Annual Review of Psychology*, *41*, 417–440.

Edwards, D. (1997). *Discourse and cognition.* London: Sage.

Gilbert, G. N., & Mulkay, M. (1984). *Opening Pandora's box.* Cambridge, UK: Cambridge University Press.

Goldberg, L. R. (1990). An alternative "description of personality": The big-five factor structure. *Journal of Personality and Social Psychology*, *59*, 1216–1229.

Goodwin, C. (1981). *Conversational organization: Interaction between speakers and hearers.* New York: Academic Press.

Gupta, S. (1990). Blood groups and personality characteristics. *Personality and Individual Differences*, *3*, 317–318.

Hasegawa, Y. (2005). *Hihanteki-shikou no tame no ketsuekigata-seikakuk-handan* [Theories of blood types and personality for critical thinking]. *Okayama University Bulletin*, *43*, 1–22.

Iino, M. (1999). Language use and identity in contact situations. In L. F. Bouton (Ed.), *Pragmatics and language learning* (Vol. 9), (pp. 129–162). Urbana, IL: Division of English as an International Language, University of Illinois at Urbana-Champaign.

Jang, K. L., Liversley, W. J., & Vernon, P. A. (1996). Heritability of the big five personality dimensions and their facets: A twin study. *Journal of Personality*, *64*, 557–591.

Lepper, G. (2000). *Categories in text and talk: A practical introduction to categorization analysis.* London: Sage.

Lerner, G. H. (1993). Collectivities in action: Establishing the relevance of conjoined participation in conversation. *Text*, *13*, 213–245.

Lerner, G. H. (2003). Selecting next speaker: The context-sensitive operation of a context-free organization. *Language in Society*, *32*, 177–201.

Lynch, M. (1985). *Art and artifact in laboratory science: A study of shop work and shop talk in a research laboratory.* London: Routledge & Kegan Paul.

Matsuda, K. (1991). *'Ketsuekigata to seikaku' no shakaishi* [History of 'blood types and personality']. Tokyo: Kawadeshoboushinsha.

Mori, J. (2003). The construction of interculturality: A study of initial encounters between Japanese and American students. *Research on Language and Social Interaction, 36*(2), 143–184.

Nishizaka, A. (1995). The interactive constitution of interculturality: How to be a Japanese with words. *Human Studies, 18*, 301–326.

Nishizaka, A. (1999). Doing interpreting within interaction: The interactive accomplishment of a "henna gaijin" or "strange foreigner." *Human Studies, 22*, 235–251.

Ochs, E., Taylor, C., Rudolph, D., & Smith, R. (1992). Storytelling as theory-building activity. *Discourse Processes, 15*, 37–72.

Oguma, E. (2002). *A genealogy of 'Japanese' self-images*. Melbourne, Australia: Trans Pacific Press.

Omori, M. (2007). *Constructing 'interculturality' in a NS-NNS English conversational exchange program*. Unpublished manuscript, University of Hawai'i at Mānoa.

Paoletti, I. (1998). Handling 'incoherence' according to the speaker's on-sight categorization. In C. Antaki & S. Widdicombe (Eds.), *Identities in talk* (pp. 171–190). London: Sage.

Potter, J. (1996). *Representing reality: Discourse, rhetoric and social construction.* London: Sage Publications.

Rogers, M., & Glendon, A. I. (2003). Blood type and personality. *Personality and Individual Differences, 34*, 1099–1112.

Sato, T., & Watanabe, Y. (1992). *Gendai no ketsuekigata seikaku handan buumu to sono shinrigakuteki kenkyuu* [The modern boom on the judgment on blood types and personality and its psychological study]. *Shinrigakutekihyooron* [Psychological Review], *35*(2), 234–268.

Schegloff, E. A. (1997). Whose text? Whose context? *Discourse and Society, 8*(2), 165–187.

Siegal, M. (1995). Individual differences and study abroad: Women learning Japanese in Japan. In B. F. Freed (Ed.), *Second language acquisition in a study abroad context* (pp. 225–244). Amsterdam: Benjamins.

Siegal, M. (1996). The role of learner subjectivity in second language sociolinguistic competency: Western women learning Japanese. *Applied Linguistics, 17*, 356–382.

Wagner, J., & Gardner, R. (2004). Introduction. In R. Gardner & J. Wagner (Eds.), *Second language conversation* (pp. 1–17). London: Continuum.

Wu, K., Lindsted, K. D., & Lee, J. W. (2005). Blood types and the five factors of personality in Asia. *Personality and Individual Differences, 38*, 797–808.

Yoshino, K. (1992). *Cultural nationalism in contemporary Japan: A sociological enquiry.* London: Routledge.

Zimmerman, D. H. (1998). Identity, context, and interaction. In C. Antaki & S. Widdicombe (Eds.), *Identity in talk* (pp. 87–106). London: Sage.

5 "Are you Hindu?": Resisting Membership Categorization Through Language Alternation

Christina Higgins
University of Hawai'i at Mānoa

Introduction

Membership categorization analysis (MCA) research has largely focused on conversational data involving the use of a single language. Only recently have studies that use MCA as their primary methodology examined how multilingual speakers use their various linguistic codes as a resource for organizing their social actions in face-to-face interaction. Among these recently published studies on multilingual conversation and MCA, the research is quite similar in that, of the various *identities-in-practice* (Antaki & Widdicombe, 1998) that might be investigated, the researchers have focused on describing the enactment of speakers' *linguistic identities.* For example, Gafaranga (2000, 2001, 2005) and Torras and Gafaranga (2002) used MCA to investigate how language preference operates as a categorization device in the social activity of 'doing being bilingual.' Gafaranga takes the view that language alternation is a social activity in its own right, so his research focused on the locally relevant linguistic identities that Kinyarwanda-French-Swahili speakers used to define themselves and others. In a similar vein, Egbert (2004) examined how speakers' turntaking practices produced regional or linguistic memberships in speaking German and in particular varieties of German. Her work shows how speakers orient to 'nativeness'

Talk-in-interaction: Multilingual perspectives, pp. 111–136, Hanh Nguyen & Gabriele Kasper (Eds.), 2009
Honolulu, HI: University of Hawai'i, National Foreign Language Resource Center

and 'nonnativeness' through repair practices that assign these linguistic memberships to themselves and their coparticipants. Similarly, Cashman (2005) showed how Spanish-English bilinguals with varying degrees of language dominance established and policed the category boundaries for their linguistic identities, which include 'competent speaker of Spanish,' 'incompetent speaker of Spanish,' and 'arbiter of Spanish usage.'

In this chapter, I use MCA to examine how multilingual speakers use language alternation to manage other identities-in-practice beyond their linguistic identities. In doing so, I seek to contribute to understanding the "procedures that members have for selecting categories" (Sacks, 1995, p. 42) and to illuminate the procedures that speakers have for contesting and disavowing category selections made on their behalf. By focusing on a naturally occurring Swahili-English conversation recorded between two journalists in a newspaper office in Dar es Salaam, Tanzania, I examine how the speakers use language alternation to propose, resist, and alter categories. Furthermore, the bilingual data provides an opportunity to examine the construction of intercultural difference through the social categories 'Hindu' and 'Christian,' categories that emerge through the participants' talk. I show how this intercultural membership categorization becomes a resource for conversational activities and how it is used to manage additional categories that emerge in the ensuing talk. The identity-in-practice of 'religious affiliation' was not chosen as an interest prior to examining the talk; instead, in the spirit of ethnomethodology, it became a topic to explore because it emerged from the participants' conversation as a significant category that organized their social actions and their language choices.

In the Swahili-English conversation below, the participants demarcate specific religious memberships for themselves and for one another through their discussion of Hinduism, Christianity, and Islam. The negotiation of their memberships involves proposing, avowing, disavowing, displaying, accepting, and rejecting particular memberships. The actions involving language alternation are those in which one of the participants, Braj (a pseudonym), contests and tries to repair the religious memberships being offered to him. This tension in negotiating memberships points to a lack of culturally shared knowledge, despite the participants' shared nationality, and hence, can be considered data in which *interculturality* (Day, 1994; Mori, 2003; Nishizaka, 1995, 1999; Sarangi, 1994) is constructed through talk. Interculturality is not a static category in interaction, however, and in the ensuing talk, the other participant, Irene (also a pseudonym), tries to establish a mutual identity with Braj. In a series of sequences, she categorizes herself as 'someone who helps children not of one's own kind,' and she offers Braj comembership in this category through a request for financial assistance regarding a child she is taking care of. Braj rejects this membership, however, and he contests Irene's categorizations through a variety of conversational structures, including language alternation.

Interculturality due to religious affiliation

Like the social constructs of gender, ethnicity, and social class, religious affiliation can be seen as a *transportable identity* (Zimmerman, 1998) that "travel[s] with individuals across situations and [is] potentially relevant in and for any situation and in and for any spate of interaction" (pp. 90–91). While religious affiliation may be a cultural or even physical indicator of identity (e.g., through clothing, hairstyles, and gestures), this categorization should be examined as an identity-in-practice (Antaki & Widdicombe, 1998) that may emerge in microlevel discourses rather than one that is relevant for people at all times. The examination of categories such as 'religious affiliation' as identities-in-practice allows for the possibility that "a participant may be aware of the fact that a co-interactant is classifiable as a young person or male without orienting to those identities as being relevant to the instant interaction" (Zimmerman, 1998, p. 91).

As the data demonstrate, one possible outcome of talk involving religious affiliations is the production of cultural difference among speakers, or the enactment of interculturality along religious lines. Sarangi (1994), Nishizaka (1995, 1999), and Mori (2003) use interculturality to mean cultural affiliations that produce cultural differences that are made relevant through conversation. As Nishizaka proposes, we should not take different cultures for granted when analyzing talk, but rather, explicate "how it is that the fact of being intercultural is organized as a social phenomenon" (p. 302). Nishizaka's (1995) research examines the ways that 'being a Japanese' is achieved interactively in the same way that 'being a foreigner' is achieved through talk. Nishizaka explains, "For instance, that I am a Japanese is correct, but the category 'Japanese' is not always relevantly applicable to me; whether I am Japanese or not might be irrelevant when I talk to students about Structural-Functionalism in a sociology class" (p. 305). Mori continues this line of research, examining question-answer sequences for the ways that interculturality organizes participation frameworks. She focuses on the description of interculturality by examining moment-by-moment shifts of participation structures for the next-speaker selection, and she shows that interculturality was treated as altogether irrelevant for some interactions. The present study contributes to this line of research by investigating the membership categories displayed and made relevant by participants regarding cultural difference and cultural similarity. Moreover, the data presented demonstrate how (inter)cultural identities are contingent on the categories constituted in talk, and hence, can easily shift from one moment to the next.

Being ascribed and resisting interculturality

Studies of talk-in-interaction have shown that categories such as gender and ethnicity are made relevant among speakers by way of explicit category naming and through *category bound activities* (CBAs; Sacks, 1966, 1979). However, the naming of these categories alone does not make them 'real' or identifiable as the cause of how someone is acting or speaking. For example, a person may be categorized as 'White' or 'African-American' by another speaker, but the person categorized that way may react against such membership as irrelevant for the context of the conversation. Moreover, the person may react against the categorization altogether because these categories and who they apply to are contestable as well. For example, in his study of talk-in-interaction among ethnic minorities in Swedish factories, Day (1994, 1998) shows how 'ethnic group' categorizations were sometimes contested by the participants. He sought to determine ethnicity not as a category pre-existing the conversational interactions he encountered, but rather, to look for "ethnification processes...through which people distinguish an individual or collection of individuals as a member of members respectively of an ethnic group" (p. 154). He gives the example in Excerpt 1 as an illustration, which is translated from Swedish. In the excerpt, three speakers who work together at a factory in Sweden are planning a party to which they will invite all of their coworkers, and they are discussing what kind of food to prepare.

Excerpt 1 (Day 1998, p.162)

```
Lars: don't we have something that, one can eat
      that, China or
Rita: Chinese food is really pretty good
Xi:   ha ha ( ) it doesn't matter, I'll eat anythings
Rita: ah (that's [what I that)
```

Lars has suggested Chinese food for the party in line 51, and Rita upgrades the suggestion, stating her positive opinion of Chinese cuisine. Xi takes the next turn by laughing, and then offers an ambivalent attitude toward the choice of Chinese food for the party. In his analysis of the talk, Day explains that Lars's suggestion and Rita's confirmation project the next turn as belonging to Xi. The turn is projected to take the shape of either an acceptance or refusal. Day explains that their talk thus far makes relevant Xi's ethnicity as Chinese, and he argues that Xi's response as the next speaker confirms this idea. According to Day, Xi's response in line 54 indicates that she heard the suggestion as particularly relevant for her, as someone who would be knowledgeable about Chinese food, thereby producing her identity as 'Chinese' by virtue of the CBA associated with the ethnic category 'Chinese,' namely, 'eating Chinese food.' Day explains that her response would not make sense without this inference, and he suggests that Xi's denial of the relevance of the ethnic category via the CBA of eating

Chinese food resists the relevance of the ethnic categorization produced by the coparticipants. Xi's response in line 54 can be seen as her intent to be viewed as a member of the social group jointly pursuing the social activity at hand, rather than to suffer the fate of 'exteriorization.' The marking of her ethnicity would prevent her from fully participating as an equal member in the group, so her aversion to being marked as culturally specific here shows her resistance to the implication that she is "not due the trust one needs to be a member of the social group constituted in the social activity" (Day, 1998, p. 168).

The actions among the Swedish factory workers provide a basis for comparison with the bilingual data I present in the ways that speakers go about displaying their acceptance or rejection of categories that mark them as culturally similar to or different from one another. This excerpt also offers an indication of where language alternation might emerge in disaffiliative actions, including rejections or downgradings of categorizations. In Excerpt 1, the rejection of the relevance of Xi's ethnicity is preceded by a laughter token, a means by which *dispreference* (Pomerantz, 1984) can be marked in the way that it delays her rejection. The laughter is similar to the use of pauses and token words such as *well* in monolingual talk before other dispreferred actions such as disagreement, as in line 02 of Excerpt 2:

Excerpt 2 (Sacks 1987, p.58)

```
A: You coming down early?
B: Well, I got a lot of things to do before
   getting cleared up tomorrow I w- probably
   won't be too early.
```

Whereas laughter or delay tactics can mark dispreference in monolingual talk, multiple studies have demonstrated that code contrasts often mark dispreferred turns in bilingual talk (Auer, 1984, 1998, 1999; Cashman, 2001; Li Wei, 1994, 1995; Shin & Milroy, 2000). Actions that have been found to co-occur with and that mark dispreference include refusals, disagreements with assessments, and disaffiliations with questions structured for yes-answers. In monolingual data, these actions are normally accompanied by hedges, pauses, delays, and other markers of dispreference. In bilingual talk, codeswitching may be the only marker, though it may also co-occur with the same features found in monolingual talk. In Excerpt 3, we see how refusals may co-occur with language alternation when a mother (A) offers her child (B) some fried rice.

Excerpt 3, codeswitching in refusals (Li Wei, 1995, p.204–205)

A: oy-m-oy faan Ah Ying a?
Want some rice?

```
2 B: ((no response))

3 A: chaaufaan a. Oy-m-oy?
     Fried rice. Want or not?

4 B: (2.0) I'll have some shrimps.

5 A: mut-ye? (.) Chaaufaan a.
     What? Fried rice.
```

The child's refusal coincides with a 2-s pause and a codeswitch, thus contextualizing it as dispreferred. Li Wei (1995) explains that the child's use of language alternation combined with a lengthy pause helps to produce an extra degree of mitigation in the refusal of food and hence can be seen as a case of dispreference through codeswitching.

In a similar fashion, the Swahili-English data below provide illustrations of how two participants manage dispreferred turns involving disagreement and downgradings of proposed membership categorizations. Whereas laughter and lexical markers of dispreference are used in monolingual conversation, the Swahili-English data show that language alternation may be viewed as another resource by which speakers display dispreferred actions, including challenges to membership categorizations. In addition to the conversational structure of language alternation, the participants in the data below also use categorial pronouns and categorial vocabulary to establish disaffiliation with each other.

Pretopical talk and topical talk

When conversational participants who do not share a great deal of familiarity with one another, such as Irene and Braj, begin an interaction, they often engage in talk that contains many occasions for membership categorization devices (MCDs) to be offered, taken up, or rejected. Maynard and Zimmerman (1984) describes such talk as *pretopical talk*, that is, sequences that involve categorization and category-activity question-answer pairs that may generate more elaborated talk. Their study of university students found that unacquainted pairs began conversations by asking about one another's year in school, academic major, home residence, and local residence. Once such knowledge was established, more elaborated talk sometimes followed. Excerpts 4 and 5 illustrate pretopical talk wherein Maynard and Zimmerman's participants are discovering and displaying their category memberships to one another. By asking questions, the participants categorize their coparticipants according to those social categories explicitly mentioned and at the same time, display the relevance of the more general category 'student' within which the other categories mentioned are subsumed.

Excerpt 4, pre-topical talk: Year in school (Maynard & Zimmerman, 1984, p.305)

```
B1: Are you a freshman
B2: No, second year.
B1: Oh.
```

Maynard and Zimmerman report that unacquainted pairs also asked each other about matters such as courses they were currently taking, as in Excerpt 5. Such actions indirectly group participants with MCDs by virtue of association with the categories; for students, CBAs might include going to classes regularly, taking tests, and having a major, as in Excerpt 6.

Excerpt 5, taking classes (1984, p.306)

```
A: What are you taking anyway?
B: Well, sociology, anthropology, and art history.
```

Excerpt 6, taking classes (1984, p.306)

```
A: Are you a soc major?
B: Um, I'm thinking of it. What're you?
A: Uh, marine geology is my major.
```

Through these question-answer sequences, Maynard and Zimmerman demonstrate how unacquainted parties establish knowledge of each other's biography and "test each other for just how close or distant their particular relationship will be" (p. 314). These categorization sequences often lead unacquainted dyads into more "personal" autobiographical talk, or what Maynard and Zimmerman term *topical talk*: talk that is generated from the biographical information and knowledge that was achieved in the pretopical sequences, as shown in Excerpt 7.

Excerpt 7, topical talk ensuing from pre-topical talk (1984, p.308)

```
B2: Where'd you come from.
B1: Sacramento.
B2: Oh Yeah? I'm from Concord. It's up north too.
B1: Yeah it's a little bit close.
B2: Yeah and I went home this weekend . . . ((story))
```

Maynard and Zimmerman found that unacquainted participants searched for opportunities to establish "common territories of self" that would enable them to develop more 'personal' autobiographical talk (p. 314). In the Swahili-English data below, I show how the participants make relevant the category 'religion,' a category that is also interdependent with ethnicity for some religions in Tanzania, namely, Hinduism. I show how Braj and Irene use this category to engage in pretopical and topical talk, thereby demarcating categories that produce their different memberships in the category 'religious affiliation.' Their interaction involves many instances of membership categorization, and both participants use language alternation as a resource for downgrading, challenging, and rejecting certain categorizations.

One important difference between my study and Maynard and Zimmerman's study is that all of their participants were Anglo speakers of American English who did not know each other prior to the conversation. In contrast, in the present data set, the participants are multilingual coworkers who are marginally acquainted, and who, on the face of it, can be said to represent different races and genders, that is, a Black woman and an Indian man. Both are Tanzanian nationals who were born and raised in Tanzania. Both speak English and Swahili, and both speak at least one other language. Irene speaks Chagga, a Bantu language spoken in Northern Tanzania, and Braj speaks Gujarati, an Indic language with a wide diaspora of speakers all over the globe. While it is tempting to draw connections to social identities and *a priori* knowledge of the participants (such as the categories 'Indian' or 'Black,' 'Hindu' or 'Christian,' 'male' or 'female'), I reiterate that these categories are not necessarily relevant to the participants because of their apparent or historic qualities; instead, I am concerned with how the participants make the relevance of these social identities visible through talk. I am also concerned with how these identities further impact the development of talk or how they might be procedurally consequential to ensuing turns of talk, particularly in reference to language alternation. As the data show, these categories are treated as the basis for cultural difference among the speakers at one point in the conversation, and at a later point, one of the participants treats cultural difference as the basis for mutual understanding. The data therefore show how cultural sameness and difference are highly dynamic because they are contingent on the categories that emerge in and through face-to-face talk; moreover, the interactional data show how the categorization of cultural sameness and difference depends on the participants' responses to the categorizations.

Data analysis

At the beginning of the conversation, the two participants are discussing Braj's religion. It becomes clear that Braj and Irene claim different memberships in this category, and Irene's efforts to display her understanding of Braj's religion are largely contested and eventually repaired by Braj. This talk results in the participants' *interculturality* despite their shared nationality. In spite of their cultural differences, Irene makes relevant specific identities-in-practice in talk to organize her interaction with Braj in ways that will allow her to follow the ritual of generating *topical talk*, that is, talk that allows her to affiliate with him. Braj resists engaging in topical talk with Irene,[1] so the talk has the feel of an interview in Excerpts 8–10. At the beginning of Excerpt 11, Irene asks Braj about his activities with charitable organizations, and this new topic leads to topical talk in which Irene makes a request of Braj. In this topical talk, she claims a shared identity-in-practice for Braj and herself, an identity that involves helping others outside of one's ethnic group. Braj resists this categorization, however, and he displays his disalignment through contrasting language, pronominal, and vocabulary choices. By producing conversational structures that contrast with Irene's talk, Braj resists the shared identity proposed for him, and in his responses, he produces an identity that indexes activities associated with a business exchange, rather than charitable or philanthropic activity.

Establishing common ground through pretopical talk

In Excerpts 8–10, the nominations of topics explicitly naming 'Indian things' make visible the participants' orientation to the interculturality of the interaction in a very direct manner through *labeling* (Antaki & Widdicombe, 1998), the practice of producing explicit membership categorizations that are locally occasioned in talk. These turns appear to be treated as part of the ritual of unacquainted participants getting to know one another. By asking questions concerning Braj's experience with, knowledge of, or perspective towards his own culture, we see that Irene is attempting to discover shared experience, or knowledge, across cultural boundaries to prompt her coparticipant to extend topical talk.

In Excerpt 8, the participants are displaying their relatively unacquainted status to one another through their short question-answer sequences, routines that provide further support for Maynard and Zimmerman's (1984) conclusions that unacquainted pairs tend to rely on categorization sequences and categorization activity sequences to establish pretopical talk before any topical talk can develop (see the Appendix for abbreviations used in the transcript).

Excerpt 8

```
01 I: nanii (.) wewe  ni:  ni   Hi↑nd↓u.
      uh        you   are  are  Hindu
      uh are you Hindu

02 B: m-mh (.) Baniani.
      m-mh     Baniani
      no I'm Baniani

03 I: eeh?
      what
      what

04 B: Baniani.

05 I: Baniani.
```

06 B: eeh Hindu yes.
right Hindu yes
right Hindu yes

07 I: Baniani (.) is it different from Hindu.

08 B: Yeah tu-na-tofautia-na kwa (kabila) mbalimbali
yes we-prs-differ-rcp by tribe various
yes we differ from one another by various tribes

09 kwa mfano Wa-sukuma,
for example pl-Sukuma
for example the Sukuma people ((a Bantu ethnic group of Tanzania))

10 I: eeh.
yes/oh
yes/oh

11 B: wa-hehe,
pl-Hehe
((or)) the Hehe people ((a Bantu ethnic group of Tanzania))

12 I: °Baniani.° Eeh u-na- you worship kwenye
Baniani um you-prs you worship at
Baniani um do you you worship at this um

13 hii nanii (.) >Jamatini pale<
this um Ismailia-mosque here
Ismailia mosque over here

14 B: Jamatini ipi?
Ismailia-mosque which
which Ismailia mosque

15 I: Jamatini ya hapo Upanga.
Ismailia-mosque of there Upanga
the Ismailia mosque in Upanga

16 B: uh: Upanga road pale?
uh Upanga road here
uh, on Upanga Road over here

17 I: hii hii ya hapa karibu na nanii,
this this of here near by um
this one nearby near the um

18 B: na,
by
by

```
19 I: na Aga Khani xx hospital.
      by Aga Khan     hospital
      by the Aga Khan Hospital

20    (0.5)

21    [au:,
       or
       or
```

In line 01, Irene proposes the categorization of Hindu for Braj, and her question (marked through its rising then falling intonation) is built for a positive response. The choice of her question can be viewed as 'setting talk' (like talk about the weather), wherein participants who are engaged in getting a conversation going talk about obvious or visible topics to get to more topical and personal talk. In this case, talk about one's religious/ethnic identity is treated as an appropriate initiating move by Irene, and this may point to the salience of these categories as highly visible ones in multiethnic, multicultural Dar es Salaam. In line 02, Braj rejects her categorization and repairs it, narrowing the category to Baniani, which historically in Hindi means 'trader/merchant' and is a word that has normally been associated with people from the Gujarat region in India. In the Tanzanian context, however, the word has come to refer to a Hindu sect local to the Dar es Salaam area.

After a confirmation request initiated by Irene, Braj unexpectedly accepts the category 'Hindu' that Irene has proposed in line 06, which can be seen as an effective way of avoiding elaboration on the repair he offered in line 02. Maynard and Zimmerman (1984) reported that during pretopical talk, speakers may produce minimal responses to avoid participating in more topical talk, and Braj's affirmative answer here may be a strategy to avoid any continued talk on the subject of his religion. However, because Braj has produced an *identity-rich puzzle* (Maynard & Zimmerman, 1984) for Irene at this point (by answering first "no" then "yes"), she inquires more about it in line 07, prompting Braj to elaborate about the difference between Baniani and Hindu in lines 08–09. His ensuing clarification uses references to categories that are non-Indian, as the Sukuma and Hehe are Black ethnic groups in Tanzania belonging to the wider category of Bantu, which Irene is sure to know. Through drawing on categories and sets of knowledge that are Bantu in nature, rather than Indian, Braj effectively maintains a cultural boundary between himself and Irene. Moreover, instead of responding directly to Irene's English-medium question by explaining about the sects of Hinduism in the same code, he offers a brief affirmative answer in English [yeah] in line 08 and then returns to Swahili as he refocuses the topic to Bantu cultures rather than Indian religions.

Braj's clarification in line 08 allows him to evade biographical information that might yield a more intimate conversation, and hence, the pretopical talk continues. Irene asks about the CBAs she associates with being Baniani or Hindu, such as where the members of these groups worship, in lines 12–13. Irene's language alternation in line 12 from *eeh una-* [and you-prs-] to *you worship kwenye hii nanii Jamatani* [you worship at this um Ismailia mosque] can be understood as a self-initiated self-repair. Here, Irene alters the Swahili utterance underway, having at least the choices of *unasali* [you pray/you recite prayers], *unaabudu* [you worship God], or possibly even *unahusudu* [you revere/adore]. She chooses the English *you worship* instead. Irene's use of *you worship* is placed within the context of pretopical talk, and it is arguable that the use of English here marks her assumption as more neutral than using the expression *unaabudu* (often used for Christian and Muslim practices), or *unasali* (often, though not exclusively, used with Muslim practices of reciting prayers). Based on the talk that follows, she clearly has little understanding of what it means to be Baniani, and therefore, the choice of the English word here can be seen as a strategy to avoid making a mistake within her pretopical moves that appear to be designed to get Braj to elaborate more fully.

The effect of Irene's clarification request regarding the Hindu/Baniani distinction, together with her knowledge of the religious practices of Baniani, based on physical buildings such as the *jamatini* [temple], categorize her as someone who is a nonknower, a novice, a nonmember. In other words, she is an 'outsider' because she only has knowledge of the features of the Baniani people that outsiders have access to, such as the buildings they use for worship. Moreover, Braj's treatment of her questions reinforces these categories, as his initial attempt to accept her misunderstanding of his religion, together with his framing of the variation in India within the indigenous Bantu ethnic group system of Tanzania, positions her as someone who does not understand the Baniani people. In this excerpt, clear boundaries are drawn between the two participants, and they are associated with the interdependent categories of religion and ethnicity.

Excerpt 9 continues this theme a few moments later in the same conversation when Braj offers to escort Irene to the building he worships at, which can be read as an offer by a member to acquaint a nonmember with a new or unfamiliar community. Irene then engages him in a set of questions about his religious beliefs, a move that appears to go beyond pretopical talk.

Excerpt 9

```
37 B: ni-ta-ku- [sindikiza.
      I-will-you-escort
      I will take you there.

38 I:           [whom do you believe in (.) Mohammed?
```

39 B: ni Wa-islamu.
is pl-muslim
that's the Muslims

40 I: nyie? Nyie m-na-believe in what.
you.pl you.pl you.pl-prs-believe in what
and you all what do you all believe in

41 B: tu-na-believe na mungu wetu.
we-prs-believe in god our
we believe in our god.

42 I: mungu wa- wa: Baniani.
god of of Baniani
the Baniani god

43 B: Yes.

44 I: ni nani huyu?
is who this one
who is this god

45 B: ku-na wa mbalimbali.
there-are of different kinds
there are different kinds

46 I: mi-ungu.
pl-god
gods

47 B: yeah. (2.0) ku-na [m-,
yes there-are m-
yes there are m-

48 I: [kama sisi Christians tuna
like we Christians we-have
like we Christians, we have

49 Jesus Christ ku-na Mohamed for Muslims,=
Jesus Christ there-is Mohamed for Muslims
Jesus Christ, there is Mohamed for Muslims

50 B: =yeah we have different ones. different

51 I: kwa hiyo you don't have one god you believe in.
for that you don't have one god you believe in
so you don't have one god you believe in

In line 38, Irene asks Braj whom he believes in, and she offers a candidate answer, Mohamed. Braj rejects her answer, grouping himself outside the label 'Muslim,' and the rejection aligns with a switch into Swahili. This question-answer pair displays a lack of cooperation or disalignment in several ways. First, Irene's question has been built for a positive response because its construction as a yes-no question seeks confirmation for Mohamed as the entity that the Baniani believe in. However, Braj's response does not confirm this categorization. Moreover, her question asks him to speak as "you," and his answer uses the ambiguously marked copula verb *ni* [is], which can take any subject in Swahili. Additionally, a disjunction with language choice coincides with the rejection of the CBA of believing in Mohamed. At this point, the conversation is not building toward topical talk because the turns comprise a sequence of categorizations in which Braj and Irene continue to "test each other for just how close or distant their particular relationship will be" (Maynard & Zimmerman, 1984, p. 314).

In line 40, Irene asks Braj to speak for his group, and she specifies the second-person plural pronoun, *nyie* [you all]; the rest of her question is in hybrid Swahili-English in the form of *mnabelieve in what*. Braj accepts this membership categorization, and his code choice is similarly hybrid when he answers *tunabelieve na mungu wetu* [we believe in our god]. His response aligns with the language choice of her question. However, his reference to *mungu wetu* [our god] uses the noninclusive first-person plural possessive pronoun, which has the effect of maintaining Irene's outsider knowledge about the Baniani because it fails to impart new information about the religious entity the Baniani believe in. As has been clear throughout the talk, Irene does not understand the religious beliefs of the Baniani, so in line 42, she initiates repair, rephrasing Braj's previous utterance as *mungu wa- wa Baniani*. This turn does not indicate that she has learned anything, but instead, marks her lack of knowledge. Moreover, through her expression, *mungu wa- wa Baniani*, she replaces Braj's *mungu wetu* [our god] with *mungu wa Baniani*, a move that shows her own alignment as an outsider of this category. Notably, the language choice is the same throughout these turns. Several questions follow, all attempts to better understand the Baniani religion, and then in lines 48–49, Irene asks for further clarification. Her question is structured so that it creates membership for herself as a Christian and opposition through pronominal usage between Christians and Muslims. She says, *sisi Christians tuna Jesus Christ* [we Christians we have Jesus Christ], followed by the existential construction *kuna Mohamed for Muslims* [there is Mohamed for Muslims]. Her use of "we Christians" marks the religious difference between herself and the Muslims as well as the difference between herself and Braj; the existential usage of "there is Mohamed for Muslims" also categorizes both herself and Braj as non-Muslims.

In the same way that Hinduism and Baniani beliefs do not conform to monotheism, Braj's line 50 does not follow the structural pattern that Irene has set up for him. In producing "we Christians, we have Jesus Christ, there is Mohamed for Muslims," Irene's nonfinal intonation leaves the final slot open with an expectation for a statement such as "and we Baniani have X," or "and there is X for the Baniani people." Instead, Braj produces *we have different ones. (.) different*, thus marking the interculturality in four ways: (a) language alternation, (b) the use of *we* to mark off the Baniani as different from the Christians and the Muslims, (c) the use of the word *different*, uttered two times, and (d) a different syntactic structure. At this point, interculturality via religious categories seems to have become a block to shared experience and has therefore precluded topical talk. This interculturality is displayed through the conflicting conversational structures portrayed in Figure 1.

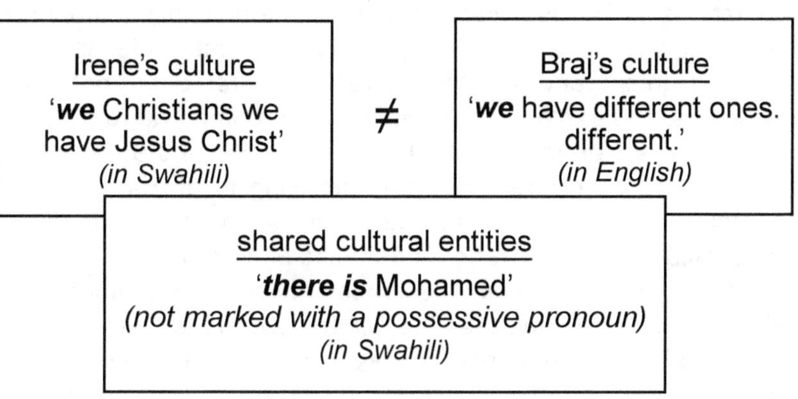

Figure 1. Conversational structures reflecting interculturality.

At this point in the talk, all that has been accomplished is a great deal of categorizing one another as different. In Excerpt 10, pretopical talk continues. Irene's outsider status is reflected in her questions to Braj about his eating practices during fasting periods.

Excerpt 10

```
83 B: yaa different kind of fasting (.)
84    throughout the year.
85 I: mhm. (.) you eat meat.
86 B: some of them (.) they eat meat.
87 I: eeh.
88 B: >they don't eat meat.< [what they eat is
      chicken fish,
89 I:                         [yaani,
                               in other words
                               in other words
90 B: we can eat meat but we eat chi- mostly
91    chicken fish,
92 I: mhm.
93 B: we don't eat the red meat.
94 I: mhm.
95 B: we don't eat the red meat.
96 I: you don't eat red meat.
```

```
97 B: yaa.
98 I: mhm.
99 B: yaa.
```

Excerpt 10 contains sequences of pretopical talk searching for shared experience, with a focus on food rituals observed for religious reasons. Of significance to the investigation of interculturality are lines 85–86, where Braj reformulates Irene's pronoun choice of "you" in "you eat meat" in line 85 as "some of them" and "they" in line 86, when he explains that only certain Indian populations in Dar es Salaam eat meat. Interestingly, although these turns involve Braj's contestation and repair of Irene's categorial assumptions regarding the Baniani and Hindu populations, Braj does not alternate languages. A possible explanation for this is that, compared to his previous responses to Irene's categorizations, his lines 86, 88, and 90 are a 'softer' rejection and repair of Irene's monolithic grouping of all Baniani or Hindu as meat eaters. The softening may be seen as an attempt to downplay the interculturality between Irene and himself. In other words, through demonstrating the diversity among the Tanzanian Indian population, all forms of interculturality may become less identifiable and hence, less significant. Irene's use of *yaani* [in other words] in line 89 is an instance of other-initiated repair, and her use of Swahili to carry out this repair can be understood as a means by which bilinguals may handle the dispreferred act of other-initiated repair. In comparison with self-initiated repair sequences, other-initiated repairs typically co-occur with dispreference markers in monolingual conversations (Schegloff, 2000), so language alternation occurring here is not surprising.

Claiming and resisting a shared membership

After a lengthy pause following line 99, Irene switches topics and continues to pursue another line of pretopical talk in Excerpt 11. Irene asks about Braj's work with UNICEF, a question that might be characterized as an educated guess about his activities. Braj's status as someone who works with children is well known in the office because his job at the newspaper is to write the "Children's Corner" for the Sunday edition. Based on my observations of his activities at the office, he often engages in conversations about events that aim at helping children with anyone who is willing to listen. Irene's question about UNICEF may also be influenced by the fact that many Indian Tanzanians are involved with philanthropic work that strives to assist needy children in East Africa. As it turns out, Braj does not actually work or volunteer his time for UNICEF, though he does volunteer for the Lions Club, a similar charitable organization. Braj does not explicitly correct Irene on this matter, however.

Excerpt 11

((18 s pause))

100 I: UNICEF u-na-fanya nanii: (.) u-na-jitolea.
UNICEF you-prs-do um you-prs-volunteer
at UNICEF do you uh do you volunteer

101 B: wapi?
where
where

102 I: UNICEF do they pay you.

103 B: no, na-jitolea.
no I-prs-volunteer
no I volunteer

104 I: u-na-jito↑lea? ((with high pitch))
you-prs-volunteer
you volunteer

105 B: mhm.

((lines omitted; Braj explains how much time has passed since he volunteered))

110 I: kwenye ile project ya: nanii Children
at that project of um Children
you didn't go to that project um Children's

111 Movement hu-ku-kwenda.
Movement you-neg.pst-go
Movement project

112 B: ipi project.
which project
which project

((lines omitted; Irene and Braj discuss the location of the event))

115 I: i-li-kuwa State House. (.) nanii wasela wa-
it-pst-be state house um streetboys they
it was at the State House um streetboys they

116 wa-ka-tengeneza skafu na caps
-they-cns-make scarf and caps
were making scarves and caps

((lines omitted; they clarify the date of the event))

120 B: I was not around.(0.5) Ni-li-kuwa Nairobi
I was not around I-pst-be Nairobi
I was not around I was in Nairobi

121 na-hudhuria mkutano
I-attend meeting
attending a meeting

122 I: mkutano wa watu gani?
meeting of people kind
what kind of people were at the meeting

123 B: wa Lions. (.) convention
of Lions convention
people meeting at the Lions convention

124 I: a ah okey kumbe nyie ni lions.
oh okay wow you.pl are lions
oh okay you all are Lions, huh

125 B: eeh.
yes
yes

126 I: nije ku-omba nini msaada kwenu
I-come-sbj to-beg what help from-you.pl
if I should come to ask for your help

127 ni-ta-pewa.
I-fut-give-psv
would I get it

128 B: msaada wa,
help of
what kind of help

129 I: kama mtoto na-m-somesha shule.
like child I-her-help-study school
for example I am sending a child to school

130 B: (0.3) ah okay. (.) you need uh school fees.

131 I: mm.

132 B: bei gani.
price type
how much

133 I: (1.0)↑si a-na-soma tu.↑ ni mtoto yaani (.)
neg she-prs-study only is child that is
she's just studying right she's a child, I mean

134 ni-li-lete-wa housegirl. U-na-elewa?
I-pst-brought-psv housegirl you-prs-understand
I was brought a housegirl do you follow

```
135 B: eeh.
       yes
       yes

136 I: housegirl mwenyewe a-li-kuwa  ni mdogo sana
       housegirl herself  she-pst-be is young very
       the house girl she herself was very young so I

137    sasa mimi ni-ka-mw-ambia  si-wezi     ku-mu-ajiri,
       now  I    I-cns-her-tell  I.neg.-able to-her-hire
       had to tell her that I couldn't hire her
```

Irene asks Braj about his work with UNICEF in an effort to establish topical talk through a set of questions. Again, Braj does not use the opportunity to offer more personal or intimate talk, such as a story about his experiences with volunteering, or a clarification that he actually volunteers for the Lions Club; instead, he offers minimal responses with no expansions. Braj's line 103 shares much with his line 06 in Excerpt 8, where he concedes to being Hindu rather than explaining about the Baniani sect of Hinduism. Both responses maintain the pretopical talk by evading elaboration.

In line 110, Irene pursues more pretopical talk by asking him about an event that took place the weekend before that focused on helping needy children in Dar es Salaam, and she asks him if he attended it. This question displays an assumption that Braj regularly goes to events planned to help needy children. It also displays her own practice of going to such events: she reports details about the event such as where it was (the state house) and what was going on there (people were selling scarves and caps). This assumption of shared experience proposes a category for both participants as 'people who attend events meant to help others in need.' It can also be seen as a move on Irene's part to pursue topical talk by finding something in common to talk about. Interestingly, in responding in the negative, Braj switches to English, a means by which the dispreferred act of a disaffiliative response can be handled by bilinguals.

Braj's response in line 120 leads to a clarification regarding his activity with the Lions Club, and this has the effect of categorizing him as a person who helps people in need, especially needy children. Irene's change of state token in line 124 seems to indicate that for her, a shared experience has been achieved that confirms that both participants are involved in charitable organizations and activities that help children. In terms of shared memberships, this confirmation of shared experience effectively moves the pair from insider-outsider in regard to the social category of 'religion' to that of insider-insider in terms of the category 'people who help those in need.' This mutual category membership is proposed by Irene's references to CBAs such as attending meetings about children's rights in Tanzania. The sequencing of the shared categorization followed by a request for help makes it appear that the mutual category membership has established a context in which such a request can be made. In line 126, Irene asks Braj for help to pay for the school fees of an orphaned child by saying, "if I should come to ask for your help, would I get it?"

In line 130, Braj offers his understanding of her request, and he displays understanding of her previous turn with his change-of-state token and reformulation in "ah okay. you need school fees." Braj's turn here shows disjunction with Irene's in several ways, similar to how line 50 displayed disjunction in Excerpt 9. He produces language alternation in relation to Irene's turn in line 129, and he reformulates the request for empathy and philanthropy into a more impersonal money-matter request that rejects the solidarity that Irene has been trying to build. In lines 126–127, Irene has framed her request as for *msaada* [help], which Braj restates as financial help when he says "you need uh school fees." This disjunction also marks a rejection of the shared interculturality that Irene had been establishing through talk. Instead of aligning with the 'people who help those in need' category, Braj produces CBAs associated with a businessperson involved in a barter. In line 132, he asks *Bei gani?* [how much?], a term used commonly in markets when buying produce, or when negotiating a taxi fare, and he does not produce any expressions of empathy or understanding in relation to helping the orphaned child.

In response to Braj's direct request for how much money she needs, Irene responds *si anasoma tu?* [she's just studying], a response delivered with a high pitch throughout, which is a way of speaking in Swahili often taken to mean something like 'don't you already know that?'[2] Through her response in line 133, Irene categorizes Braj as someone who knows how much things cost in Tanzania, as an 'insider' in these matters. In lines 133–134, Irene moves into an account for the financial request, explaining the history of the young girl whose school fees she is paying and for whom she is seeking assistance. She tells a hard-luck story about the girl, and she seeks Braj's shared cultural understanding of such stories through her question in line 134, *unaelewa* [do you follow?]. She also invokes the CBA for herself of 'not hiring a girl who is very young to do housework' (lines 136–137), an activity that indexes the category of 'someone who helps children in need.'

Irene's story continues for 20 lines of talk (omitted here) in which she continues making the case for her request. As we see in Excerpt 12, she adds the CBA of 'helping an orphaned child' (lines 151–154) to her own membership in the category of 'someone who helps children in need.' Irene then moves into the arena of interculturality in lines 157–161, where she explains that she is helping a young orphaned girl in spite of the fact that the girl is 'not of [her] ethnic group' (line 159).

Excerpt 12

```
151 I: u-na-ona. (.) kama sasa hivi  na-hitaji
       you-prs-see   like now  right I-need
       look like right now I need to pay for
```

152 uniform na-hitaji ma-daftari na-hitaji(.)
uniform I-need pl-notebook I-need
a uniform notebooks

153 nini nauli na school fees
what travel and school fees
and what else travel and school fees

154 >ni kama yaani< huyo mtoto ni kama
it.is like that.is this child is like
it's like this child I mean this child is like an

155 orphan sasa hivi
orphan now right
orphan right now

156 B: Aah okay.

157 I: yaa kwa hiyo a-li-kuwa a-na-kaa na
yes for this she-pst-be she-prs-live with
yes, and so she was living with

158 shangazi yake, both parents wa-me-kufa
aunt her both parents they-pfc-die
her aunt (since) both parents had died

159 na wala siyo kabila langu,
and though neg. ethnicity my
and even though she's not of my ethnic group

160 she is from Tabora kwa hiyo yaani
she is from Tabora- for that I-mean
as she is from Tabora, so that's why

161 a-na-kaa na kijiji-ni mama-ngu.
she-prs-live with village-loc mother-my
she is living in the village with my mother

162 B: now let me talk with my board, board of members.

Here, the reference to helping someone who is outside of one's own ethnic group in line 159 intertextually relates to the category memberships that have been built so far in the conversation. Through her CBAs that affiliate her with the categorization 'someone who helps those in need,' she associates the practice of helping those outside one's ethnic group as something charitable people do. This identity work neatly ties back to the interculturality that was based on religious difference that had been so clearly established earlier in the talk. In other words, through her categorization moves involving herself and Braj in lines 100–124 and 159, she implicates Braj as 'someone who helps those in need who are not of one's own kind' and as someone who can offer an act of charity in spite of ethnic and/or cultural difference. In contrast to the previous talk (Excerpts 8–11), Irene uses interculturality in Excerpt 12 as a device to achieve mutual understanding. The use of interculturality here allows her to achieve a shared personal biography with Braj because her own relationship with the orphaned girl of a different ethnic background groups her with people like Braj, that is, people who help those in need, no matter what their background may be. By virtue of asking Braj to help those not of his ethnic group, Irene offers Braj membership in the category of people who help others, not because of a sense of duty based on kinship or ethnic ties, but based purely on humanitarianism and philanthropic, and even religious, ideals.

However, Braj resists this categorization. His response to the request comes in line 162, where he adheres to his pattern of using language alternation to mark a disjunction with the previous talk, and hence, he marks a disjunction with the CBAs and MCD that Irene has been attributing to him. His response is noncommittal, and it does not immediately fit into the CBAs that fit the category of helping those in need, being charitable to orphans, helping destitute children, placing an orphan with one's mother, and so on. Instead, his response orients to the practical aspect of the activity he can offer her, and he reframes the conversation into a more impersonal and business-like exchange, rather than one that shows that the two participants share the same worldview in regard to helping children. In line 162, Braj delicately avoids becoming obligated by Irene's categorization of him as someone who should help the girl she is sending to school by indicating that the board will make the decision, by avoiding expressions of alignment with the category Irene has constructed, and through his language switch, which co-occurs with the disjunction in MCDs. While his offer to talk to the board of members is a sign of possible assistance to Irene, it is neither a rejection nor a personal financial commitment from Braj himself.

Conclusion

This chapter has examined the ways that participants use bilingual conversation to produce and resist membership categorizations. I have argued that among bilinguals, resisting, downgrading, and rejecting categorizations are disaffiliative actions that may be understood as dispreferred acts. In a manner similar to the ways that bilinguals use codeswitching to manage dispreference in refusals and disagreements (Cashman, 2001; Li Wei, 1995; Shin & Milroy, 2000), the data in this chapter have shown that codeswitching appears to be a resource available to bilinguals for managing the dispreferred action of challenging a membership categorization that has been proposed by others. Throughout the data, language alternation is used as a resource by both Braj and Irene to disaffiliate with proposed memberships and to manage other dispreferred actions, such as providing disaffiliative answers to questions structured for positive responses, initiating other-repairs, and responding in noncommittal ways to requests for assistance.

The data also reveal how interculturality can be both an obstacle and a resource for participants in their efforts to develop topical talk. In the first set of excerpts (8–10), intercultural difference based on religious categories was an obstacle because it created 'outsider' status for both participants and made topical talk difficult to achieve, given the lack of shared experience with religious practices. However, interculturality became a resource when Irene proposed the MCD of 'those who help others in need,' using the CBA of 'helping others not of one's own ethnicity,' which allowed her to pursue topical talk and make a request of Braj that involved financial assistance for a young girl she was taking care of. In spite of Irene's efforts to bridge the intercultural boundaries, however, Braj skillfully downgraded, resisted, and even rejected these categorizations through a variety of methods, including language alternation. Braj's responses to Irene's proposed categorizations show how language alternation was a highly effective means for resisting categorizations and redirecting potentially 'unwelcome' topical talk while skillfully managing preference organization at the same time.

While past studies of Swahili-English alternation in East Africa have argued that switches to English systematically index social distancing (e.g., Myers-Scotton, 1993), the data in this chapter do not support this claim. In fact, the data show that language switches for Irene and Braj are bidirectional. As we saw in Excerpts 8–10, Braj used language alternation to disaffiliate with Irene in both directions, that is, moving from Swahili to English and from English to Swahili. In Excerpts 11–12, Braj used English in response to Irene's Swahili-medium talk. Though it might be tempting to interpret Braj's use of English here as indexical of a 'business-like exchange,' through use of the 'they code' (Gumperz, 1982), this conclusion cannot be draw because Irene's turns in Excerpts 11–12 were all in Swahili. Instead, Braj's use of English can be seen as a marker of disaffiliation and dispreference. Of course, additional data of conversations between Braj and Irene containing similar requests carried out in English would be needed to determine whether rejections were more or less likely to be done through language alternation. Finally, it should be noted that these data cannot predict how other Tanzanian bilinguals use language alternation to affiliate or disaffiliate with one another's membership categorizations. Further comparative work on additional speakers in Dar es Salaam and among other bilingual populations is needed to illuminate our understanding of how they use their 'extra' conversational structure of language alternation to propose, accept, and contest identities-in-practice.

Notes

1 The history of political, economic, and social tension between the Indian population and the Black Tanzanian population may be affecting the conversational dynamics,

but such information is not normally considered relevant in analyses of membership categorizations. Interviews that I carried out with Irene and other Black Tanzanians show a common belief that Indian Tanzanians will not freely share information about themselves. From another view, however, Braj's reluctance to elaborate can be understood as the result of his minority culture being repeatedly poorly understood by many Black Tanzanians over time, leading him to be less-than-enthusiastic about clarifying it, especially when it involves the uncomfortable issue of explaining polytheistic beliefs in a society where monotheism is highly valued by the majority. In this data, the interview-style interaction may very well be due also to age and status differences because Braj is a freelance journalist in his 20s, while Irene is a senior editor in her 40s.

2 This way of speaking is known by many Tanzanians, and this interpretation was confirmed by Braj and Irene themselves as well as a group of scholars who participated in a data session at the University of Dar es Salaam.

References

Antaki, C., & Widdicombe, S. (1998). Identity as an achievement and as a tool. In C. Antaki & S. Widdicombe (Eds.), *Identities in talk* (pp. 1–14). London: Sage.

Auer, P. (1984). *Bilingual conversation.* Amsterdam: Benjamins.

Auer, P. (1998). Bilingual conversation revisited. In P. Auer (Ed.), *Codeswitching in conversation: Language, interaction, and identity* (pp. 1–24). New York: Routledge.

Auer, P. (1999). From codeswitching via language mixing to fused lects: Toward a dynamic typology of bilingual speech. *The International Journal of Bilingualism, 3*, 309–332.

Cashman, H. (2001). *Doing being bilingual: Language maintenance, language shift, and conversational codeswitching in Southwest Detroit.* Unpublished doctoral dissertation.

Cashman, H. (2005). Identities at play: Language preference and group membership in bilingual talk in interaction. *Journal of Pragmatics, 37*, 301–315.

Day, D. (1994). Tang's dilemma and other problems: Ethnification processes at some multicultural workplaces. *Pragmatics, 4*, 315–336.

Day, D. (1998). Being ascribed, and resisting, membership of an ethnic group. In C. Antaki & S. Widdicombe (Eds.), *Identities in talk* (pp. 151–170). London: Sage.

Egbert, M. (2004). Other-initiated repair and membership categorization—some conversational events that trigger linguistic and regional membership categorization. *Journal of Pragmatics, 36,* 1467–1498.

Gafaranga, J. (2000). Medium repair vs. other-language repair: Telling the medium of a bilingual conversation. *International Journal of Bilingualism, 4,* 327–350.

Gafaranga, J. (2001). Linguistic identities in talk-in-interaction: Order in bilingual conversation. *Journal of Pragmatics, 33,* 1901–1925.

Gafaranga, J. (2005). Demythologising language alternation studies: Conversational structure vs. social structure in bilingual interaction. *Journal of Pragmatics, 37,* 281–300.

Gumperz, J. (1982). *Discourse strategies.* Cambridge, UK: Cambridge University Press.

Li Wei (1994). *Three generations, two languages, one family: Language change and language shift in a Chinese community in Britain.* Clevedon, UK: Multilingual Matters.

Li Wei (1995). Code-switching, preference marking and politeness in bilingual cross-generational talk: Examples from a Chinese community in Britain. *Journal of Multilingual and Multicultural Development, 16,* 197–214.

Maynard, D., & Zimmerman, D. (1984). Topical talk, ritual and the social organization of relationships. *Social Psychological Quarterly, 47,* 301–316.

Mori, J. (2003). The construction of interculturality: A study of initial encounters between Japanese and American students. *Research on Language and Social Interaction, 36,* 143–184.

Myers-Scotton, C. (1993). *Social motivations for codeswitching: Evidence from Africa.* Oxford, UK: Oxford University Press.

Nishizaka, A. (1995). The interactive constitution of interculturality: How to be a Japanese with words. *Human Studies, 18,* 301–326.

Nishizaka, A. (1999). Doing interpreting within interaction: The interactive accomplishment of a "Henna Gaijin" or "Strange Foreigner." *Human Studies, 22,* 235–251.

Pomerantz, A. (1984). Agreeing and disagreeing with assessments: Some features of preferred/dispreferred turn shapes. In D. Atkinson & J. Heritage (Eds.), *Structures of social action: Studies in conversation analysis* (pp. 79–84). Cambridge, UK: Cambridge University Press.

Sacks, H. (1966). The search for help: No one to turn to. Doctoral dissertation, University of California, Berkeley, CA.

Sacks, H. (1979). Hotrodder: A revolutionary new category. In G. Psathas (Ed.), *Everyday language: Studies in ethnomethodology* (pp. 7–14). New York: Irvington.

Sacks, H. (1987). On the preferences for agreement and contiguity in sequences in conversation. In G. Button & J. Lee (Eds.), *Talk and social organisation* (pp. 54–69). Clevedon, UK: Multilingual Matters.

Sacks, H. (1995). Lecture 6: The MIR membership categorization device. In G. Jefferson (Ed.), *Harvey Sacks lectures on conversation* (Vol. 1), (pp. 40–48). Malden, MA: Blackwell.

Sarangi, S. (1994). Intercultural or not? Beyond celebration of cultural differences in miscommunication analysis. *Pragmatics, 4,* 409–427.

Schegloff, E. (2000). When 'others' initiate repair. *Applied Linguistics, 21,* 205–243.

Shin, S., & Milroy, L. (2000). Conversational codeswitching among Korean-English bilingual children. *The International Journal of Bilingualism, 4,* 351–383.

Torras, M., & Gafaranga, J. (2002). Social identities and language alternation in non-formal institutional bilingual talk: Trilingual service encounters in Barcelona. *Language in Society, 31,* 527–548.

Zimmerman, D. (1998). Discourse identities and social identities. In Antaki & Widdicombe (Eds.), *Identities in talk* (pp. 87–106). London: Sage.

Appendix: Abbreviations in gloss translations

adv	adverbial
cns	consecutive marker
fut	future tense
loc	locative
neg	negative
pl	plural
pfc	perfective
prs	present tense
pst	past tense
psv	passive
rcp	reciprocal
sbj	subjunctive

6 A Practice for Avoiding and Terminating Arguments in Japanese: The Case of University Faculty Meetings

Scott Saft
University of Hawai'i at Hilo

Introduction

In one of the defining papers of the conversation analytic program, Schegloff and Sacks (1973) observed that conversations do not merely end but rather need to be brought to conclusion through the collaborative efforts of the participants themselves. Noting the existence of a turn-taking organization that typically provides a slot for a next speaker to take a turn at talk, they set out to describe the practices used by participants to suspend the relevance of next turns and thereby bring conversations to a close.

Subsequent CA research has examined a variety of social actions, but analysts have continued to study closings not only in everyday conversation (Button, 1987; Clayman, 1989) but also in institutional settings such as physician-patient interactions (Heath, 1986; Robinson, 2001), news interviews (Clayman, 1989; Clayman & Heritage, 2002) and business meetings (Bilmes, 1995). Research on institutional settings has shown that beyond a need to bring interactions to conclusion, participants also often orient to specific features of the institution. Clayman (1989), for example, in his study of news interviews, showed that interviewers orient to a punctuality requirement by unilaterally managing closings. By doing so, interviewers preserve the time constraints and thereby maintain the institutional structure of the news interview.

Talk-in-interaction: Multilingual perspectives, pp. 137–156, Hanh Nguyen & Gabriele Kasper (Eds.), 2009
Honolulu, HI: University of Hawai'i, National Foreign Language Resource Center

In addition, analysts have been interested in the closings of particular interactional activities, especially arguments (Bilmes, 1995; Dersley & Wootton, 2001; Greatbach & Dingwall, 1997; Vuchinich, 1984, 1990). For instance, in his examination of talk in a meeting at the Federal Trade Commission, Bilmes (1995) described how an argument about the pursuit of penalties against a particular company came to a close when one of the participants failed to produce a counterargument. Not only did this result in one participant "losing" the argument, but like the closings of news interviews, it also had ramifications for the institutional setting in which it occurred. With one position prevailing over another, the closing of the argument strongly influenced the next course of action in pursuing and collecting the penalties.

In this chapter, I build on prior research by examining how arguments are avoided and terminated in a particular setting, Japanese university faculty meetings. Understanding arguing as an interactional activity constituted by the exchange of opposition by two or more participants (Greatbach & Dingwall, 1997; Hutchby, 1996), I describe a particular practice prefaced with the linguistic item *maa* ("well"), which was often used in the meetings to move the talk away from the expression of opposition. Basing the analysis on audio-recordings of 16 hours of naturally occurring faculty meeting interaction, I demonstrate that this *maa*-prefacing practice, by enabling participants to bring arguments to conclusion, makes it possible to shift the interaction from the arguing activity, which typically involves only two or three participants, to a different interactional activity: the reporting of information by one participant to the entire set of remaining participants. Although I do not claim that this practice is specific only to faculty meetings—*maa* is prevalent in casual conversation (Fukuda-Carlin, 2002)—the analysis further shows that this move away from arguing is important to the university as an institution in that it allows the participants to accomplish important work related to their jobs as university faculty members. The analysis, in other words, makes a connection between the institutional setting of the university and the termination practice; the practice enables the participants to engage in the interactional work that helps maintain the institutional structure.

Two closing problems

To understand the closing of any interactional activity, beginning with the two closing problems noted by Schegloff and Sacks (1973) is instructive. The first problem, alluded to above, derives from the structure of turn-taking in general because participants must figure out how to suspend the relevance of a next turn so that the conversation may be brought cooperatively to a conclusion. The general solution to this initial problem, as Schegloff and Sacks (1973) pointed out, is the "terminal exchange," most frequently characterized by the use of the term *goodbye*. By exchanging goodbyes, participants display a willingness to allow the conversation to end.

The second problem concerns the placement of the terminal exchange. Given the turn-by-turn structure of interaction, an abruptly placed farewell on the part of one of the participants can impinge on other participants' desire to use some subsequent turn to add further talk. How then can participants create a situation where the terminal exchange will be appropriate? The solution to this problem, according to Schegloff and Sacks (1973), is the construction of a "pre-closing" exchange through the use of terms such as *okay*, *well*, and *alright*. The fragment in Excerpt 1 provides an illustration of a preclosing and a terminal exchange.

Excerpt 1 (Schegloff and Sacks, 1973, p.307)

```
Dorrinne: Uh-you know, it's just like bringin the-
          blood up
Theresa:  Yeah well, things uh always work out for
          the [best
Dorrinne:     [Oh certainly alright [Tess
Theresa:                            [Uh-huh, okay
Dorrinne: G'bye
Theresa:  Goodnight
```

After her phrase of agreement, "oh certainly," in line 05, Dorrinne offers a possible preclosing with the phrase "alright Tess." In the next turn in line 06, Theresa, rather than take up a new topic or offer talk that would require a fuller response from Dorrinne, returns the preclosing with the phrase "Uh-huh, okay." Both participants have thus "passed" on their opportunities to extend the conversation, hence warranting the production of the terminal exchange in lines 07 and 08.

Terminating arguments and two additional problems

Similarly to conversations, arguments must be brought to conclusion. To be sure, people can have running feuds that last for days, months, and even years, but argument episodes, like the interactions in which they occur, must end at some point. However, an argument is different from other interactional activities (such as requests and invitations) in that it is constituted by a specific type of action: an opposition. This difference raises at least two additional closing problems that are specific to an opposition-relevant activity such as an argument. The initial problem directly follows from Schegloff and Sacks's first concern; namely, participants must find a way to discontinue the relevance of further talk. In the case of an argument, the situation is slightly more complex in that participants must figure out how not just to suspend the relevance of a next turn but more specifically, in the words of Vuchinich (1990, p. 121), to bring the argument to "a point where one speaker's oppositional turn will not elicit an oppositional turn from the other."

One seemingly simple way to resolve this problem is for a next speaker to refrain from pursuing the point of opposition. Excerpt 2 provides an example from the Japanese faculty meeting data. It begins as Sasaki is in the middle of putting forth a suggestion.[1]

Excerpt 2, 1–22–98

```
01 Sasaki: soo  yuu  fuu na jooken      o tsukechaeba
           that say type LK requirement O if add
02         (.) sono nandaka kenkyuu  o yaru koto  mo
               that somehow research O do   thing also
03         dekiru to omoimasu.
           can do QT think
           "if you add that kind of requirement then
           it will somehow become possible to do the
           research"

04 Ogawa:  iya dekinai  to yuu jikanwarijoo dekinai
           no  can't do QT say schedule     can't do
05         koto  ni natteru  kara.
           thing is becoming because
           "no we can't do it that way, according
           to the schedule"

06         (.)

07 Ogawa:  dakara son- sonna koto  yuu to yokei
           thus   that kind  thing say if extra
           yayakoshiku naru,  soo ja nakute sotsuken wa:
           confusing   become that  not     thesis   TM
           (.) kyooin  ga: yarasenai tte ieba   sore de
               teacher S   have do   QT  if say that
           oshimai desu kara    ne.
           end      COP because FP
          "so if you start saying that kind of a thing it
           just gets more confusing, instead of that, as
           for the thesis, if the teacher says the
           student can't do it, then that is the end
           of it"

11        (1.0)

12         de  hoka ni wa hookoku jikoo arimasu ka.
           and besides TM report  item  have    Q
           "are there any other matters to report?"
```

After Sasaki finishes his suggestion in line 03, Ogawa enters in lines 04–05 to express opposition. Sasaki, however, does not provide a verbal response, even though he could have done so at certain points in the interaction. The micropause in line 06 and the longer pause in line 11 could have provided Sasaki with ample space for taking a turn and making a rebuttal. In terms of opposition, then, Sasaki's lack of response does not lead to any pursuit of opposition. Sasaki's silence indicates that he is passing on any chance of convincing Ogawa and the other participants of the validity of the suggestions he made in lines 01–03. Ogawa, who also serves as the chair of the meeting and chair of the department, uses the lack of response to move away from this exchange with Sasaki and to solicit matters from the other participants. Based on this excerpt, a simple method for avoiding as well as terminating arguments would seem to be to refrain from responding to statements of opposition.

However, a nonresponse to a statement of opposition may have undesirable consequences. In Bilmes's (1995) analysis of a Federal Trade Commission meeting mentioned above, a participant's failure to respond to a statement of opposition with a counterargument led her to "lose" the argument. Hence, for a participant not willing to concede a point, a lack of response may not be a viable option or may be only a last resort if winning the argument proves impossible. The problem, then, is how participants can continue stating their oppositions and still bring an argument to conclusion. How, in other words, can they exit or avoid arguments without conceding their points?

To further understand this second problem, we may invoke Bilmes's concept of priority response (1993, 1995) and note that a statement of opposition is a first priority response. Developed from earlier ideas of Sacks (1992), Bilmes (1993) defined a priority response as follows: "if X is the first priority response, then any response other than X (including no response) implicates (when it does not explicitly assert) that X is not available or in effect, unless there is reason to suppose that it has been withheld" (p. 391). Hence, unless a participant wants to imply that he or she does not have a rebuttal available, the first priority is to respond to a statement of opposition by producing a rebuttal or refutation or at least a restatement of his or her position. This would help explain why Sasaki's lack of response in Excerpt 2 resulted in Ogawa's inference that the appropriate next move was to move the interaction in another direction. Based on the recognition of the pursuit of opposition as a first-priority response, we can combine the two problems and formulate our closing problem as follows: How do participants cease to utter oppositions and thereby bring an argument to a close without implying that they lack the ability to provide the first-priority response, that is, another opposition-relevant utterance?

One possible strategy for solving both "argument problems" is for a participant to utter a rebuttal and then declare withdrawal from the argument. An example of this, which comes from Vuchinich (1990), is shown in Excerpt 3.

The exchange represented in this fragment occurs after the participants have already been arguing for several minutes.

Excerpt 3 (Vuchinich, 1990: 132)

```
Husband: Now that ain't really ah no- no trouble
         to put up a ( )
Wife:    That's a lot of trouble to me. I ain't
         arguin
```

The wife in line 03 first contradicts the husband's previous utterance, thus indicating that she has a response available by directly refuting his opinion. Then, when she declares "I ain't arguin'," she announces her withdrawal from the argument. The husband does try in the talk that follows (not shown in the transcript) to pursue the argument, but in response to these pursuits, the wife does not reply except for once when she repeats her refusal to argue. She is able to refuse to argue without implying that no response is available because she had earlier canceled such implications by sequencing her response in the way that she did. She is therefore able to resolve the two closings problems noted above. The moves made by the wife in this excerpt to deal with these two problems are very different from the conversational closings originally described by Sacks and Schegloff (1973). There is no preclosing, nor is there a terminal exchange. Instead, the wife accomplishes termination with a phrase that by itself declares her withdrawal. This move is relevant to the present study because it contains both similarities to and differences from the moves made by the participants in the Japanese faculty meetings.

Arguments in the Japanese faculty meetings

The faculty meetings examined here occurred at a 4-year private Japanese university located in the northern part of Japan. The data were collected over a period of 14 months, while I served as a full-time faculty member at the university. The meetings were departmental, involving 11 full-time faculty members belonging to the International Department, a pseudonym for the department to which I belonged. The meetings typically centered on reports from the participants who brought with them various pieces of information to disseminate to the other faculty members. When the participants began making their reports, the interaction was organized in a "reporting framework," with one participant reporting information to the other nonreporting participants. However, as the participants made their reports, it was not uncommon for nonreporting participants to interject talk into the middle of others' reports to make corrections, elaborate on the information being given, ask clarification questions, and express opposition, among other purposes. Occasionally, these interjections resulted in the exchange of opposition among the participants, which meant a shift in the organization away from a reporting framework to a framework where two or more of the participants directly exchanged talk with another. Excerpt 4 provides an example. It begins as Tanaka is in the process of outlining the procedures for judging prospective students who will be coming to the university for interviews.

Excerpt 4, 1–22–98

```
01 Tanaka: shinsa o suru wareware kyoogi  suru naka de
           judge  O do   we       discuss do   within
02         ee su- kono sanjutten da  keredo mo
           SF     this 30 points COP but
03         sanjuugoten ni chikai are  da  toka        kedo
           35 points      near   that COP and the like but
04         choosei  shi[masu.
           regulate do
           "in the process of judging the students, um, we
           might find that although we gave them 30
           points,  the students are closer to 35, so we
           can adjust  their scores"

05 Ogawa:              [soo  yuu no  wa dame na  n  [desu.
                        that say NOM TM bad  NOM NOM COP
                        "we can't do that"

06 Tanaka:                                          [so-
                                                     so
07         iya iya un- sore wa so- sore wa kyooshitsu
           no  no      that TM that     TM classroom
08         kaigi ni suru n   da  kara (.) daiji
           meeting  do   NOM COP because  important
09         nan da (.) datte sonoba tensuu tsukeru wake
           NOM COP    that  place  points mark    reason
10         desu.
           COP
           "so no, no, about that, as for that, we can do
           it during the classroom meeting, it is
           important, because we will be grading them
           right there at the interview"

11 Ogawa:  aa tensuu=
           oh points
           "oh the grading"

12 Tanaka: =ee=
            yes
            "yes"

13 Ogawa:  =tsuke- iya tsukerarenai n   da  yo tensuu
            do     no  can't mark   NOM COP FP score
```

```
14          wa moo     uchidasarete dete   kuru n   desu
            TM already come out      go out come NOM COP
15          kara    hantei   kaigi   no toki
            because decision meeting LK time
            "grad- no we won't be able to grade them
            there, the grades will be decided and merely
            handed to us, ((what you are referring to are))
            the procedures for the judgement meeting"
```

As Tanaka is in the middle of his report in lines 01–04, Ogawa interjects in line 05 the phrase *soo yuu no wa dame nan desu* ("we can't do that") to oppose Tanaka's proposal that they adjust the scores of the candidates. After a brief false start in lines 06–07, Tanaka responds by supporting his original point; they will be able to change the scores during the *kyooshitsu kaigi* ("classroom meeting"). In line 11, Ogawa appears for a moment to concede the point, but before this can be confirmed, we see that he further pursues the opposition by expressing another opposition in lines 13–15.

As this excerpt indicates, an argument sequence prompts the reporting participant to move away from the action of reporting and to the action of arguing with one particular coparticipant. Thus, in addition to the two termination problems for arguments noted above, one other related issue for the participants in this particular setting is how to bring argument sequences to an end so that they can move on with their reports.

Avoiding and terminating arguments in the Japanese faculty meetings

Just as the wife in Excerpt 3 used the short phrase "I ain't arguin'" to attempt to terminate the argument, participants in the Japanese faculty meetings commonly attempted to terminate or avoid arguments with one phrase.[2] Excerpt 5 offers an example. It comes at a point when Tanaka is reporting that the university has decided to allow a student who had dropped out earlier in the semester to return to school in the same semester and attempt to gain credit for all of her classes.

Excerpt 5, 5–15–98

```
01 Tanaka:  mada  juubun jikan aru  to (.) yuu koto
            still enough time  have QT      say thing
02          na no   de  kore kara ganbatte yareba
            because COP this from try hard if do
03          nantoka naru   n   ja nai ka na: to=
            somehow become NOM NEG    Q  FP  QT
            "it's that there is still enough time ((for her
            to get credit)) and so if she tries hard, I
            think it will somehow work out"
```

04 Kida: =demo soo kantan ni yurushite yaru to yuu
but that easily forgive do QT say
05 no wa yoku nai tsumari nani yatte mo ii
NOM TM good not basically what do even good
06 to yuu koto ni naru kara.
QT say thing become because
"but it's not good to let them come back so easily basically it means that they can do anything they want"

07 Tanaka: kimochi wa wakaru kedo mo konkai
feeling TM understand but this time
08 wa ne chanto X san to atte hanashi o kiite
TM FP closely X AT meet talk O listen
09 daijoobu da to handan shita [(wake)
okay COP QT judge did reason
"I understand your feelings but on this occasion we met with Ms. X, talked closely with her and then made the judgment"

10 Kida: [ikura gakusei to
how much students
11 hanashite mo wakaranai yo (.) tekitoo na
talk even not know P whatever LK
12 iiwake o yuu kara. kore kara dandan
excuse O say because this from gradually
13 yamasu yoo ni naru (.) ka mo wakaranai
leave become maybe not know
"however much you talk to a student you never know, they say whatever as an excuse, from now they are going to start taking breaks more and more, probably"

14 Tanaka: demo X san no jijoo wa futsuu ja nai
but X AT LK circumstance TM typical not
15 shi,(.)kimatta koto da kara ima sara giron shite
and decided thing because now even argue do
16 mo ne: maa: ii n ja nai? am- a- (.) ato
even FP well good NOM not after
17 wa moo itten hookoku arimasu ga konoaida
TM more one report have but before
18 Takano-san kara hookoku ga atta yoo ni kondo
Takano-Mr. from announcement S had as soon
19 XXXkoo ni taisuru shisutemu ga kawatte ...
XXX-school toward system S changed
"but Ms. X's circumstances were not typical, plus, it's already been decided and so it makes no sense to argue now well, it should be okay am- I have one more point I want to report on. As Mr. Takano reported on before our system of dealing with prospective students from XXX-school has changed ..."

As Tanaka expresses his belief through line 03 that the situation will work out for the student if she works hard, Kida enters the interaction in line 04 to state that letting students return so easily is not good, thereby implying that the decision to allow this particular student to come back was too hasty. Tanaka responds in line 07 first with an agreement, *kimochi wa wakaru* ("I understand your feelings"), but then offers further support for the decision; they had met and talked closely with the student before deciding to re-admit her. Kida, however, continues his opposition in lines 10–13 by suggesting that students in general cannot be trusted and that this particular decision will result in more students deciding to take semesters off. Tanaka offers one more rebuttal in lines 14–15, when he claims that this particular student's situation was special, and then he asserts that arguing over this issue makes no sense because it has already been decided. Tanaka's statement that arguing makes no sense in lines 15–16 is not unlike the wife's refusal to argue in Excerpt 3 but with two differences. First, Tanaka does not specifically refuse to argue, and second, Tanaka, rather than allowing a pause that could result in a speaker transition, follows this statement in line 16 with a phrase that seems to accomplish the work of terminating the opposition. He utters the linguistic item *maa* ("well") and the fixed expression *ii n ja nai?* ("it should be okay") before making a move, after two false starts and a micropause, to completely leave the matter.[3] He states in lines 16–17 that he has one more point to report on and proceeds to introduce a new issue. This practice of using *maa* plus *ii n ja nai?* has, in effect, served as a bridge away from the previous issue and toward a new one. This practice is different from the wife's declaration of "I ain't arguin'" in Excerpt 3, but notice at least one similarity. Like the wife, Tanaka is able to offer a further refutation of Kida's contention concerning the student. He has made known explicitly that he has a response available before using the practice, prefaced by *maa*, to move the talk in a different direction.

At the same time, the moves made by Tanaka and the wife in Excerpt 3 have at least one important difference that highlights the efficacy of the *maa*-prefacing practice. As noted previously, after the wife announced her withdrawal from the argument, the husband still had an opportunity to use a next turn to pursue the point of opposition. In contrast, Tanaka in Excerpt 5 never allows Kida or any other participant an opportunity to occupy a next turn. The phrase *maa: ii n ja nai?* in line 16 ends with a rising, question intonation, but note that Tanaka's two false starts, *am-* and *a-*, directly after this phrase, display that he has more to say. A micropause occurs after these false starts, but Tanaka never indicates that he is ready to give up his turn. Instead, he moves quickly not only away from the argument but also to shift the interaction into a different organization. The exchange of opposition, though relatively brief, has involved only two participants, Tanaka and Kida. Yet, in lines 16–18, Tanaka, by announcing that he has one more point to report on, returns the interaction to a reporting framework, through which he will report to the entire set of participants about a change in the way that the school will deal with prospective students from a particular high school. In this sense, the efficacy of the *maa*-prefacing practice extends beyond mere termination of an argument. It has enabled Tanaka to show that he has a rebuttal available and then quickly shift the organization of the interaction.

Excerpt 6 provides another example that highlights the effectiveness of this practice. The excerpt occurs at a point in Ogawa's report after he has nominated one of the participants to serve as the departmental representative for the university's employment committee and as he is describing the limited number of activities that the committee actually engages in.

Excerpt 6, 1–22–98

01 Ogawa: toku ni yaru koto wa i-ichinen ni ikkai,
especially do thing TM in one year one time
02 tada iinkai ni dete, gohan issho ni taberu
only committee take part meal together eat
03 dake desu kara.
only COP because
"there is nothing much to do, in one year, on one occasion, you just take part in the committee and eat a meal together, that is it"

04 Kida: sore ja komaru n da yo [(ne)
that COP problem NOM COP FP FP
"if that's it, then it is a problem, isn't it"

05 Ogawa: [hontoo sore ja
really that COP
06 komaru n da kedo mo: jissai wa hotondo i-
problem NOM COP but actually TM almost
07 imi nai n da mon. kore (.) hontoo ni
meaning not have NOM COP thing this really
08 u-imi no nai iinkai da to omou kedo
meaning LK not have committee COP QT think but
09 na: kore. shuushoku shidoo shitsu mo warui
FP this employment guide room also bad SF
10 n da yo. maa ii ya toriaezu jaa sore de
NOM COP FP SF ok FP for now then that
11 shoonin to yuu koto de yoroshii desu ne, eeto
accept QT say thing ok COP FP SF
12 moo itten arimasu kedo mo kondo netwaaku ga
more point have but this time network S
13 dekiagarimasu no de ....
completed because
"in reality, it is a problem but in actuality, it is almost meaningless this, I think that it is really a meaningless committee and, the employment guidance office is also at fault, well, never mind, for now then, it is okay to consider this an accepted point, right, um, I

    have one more point, soon the network will be
    completed and so..."

Just after Ogawa explains in lines 01–03 that the committee does not do much, Kida enters in line 04 to express his dissatisfaction. To Kida, it is a problem if the committee only gets together and eats a meal. Ogawa in line 05, beginning his turn in overlap, produces first a preface of agreement that it is in fact a problem, but then goes on to claim that the committee really is useless and assign blame to the university guidance office. He then utters *maa* ("well") followed immediately by another set expression, *ii ya* ("never mind"), in line 10 and proceeds to change the direction of the interaction; he suggests that this matter (the appointment of the faculty member to the committee) be accepted, and then he moves on to a completely different issue, the status of the university's new computer network. In this excerpt, saying that an actual argument occurs is difficult. Kida expresses his opposition to Ogawa's description of the committee, and Ogawa responds by criticizing the committee as meaningless. Nonetheless, the *maa*-prefaced utterance being examined here has the same effect as in Excerpt 5 in that it effectively terminates any pursuit of opposition. Instead of concluding an argument, we might call this "avoiding" an argument, but the power of the particular practice being described is essentially the same. In terms of the two exit problems, this *maa*-prefacing practice has allowed Ogawa to display that he has a rebuttal available and then prevent his coparticipant, Kida, from further pursuing the issue.

By shifting the interaction away from opposition, Ogawa ensures that the organization of the interaction in the meeting remains in a reporting framework. In lines 12–13, he informs the rest of the participants about the soon-to-be completed computer network. That he is able to continue on with his report follows from his successful avoidance of any further pursuit of opposition about the previous matter. Thus, as in Excerpt 5, the *maa*-prefacing practice has served as a transition from the activity of argument to the activity of reporting.

One question that arises is how this *maa*-prefacing practice can serve such a purpose. The answer lies at least partly in the item *maa* itself. In the few instances in which *maa* has been treated in the literature, it has often been quickly described as a hedge or speech filler that is void of any significant propositional content (Kamio, 1994; Peng, 1981). Based on its appearance in the data extracts, it is difficult to build a characterization of *maa* that refers to participant orientations. As part of moves used to change topics, *maa*-prefaced items are not directly responded to by participants in subsequent turns. Nonetheless, noting its sequential position between statements of oppositions and changes in topic, we may suggest that the hedge-like quality of *maa* makes it such a resource in the accomplishment of these moves. As a hedge, its use directly after the opposition may allow the participant to make a display of the fact that he or she is about to relent on or move away from the opposition just uttered. In other words, *maa*, as a hedge or a speech filler, can make it visible that the participant, instead of continuing on with opposition, is about to change the course of his or her talk and shift away from the opposition.

At the same time that we note the import of *maa*, we cannot ignore the occurrence of the set expressions that follow it. Both expressions, *ii n ja nai?* ("it should be okay") in Excerpt 5 and *ii ya* ("never mind") in Excerpt 6, while different in meaning, play an important role in allowing the speaker to disengage from the opposition. In Excerpt 5, *ii n ja nai?* displays the attitude toward the preceding interaction that it is not such a big problem—that it is a not an issue worth arguing over. Thus, Tanaka is able to offer his rebuttal and then use this phrase to help distance himself from the point of opposition, thereby making it possible to shift entirely to a different issue. In Excerpt 6, *ii ya* appears to be a comment by Ogawa directed specifically at his own opposition, in a sense downplaying the criticism he just made about the committee being unimportant. After downplaying the potential point of opposition, Ogawa, like Tanaka in Excerpt 5, is then in a position to move the interaction in a very different direction. Hence, despite the different nuances of these two set expressions, they both lead the speaker away from the opposition, and when put together with *maa*, allow a participant to accomplish a noticeable shift in the interaction.

Excerpt 7 provides one further example of *maa*-prefacing that features still another set expression. It begins as Tanaka suggests that the best way to deal with a current problem, which is the decreasing number of students being sent to the university from a local high school, is to have the members of a particular committee come up with a solution.

Excerpt 7, 1–20–99

```
01 Tanaka: iin       no sensei   ga yappari kangaete
           committee LK teachers S  indeed   think
02         moraenakerya ikenai, sore shika kaiketsuhoo ga
           must have            that only  solution    S
03         nai tte yuu jookyou   da  kedo mo
           not QT  say situation COP but
           "the teachers on the committee have to come up
           with a solution, we are in a situation where
           that is the only solution"

04 Ogawa:  tada uchi no gakkoo no warui tokoro ne, nandemo
           but  our  LK school LK bad   place  FP everything
05         sono iinkai    ga iinkai    ga tte yutte sono
           that committee S  committee S  QT  say   that
06         ikkankyouiku      ikkankyoiku       tte yuu shi.
           unified education unified education QT  say and
07         de  kooho     wa kooho      tte  kanji   ni
           and candidate TM candidate  QT   feeling
08         shichau n   desu ne (.) de  renkei     shinaku
           make    NOM COP  FP     and connection not do
```

09 natchau to yokei hen na koto ni natchau no
become if extra strange LK thing become NOM
10 ne: maa (.) komatta mondai da ne. yo:shi sore
FP SF troubling problem COP FP okay that
11 kara eeto hoka hoka wa nanika
from SF in addition in addition TM something
12 arimasen ka. sasaki-san (.) XXX daigaku to
not have Q Sasaki AT XXX university with
13 no kookan ryuugaku ni tsuite hookoku arimasu
LK exchange study about report have
14 yo ne
FP FP
"but one bad thing about our school is that it always relies on committees and more committees and it always talks about unified education, and it is always talking about candidates, if we lose our connection ((with this school)) will become an even worse situation, (.) well it, it is a problem, okay, next, are there any additional, additional issues to be raised Mr. Sasaki, you have a report about the exchange program with XXX University"

15 Sasaki: hai, sore de desu ne ...
yes that COP FP
"yes, about that ..."

Ogawa reacts to Tanaka's suggestion by complaining in lines 04–08 about the university's tendency to rely on committees and worry about appointing candidates for those committees. He is in a fairly strong sense arguing against or at least offering a complaint in relation to Tanaka's suggestion. However, in a manner similar to those in Excerpts 5 and 6, Ogawa utters *maa* in line 10, follows it with a set phrase, this time *komatta mondai* ("it is a problem"), and then shifts away from this issue to solicit in lines 11–14 a report from another participant. Because Tanaka does not reply to Ogawa's complaint, the opposition is not pursued in this excerpt, but such an observation highlights the main point of the analysis. Ogawa's use of the *maa*-prefaced phrase allows him to first display his complaint and then create a bridge to a next activity without offering Tanaka or any of the other participants an opportunity to respond, thus avoiding any pursuit of opposition.

Like the phrases *ii n ja nai?* ("it should be okay") and *ii ya* ("never mind") *komatta mondai* is a fixed expression occurring regularly in Japanese conversation that contributes greatly to the interactional shift being accomplished in the faculty meetings. With the combination of *mondai* ("problem") and *komatta* ("troubling"; literally, "a troubling problem"), this expression in Excerpt 7 displays Ogawa's recognition of a serious problem. In that sense, rather than function as a move away from opposition, inclusion of this fixed expression would seemingly emphasize Ogawa's complaint. Yet, at the same time, we need to note that in conversation analytic terms, Ogawa's usage of *komatta mondai* serves as a formulation, an action in which "a member may treat some part of the conversation as an occasion to describe that conversation, to explain it, to characterise it, or explicate, or translate, or summarise, or furnish the gist of it . . ." (Garfinkel & Sacks, 1970, pp. 350–351). In Excerpt 7, Ogawa's use of this fixed expression seems to do the work of summarizing the issue as a problem. Heritage and Watson (1979, 1980) have suggested that a formulation can make it relevant that another participant occupy a next turn to confirm (or disconfirm) the formulation, but Saft (1997, 2003) has noted that a formulation can indicate a readiness to end a current topic and move on to a next one (see also Drew & Holt, 1995). In Excerpt 7, a micropause in line 10 after the expression *komatta mondai* ("it is a problem") could allow another participant to take a turn. Yet, none of the participants make a move to speak. Moreover, we can also see that Ogawa does in fact make a move to shift the interaction in a different direction as he uses the talk in lines 10–14 to change the topic and allocate a turn to another participant. This phrase would seem, then, to work as indication of topic change in this particular case. Thus, while the expression *komatta mondai* is quite different from both *ii n ja nai* and *ii ya* in terms of meaning, nonetheless, as a formulation, it appears to work as a bridge that helps move the interaction away from Ogawa's complaint and reinvoke a reporting framework.

Further support for referring to this move by Ogawa in line 10 as an interactional bridge is the fact that the expression *komatta mondai* was prefaced by *maa*. As a hedge-like item that heads the phrase *maa komatta mondai*, *maa*, as it does in Excerpts 5 and 6, serves as an indicator that the speaker is about to move to disengage himself from the complaint that was just made. This then allows him to proceed with the summary, *komatta mondai*, and then to shift the interaction.

Note that in each of the excerpts in which the participants used this *maa*-prefacing (Excerpts 5–7), not once did the participants whose utterances were opposed attempt to pursue the point of opposition. Unlike Excerpt 3, in which the husband still tried to argue despite the wife's utterance "I ain't arguin'," the participants in the faculty meetings, by not responding to the *maa*-prefaced utterances, indicated a willingness to accept the subsequent moves to a different issue. Such an outcome suggests that the participants themselves were treating this *maa*-prefaced utterance as an acceptable move away from the expression of opposition. In other words, at least in the faculty meeting data collected for this study, the combined usage of *maa* and set expressions such as *ii n ja nai*, *ii ya*, and *komatta mondai* serves as an effective resource for the termination and/or avoidance of arguments.

Terminating and avoiding arguments and the work of the institution

In Excerpt 7, Ogawa, after first expressing opposition to Tanaka's assertion that the faculty should come up with a solution to the problem, uses a *maa*-prefaced utterance to move the interaction completely away from Tanaka. In lines 12–14, he prompts another participant, Sasaki, to begin a report about an exchange program with a particular university. In doing so, Ogawa has preempted any further statement of opposition about Tanaka's report and made it possible for the participants to attend to another piece of university business. Indeed, to fully appreciate the role played by the *maa*-prefaced termination sequence in the faculty meetings, it must be viewed not just as a device for avoiding or terminating arguments but also as a resource for accomplishing the institutional work of the university.

To make this point, note that the occurrence of arguments does not necessarily prevent the participants from accomplishing their job. In fact, as I have maintained elsewhere, arguments can sometimes allow them to discuss and even decide issues that are important aspects of the university (Saft, 2004). Nonetheless, the onset of arguments tends to prolong meetings and make it difficult for participants to attend to all of the business of the day. If we examine Excerpts 5–7 again, we can see that the *maa*-prefaced utterances for avoiding and terminating arguments facilitate quick and smooth transitions to issues that are important to the institutional structure of the university. In Excerpt 5, Tanaka, after moving away from the argument, initiates a report about the procedures for dealing with prospective students from a high school that used to send but no longer sent many of their graduates to the university. Without students, a university cannot function, which means that any failure to attend to such a matter could adversely affect the very existence of the university.[4] In Excerpt 6, where Ogawa makes a transition to a report about the completion of a new computer network, the connection is perhaps not as dramatic as in Excerpt 5, but the issue is nonetheless important to the jobs of the faculty as well as the institution as a whole. The new network was to enhance communication among the faculty, thereby facilitating their ability to carry out the work of the institution. In Excerpt 7, Ogawa moves away from opposition to prompt Sasaki to make a report about another important aspect of the university, exchange programs. Like prospective students and computer networks, exchange programs are an integral component of a university as a particular type of social institution, one that offers various kinds of services to students, including study-abroad programs. By avoiding any further expression of opposition, the participants were able to focus on this aspect of the university, thereby attending to a piece of business that helps maintain the institutional structure of the university.

Moreover, this practice enabled Ogawa to carry out the institutional role assigned to him. As noted previously, Ogawa served as the chair of the department at the time the recordings were made. Accordingly, his job was to make sure that the faculty members used the meeting to attend to the matters that were important to how the department functioned as a part of the university. Therefore, that Ogawa is able to use the *maa*-prefacing practice in Excerpt 6 to report the completion of the computer network and in Excerpt 7 to allow Sasaki to give his report about the exchange programs contributes greatly to the accomplishment of his institutional role as chair.

Of course, even if the participants had failed to avoid or terminate arguments in Excerpts 5–7 when they did, they might have still been able to attend to all three of these pieces of university business, and Ogawa may have been able to perform his functions as the chair. Nonetheless, the data makes evident that the *maa*-prefacing practice, because it facilitated a prompt shift away from the expression of opposition, ensured that the participants would be able to focus the meeting on a variety of issues that were pertinent to the university as an institution. In short, the practice described here assisted the faculty members in carrying out their roles as employees of the university and maintaining the university's institutional structure.

Conclusion

This chapter began by describing the two closing problems in mundane conversation observed by Schegloff and Sacks (1973). I next noted that the activity of arguing, because it centers on the expression of opposition, can create two problems in terms of termination. On the one hand, participants must arrive at a point in the interaction where they cease exchanging expressions of opposition, and on the other hand, they often need to do so while still displaying that they have rebuttals available. The analysis then focused on one particular setting, faculty meetings at a Japanese university, in which the participants sometimes used a practice that allowed them to handle both of the problems involved in closing arguments. Prefaced by the linguistic item *maa* ("well"), the utterances enabled the participants to put forth rebuttals and then move unilaterally to terminate the expression of opposition. I further suggested that this practice did more than just avoid or terminate arguments in the faculty meetings. It provided the participants with a means for accomplishing the work of the university and thereby helped the faculty members maintain the university's institutional structure. By way of conclusion, I emphasize that although the analysis has shown that the *maa*-prefacing practice is used by the faculty members to engage in university-specific work, I do not claim that the practice is unique to university faculty meetings. Nothing is so specialized about the organization of interaction in the meetings that would lead us to expect to see this practice used only there. Further research on Japanese interaction may show a similar type of practice being used to avoid or terminate arguments in other settings. Nonetheless, the analysis did demonstrate that in this particular setting, *maa*-prefaced utterances served the faculty members as important resources for accomplishing their jobs. They allowed them to shift their attention away from the expression of opposition so that they could attend to a variety of issues that were of importance to the internal workings of the university.

Acknowledgements

An earlier version of this paper was presented at the 2005 International Conference for Ethnomethodology and Conversation Analysis at Bentley College, MA. I especially thank Anne Rawls, David Francis, and Aug Nishizaka for their comments at the time of the presentation.

Notes

1 The symbols appearing in the interlinear gloss of the Japanese transcripts can be found in the Appendix. All names of people and places appearing in the transcripts are pseudonyms.

2 I emphasize that the practice described here is only one of the means used by the faculty members to terminate argument sequences in the meetings. Saft (2001) described another strategy used by participants to deal (or not deal) with the expression of opposition.

3 In terms of structure, the expression *ii n ja nai?* is a negative question, and hence, a more literal translation might be "isn't it okay?" However, as a fixed expression, it does not always clearly function as a question, and hence, the pragmatic force seems to be closer to the statement "it should be okay."

4 In fact, at the time of these recordings, the university was facing an enrollment crisis. The number of students applying to the university had decreased significantly in the previous 2 years.

References

Bilmes, J. (1993). Ethnomethodology, culture, and implicature: Toward an empirical pragmatics. *Pragmatics, 3*, 387–409.

Bilmes, J. (1995). Negotiation and compromise. In A. Firth (Ed.), *The discourse of negotiation: Studies of language in the workplace* (pp. 61–81). Oxford, UK: Pergamon.

Button, G. (1987). Moving out of closings. In G. Button & J. R. Lee (Eds.), *Talk and social organization* (pp. 101–151). Clevedon, UK: Multilingual Matters.

Clayman, S. (1989). The production of punctuality: Social interaction, temporal organization, and social structure. *American Journal of Society, 95*, 659–691.

Clayman, S., & Heritage, J. (2002). *The news interview: Journalists and public figures on the air.* Cambridge, UK: Cambridge University Press.

Dersley, I., & Wootton, A. (2001). In the heat of the sequence: Interactional features preceding walkouts from argumentative talk. *Language in Society, 30*, 611–638.

Drew, P., & Holt, E. (1995). Idiomatic expressions and their role in the organization of topic transition in conversation. In M. Everaert, E. Van der Linden, A. Schenk & R. Schreuder (Eds.), *Idioms: Structural and psychological perspectives* (pp. 117–132). Hillsdale, NJ: Lawrence Erlbaum Associates.

Fukuda-Carlin, A. (2002). Functions of the attitudinal discourse marker *maa* in Japanese conversation. In P. Clancy (Ed.), *Japanese/Korean Linguistics* (Vol. 11). Stanford, CA: CSLI.

Garfinkel, H., & Sacks, H. (1970). On formal structures of practical actions. In J. C. McKinney & E. A. Tiryakian (Eds.), *Theoretical sociology* (pp. 337–366). New York: Appleton-Century-Crofts.

Greatbach, D., & Dingwall, R. (1997). Argumentative talk in divorce mediation sessions. *American Sociological Review, 62*, 151–170.

Heath, C. (1986). *Body movement and speech in medical interaction.* Cambridge, UK: Cambridge University Press.

Heritage, J., & Watson, D. R. (1979). Formulations as conversational objects. In G. Psathas (Ed.), *Everyday language: Ethnomethodological approaches* (pp. 123–162). New York: Irvington Publishers.

Heritage, J., & Watson, D. R. (1980). Aspects of the properties of formulations in natural conversations: Some instances analysed. *Semiotica, 30*, 245–262.

Hutchby, I. (1996). *Confrontation talk: Arguments, asymmetries, and power on talk radio.* Mahwah, NJ: Erlbaum.

Kamio, A. (1994). The theory of territory of information: The case of Japanese. *Journal of Pragmatics, 21*, 67–100.

Peng, F. (1981). *Nihongo no danjosa* [Gender differences in Japanese]. Tokyo: The East-West Sign Language Association.

Robinson, J. (2001). Closing medical encounters: Two physician practices and their implications for the expression of patients' unstated concerns. *Social Science and Medicine, 53*, 639–656.

Sacks, H. (1992). *Lectures on conversation.* Oxford, UK: Blackwell.

Saft, S. (1997, August). *Interaction and the 'local achievement' of identity: A single case analysis of a Japanese mental patient.* Paper presented at the Ethnomethodology and Conversation Analysis: East and West Conference, Waseda University, Tokyo.

Saft, S. (2001). Displays of concession in university faculty meetings: Culture and interaction in Japanese. *Pragmatics, 11*, 223–262.

Saft, S. (2003, September). *From grammar and interaction to grammar, interaction, and identity: An analysis of an episode of talk in a Japanese mental hospital.* Paper presented at the 11th Japan Association of Sociolinguistic Sciences, Sendai, Japan.

Saft, S. (2004). Conflict as an interactional accomplishment in Japanese: Arguments in university faculty meetings. *Language in Society, 33*, 549–584.

Schegloff, E. A., & Sacks, H. (1973). Opening up closings. *Semiotica, 8*, 289–327.

Vuchinich, S. (1987). Starting and stopping spontaneous family conflicts. *Journal of Marriage and the Family, 49*, 591–601.

Vuchinich, S. (1990). Sequencing of termination of family disputes. In A. D. Grimshaw (Ed.), *Conflict talk: Sociolinguistic investigations in conversation* (pp. 118–138). Cambridge, UK: Cambridge University Press.

Appendix: Abbreviations used in the interlinear gloss

(see also Transcript Conventions, p. xiv)

COP	forms of the copula be-verb
FP	sentence-final particle
LK	linking nominal
NOM	nominalizer
QT	quotative marker
SF	speech filler
O	object marker
S	subject marker
TM	topic marker
Q	question marker
AT	address term

7 Third Party Involvement in Japanese Political Television Interviews

Keiko Ikeda
Kansai University

Introduction

This study uses conversation analysis to examine a particular genre of contemporary broadcast journalism in Japan, namely, public affairs interview programs. These shows are similar in many respects to those broadcast regularly in the United States, such as ABC's "This Week," NBC's "Meet the Press," and CBS's "Face the Nation," all of which have become staples of Sunday morning fare. The focus of this study is a particular interactional resource deployed by the Japanese media for political journalism, which constructs what the audience would see as fundamental attributes of this genre (Clayman & Heritage, 2002).

An interest is growing in the important relationship between politics and television in Japan today (Altman, 1996; Gatzen, 2003; Krauss & Pharr, 1996; Watanabe, 2000). As television and the Internet have become central to the contemporary Japanese lifestyle, public affairs broadcasting has become influential with the Japanese electorate.[1] I argue that this can partly, but importantly, be explained by the discursive design of talk shows, which is well crafted for the satisfaction of viewers who seek a dramaturgical performance in politics.

To understand the attributes of this particular genre, we must realize that interviews and talk shows, regardless of the language or cultural setting, are ultimately sites of interaction. Conversation

Talk-in-interaction: Multilingual perspectives, pp. 157–180, Hanh Nguyen & Gabriele Kasper (Eds.), 2009
Honolulu, HI: University of Hawai'i, National Foreign Language Resource Center

analysis (CA) enables us to study in detail the relevant processes of how political affairs talk is organized in media discourse. It can also help us identify practices distinctive to Japanese broadcast journalism.

The chapter begins with a review of relevant CA scholarship on political talk shows in North America and Western Europe, which have become the touchstones for the study of this genre in the Japanese context. It proceeds to discuss two important studies that deal with Japanese current affairs programs in particular (Furo, 1998; Honda, 1999). It then seeks to broaden and enrich our understanding of the Japanese case by focusing on a particular interactional pattern, namely, third-party involvement in the process to complete a question-answer sequence in political news interviews. Japanese public affairs talk shows commonly adopt an interview format and have multiple participants present.[2] This particular feature of Japanese public affairs shows enables participants other than the primary questioner and answerer to be readily involved in the interaction. The study illustrates how third-party involvement is invoked and accepted by the original participants as well as the incoming participant. A social consequence of third-party involvement is that the question-answer sequence that is typical of interviews develops in an unorthodox fashion, but one that is welcomed and encouraged for the ulterior purpose of entertainment.

Background

Public affairs shows

The public affairs show is a familiar genre in broadcast journalism, at least in North American and British settings (Clayman, 1992; Clayman & Heritage, 2002; Heritage, 1985; Heritage & Greatbatch, 1991). The nature of turn-taking and other interactional features of broadcast interviews have been well reported in the literature. Talk in television interviews not only belongs to the participants but also to the audience or “overhearers” (Goffman, 1981). CA has enabled us to appreciate the highly crafted details of broadcast interviews. It can show us how interviewers attempt to maintain objectivity and neutrality (Clayman, 1992; Greatbatch, 1998), how speakers index overhearer-orientation in their interaction (Heritage, 1985), and how interviewees construct or evade answers (Clayman, 2001).

Public affairs shows come in a variety of formats. One type is the panel interview, in which multiple participants come together to face an interviewer (Clayman & Heritage, 2002; Greatbatch, 1992, 1998). Because the selection of interviewees is intended to reflect a variety of interests, ideologies, and views on the topics under discussion, this particular format tends to produce highly conflictive interaction. Various studies (e.g., Clayman & Heritage, 2002; Greatbatch, 1998; Greatbatch & Heritage, 1990) have shown how the interviewer solicits interplay among the interviewees to generate disagreement while maintaining the interview framework. A common technique, for example, is for an interviewer to ask a question of the first interviewee, retrieve the turn after the answer, comment on the answer with an embedded adversarial formulation, and invite the next interviewee to comment. Clayman and Heritage (2002, p. 313) provided an example:

Excerpt 1, (United States), PBS News Hour, 25 July 1985: South Africa Sanctions

```
IR:  Jim Lehrer (interviewer)
IE1: Sheena Duncan (first interviewee)
IE2: John Chettle (second interviewee)

IE1: ... and if: one can: .hh put sufficient
     pressure. .hhh on them to re:ally in-
     int=hh=end. (.) .h uh: to::: pursue: de the
     Government to change, .h and if that pressure
     Is also coming from the West at the same time
     .hh then: <our: Government is faced with: very
     real:: .h real persuasive forces.>
     (0.4)
IR:  You don't think the Government would react
     that [way,] [(Mr. Chettle,)]
IE2:      [tch ] [No:          ] every time the:
     Government has been pressured in a crass way.=
     = For example in the arms embargo. .h They
     promptly set about, (e)=stablishing : ay major
     arms industry, and in fact it's the tenth
     larger ar:ms industry in the world today:.
     ((continues))
```

In lines 09–10, the interviewer (IR) turns to the next interviewee (IE2). "You," addressed to IE2, and the anaphoric expression "that" in "you don't think the Government would react that way, [Mr. Chettle]" effectively sets up the first interviewee (IE1) for an oppositional response. By using a negative declarative in his question, the IR invites IE2's immediate disagreement.

Panel interviews in the United States and Britain are most often used when less distinguished public figures appear and are chosen largely for their entertainment value for viewers. If an interviewee is highly recognized or newsworthy in his or her own right (a president, a prime minister, or a senior cabinet official, for instance), a one-on-one interview hosted by a well-established anchor is more common. In Japan, at least as a trend in the last decade, important figures such as the prime minister or senior cabinet ministers also appear solo as guests; however, there is often more than one interviewer. In such a case, a group of professional commentators joins the main interviewer, who is typically a highly recognized anchor, just as in the United States and Britain. A multiple participant interview format like this simulates a crowd gathered to hear an important person talk and offers ample opportunity for the participants, including the host of the show, to find moments in which to challenge the interviewee and attempt to generate news.[3]

Political TV interviews in Japan

Many existing studies of Japanese political affairs talk shows have evolved out of the discussion of conflict management (Eisenstadt & Ben-Ari, 1990; Lebra, 1984). Furo (1998) and Honda (1999), for instance, discussed interactional sequences that both produce and seek to manage conflict. Honda (1999) examined three different political affairs talk shows[4] for patterns of enactment and treatment of disagreement between the participants. Her study revealed a set of effective ways of managing conflict, such as the insertion of mitigation and mollification markers in opposing statements—a rather common feature of conflict management previously identified in the English-language-based literature. She also documented instances of the moderator or a third party to the argument inserting his or her turns in the interstices of unresolved disagreement, momentarily producing a three-way participation structure.

Furo (1998) compared the program *Sandee Purojekuto* [Sunday Project] with a socially "equivalent" American show, "Meet the Press". Inspired by the observations of Japanese politicians' "interactional frame" (Tannen, 1993), which is supposedly indirect and nonconfrontational, Furo's analysis of turn-taking patterns showed that, whereas in the American data the interviewee frequently interrupted the moderator to make counterarguments, in the Japanese case, the moderator's interactional control was the dominant preference. In Furo's understanding, interruptive moves indicated the agent's intent to control the floor.

These two studies both remarked on the involvement of a third person—either the moderator or another participant—during the course of Japanese interviews. The third party inserted him- or herself in the sequence between two protagonists to ameliorate tension and to steer the argument toward an end. According to their analyses, this was one of the conflict management strategies that supposedly represented Japanese "irenistic," or conflict-avoidance, tendencies (Ong, 1981).

I believe that these observations warrant critical scrutiny. First, we should not assume that U.S. and Japanese political TV interviews are equally valued social practices in the local communities or that the features of news interviews familiar to a North American audience map directly onto the Japanese case. The more prevalent use of a multiple-interviewer format in Japan, which is the object of this study, may indeed itself be an indication of a significantly different social purpose of the activity.[5] Second, while third-party involvement may be useful for conflict management in certain circumstances, it can also have other functions in other contexts. The television programs examined in these studies derive their entertainment value from being conflict-laden and highly combative. In such a context, resolving tension among the participants, as Honda (1999) and

Furo (1998) suggested, need not be a priority. Finally, the search for evidence of conflict avoidance may lead us to overlook certain aspects of the data that point toward other implications. If we begin by analyzing sequences of interview talk without preconceptions as to their pragmatic purposes, that is, through "unmotivated looking" (see Sacks, 1992 on methodology), we may discover a richer set of goals and functions. This study suggests that third-party involvement can also be a resource to *trigger* a conflict and to invoke unexpected outcomes, and it illustrates a case in the context of Japanese broadcast journalism.

Sandee Purojekuto [Sunday Project]

This study examines a total of nine occurrences of third-party involvement patterns from a collection of recordings of the weekly TV Asahi political affairs program, The *Sandee Purojekuto* (Sunday Project). The interviews selected for this study were aired in July, November, and December 2003; April 2004; and February 2005. A total of 25 interviews in this collection specifically used the multiple-interviewer/single-interviewee format. With either 1 or 2 interviews per broadcast, third-party involvement in the completion of a question-answer sequence was found approximately 65% of the time. In all cases, the single interviewee was a well-established, well-known public figure.

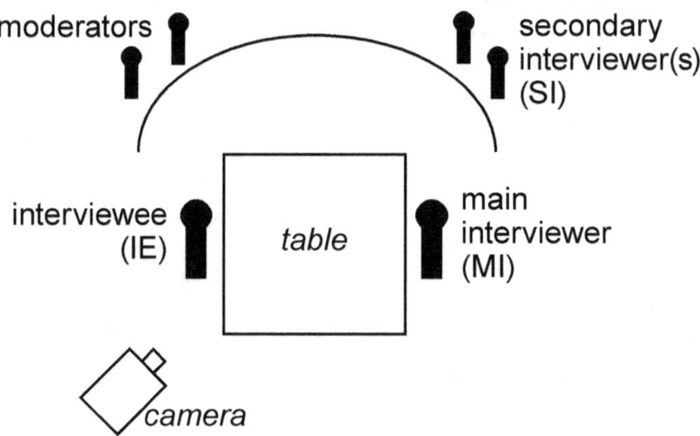

Figure 1. A typical seating arrangement for Sunday Project interviews.

Sunday Project is a program well known to the general Japanese television audience. It is broadcast live, with no editing of language. The host of the show, Sooichiroo Tawara, has interviewed prominent political figures such as former prime ministers, the vice-chief secretary of the Japanese cabinet, the minister of finance, and the chairman of the health and welfare committee of the Lower House of the Diet. The show began in 1993 and has been one of the longest-running political affairs talk shows in Japan. The seating arrangement is shown in Figure 1.

Television is one of the most effective media for "advertising" Japanese politicians. Since 1952, the central government and Japan's public broadcasting system (NHK) have had a close relationship, but in the last two decades, an increasing number of programs on commercial TV networks have begun to deal with political issues, and they have given politicians more opportunities to appear on the air. These shows have had such a strong impact on the electorate that some have described the 1990s as the decade of "television politics" (Altman, 1996, p. 175). In this media-rich society, prominent interviewees' words are never taken lightly; significant remarks may make headlines in Japanese newspapers or reverberate through the government or public service. While the competition for Sunday morning television audience share is extremely intense, political affairs shows do rather well. In 2001, for example, Sunday Project earned on average a 13% audience share in its time slot only in Eastern Japan (Video Research Ltd., 2001). Appearing as a guest on shows such as Sunday Project has become a vital part of politicians' public lives.

Third party involvement

In the multiple-interviewer/single-interviewee format, one interviewer is commonly dominant, while the other interviewers (or, as they are called in Japanese, the *komenteitaa* [commentators]) participate when invited to do so. The seating arrangement clearly indicates who possesses dominant control of the interaction. A prototypical seating arrangement for this type of interview is illustrated further in Figure 2.

Figure 2. A scene from Sunday Project (TV Asahi).

The general course of the interaction is, not surprisingly, a series of question-answer sequences. However, the presence of multiple interviewers makes possible a rich variety of interaction patterns. This study focuses on one of them, in which a third party, often played by the secondary interviewer, becomes involved in a sequence initiated by the main interviewer, addressing the interviewee (IE). An outline of the pattern is shown in Figure 3. To capture the general picture, instead of determining the main or secondary roles of the interviewers, the outline simply indicates a case in which one of the multiple interviewers (i.e., IR2 in turn 4) takes over the turn.

turn 1	IR1	to IE1	projection of question
turn 2	IE	to IR1	refusal to answer/initiation of answer
turn 3	IR1	to IR2	invitation for third-party involvement
turn 4	IR2	to IR1	acceptance and emergence of side-play
turn 5*	IE	to IR1	commentary against the side-play

Note: IE=interviewee; IR1=interviewer 1; IR2=interviewer; 2*=optional

Figure 3. Third-party involvement pattern in question-answer sequence

Third-party involvement has been recognized in interactional sequences outside of political interview contexts. For instance, the pattern was observed by Kang (1998) as a part of a "triadic speech pattern." A triadic exchange occurs when one participant indirectly communicates a message to another (the target) by directly addressing a third party (the mediator). In Kang's data—a meeting among several Korean-American youth group members—this particular exchange pattern was used to carry out face-threatening acts, such as accusing and blaming. The triadic exchange created space for side-participants (Clark & Carlson, 1982) in the interaction to display alignment and/or rebuttal, enabling the group as a whole to negotiate and re-establish their social relationships. Kang presented the data in Excerpt 2:

Excerpt 2 (Kang, 1998: 143)[6]

```
Participants: Ralph, Dave, Jill, Andy, Hank, Mark, Agnes
They are Korean-American teens at a youth meeting.
1  Hank: ((pointing at Mark))
         Don't work with him on anything
2        like tapes or something <@ because like @>,
3        ((gaze at Dave, Ralph, and Jill))
4        You'll give a suggestion and he'll be like,
5        yeah but,
6        and then he'll put his own suggestion down.
7        ((gaze goes to Mark by the end of utterance,
8        then back to others))
9  ALL:  @@@@
10 Jill: Oh. ((sympathetically))
11 Mark: Come on.
```

```
12 Hank: ((pointing to Mark)) He's the most anal
13       person I've ever met in my life.
```

In this example, a triadic exchange was formed among Hank (the speaker), the other participants (including Jill) as the mediating receivers, and Mark (the target). Hank engages in a "side-play," in Goffman's (1981) sense, on the matter with Jill, while Mark listens as an "overhearer" to their exchange. Mark and the others present are not ratified participants (Goffman, 1976, 1981) in this particular interaction. Hank chose Jill as his addressee despite the fact that Mark is the main referent of the talk. Hank's gesture, pointing towards Mark (the target), also indicates that Hank designed his utterance to be overheard by Mark. Kang's interpretation is that this indirect triadic pattern is used to threaten Mark's face.

Kang stressed the importance of a third phase of the interaction, in which the target responds directly to the first speaker, completing the pattern. Not all studies show this, however. An insightful study of the triadic speech pattern in an African-American community by Morgan (1996), for example, demonstrated how the social purposes of the interaction may be accomplished without this closure. Morgan noted that the pattern is actually known as the act of "signifying" in the community, and she identified two major enactments of the pattern. The first, termed "pointed indirectness," occurs when a speaker ostensibly says something to a mock receiver, intending the message to be heard by someone else. The second, called "baited indirectness," occurs when a speaker attributes something (often a negative feature) to an unspecified target, rather than to a specific mock receiver. The targeted hearer may or may not provide any direct response, but if he or she does so, this confirms the baited indirectness (Morgan, 1996).[7] The act of signifying (Mitchell-Kernan, 1972; Morgan, 1996) is easily recognized because of the speaker's use of special lexical and grammatical features available to the members of the community. Because the third person's direct response only *confirms* the pattern completion, it is not always required. In both cases, however, we can see relevant displays of the pattern by the participants. The third-party involvement patterns examined in this study also demonstrate the availability of linguistic resources in Japanese for making the patterns salient, in a manner similar to the participants' orientation to signifying.

Analysis

Seven of the nine instances observed in the data share a similar placement of third-party involvement in the ongoing interaction. In these seven cases, the third party was played by the secondary interviewer, engaging in talk with the MI, immediately after the interviewee's turn. In some of these sequences, the interviewee explicitly responded to the MI-SI side-play (Goffman, 1981) as analyzed by Kang (1998); in the others, the interviewee did not react. These latter cases lacked uptake (e.g., self-defense or rebuttal) by the target in the third position, and are therefore reminiscent of Morgan's (1996) signifying act. Two other cases, which I discuss in a separate section, exhibited a different placement of the pattern: the third-party involvement was initiated in the turn where the interviewee had the interactional obligation to speak.

Counterargument through third-party involvement

The first excerpt illustrates the attested triadic speech pattern. The interviewee (IE), Katsutoshi Kaneda, was at the time a Lower-House representative and the Liberal Democratic Party chair of the Health and Welfare committee. Prior to the exchange in Excerpt 3, Kaneda was asked to comment on his view of a new health care policy, which the Koizumi cabinet had recently proposed in 2003. Kaneda indicated that he opposed the government's decision to increase the copayment for senior citizens.

Excerpt 3, health care 1

```
IE: Kaneda (interviewee)
MI: Sooichiroo Tawara (main interviewer)
SI: Hiroshi Hoshi (second interviewer)

01 IE: e (.) soko  de desu      [ne
       SF    there at CP-polite IP
       "uh, at that point"

02→MI:                          [Hoshi san
                                 Hoshi  Mr.
                                 "Mr. Hoshi"

03 SI: hai
       yes
       "yes"

04→MI: dotchi ga tadashii no?
       which  SB correct  N
       "which one is correct?"
```

In line 01, the IE begins to elaborate the argument. He prefaces the turn with *e* [uh], displaying that he is still engaged in the talk. He then says *soko de desu ne*[8] [at that point], prefacing his continuation, but before he gets to the end of a transition-relevant place (TRP; Sacks, Schegloff, & Jefferson, 1974),[9] the MI, Tawara, inserts his turn (line 02) in a short overlap. In line 02, the MI summons the SI (Hoshi).[10] The SI answers the summons, showing his availability for further interaction (Schegloff, 1968). In line 04, the MI poses a question to the SI, asking which of the views (for or against the policy change) is the "correct" one. By doing the summons-answer sequence prior to the question, the MI elicits a response from the SI, the ratified addressee (Goffman, 1981), to the first pair part in particular. The IE is not a ratified participant for the moment, and this question-answer sequence results in a total of 29 lines of exchange between the MI and the SI. In their exchanges, as shown in Excerpt 4, they accuse the IE of opposing the new policy to satisfy his favored interest group (doctors and medical enterprises). Excerpt 4 starts with line 22:

Excerpt 4, health care 2[11]

```
22 MI: (a) kekkyok[u K]aneda san tachi no:: (.)Niwa=
       oh  after all Kaneda  Mr. etc.  LK      Niwa
23 SI:            [hai ]
                   yes
                   "yes"
24 MI: =san tachi no itteru::, sono sanwari hutan  o:,=
       Mr. etc.  LK saying    that 30%     co-pay O
       "after all, Mr. Kaneda's group is the same as
       Mr. Niwa and others are saying that 30%
       co-pay should be"

25 SI: =ee
        yes
       "yes"

26 MI: (.5) ma (.) bappon      kaikaku shite kara (.)yare
            SF     fundamental reform  doing after   do
27     to yuu no wa .hh kekkyoku  bappon kaikaku
       QT say N  TP .hh after all basic  reform
28     sonomono no SAKIokuri  da to=
       itself   LK postponing CP QT
       "well, doing it after the basic political reform
       would after all mean .hh the same thing as
       postponing the reform, is that what you're
       saying"

29 SI: =hh hai jissai mondai wa
        hh yes real   concern  TP
30     desu n[e: sono sanwari: hutan  ga doonyuusareru TO
       CP    IP  that 30%      co-pay SB introduce    when
       "hh yes the reality is, once the 30% co-pay takes
       place,"

31 MI:       [n
              uh huh
             "uh huh"

32 SI: moo     oyakunin  no hoo  wa soko  de moo
       already officials LK side TP there at already
33     a(h)njyuu-shichaimashite desu      [ne
       settle-happen            CP         IP
       "the government bureaucrats would be satisfied
       and stay unimproved."
```

```
34 MI:                                                [hmm
                                                       hmm
                                                       "hmm"
```

Despite the extensive criticism the IE endures from both interviewers, he does not respond immediately to the accusation. In mundane conversation, an immediate response by Kaneda would have been a first-priority response (Bilmes, 1981), that is, the preferred action in this context. However, the sequence is confined entirely to the two interviewers until line 42 in Excerpt 5, where Kaneda finally gets in to defend himself.

Excerpt 5, health care 3[12]

```
42 IE: (iya)sore wa nai desu [ne(.) sore wa ]
        no  that TP NG  CP     IP    that TP
       "no, that would not be true, that"

43 MI:                       [isha    ya (.5)]
                              doctors and
44     isha ya
       doctors and
45     kusuri[ya sorera o mamoru  tame    ni
       pharmacy  them   O protect purpose GL
       "doctors and doctors and pharmacy, in order to
       protect these"

46 IE:       [(*) hutan  o kichinto (**)
                  co-pay O properly
       "doing the right thing about co-pay"

47 MI: chotto    matte=
       a little  wait
       "just a minute"

48 IE: =hai °h[ai°
       yes yes
       "okay, okay."

49 MI:        [anata ga iru   kara
               you   SB exist because
50     itteru °no mae   de°
       saying  N  front at
       "I am saying this because you are here in
       front of us."

51( ): e:: yaroo to shiteru n da to. (.)
       SF  do    Q  doing   N CP QT
52     hai  hanron.
       okay counterargument
       "((They)) intend to do it((dissolving the policy)),
       you say. Okay, counter argument."
```

The IE inserts a rebuttal preface (line 42) but is thwarted by the MI. Between lines 43 and 46, we see the IE and MI compete for the next turn. In line 43, the MI wins the turn over the IE by overlapping and recycling the initial phrase *isha ya* [doctor and]. The IE also overlaps in line 45 with the MI's turn (line 44) and speaks through the overlap, saying *hutan o kichin to* [doing the right thing about copay]. The MI halts the IE at this point by explicitly stopping his speech with *chotto matte* [wait a minute] (line 46). The MI then adds *anata ga iru kara itteru no mae de* [I am saying this because you are here in front of us] (line 48).[13] Finally, he explicitly yields the floor to the IE (line 50) by inviting a *hanron* [counterargument]. This segment clearly illustrates that the purpose of the MI-SI interaction (prior to line 42) was to articulate opposition to the IE's argument. The IE's long abstention during the two interviewers' talk, all the while paying very close attention to it, was recognized and respected by all of the participants.

In yet another excerpt, the IE is Heizoo Takenaka.[14] The MI has just asked him about the government's desire to control local banks when they receive financial aid from the national budget:

Excerpt 6, finance 1

```
IE: Takenaka (interviewee)
MI: Tawara (main interviewer)
SI: Takarabe (second interviewer)

((IE is ending his remark))

01 IE: zeikin o tsukau koto wa dekimasen
       tax    O use    N    TP can-Neg
02     ne! (.4) sore wa: >yappari<  shikkari yaranai
       IP       that TP   after all properly do-Neg
03     to: (.) masani moraru hazaado ni narimasu
       if       truly  moral  hazard  GL  become
04     .hh o- soo yu[u: kiju ° n °
           O  so  say   standard
       "we cannot use tax for that. For this, as you see,
       we must do it right. Otherwise it'll be indeed a
       moral hazard. The criteria for that,"

05→MI:               [ano: Takenaka san wa
                      SF  Takenaka  Mr. TP
06     koo  yuu huu ni ossharu to omou. (1.0)
       this say like   say-HON QT think-PLAIN
07→    Takarabe san doo=dakedo <yappari>  ne,(.)
       Takarabe Mr. how but     after all IP
08     chigin      ga sorezore shutaitekini tte yappari
       local banks SB each     autonomously QT  after all
```

```
09      kinyuuchoo ga omae koko to >koto to< kuttsuita
        Min. of F  SB you  this GL  this GL  merge
10      hoo ga ii yo to (.) koo yuu n janai  ka na
        way SB good  IP QT this say N CP-Neg Q  IP
        "uhm, I think Mr. Takenaka would say it like
        this. Mr. Takarabe how about this, but you
        see, even they tell local banks to be
        autonomous, the Ministry of Finance will say, you,
        it's best that your bank merges to this bank.
        Wouldn't they say it like that, I wonder."
```

A pattern similar to that evident in the first excerpt is also evident here. The IE has just made a remark that local banks should be autonomous, not under the direction of the national government. At the end of the IE's turn, when he is about to form another TRP (line 04), the MI cuts in. Because the IE's turn has already begun, the MI prefaces his turn with an attention getter, *ano:* [uhm] to indicate his move in overlap, and this leads the IE to cease his turn construction (see a truncation in line 04). Competitive overlapping talk is a sequential practice used to claim a turn (Sacks et al., 1974; Schegloff, 2000). In lines 05–06, the MI first states *Takenaka san wa koo yuu huu ni osshari to omou* [I think Mr. Takenaka would say it like this]. In this utterance, the speaker used the demonstrative pronoun *koo* [this]. Usually, the speaker would use a demonstrative pronoun *soo* [that] to refer to the content of the *addressee's* utterance. I argue that this deictic shift here suggests a shift in the speaker's footing (Goffman, 1981): that is, he is now speaking to another interlocutor. A nonverbal cue also supports this argument. While uttering line 05, the MI looks down at the documents on his desk, disengaging from eye contact with the IE. After a 1-s pause, he turns away from the IE, then calls on the SI, Takarabe—an economic journalist—summoning him by name (line 07). While speaking to the SI, the MI shows disagreement with the IE, stating that the government *would* control the banks unofficially (line 07–10) despite the IE's claim to the contrary.

The MI's lines 07–10 also evince a change in terms of linguistic style. The MI's utterance is ostensibly more casual. For instance, he uses the plain form *doo* [how is it] in line 07 to form a question, instead of the polite speech style alternative, *doo desu ka* [how is it]. At the end of line 10, where he says [..] *koo yuu n janai* [[he] would say like this], he might instead have used a polite style alternative, *koo yuu n janai deshoo/desu*. Finally, he uses *ka na*, a combination of the question marker *ka* and the interactional particle *na*, which is not used when addressing someone formally. The addressee for the MI's turn is now someone else (the SI in this case), not the IE. While the two interviewers talk, the camera shows the IE following the side-play interaction closely with his eyes; yet he says nothing. In response to the question from the MI, the SI answers in Excerpt 7, where he picks up his turn.

Excerpt 7, finance 2

```
IE: Takenaka (interviewee)
MI: Tawara (main interviewer)
SI: Takarabe (second interviewer)

11 SI: .hh ano:::(.)ma-(.)Takenaka san wa otachiba aru
           SF       SF    Takenaka Mr. TP position have
12      kara  ienai  to omou  n desu kedomo
        since say-NG QT think N CP   but
13      >sore wa< yaru to omoimasu. .hh (.)
         that TP  do   QT think
14      boku wa jitsuwa  ne?(.)Takenaka san no: zutto  kono:
        I    TP actually IP    Takenaka Mr. LK  always this
15      suunen kan  no shuwan   mitekite:,
        some   years LK strategy have watched
16      (.) MA- sono tsudo      sono tsudo
            SF  that every time that every time
17      boku monku     mo   iimashita kedomo:(.).hhh>demo
        I    criticism also said      but            but
18      ano< Risona ginkoo no shuhoo   miteru   to
        SF   Resona bank   LK strategy watching when
19      >desu ne:<yahari nihon o sukutta sono seijiteki na, .h
         CP   IP  again  Japan O saved   that political CP
20      ketsudan ga atta    to sureba: (.)
        decision SB existed if do-if
21      boku wa  Risona da to omotte   n desu yo.
        I    TP  Resona CP QT thinking N CP   IP
22      (.).h >are demo< zuibun hihansaremashita
        (.).h  that but  quite criticized-PAS
23      yo ne:,=
        IP IP
        ".hh well, um, since Mr. Takenaka has his
        responsibility for his position I don't think he
        can say it but, I think he will do it[15]. .hh I
        actually think, you know, I've watched his
        actions  for awhile, well, every time I've
        made some criticisms about them but .hhh but,
        well, when I observe the strategy taken for Resona
        Bank, you see, if there are any political decisions
        that saved Japan, I believe it was the one for
        Resona Bank. .h but that was criticized, wasn't it."

24 MI: =soo:   mecha[kuchani iwareta
        so     heavily        said-PAS
       "Right. Heavily criticized."

25 SI:              [ii toka warui toka tte
                     good like bad like QT
26      ↓yuu .hh tokoroga
         say     however
27      (.) are  wa (.) asoko de are  o *yatta kara*[16]
            that TP     there at that O  did because
```

```
28      (.2)jissai keizai  no yosa     ga >desu ne<
            actual economy LK goodness SB  CP   IP
29      ashi o hippararezu ni    nobita! tte no ga
        legs O pull-PAS-NG while grew    QT  N  SB
30      ichiban ookikatta n desu ne:,(.)
        most    effective N CP   IP
31      >desukara< Takenaka san wa yarimasu yo.(.)
         so        Takenaka Mr. TP do       IP
32      nanika    attara .hh
        something happen-if
33      ↑nandemo  ↑yaru to omoimasu.
         anything  do   QT think
        "people said it's good, no it's bad. .hh however
        that[17] was because he made that happen
        then, actually the economy status improved
        without being interrupted. That was the most
        effective, as you know, Mr. Takenaka will do
        it. If anything happens. .hh he'll do anything,
        I believe."

34 MI: nandemo.
       anything
       "anything"

35 SI: >yaru to omoimasu<=
        do   QT think
       "I believe he will do it."

36 MI: =kowai      hito   da.
        incredible person CP-Plain
       "what an incredible person."
```

The SI answers the MI's question by recalling the precedent case of a specific bank (Resona Bank[18]), which the IE handled as the Finance Minister in 2003. The SI then clearly affirms the MI's assertion by saying *nandemo yaru to omoimasu* [I think (Takenaka) will do anything] (line 33). While the SI holds the floor at some length (between lines 11–33), the MI inserts only a single alignment (line 24), while the IE never seeks a speaker turn. In this excerpt, too, we see third-party involvement supporting the MI's opposition to the IE.

What has been accomplished by third-party involvement in these cases? In interview settings in the US and the UK, a common practice by which interviewers produce counterarguments is to change footing (Clayman, 1992; Goffman, 1981). When confronting the interviewee with an oppositional view, the interviewer may preface it with expressions such as "Some say that..." or "It has been said that..." to dissociate him- or herself from the conflictive stance. The maintenance of a neutral footing is a critical foundation for broadcast journalism. This is as true in Japan as it is elsewhere, but a substantive interview does at times require that interviewers embrace a devil's advocate role. In contrast to the American and British cases, where the interviewers fulfill this role by, in effect, serving as 'spokespersons' for a generic opposition, in the Japanese case the interviewers fulfill the function in a much more theatrical way by having a third party involved in the interview. The use of side-play (Goffman, 1981) with the third party cultivates controversy—an element of entertainment for the show—by sanctioning the subjective views expressed by the interviewers.

Third-person involvement to answer a challenging question

Most of the cases observed show that a third party inserts him- or herself immediately after the interviewee's first opportunity to state an argument so that the side-play between the interviewers is understood as conditionally relevant (Schegloff, 1968) and, in the cases examined, as an opposing move to the interviewee's most recent point. However, two cases do not conform to this sequential pattern. In these two cases, the third-party involvement occurs where the interviewee should have taken a turn. Let us examine these two cases in detail.

In the first case, the IE is Ki'ichi Miyazawa,[19] a former prime minister of Japan. In addition to the MI (Tawara), the current governor of Nagano prefecture (Yasuo Tanaka[20]) is serving in an interviewer role (SI).

Excerpt 8, Katoo Kooichi

```
IE: Ki'ichi Miyazawa (interviewee)
MI: Tawara (main interviewer)
SI: Yasuo Tanaka (second interviewer)

01 MI: ima Katoo Kooichi san taibooro[n
       now Katoo Kooichi Mr. wanted
       "we have hypothesized that Katoo Koichi is
       desired ((for the prime minister position))"

02 SI:                                [n:     sore koso
                                      right  that very
03     watakushi wa shin no Katoo no ran    ni naru
       I          TP true LK Katoo LK revol.GL become
04     n janai ka to ↓omotte    n desu kedo ne.
       N CP-NG Q QT   thinking N CP   but  IP.
       "right, that's what will truly be 'Katoo's
       rebellion,'[21] I would think."

05     (1.0)

06     kisetsu hazure no.
       season  off    one
       "off season one."

07     (1.5)
       ((KM grins at IE, displaying subtle shoulder
       movements))
```

```
08 MI: Miyazawa san.
       Miyazawa Mr.
       "Mr. Miyazawa"

09     (1.0)

10 SI: ne:.(.5) Miyazawa san mo:: uh: sono katachi o
       IP       Miyazawa Mr. also uh  that form   O
11     jitsuwa:(.) sukoshi  nozonde irassharu n janai
       actually    a little wishing-HON       N CP-NG
12     ka na: tte ki      ga: watashi [wa]
       Q  IP  QT  feeling SB  I        TP
       "you see, Mr. Miyazawa would actually also wish
       a bit for this outcome wouldn't he, I have that
       feeling"

13 MI:                                [a!]
                                       oh
14     nozonderu kara!  kotaerarenai  to.
       wishing   because answerable-NG QT
       "Oh, because he wishes that he cannot answer,
       you say."

15 SI: ah ↑a::↓ (.)[kamo     shirenai desu keredomo ne.
       oh  oh::,(.) perhaps  maybe    CP   but      IP
       "Oh, oh:: yeah, perhaps so, maybe."

16                 [((gazing with T))

17 MI: soo ka.
       so  Q[22]
       "I see."
```

In this segment, in lines 01–05, the MI and SI suggest a rather unexpected candidate for the next prime minister (Kooichi Katoo) as a method of seeking the IE's opinion. In the interview, suggestions, assertions, and other interviewers' actions are normatively heard as questions addressed to the IE. With the answer from the IE on hold, the SI pursues the idea further: line 06 *kisetsu hazure no* [off season] can be seen as an "extension" (Ford, Fox, & Thompson, 1996; Schegloff, 1996), an increment utterance that is interpretable as a continuation of the immediately prior, possibly completed turn.[23] In the recorded data, the camera shot shows the SI gazing at the IE while so doing. Despite the fact that the question is on the table, through these intermediate turns by the MI and SI, the IE provides only nonverbal grins and subtle shoulder movements for 1.5 s as a response (line 07). At this point, the MI once more presses the IE using a summons (line 08), but the IE resists, whereupon the SI self-selects for the next turn, addressing the MI. At this point, a dyadic interaction between the SI and MI begins. The SI prefaces his turn with a solo-standing *ne:* [you see?],[24] claiming the turn next. Then he speaks on the IE's behalf: "Mr. Miyazawa may be wishing for this outcome (i.e., Kooichi Katoo as the next Prime Minister), wouldn't he? I have that feeling." Upon this, in lines 13–14, the MI replies "oh! because [Miyazawa] wishes that, he cannot answer, you say." The MI's receipt of the SI's self-selected turn in line 08 establishes the side-play exchange between the interviewers. During the sequence, the camera captures the IE sitting in his seat silently with a rather ambivalent-looking expression on his face. In this case, the third-party involvement begins at the IE's turn to respond, yet he declined the opportunity. The result is that the side-play between the interviewers provides an answer (second pair part) to the question (first pair part) initially given by the MI.

Excerpt 9 is another case of a third party becoming involved to speak on behalf of an IE—in this case, Heizoo Takenaka, the minister of finance in 2005. Notably different here is how the interviewers' side-play develops. Unlike the cases discussed thus far, the side-play here does not challenge the IE but instead saves his face when he does not answer a question posed to him. In Excerpt 9, Matsubara (SI) attacks the IE by saying that the ministry must carry out a much more radical policy to enforce changes for local banks in Japan (lines 01–06):

Excerpt 9, local banks

```
IE: Takenaka (interviewee)
MI: Tawara (main interviewer)
SI: Matsubara (second interviewer)

01 SI: >dakara< tonariatta chigin      dooshi ga gappei
       >so<     neighbored local banks each   SB merge
02     suru yoo  na (.)
       do   like CP
03     sono gurai no daikaikaku   o chihoo de mo
       that about LK large reform O local  at also
04     yaranai to (.)
       do-NG   if
05     $kekkyoku$ chihoo keizai  mo   huyoo shinai
       after all local  economy also rise  do-NG
06     n janai [ka
       N CP-NG  Q
       "So, if the neighboring local banks merge, if they
       did not do such a large scale reform in the
       regions, then the regional economy won't improve
       after all, will it"

07     ((N turns around and gazes towards M))

08 IE:           [sore-] sore wa >desu ne<=
                  that   that TP  CP   IP
                  "That, that you see"
```

```
09 MI:          [iya  ]
                 no
                 "no"

10 SI: =[tarinakya-
          short-if
          "if (the banks) are short (of money),"

11 MI: =[sore wa Takenaka san ga yuu no wa
          that TP Takenaka Mr. SB say N  TP
12      muri      de:,=
        impossible CP
        "for Mr. Takenaka to say that would be impossible"

13 IE: =((laughs quietly))

14 MI: yaroo    to shite n da       tte
       do-Plain QT doing N CP-Plain QT
15     >kono hito   wa!< (.2) de  tabun   ne!
        this person TP        and perhaps IP
16     kinyuuchoo            mo   yaru     no!
       Ministry of Finance also  do-Plain N
       "he intends to do it, this guy. And, perhaps
       The Ministry of Finance will do it too!"
```

As the SI directly addresses his turn to the IE, he starts to answer in line 08, *sore- sore wa desu ne* [about that, you see], which projects further development of his turn. A recycled turn-beginning (Schegloff, 1987) of the deictic word *sore* [that] into the opening is also indicative of his move. Despite the IE's initiation of an answering turn, in this segment, the MI jumps into the talk and begins addressing the SI. When the SI speaks before the IE is able to continue with his turn (line 09), the MI overlaps with the SI's turn (line 11) and wins the competition over the next turn. The MI's turn-beginning appropriates the phrase used in the IE's aborted turn, *sore wa* [that is], which can be heard as answering on behalf of the IE. Indeed, the MI halts the interaction between the SI and IE and invokes instead an interviewers' side-play. Exactly as we observed in the earlier excerpt, the MI uses a casual speech style in line 14; for example, in the phrase *yaroo to shite n datte* [he intends to do it], we find the choice of verb *yaru* [do] (plain style, tentative form), which is a less formal register than *suru* [do].[25] It also has a phonologically contracted articulation and uses the plain style copula *da* in *shite n da* [doing] (nominalized), which would be, if not contracted, *shite iru n da* [doing] (nominalized). These forms index that the MI is shifting his footing (Goffman, 1981) to engage in interaction with a different addressee, that is, the SI in this case. In the side-play talk (lines 14–16),[26] the MI asserts that the IE) would indeed control the local banks even though he cannot say as much on television. The IE, the subject of this attribution, inserts his laughter in line 13, exactly when the MI finishes stating, "For Mr. Takenaka to say that [he would control the private banks] would be impossible" (lines 11–12). This laughter, projected at this precise point, neither confirms nor denies the truth of the MI's attribution—which is, after all, the best possible response given his position as the minister of finance.

In this case, the third party that becomes involved in the talk is the MI, not the SI. The development of the pattern differs from the previous excerpts in that it emerges at a point where the IE has already claimed and initiated a speaker turn (line 09). If the IE were to go ahead with his turn at this point, he would be left with no option other than to evade the question. Instead of forcing the IE to endure this awkwardness, the MI simply takes over and provides the answer on behalf of the IE. This proxy answer is, as it happens, more radical and more provocative than any answer the IE could possibly provide. Not only does the third-party involvement save the IE's face here, it also enhances the entertainment value of the show.

Conclusion

In this chapter, I have examined a series of cases in which televised Japanese political interviews exploit third-party involvement to accomplish a series of social purposes. The analysis showed that the pattern enables interviewers both to challenge interviewees and to arrange the development of the interaction in a more provocative way than would otherwise be possible. When using the pattern, interviewers can play devil's advocate roles, enabling them to push the envelope of journalistic neutrality. By using the pattern in the unfolding process of an interview, they generate informative and entertaining products.

While the pattern observed in this study is not unique to Japanese, its use in the particular genre of political television interviews is perhaps more common in Japan than in the United States or Britain.[27] This study showed that while third-party involvement and the emergent side-play are useful for avoiding direct conflict and challenges to face as documented elsewhere in the literature, they can also perform pragmatic functions other than conflict management. They can enable more argumentative and theatrical discussions, thus enhancing the discussions' entertainment value. Televised politics, at least in contemporary Japan, is intended to have substantial entertainment value. The conversation analysis carried out here has enabled us to see precisely how journalists construct substantive and informative talk without violating interviewers' normative interactional roles and while cultivating and maintaining a desired level of conflict. In the Japanese case, the observed pattern is a valuable interactional resource commonly used for these superficially inconsistent purposes.

A question naturally arises at this point: why do Japanese political television programs adopt this particular pattern? Why is the one-on-one interview not as popular a format as in the United States and elsewhere? Fundamentally, this may be an anthropological question that cannot be answered definitively using conversation analysis. However, I can at least suggest that one-on-one interviews in Japan are often handled very differently than in other settings. One-on-one interviews with political figures are often aired as special events with titles such as *tandoku intabyuu* [one-to-one interviews]. A notable difference is that Japanese interviewers in one-on-one interviews tend not to challenge interviewees but instead largely relinquish control of the floor to them—in effect, offering them platforms for their views. Japanese interviewers, often prominent journalists and anchors, thus assume a different social stance from their North American or British counterparts in a one-on-one context. Interviewees can be challenged much more readily in a multiple-participant setting. This study demonstrates one way in which combative journalism can be engineered within a social context otherwise highly constrained by norms of propriety: through third-party involvement, interviewers are able to mount challenges while simultaneously enhancing the entertainment value of the program. Conversation analysis enables us to see the development of these dynamics in the talk.

Notes

1 According to a 1995 NHK survey (*Kokumin Seikatsu-Jikan Choosa* [National Lifestyle Research]), the average Japanese watches television for 3 hours and 28 minutes a day (Watanabe, 1995).

2 As of the year 2007, shows of this kind included TV Asahi's *Sandee Purojekuto* [Sunday Project], Fuji TV's *Hoodoo 2001* [Broadcasting 2001], and NHK's *Nichiyoo Tooron* [Sunday Debate]. They devote most of their air time to interviewing important contemporary political figures.

3 This pattern has exceptions. For instance, a program, *Nichiyoo Tooron* [Sunday Debate], aired by the public broadcasting institution called NHK (National Broadcasting Association), is mostly managed by a single host with one or more guests.

4 The programs were the same programs referred to in endnote 2.

5 The multiple interviewers may not share equally in the act of interviewing. As I show later, it is common to have a main interviewer and several others playing merely supporting roles. Nevertheless, they engage in interviewing as a team, which is not as common in a North American setting, particularly for political television interviews.

6 @ indicates laughter in Kang's (1998) transcript.

7 Even in a case when the bait is not explicitly confirmed by the target using words, the target's following action, which may be a long while later, may display an effect of receiving the signifying.

8 The phrase *desu ne* (copula + IP) is often placed in transition-relevant places in Japanese conversation, creating a space for interaction (Morita, 2005). The copula

desu indicates a speech style (polite) but does not function grammatically as a copula. The interactional particle *ne* is used when the speaker solicits the listener's cooperation, and it emphasizes recipient design of the utterance.

9 In Japanese, the interactional particle *ne* is often inserted to mark the end of a TCU (Tanaka, 1999).

10 Hoshi is the chief editor of a major Japanese newspaper publisher (Asahi Shimbun), and his expertise in "reading" the political current is well known in the media.

11 Lines 05 to 21, in which the exchange between the two interviewers continues, are omitted.

12 Lines 34-41, in which the exchange between the two interviewers continues, are omitted.

13 The MI indicates here that he is not criticizing the IE behind his back.

14 Minister of State for Economic and Fiscal Policy and Minister of State for Privatization of the Postal Services.

15 "It" in this line refers to the national control of private businesses banks, companies, etc.).

16 *Word* indicates a creaky voice.

17 "That" here and the next "that" in line 24 both refer to Takenaka's decision to use national funds in 2003 to bail out the private nation-wide Resona Bank. See following note.

18 In 2003, to rebuild its capital base, Resona Bank had to apply for national funds of ¥1.96 trillion. Takenaka, at the time Minister of Finance, opted to place it under government control of a private bank. This violated a strong norm of public/private disentanglement in the financial sector.

19 Miyazawa was a long-time leader of one of the largest factions of the Liberal Democratic Party (LDP). He was elected party leader in 1991 and served as Japan's prime minister from 1991 to 1993, when he resigned after a failure to pass reforms that led to the LDP's first defeat in national elections since 1955. From 1998 to 2001, he was the finance minister; during this period, he led Japan's efforts to help alleviate the 1997–1998 Asian economic crises. He retired from the Diet in 2003.

20 A novelist who became governor of Nagano prefecture in 2000 without the support of a major political party, Tanaka helped found the New Japan Party in August 2005.

21 "Katoo's rebellion" refers to Kooichi Katoo, a senior member and a former Secretary-General of the ruling Liberal Democratic Party, who in 2000 attempted to move a non-confident vote against Prime Minister Yoshiroo Mori. Katoo's rebellion failed and his status in the LDP has been greatly diminished.

22 The question particle *ka* here is not used to form an interrogative; instead, it indicates that this utterance is a "response cry" (Goffman, 1981).

23 The ending of the prior turn (line 03), [clause] + *to omou n desu kedo ne* [I think that (clause)], is also indicative of this observation. The formulaic sequence *n desu kedo* (nominalizer *n (no)* + copula + conjunctive marker) marks a clear TRP to the other speakers. Therefore, it has been recognized as a turn-final discourse marker.

24 Tanaka (1999) remarked that *ne* in the utterance-initial position functions as a turn-grabbing device.

25 A bare predicate used to refer to a person to whom one would normally use honorific forms (if speaking to him or her directly) is a good indication that the speaker does not treat this utterance as a direct address.

26 The MI now uses the plain style of the verb *yaru* [do] to refer to the IE's action in this side-play, which also indicates that the MI is addressing the SI, not the IE directly.

27 While cases of multiple IEs versus a single IR have been discussed in the English-language literature on political interviews (Clayman & Heritage, 2002; Greatbatch, 1992), multiple IR/single IE interviews have not.

References

Altman, K. (1996). Television and political turmoil: Japan's summer of 1993. In E. S. Krauss & S. J. Pharr (Eds.), *Media and politics in Japan* (pp. 165–186). Honolulu, HI: University of Hawai'i Press.

Bilmes, J. (1981). Proposition and confrontation in a legal discussion. *Semiotica, 34*, 251–275.

Clark, H., & Carlson, T. (1982). Speech acts and hearer's beliefs. In N. V. Smith (Ed.), *Mutual knowledge* (pp. 1–36). New York: Academic Press.

Clayman, S. (1992). Footing in the achievement of neutrality: The case of news interview discourse. In P. Drew & J. Heritage (Eds.), *Talk at work: Interaction in institutional settings* (pp. 163–198). Cambridge, UK: Cambridge University Press.

Clayman, S. (2001). Answers and evasions. *Language in Society, 30*, 403–442.

Clayman, S., & Heritage, J. (2002). *The news interview: Journalists and public figures on the air.* Cambridge, UK: Cambridge University Press.

Eisenstadt, S. N., & Ben-Ari, E. (1990). *Japanese models of conflict resolution.* London: K. Paul International.

Furo, H. (1998). Turn-taking in Japanese political debate: Syntax, intonation, and semantics. In D. Silva (Ed.), *Japanese/Korean linguistics* (Vol. 8), (pp. 31–44). Stanford, CA: Stanford Linguistics Association.

Gatzen, B. (2003). Japan media: The stone unturned. *Japan Media Review.* Retrieved April 4, 2007, from http://www.japanmediareview.com/japan/media/1043974972.php.

Goffman, E. (1974). *Frame analysis: An essay on the organization of experience.* Cambridge, MA: Harvard University Press.

Goffman, E. (1981). *Forms of talk.* New York: Pantheon Books.

Greatbatch, D. (1992). On the management of disagreement between news interviewers. In P. Drew & J. Heritage (Eds.), *Talk at work: Interaction in institutional settings* (pp. 268–301). Cambridge, UK: Cambridge University Press.

Greatbatch, D. (1998). Conversation analysis: Neutralism in British news interviews. In A. Bell & P. Garrett (Eds.), *Approaches to media discourse* (pp. 163–185). Oxford, UK: Blackwell.

Heritage, J. (1985). Analyzing news interviews: Aspects of the production of talk for an overhearing audience. In T. A. van Dijk (Ed.), *Handbook of discourse analysis* (Vol. 3), (pp. 95–117). London: Academic Press.

Heritage, J., & Greatbatch, D. (1991). On the institutional character of institutional talk: The case of news interviews. In D. Boden & D. H. Zimmerman (Eds.), *Talk and social structure: Studies in ethnomethodology and conversation analysis* (pp. 93–137). Cambridge, UK: Polity Press.

Honda, A. (1999). *Managing conflict talk in Japanese public affairs talk shows.* Unpublished doctoral dissertation, Georgetown University, Washington, DC.

Krauss, E. S., & Pharr, S. J. (Eds.) (1996). *Media and politics in Japan.* Honolulu, HI: University of Hawai'i Press.

Lebra, T. (1984). Non-confrontational strategies for management of interpersonal conflicts. In E. S. Krauss, T. P. Rohlen, & P. G. Steinhoff (Eds.), *Conflict in Japan* (pp. 130–142). Honolulu, HI: University of Hawai'i Press.

Morgan, M. (1996). Conversational signifying: Grammar and indirectness among African American women. In E. Ochs, E. A. Schegloff, & S. A. Thompson (Eds.), *Interaction and grammar* (pp. 405–434). Cambridge, UK: Cambridge University Press.

Ong, W. J. (1981). *Fighting for life: Contest, sexuality, and consciousness.* Ithaca, NY: Cornell University Press.

Sacks, H., Schegloff, E. A., & Jefferson, G. (1974). A simplest systematics for the organization of turn-taking for conversation. *Language in Society, 50*, 696–735.

Tanaka, H. (1999). *Turn-taking in Japanese conversation: A study in grammar and interaction.* Amsterdam: John Benjamins.

Tannen, D. (1993). *Framing in discourse.* New York: Oxford University Press.

Video Research Ltd. (2001). TV rating research. Retrieved July 7, 2003, from http://www.videor.co.jp/index.htm

Watanabe, T. (1995). *Media tricks no shakaigaku* [Sociology of media tricks]. Tokyo: Sekai-Shisosha Shuppan.

Watanabe, T. (2000). *Terebi: Yarase to jōhō-sōsa* [Television: Its fiction and information control]. Tokyo: Sanseido.

8 Resisting ESL: Categories and Sequence in a Critically "Motivated" Analysis of Classroom Interaction

Steven Talmy
University of British Columbia

Introduction

The following data, from Sacks (1992), come from an adolescent boys' group therapy session:

Sacks (1992, p. 461; cf. p. 597)

```
Ken:        Did Louise call or anything this morning?
Therapist:  Why, did you expect her to call?
Ken:        No. I was just kind of hoping that she
            might be able to figure out some way of
            coming to the meetings. She did seem like
            she wanted to come back.
Therapist:  Do you miss her?
Ken:        Oh in some ways, yes. It was nice having
            the opposite sex in the room, ya know,
            having a chick in the room.
Roger:      ((sarcastically)) Wasn't it nice?
Ken:        In some ways it was. I really can't say
            why, but it was.
```

Sacks's analysis of these data concerns how the substitution of a locational category such as "in the room" for "in the group" (line 9) and the use of "opposite sex" (line 9) for "Louise" work to weaken any interest or "compliment" about the adolescent girl, Louise, that may be implied by Ken's inquiry into her absence. As Sacks makes clear, Ken's choice of categories here allows for

Talk-in-interaction: Multilingual perspectives, pp. 181–213, Hanh Nguyen & Gabriele Kasper (Eds.), 2009
Honolulu, HI: University of Hawai'i, National Foreign Language Resource Center

his "safe" reply: Louise's absence is a *categorical* loss (i.e., as a member of the "opposite sex"), not a personal one (p. 464; cf. pp. 597–599).

Missing from Sacks's analysis, however, is a consideration of sexism (cf. Edwards, 1998). This is perhaps unsurprising because neither the boys nor therapist appear to orient to it in the data, and a defining characteristic of conversation analysis (CA) and membership categorization analysis (MCA), is an insistence on participant orientations rather than those of the analyst. Arguably, however, consideration of sexism could advance Sacks's analysis of "weak and safe compliments" here. As he notes, use of "opposite sex" is key in downgrading Ken's implied compliment such that it is not a specific member (Louise) who is missed; it is any member. The replaceability attributed to women—like interchangeable parts, one member easily substitutes for another—signifies an unexamined objectification that could warrant a claim of sexism. Further, if one considers that "chick" serves as a second downgrade—from "Louise," to "opposite sex," to "chick"—one can see that the "safety" of Ken's reply comes not just through the categorical substitutions, but from his objectification and disparaging reference, that is, from the sexism these substitutions are imbued with. This provides added insight into why the boy's reply might be considered "weak and safe" in the context of an audience of adolescent male peers and allows analysis beyond the local situation to matters of wider sociological significance, including, for example, how sexism is achieved in talk, why it might serve as a *resource* for an adolescent boy on an occasion such as this, as well as why, crucially, *it remains unoriented to* in this interaction.

This discussion recalls an ongoing debate between scholars in CA and in branches of feminist and critical discourse studies (see, e.g., Billig, 1999a, 1999b; Blommaert, 2005; Fairclough, 1989; Kitzinger, 2000; Schegloff, 1999a, 1999b; Wetherell, 1998; Wooffitt, 2005). As I discuss in more detail below, the debate concerns criticisms that conversation analysts have made about "politically motivated" discourse research suffering from the "imposition" of analysts' critical/feminist "agendas."[1] Many of these studies, they maintain, lack rigor and warrants for claims and tell more about the analyst's politics than how sexism, for example, is achieved in talk. Conversely, critical and feminist researchers argue that *no* analysis can be free of the analyst's interests, however explicitly political or implicitly "neutral" they may be. CA's insistence on "unmotivated looking" (Sacks, 1992), they claim, speaks to CA's scientism and "naïve epistemology" (Billig, 1999b) and results in analyses that are overly focused on the details of talk rather than on matters of greater analytic consequence to critical researchers, such as social injustice, discrimination, and inequality (but see Wooffitt, 2005).

This paper joins an emergent line of enquiry that works to transcend these differences by harnessing the powerful methods of CA and MCA (M/CA) for "openly ideological" (Lather, 1986), or explicitly "motivated" discourse research. The paper concerns the "cultural productions of the ESL student" (cf.

Levinson, Foley, & Holland, 1996) in an English-as-a-second-language (ESL) class at Tradewinds High School.[2] I undertake, from a critical/cultural studies framework,[3] an analysis of membership categories and sequential organization in classroom talk. Specifically, this work examines two back-to-back interactions involving "oldtimer" (Wenger, 1998), "generation 1.5" (Harklau, Losey, & Siegal, 1999) or "Local ESL" students (Talmy, 2008),[4] and their teacher, in which Local ESL students were ascribed and resisted membership to the category of "ESL student" (cf. Day, 1998).

Before undertaking that analysis, I first consider some of the challenges that attend the use of ethnomethodological approaches in a critical analysis of discourse. Afterward, I briefly describe the critical ethnography that the data I analyze below are drawn from and then use the bulk of the paper to engage these data. Following this, I discuss how the analysis works to substantiate and elaborate several "political" arguments from the larger study, before concluding with reconsideration of certain benefits that M/CA can bring to critical discourse research.

Of (in)compatibilities and oxymorons: CA, MCA, and "motivated looking"

Billig (1997, p. 205) has asserted that despite its broad interests in the intersections between power, ideology, and cultural and social (re)production on the one hand, and race, class, gender, and sexuality on the other, that critical/cultural studies research often appears "depopulated," with analyses involving "manufactured artifacts, such as magazines, films, or academic books" rather than the social actions of "recognizable women and men" (see, e.g., Fairclough, 1989; Grossberg, Nelson, & Treichler, 1992; cf. Barker & Galasiński, 2001). Even in "populated" critical/cultural studies research, however, claims may not be clearly and accountably drawn because these studies often do not include analyses of social interaction. As Wetherell (1998, p. 35) has argued:

> [p]ost-structuralist theorists, with their more global view, rarely have their noses pressed up against the exigencies of talk-in-interaction. Rarely, are they called on to explain how their perspective might apply to what is happening right now, on the ground, in this very conversation. Theoretical concepts emerge in abstract on the basis of often implicit assumptions about the nature of interaction, language, or social life.

However, Widdicombe (1995, p. 107) maintains that even in critical discourse studies that do include analyses of social interaction, the "pressure to produce political conclusions" can have "unfortunate conceptual, methodological and practical consequences." Although critical researchers argue that all conclusions are political, not just those that aspire to be (see, e.g., Kincheloe & McLaren,

2000), Widdicombe (1995, p. 111) makes an important point: "by elevating their own political agendas as the pre-established frame, [critical] researchers may actually undermine the practical and political utility of the analyses they undertake." Put another way, an overriding commitment to an agenda—*any* agenda—can obscure analysis.

One way forward that Widdicombe (1995) suggests for critical/cultural studies analysts is through M/CA, which shifts focus away from the broad sweep of macro-abstraction to the detail of everyday talk. As she argues, "it is precisely in the mundane contexts of interaction that institutional power is exercised, social inequalities are experienced, and resistance accomplished" (p. 111). However, just as cultural studies has been criticized for its more "global view," ethnomethodological approaches to analyses of discourse have been condemned for not adequately dealing with issues of "social relevance" (van Dijk, 1985), and in CA's case in particular, for being too narrowly focused on the mechanics of talk.[5] As Wetherell (1998, p. 402) puts it, "the problem with conversation analysts is that they rarely raise their eyes from the next turn in the conversation." Thus, bringing a cultural studies perspective to M/CA would appear to offer potential for an analysis concerning the ways that, for example, homophobia or sexism is achieved in interaction: cultural studies might address criticisms concerning M/CA's overly microanalytic orientation, its restricted view of "context," its formalism, and its objectivism as evident in the insistence on approaching data with a "clean gaze"; and M/CA could help critical discourse studies, and cultural studies more generally, answer criticisms concerning analytic inattention to social interaction, *a priori* contextualization, theoretical "imperialism," and inadequate warrants for claims.

It is, of course, more complicated than simply "mixing and matching" theories and methodologies, particularly in terms of the paradigmatic tensions and epistemological incommensurabilities that arise when attempting to integrate scientistic methodologies into a "political" theoretical framework. However, an increasing number of efforts, particularly (but not exclusively) by feminist psychologists, have successfully overcome the apparent "oxymoron" (Speer, 1999) of what might be called a "motivated M/CA."

Before reviewing several recent feminist M/CA studies that demonstrate how M/CA could benefit critical/cultural studies research, it may be useful to consider feminist M/CA (or any "motivated" M/CA) as a form of so-called "applied CA." In remarks that signpost some of the difficulties of integrating CA with a political agenda, ten Have (1999, p. 162) notes that "CA was originally developed as a 'pure' science, motivated by the wish to discover basic and general aspects of sociality." In contrast to its "pure" predecessor, "applied CA," which developed in earlier CA studies of institutional talk (see, e.g., Heritage, 1984), "denote[s] the implicit or even explicit use of CA...to support efforts to make social life 'better' in some way" (ten Have, 1999, p. 162; see also 2001). Stokoe and Smithson (2001) advance this contrast in their paper on M/CA and gender when they argue that

> although CA provides the tools to explore in fine detail how issues around gender are occasioned in talk, a Schegloffian [or "pure" CA] is of limited use if one wishes to comment on the wider social significance of such occasioning... [In a "pure" CA, we] can point to speakers shifting between gender categories, repairing their use of gendered terms, challenging each other on the upshot of invoking gender and resisting 'sexist' identities, but we cannot draw upon our background knowledge as feminists to produce commentary on such matters... [This] leaves a gap between technical analysis and that which is relevant socially for speakers. (p. 238)

Kitzinger and Frith (1999) offer one example of how the "tools" of CA can be used to warrant observations of "wider social significance" when they apply insights from CA's extensive literature on refusals to complicate the "just say no" maxim prescribed in date rape prevention training seminars. Kitzinger and Frith argue that "just say no" is in fact "counter-productive" because it privileges a "conversationally abnormal action" (just saying "no") and derogates other, more common but indirect ways of refusing that include delays, mitigations, and accounts. They also note that this simplistic saying, which is intended to "empower" women, "allows rapists to persist with the claim that if a woman has not actually said 'NO'...then she hasn't refused to have sex with him" (1999, p. 310). Kitzinger (2000), too, uses CA for her analysis of gay and lesbian students' "coming out stories" in university seminars. She traces other students' lack of uptake to these stories to how they are embedded in extended turn-constructional-units, arguing that the storytellers' use of turn-taking organization allowed them to avoid topicalizing their sexuality. Kitzinger extends these conclusions to comment on homophobic social attitudes, such as negative ideologies about "flaunting" one's gay/lesbian sexuality. In their CA-informed analysis concerning class and gender, Stokoe and Smithson (2001) illustrate not only how interviewees oriented to these "abstract" topics but also constructed them in interaction. However, in arguing for the need to go beyond participants' displayed orientations, they also illustrate the importance of a feminist analysis even when gender was "not oriented to except by us as analysts" (p. 233). In addition to CA, they undertake an MCA analysis concerning ascription of and resistance to gender categories and similarly demonstrate the need for analysis that moves beyond the local interaction since neither CA nor MCA helped to problematize unoriented-to sexism in their data (e.g., the unproblematic binding of "ironing" and "washing" activities to the category "wife"). Similarly, Ohara and Saft (2003) use M/CA to examine how the interactional structure of a call-in TV show facilitated a shift in responsibility for problems that women callers noted about their husbands' behavior from the men to the women. They note that such shifts were evidence of particular gender ideologies in Japan, which were reproduced in these calls. As well, in her reanalysis of an earlier, non-CA feminist interview study, Widdicombe (1995) uses the same data the author did to undermine the original analysis and arrive at demonstrably different conclusions concerning an interviewee's account of an aspect of her sexual history.

This selective review hints at the potential for a critical/cultural studies analysis that examines in detail the competing cultural productions of a stigmatized institutional identity category: "ESL student." As Speer (1999, p. 476) notes, "there is nothing intrinsic to...CA...that would prevent feminists—and others with a critical agenda—from using it to ask politically motivated questions, or to reach politically efficacious outcomes." In fact, Kitzinger (2000) concludes, M/CA "offers a *method* for...social constructionist, postmodern and queer" research that treats abstractions such as race, class, gender, and sexuality "as *accomplishments* rather than as pre-given categories" (p. 170, my emphasis; also see Cameron, 2005).

This study

The data come from a 2.5-year critical ethnography (Talmy, 2005) concerning two broadly competing "cultural productions of the ESL student": one "official," or school-sanctioned, manifest in curriculum, instruction, and policies regulating ESL, which constructed ESL students as an undifferentiated group of exotic newcomers; and the other generated by a Local ESL student "community of practice" (CoP; Lave & Wenger, 1991) that was evident in each of the eight ESL classes I observed in the study.[6] The "joint enterprise" of this CoP, produced as Local ESL students "mutually engaged" in a "shared repertoire" of oppositional social practices (Wenger, 1998), was the subversion of the "official" cultural productions of the ESL student.

Mr. Day's ESL class

The interactions I analyse took place in a first-year "ESL-A" class, which I observed for 64 hours and audio-recorded for 29 hours over an academic year. This was a large, diverse class, attributable in part to a school policy that mandated that ESL course placements be determined by how long students had been enrolled at the school, rather than, for example, L2 English expertise. Thus, Mr. Day's class was for ESL students in their first year at Tradewinds, regardless of age, grade-level, formal schooling experience, or L2 proficiency. Significantly, despite the substantial differences in student backgrounds in this class, there was only one curriculum, which was centered on novels written for an L1-English audience of 2nd–6th graders. The interaction below concerns the "bookwork" assignments for one of these novels.

Participants

At the time of these interactions, Mr. Day was in his first year teaching at Tradewinds. An industrial arts instructor with no experience or education in teaching ESL, he had reluctantly agreed to teach the ESL-A class only days before the school year began. The two students in the interaction, Jennie and CJ, were both Local ESL students. Jennie, a 9th grader from Korea, had been in school in the US for 2.5 years; CJ, also a 9th grader, was from the Philippines and had lived in Hawai'i for 7 years. Also co-present were Computer, a Korean boy who had lived in the US for 6 years, and Iwannafuckalot (IwannaFAL), a 9th grader who had moved to Hawai'i from Vietnam when he was 5 years old and who was carrying the machine that recorded these interactions. I have argued elsewhere that each of these students was a member of the Local ESL CoP in this class, although Jennie's participation in it was more peripheral.

Analysis: "Work"ing it in ESL

The interactions occurred midway through the final quarter of the school year. Jennie, CJ, Computer, and IwannaFAL were among the approximately two-thirds of the students who had not brought to class their copies of *Sadako and the thousand paper cranes* (Coerr, 1977), an award-winning novel intended, according to the publisher's estimation (printed clearly on the cover), for readers in the 3rd–5th grades.

The lesson to this point had consisted of a 15-item cloze vocabulary quiz that students had been given 45 minutes to complete and a 21-item cloze grammar exercise on negative forms of "have to" (e.g., "1. He has to work late tonight. (does not have)"; Dixon, 1956, p. 34) that had been allotted 30 minutes. Students were then to have been "working ahead or behind" to complete one of a number of "bookwork" assignments from *Sadako*. Five minutes prior to this interaction, Mr. Day had specifically directed Jennie, IwannaFAL, CJ, and Computer to stop playing cards, as they had been, and to (finally) get to work on this "bookwork."

Excerpt 1, ELA42XmdS15: 1972–1996

```
01 Mr. Day:     Jennie where's your work.
02              (0.9)
03 Jennie:      I don't know.
04              (2.5)
05 Jennie:      I've been doing it.
06 Mr. Day:     ↑where's your book.
07              (1.1)
08 Jennie:      at home.
09              (2.0)
10 Mr. Day:     ↑what do you expect to do ↓in class.
11 Jennie:      no[thing.
12(Computer):     [play.
13 Mr. Day:     and you think that's o↓kay.
```

14 (1.2)
15 Mr. Day: what do you do in your other classes.
16 (0.5)
17 (Computer): play.=
18 Jennie: =work.
19 Mr. Day: so how come in my class you don't ↓work.
20 (2.7)
21 Jennie: I did. I did the grammar (and the quiz).
22 (0.7)
23 Mr. Day: ↑yeah, I know, ↓but we're supposed to be
24 doing other works yae {yeah},[7] it's a long
25 period, ((states extended duration of
26 class session)).[8]
27 (0.6)
28 Mr. Day: you have to get bookwork done, class work,
29 all this type of stuff. you should be
30 reading the book, yae {yeah}.
31 (3.3)
32 Mr. Day: so you need to do five assignments.
33 (2.3)
34 Mr. Day: one vocabulary,(.) two summaries, (.) and
35 two ((sets of comprehension)) questions.
36 five assignments. on Tuesday ((i.e., next
37 class)). and bring your book.
38 (1.2) ((Mr. Day turns to address CJ,
39 sitting next to Jennie))
40 Mr. Day: so how are you=
41 CJ: =awesome.
42 Mr. Day: where's your folder?
43 (0.5)
44 CJ: I put it back there.
45 Mr. Day: did you do any work today?
46 CJ: yeah.
47 Mr. Day: (how much work?)
48 CJ: the:: (.) quiz?
49 Mr. Day: quiz? yeah you had to do the quiz. did you
50 finish the grammar?
51 (0.2)
52 (Computer): no.
53 CJ: no.
54 Mr. Day: did you do any bookwork?
55 (0.7)
56 CJ: my book is at home.
57 (0.5)
58 CJ: I do it at home.
60 (.)
61 Mr. Day: you bring your book to class everyday.
62 (1.6)
63 Mr. Day: fits in the pocket. real small. you put it
64 right here. ((gestures to a pocket on CJ's
65 backpack))

Lines 01–14: "Good teacher/bad student" version

In line 01, Mr. Day invokes his situational identity (Zimmerman, 1998) of teacher, making the standardized relational pair (SRP) of "teacher/student" relevant to the interaction. His question calls attention to an evident problem: that a student who 5 minutes earlier had been told to do "bookwork" has none on her desk, with the utterance thus implicative of a negative assessment. The silence in line 02 is attributable to Jennie, as the question in line 01 is both directed to her and has made conditionally relevant an account of not having "work" on her desk. This silence displays Jennie's orientation to her reply in line 03 as dispreferred (Pomerantz, 1984a), and thus projects potential disaffiliation with Mr. Day's question. Jennie's reply in line 03 is indeed nonaligning because it does not provide the information that the question seeks, even though such information would quite reasonably be available to her (cf. Pomerantz, 1984b). The absence of an account here, following "I don't know," is also disaffiliative, as accounts are the preferred or aligning action following a "no" answer or its equivalents (Ford, 2001). Jennie treats the line 04 delay as a lack of uptake by Mr. Day and thus an apparent rejection of her line 03 response as adequate (cf. Davidson, 1984), as she formulates (line 05) a "remedy pursuit" (Pomerantz, 1984b), revising the position she asserted in line 03 to "I've been doing it." The contrastive stress on "doing," however, also suggests she has oriented to the evaluatory implication in Mr. Day's question and is protesting it.

Excerpt 1a

```
01 Mr. Day:    Jennie where's your work.
02             (0.9)
03 Jennie:     I don't know.
04             (2.5)
05 Jennie:     I've been doing it.
06 Mr. Day:    ↑where's your book.
07             (1.1)
08 Jennie:     at home.
```

However, in line 06, Mr. Day again provides no uptake to Jennie's reply and instead makes relevant another apparent problem when he asks Jennie where her copy of *Sadako* is. Following the lengthy delay in line 07, another apparent display of disaffiliation, Jennie offers a second unelaborated disagreeing action, this time by minimally stating that her book is "at home." Jennie once again gives her answer as if no further account is needed. This is in contrast to the disapproval Mr. Day has displayed toward Jennie's actions, both by making relevant the absence of materials needed to carry out the "(book)work" he had earlier assigned, and his lack of uptake to Jennie's "answers" about it.

From the first few lines in this extract, Mr. Day has constructed a particular "version" (Cuff, 1993) of the SRP "teacher/student." Included among the predicates constituting the teacher category are the rights, obligations, and competencies that warrant the category bound activities (CBAs) of assigning "work" to students, monitoring classroom performance, making assessments about that performance, and if deemed problematic, requesting accounts to pursue some form of remedy. Mr. Day has tied to the student category the implied CBAs of following the teacher's instructions and doing whatever work has been assigned; specifically, here, bookwork, which necessarily entails reading the book.[9] That both of these CBAs are implied by the absence of the materials needed to carry them out implies a negative evaluation of this absence and by extension, the person responsible for it. Thus, in addition to demonstrating Mr. Day's association of these CBAs to the "student" category, the questions in lines 01 and 06 also embed two morally-qualified versions of it: a (default) "good student" category for those who are reading their books and doing bookwork, and a "bad student" category for those who are not.[10] Of these two categories, Mr. Day is evidently constructing Jennie as an incumbent of the latter, and at the same time, formulating a moral construction of himself as a "good teacher," rightly engaging in the CBAs he has attached to the "teacher" category (cf. Baker, 2004). Jennie, for her part, has displayed a disaffiliative stance to this point, with delay-prefaced turns, evasive answers, and an absence of elaborating accounts. She has, in other words, displayed nonalignment with Mr. Day's actions that is *consistent* with his candidate categorization of her as a "bad student": she apparently refuses to orient to the problematicity that Mr. Day has implied of her actions.

Excerpt 1b

```
06 Mr. Day:      ↑where's your book.
07               (1.1)
08 Jennie:       at home.
09               (2.0)
10 Mr. Day:      ↑what do you expect to do ↓in class.
11 Jennie:       no[thing.
12(Computer):      [play.
```

The emergent dispute becomes more explicit in the next series of turns as Mr. Day intensifies his challenge of Jennie's actions with the question, "↑what do you expect to do ↓in class." This question appears to be a "*wh*-question challenge" (Koshik, 2003), a class of "reversed polarity questions" (RPQ) also known as rhetorical questions. *Wh*-question challenges are formatted as *wh*-questions but do not make answers relevant because they are implicative of a challenge to a prior utterance, generally in talk characterized by disagreement. These questions are often used disaffiliatively and "are able to do challenging because, rather than asking for new information, they are used to convey a strong epistemic stance of the questioner, specifically a negative assertion... [about] the utterances they challenge" (p. 68).

A case can be made for the candidacy of Mr. Day's question as a *wh*-question challenge. The talk to this point has been characterized by conflict, with Mr. Day indexing an affective stance of disapproval about Jennie's violation of the predicates he has attached to the "good student" category, violations which centrally figure in his developing categorization of her as a "bad student." The extended, 2-s pause that prefaces Mr. Day's question, its intensified pitch and intonational contour, and the contrastive locational formulation (Schegloff, 1972) of "↓in class" (line 10) with "at home" (line 08) also signal disapproval of Jennie's unelaborated answer in line 08. With her book "at home," and her ability to do the required CBAs constituting the "good student" category "in class" thus compromised, Mr. Day ups the interactional ante by challenging Jennie about what she expects to do there.

Despite the evidence that Mr. Day has formulated his utterance in line 10 as a *wh*-question challenge, Jennie does not appear to treat it as one. As Koshik (2003; see also 2002) points out, although answers to *wh*-question challenges are not necessarily relevant, they can be given. However, Koshik continues, answers to candidate *wh*-question challenges must be in terms that display the answerer's orientation to the implied negative assertion, the epistemic stance of the questioner, and to the question as "doing a challenge" (2003, pp. 57, 68). That is clearly not the case with Jennie's line 11 reply, "nothing." In fact, this answer is precisely the "negative assertion" that the question in line 10 implies. However, regardless of whether Jennie treats the question as a challenge or as information-seeking, her answer is disaffiliative: "nothing" is hardly an aligning response from a student to a teacher in a classroom where students are expected to be doing classwork, particularly when "doing nothing" (as implied by an absence of bookwork) has just been characterized as problematic. Through this answer, Jennie further exhibits her disaffiliative stance toward the "good student" category that Mr. Day has implied is desirable, and displays alignment with her incumbency as a "bad student."

I have attributed the overlapped utterance of "play" in line 12 to Computer.[11] Mr. Day and Jennie do not orient to this utterance, which suggests that they treat it as irrelevant. Regardless, "play" works as an important denotative counterpoint to Jennie's "nothing." As I discuss below, it also signals the co-presence to this interaction of other Local ESL students: IwannaFAL (carrying the recorder), who moments earlier had himself been queried by Mr. Day about what he was (not) doing; CJ, who was sitting next to Jennie and is similarly questioned by Mr. Day moments later (see lines 40 on); and possibly, Computer, whose *sotto voce* asides are interspersed (though apparently ignored) throughout this extract.

Excerpt 1c

```
10 Mr. Day:    ↑what do you expect to do ↓in class.
11 Jennie:     no[thing.
```

```
(Computer):    [play.
Mr. Day:      and you think that's o↓kay.
              (1.2)
```

In line 13, Mr. Day utters another RPQ, this one formatted as a yes-no question: "and you think that's o↓kay." "That" refers anaphorically to Jennie's answer in line 11; given the context and the sequential position of the question, the polarity of the question is clearly reversed. Thus, the negative assertions implied in this question and the preceding *wh*-question challenge "formulate a failure" on the part of the student and can thus "be heard as a complaint" (Koshik, 2002, p. 1863). Further, this question is prefaced by the conjunction "and," which as Heritage and Sorjonen (1994, p. 5) have detailed, "play[s] a role in constituting and sustaining a joint orientation to the larger activity-focused courses of action which [such 'and-prefaced'] questions implement." Interestingly, Mr. Day's intonation here falls, too, when more commonly it rises for yes-no questions, even when their polarity is reversed (Koshik, 2002). This may be an example of Mr. Day accommodating to Pidgin, which he increasingly did over the course of the year,[12] though it may also have been a falling intonational contour in standardized English, which would signal stronger expectation regarding the anticipated answer (Celce-Murcia, Brinton, & Goodwin, 1996, p. 202). With this question, Mr. Day continues to challenge Jennie about her nonaligning classroom behavior and her disaffiliative stance toward it.

However, rather than reply, Jennie remains silent throughout the 1.2-s pause in line 14. Koshik (2002) has noted that the preferred response to a reversed polarity yes-no question would, in contrast to non-RPQs, be "no" or its equivalents. Thus, Jennie's lack of response here is somewhat ambiguous: it could, on the one hand, be a "no equivalent" and thus be an aligning move. However, and perhaps more likely given the trajectory of the interaction to this point (also see line 18), it could also be another display of Jennie's nonalignment to the negative assertion implied in Mr. Day's RPQs.

Lines 15–20: "Good student/bad teacher" version

Mr. Day appears to treat the silence in line 14 as Jennie's and as a nonaligning nonresponse because he continues in line 15 to pursue elaboration about her apparent alignment with the "bad student" category. With this next question ("what do you do in your other classes."), Mr. Day invokes another contrastive locational category, now making relevant what Jennie does in her "other," that is, mainstream and content-based ESL classes, versus what she does (not do) in his dedicated-ESL class. This allows for a concomitant "category contrast" (Hester, 1998), with the morally-qualified categories of "good/bad student" discussed to this point now delimited to *Mr. Day's ESL class* (i.e., "good/bad student in ESL class"), which thus opens up the possibility for a *new* teacher/student SRP version specific to "other classes." Sequentially, the opportunity for such a formulation falls to Jennie, placing her in a delicate position since Mr. Day has now projected at least two new candidate categories that her answer must somehow respond to: "good student in other classes" and "bad student in other classes." This latter category in fact implies a sort of *über* "bad student in *all* classes" category and is arguably the candidate categorization Mr. Day is pursuing: "good student in other classes" would conflict with the categorization of Jennie as a "bad student in ESL class." This conflict would be consequential—and accountable—because it would raise questions about her "bad" performance in ESL.

Excerpt 1d

```
13 Mr. Day:      and you think that's o↓kay.
14               (1.2)
15 Mr. Day:      what do you do in your other classes.
16               (0.5)
17(Computer):    play.=
18 Jennie:       =work.
19 Mr. Day:      so how come in my class you don't ↓work.
20               (2.7)
```

Following Mr. Day's question in line 15, a 0.5-s pause occurs, then "play" is repeated, an utterance I have also attributed to Computer. As in its first voicing, it is *sotto voce* here and is not oriented to by either Jennie (cf. the latching and contrasted content of her reply) or Mr. Day (cf. line 19). As well, the answer "play" is consistent with and corresponds to the "bad student" category that Mr. Day initially formulated: "bad students" do not have their work out, have left their books at home, and so must either be doing "nothing" (Jennie) or "playing" (Computer) during class time. Although consistent with the original "bad student" category, however, the activity "play" here follows the category contrast made relevant in line 15, and so binds to the *new* "bad student" category specific to "other classes." In other words, Computer's utterance in line 17 implies precisely the candidate categorization of Jennie as a "bad student in all classes" that Mr. Day appears to be pursuing with his question in line 15.

Significantly, however, Jennie rejects this categorization, indicating instead her incumbency as a "good student in other classes" when she states that she does not "play" in them but does "work." Including the 0.5-s pause in line 16 and the unoriented-to utterance in line 17, a 0.9-s pause occurs between the completion of Mr. Day's question in line 15 and Jennie's answer in line 18, indicating Jennie's likely orientation to her answer as nonaligning. Significantly, by maintaining that she "works" in other classes, she has suddenly and remarkably shifted the "problem" of doing "nothing" in ESL from herself to the *ESL class*. That is, any inference that Jennie is "deficient" is transformed in line 18 as she implicates instead

- *the activity of "work"* as it is differentially realized in "other classes" versus ESL and/or
- *the contexts themselves* that allow for the generation of the contextually specific category (and predicate) iterations of "student in ESL class" and "student in other classes."

Both points suggest that Jennie's actions to this point are indexes of resistance to her categorization as a "good student in ESL class," to the desirability imputed to the category, and to the activities that are bound to it (cf. Day, 1998). Further, by shifting the problem of doing "nothing" from herself to the ESL class, Jennie makes relevant at least two other candidate sources of that problem:

- *Mr. Day*, who as a member of the "teacher" category mediates the instantiation of social structures, ideologies, and beliefs about ESL as codified, for example, in policy and curriculum, through his own particular pedagogical practices (first bullet above),
- *ESL* as a class, a program, or an institution (second bullet above).

For the first point, Jennie has implied a new morally-qualified SRP version of "good *student*/bad *teacher*," the latter of which Mr. Day is an obvious incumbent. For the second point, she has implied that no matter the teacher, something about ESL "work"—specifically the bookwork she is to be doing currently—would lead her instead to do "nothing." All of this speaks to the power that Jennie has claimed, as it was made available sequentially by Mr. Day's question in line 15, both to subvert her candidate categorization as a "bad student in all classes," and instead implicate alternative trouble sources, either in terms of a new "bad teacher" category, or ESL itself as an institutional or programmatic category.

Excerpt 1e

```
(Computer): play.=
Jennie:     =work.
Mr. Day:    so how come in my class you don't ↓work.
            (2.7)
Jennie:     I did. I did the grammar (and the quiz).
            (0.7)
Mr. Day:    ↑yeah, I know, ↓but we're supposed to be
            doing other works yae {yeah},[7] it's a long
            period, ((states extended duration of
            class session)).[8]
            (0.6)
Mr. Day:    you have to get bookwork done, class work,
            all this type of stuff. you should be
            reading the book, yae {yeah}.
            (3.3)
Mr. Day:    so you need to do five assignments.
            (2.3)
```

Mr. Day: one vocabulary,(.) two summaries, (.) and
two ((sets of comprehension)) questions.
five assignments. on Tuesday ((i.e., next
class)). and bring your book.

In line 19, Mr. Day pursues an account from Jennie about working in other classes, but not in ESL: "so how come in my class you don't ↓work." Whereas in line 10, he queried Jennie about what she expected to do "in class," here, following the contrast made relevant in line 15, he introduces the determiner "my": it is no longer a generic class, it is Mr. Day's. This also suggests he has oriented to the implication that Jennie not doing work in ESL is attributable not to her but to the class or perhaps even him. Significantly, this question also includes an expansion in Jennie's accountable "bad student in ESL class" behavior: whereas at the beginning of the interaction, Mr. Day was pursuing an account concerning a specific instance of Jennie doing "nothing," the accountable topic has morphed, as evident in the question's habitual-factual present tense format, into Jennie *never* working in his class. I consider the implications of this next.

Lines 21–64: "Friendly, facilitative teacher/forgetful student" version

Jennie remains silent throughout the extended, 2.7-s pause in line 20. When she does finally reply, she does not provide the account that Mr. Day seeks, but instead orients to and rejects the underlying expansion in accountable behavior that the question encompasses: instead of never working in the ESL class, she states, "I did. I did the grammar (and the quiz)." This reply returns Jennie to her earlier asserted position (line 05) that she has in fact done "work" in Mr. Day's class. Thus, the protest that was implied there is here resumed: Jennie appears to be resisting her incumbency as a "bad student in ESL class" after all.

Or is she? Jennie's "nonanswer" in line 21 is, on closer analysis, a highly skilled piece of interactional work. By rejecting the underlying expansion of "bad student" behavior in Mr. Day's line 19 question, Jennie is not only released from having to account for it, but the accountable topic is returned to the more narrowly circumscribed matter of what she was doing earlier. What is of significance here is which particular earlier period is being referenced.

Excerpt 1f

Mr. Day: Jennie where's your work.
(0.9)
Jennie: I don't know.
(2.5)
Jennie: I've been doing it.
Mr. Day: ↑where's your book.
(1.1)
Jennie: at home.

(2.0)
Mr. Day: ↑what do you expect to do ↓in class.
Jennie: no[thing.
(Computer): [play.
Mr. Day: and you think that's o↓kay.
(1.2)
Mr. Day: what do you do in your other classes.
(0.5)
(Computer): play.=
Jennie: =work.
Mr. Day: so how come in my class you don't ↓work.
(2.7)
Jennie: I did. I did the grammar (and the quiz).
(0.7)
Mr. Day: ↑yeah, I know, ↓but we're supposed to be
doing other works yae {yeah},[7] it's a long
period, ((states extended duration of
class session)).[8]

Returning momentarily to the beginning of the interaction, Mr. Day's line 01 question seeks an account about where Jennie's "work" is *now*, which is implicative of the bookwork she has been assigned that she is *not now doing*. However, Jennie exploits the referential ambiguity of "work" and instead implies the grammar exercise and vocabulary quiz (cf. the present perfect progressive in line 05), that is, the "work" assigned *earlier* in the class. In line 06, Mr. Day rejects this answer as acceptable for what Jennie is to be doing *now* though, evident in his lack of uptake and explicit query about the absence of her book. However, in line 21, Jennie effectively recycles the same account, with a much different result, as Mr. Day's affirmative response in line 23 indicates. This difference is attributable to the expansion of and thus, shift in accountable topic, from why Jennie is not doing bookwork *now* to why she does not do *any* work *ever*; this shift allows the same account to accomplish much different interactional and categorical business: it not only works to interrupt Mr. Day's candidate categorization of Jennie as a "bad student in ESL class" and to restore her incumbency as a "good student in ESL class," it interrupts *his* candidacy as a "bad teacher" because she indicates that she does some work that he assigns. Thus, Jennie's utterance in line 21 signals what the trouble source of her doing "nothing" apparently is: the children's bookwork. However, the shift in accountable topic removes from consideration the problematicity of the bookwork (because Jennie is "accounting" for a different topic), even though this was implicated as the accountable problem in the first place. It is ironic that Jennie recycles the very account that was in part constitutive of Mr. Day's earlier categorization of her as a "bad student in ESL class" to restore her incumbency as a "good student in ESL class," to implicate the bookwork rather than Mr. Day as the trouble source of doing "nothing," and perhaps most important, to remove from accountability the fact that she is *still* not doing the bookwork she is to be doing *now*.

Excerpt 1g

Jennie: I did. I did the grammar (and the quiz).
(0.7)
Mr. Day: ↑yeah, I know, ↓but we're supposed to be
doing other works yae {yeah},[7] it's a long
period, ((states extended duration of
class session)).[8]
(0.6)
Mr. Day: you have to get bookwork done, class work,
all this type of stuff. you should be
reading the book, yae {yeah}.
(3.3)
Mr. Day: so you need to do five assignments.
(2.3)
Mr. Day: one vocabulary, (.) two summaries, (.) and
two ((sets of comprehension)) questions.
five assignments. on Tuesday ((i.e., next
class)). and bring your book.
(1.2) ((Mr. Day turns to address CJ,
sitting next to Jennie))

Mr. Day's acceptance in line 23 of Jennie's account marks a distinct shift in the interaction, one attributable both to the initial candidacy of Jennie's "good student/bad teacher" SRP version and its subsequent termination as Mr. Day now formulates a new candidate SRP version of "friendly, facilitative teacher/forgetful student." In terms of the "friendly, facilitative teacher" category, his talk before this point was characterized by interactional features that displayed disapproval of Jennie's actions. Though similar features are still evident—for example, the higher pitch at the beginning of the turn in line 23, the directive in line 37—other, more aligning features are also present. Primary among them is his acceptance of an account he had previously rejected; beyond this, Mr. Day mentions (and extends) a list of CBAs Jennie should be engaged in for her to be considered a "good student in ESL class," two of which (the bookwork and reading) he indicated earlier she should have already been doing. These CBAs take form as mitigated directives (lines 23–24, 28–30, 32), with the latter two prefaced by an account ("it's a long period . . ."). Mr. Day uses the plural pronoun "we" in line 23, adds a colloquialism in line 29 ("all this type of stuff."), and does not hold Jennie accountable for her subsequent silences (lines 27, 31, 33, 38). A final indication that Mr. Day is "doing being" a different sort of teacher here from the one earlier comes with what I interpret to be his use of the Pidgin discourse marker *yae* [yeah], which as Sakoda and Siegel (2003, p. 92) assert, "soften[s] a comment."[13] In fact, Cashman (2005) and Gafaranga (2001, 2005) argue that codeswitches such as this (also see line 30; cf. the intonational contour in line 13) can be analyzed as membership categorization devices in their own right, with Mr. Day talking into relevance his membership in a new candidate category in which standardized English and Pidgin, the language of Local identity and culture, are spoken. However, Jennie provides no uptake to it.

Mr. Day's "friendly, facilitative teacher" is relationally constructed against a candidate "forgetful student" category that Jennie is made an incumbent of: this teacher, instead of reprimanding a student who has no work on her desk, now appears to interpret this absence as a manifestation of her having forgotten it. Thus, Mr. Day in lines 23–37 "reminds" Jennie of the work she is to be doing. Although I provide only a brief analysis of the remainder of the interaction between Mr. Day and CJ (lines 37–64), Mr. Day appears to maintain an orientation to this particular version of the teacher/student SRP, which has important interactional consequences for CJ, the student he addresses next.

Excerpt 1h

38		(1.2) ((Mr. Day turns to address CJ,
39		sitting next to Jennie))
40	Mr. Day:	so how are you=
41	CJ:	=awesome.
42	Mr. Day:	where's <u>you</u>r folder?
43		(0.5)
44	CJ:	I put it <u>ba</u>ck there.
45	Mr. Day:	did you do any work today?
46	CJ:	yeah.
47	Mr. Day:	(how much work?)
48	CJ:	the:: (.) quiz?
49	Mr. Day:	quiz? yeah you had to do the quiz. did you
50		finish the grammar?
51		(0.2)
52	(Computer):	no.
53	CJ:	no.
54	Mr. Day:	did you do any bookwork?
55		(0.7)
56	CJ:	my book is at home.
57		(0.5)
58	CJ:	I do it at home.
60		(.)
61	Mr. Day:	you bring your book to class everyday.
62		(1.6)
63	Mr. Day:	fits in the pocket. real small. you put it
64		right here. ((gestures to a pocket on CJ's
65		backpack))

CJ's and Jennie's actions have evident parallels in these interactions: like Jennie, CJ does not have any "work" on his desk. He has done no bookwork; the work he has done consists only of what was assigned earlier—in fact, he has done just one of those activities (the vocabulary quiz), not both (the quiz and the grammar); and his book is "at home." CJ also displays similar disaffiliation regarding the queries about his classroom performance, through delay-prefaced replies, minimal answers, and lack of accounts. Yet, although CJ has committed comparable violations of the "good student in ESL class" predicates that led to Jennie's earlier incumbency as a "bad student in ESL class," Mr. Day treats him differently, starting with how he greets him (line 40; cf. line 01). The differential treatment becomes particularly plain after Mr. Day pursues answers from CJ about the "work" he has (not) done in class (lines 45, 47, 49–50, 54). After CJ replies in line 53 with a delay-prefaced, unelaborated "no" to the question regarding the grammar assignment, Mr. Day utters no rejoinder or pursuit of elaboration. Instead, he continues by asking about the "bookwork" but with a different affective stance than with Jennie (cf. the higher pitch and stress of line 06).[14] When CJ replies in line 56 that his book is at home and provides a minimal elaboration, there is little in Mr. Day's talk approaching the strong disapproval he displayed earlier: there is no pursuit of an account, no RPQs, and little evidence of negative affect. In fact, Mr. Day's lone directive (line 60) is mitigated and formulated as a reminder: CJ needs to bring his book to class every day, and Mr. Day even helpfully points out where to carry it in his backpack. Thus, following Jennie's ultimate rejection of the initial SRP version of "good teacher/bad student" and the candidacy of her "good student/bad teacher" SRP version, the "friendly, facilitative teacher/forgetful student" SRP version prevails, despite CJ's disaffiliative interactional work. This is suggestive, certainly, of the power that categories have in shaping the trajectories of a given interaction; it also indicates that the power to make such category formulations does not necessarily fall along lines of institutionally-ascribed status.

"Motivating" the analysis

Next, I consider how the analysis above provides warrants for and elaborates several critically-oriented arguments in the larger study from which the data are drawn. My goal is not to provide an exhaustive account of these arguments or how the analysis above supports them but instead to point to ways that "applied M/CA" might benefit a critical/cultural studies analysis, and vice versa, how a critical/cultural studies perspective can amplify a sequential and categorization analysis. Note that although my claims concerning the scope of these phenomena (i.e., across the ESL program) cannot be supported by analysis of two interactions, M/CA helps to warrant these arguments by elaborating the interactional dynamics of (at least) two instances of their occasioning (cf. Moerman, 1988).

The cultural productions of the ESL student

As mentioned above, the study these data are drawn from concerns two competing "cultural productions of the ESL student." One I glossed as school-sanctioned or "official," manifest, for example, in ESL policy, curriculum, and instruction, which constructed ESL students as an undifferentiated group of cultural and linguistic newcomers. The other I called "oppositional," produced by Local ESL students as they variously resisted accommodating the production of this "official" student identity. Both productions are evident in the interactions between Jennie, CJ, and Mr. Day.

Perhaps the clearest way that the "official" cultural productions of the ESL student were instantiated in these interactions is in terms of the predicates that Mr. Day and the students bound to the "good student in ESL class" category, which Jennie's ("bad") behavior was evaluated against. This was a student who brought his or her work to class, completed the grammar and vocabulary exercises, and did the bookwork associated with the children's novels that formed the centerpiece of the ESL curriculum. More to the point, this was a student who accommodated the language (learning) ideologies about ESL and ESL students as determined most immediately by the teacher[15] but also the ESL program and the high school. These beliefs were variously instantiated, from the undifferentiated ESL curriculum and the ESL placement policy, which implied that ESL students were more or less the same, to the use of below-grade-level juvenile fiction, which signified an evident conflation of L2 proficiency with cognitive capacity and chronological age as it essentially positioned ESL students as co-members of *Sadako*'s 3rd–5th grade audience.

Just as students who brought their books and did bookwork produced the "good student in ESL class" category and their memberships in it, not bringing books and not doing bookwork served as important resources in students' resistance to it. By refusing to accommodate the production of the "good student in ESL class" category, Jennie indexed her lack of "investment" (Norton, 2000) in the class, signaling that the range of symbolic and material resources made available for learning did not have and would not contribute to the sorts of cultural, linguistic, and symbolic capital she desired or needed (Bourdieu, 1991). Thus, predicate violations of the "good student in ESL class" underscored the fundamentality of student agency and power in classroom processes as well as the limits of the power of the institution: that the material and symbolic manifestations of educational, societal, and language ideologies about ESL education and ESL students required for their realization these students' participation.

At the same time, withdrawal of participation from these predicates and the occasionally direct conflict between the teachers and students that resulted from it meant that Local ESL students at Tradewinds who engaged in opposition were often ascribed incumbency as "bad students in ESL class." My data indicate that although Local ESL students would at times align with their incumbency in this category (cf. Jennie in lines 01–14 above), most often they would signal that they were not lacking, but the ESL teacher and/or program was instead lacking (cf. lines 18–20 above). Thus, as the data above suggest, Local ESL students' cultural productions of the ESL student involved delicate interactional work in at least three senses: in terms of violating predicates associated with the production of the "good student in ESL class" category, in terms of explaining and justifying these violations, and in terms of casting the ESL teacher or program as deficient rather than the students themselves. Such work was made all the more delicate because it occurred within a setting that cast them as members of a category ("student") that was ascribed less institutional power and fewer rights, privileges, and competencies than teachers.

Local ESL students' exercise of power in their oppositional cultural productions of the ESL student thus involved considerable L2 interactional competence (J. K. Hall, 1995, 1999). This is indicated in the interaction above, in Jennie's (and later, CJ's) exploitation of the ambiguity of "work." Data from the larger study (Talmy, 2005) include scores of instances in which Local ESL students similarly exploited some imprecision in talk, from referential shifts such as Jennie's, to uptake to locutionary rather than illocutionary meanings of utterances (and vice versa), to recourse to the students' status as L2 speakers, in which the potential omnirelevance for "misunderstanding" (e.g., of a teacher's instructions) was made use of. Each of these communicative practices allowed for what I call "defensible fall-back accounts" such as Jennie's in lines 05 and 21 and CJ's in lines 46 and 48, whereby Local ESL students could "justify" their resistance and nonaligning actions by pointing to some evidence for their potential alignment: for example, by doing one aspect of an assignment and/ or indicating that they would have done more had they simply understood the instructions to do it.

When considered together, the Local ESL students' cultural productions of the ESL student indicate that these students were not so much "bad students in ESL class" as fundamentally *different kinds of students* in ESL class. These were students who signaled in myriad ways, in their classroom behavior, in their interactions with classmates, teachers, and me, and in their schoolwork, that they did not like ESL, did not need ESL, were aware of the low prestige associated with the category, and had the L2 English expertise required to make this clear, either indirectly (e.g., in terms of justifying nonaligning behavior) or directly (e.g., in explicitly stating their negative assessments of ESL). In this respect, then, the public displays of difference that constituted Local ESL students' oppositional cultural productions of the ESL student worked to *disrupt* the monolithic homogeneity connoted by the "official" productions of ESL. At the same time, however, these public displays wound up *reproducing* the negative ideologies about ESL that constituted the stigma of the category "ESL student."

Contingency and multidirectionality in L2 socializing processes
Related to these competing cultural productions of the ESL student, the analysis above warrants and elaborates arguments that I have made concerning contingency and multidirectionality in L2 language socialization (LS) (see Talmy, 2008). Although LS is commonly asserted to be contingent and "bidirectional" (see, e.g., Garrett & Baquedano-López, 2002; Schieffelin & Ochs, 1986), the focus in much LS research on "successful" first language socialization of children by caregivers has, according to some scholars, obscured these themes.

However, the fundamental contingency of LS is clearly exemplified above in terms of the (lack of) accommodation of the "official" ESL student category. Mr. Day, Jennie, and CJ orient to a network of "good student in ESL class" predicates, some of which the two students participated in and several others of which they did not. By indicating that they had done the earlier-assigned vocabulary quiz (Jennie and CJ) and grammar exercise (Jennie), the official version of the category appears to have been at least partially accommodated. However, completion of such comparatively "simple" work as cloze vocabulary and grammar exercises and similar sorts of worksheet assignments served as important resources for the production of the "defensible fall-back accounts" mentioned earlier. Thus, although the official ESL student category appears to be partially accommodated, it was less accommodated than transformed, becoming a constitutive feature in Jennie's and CJ's oppositional cultural productions of the ESL student. Jennie's and CJ's actions above, in short, highlight how contested socialization can be (i.e., in terms of the categorical ascription of "ESL student"; cf. Day, 1998): that it never proceeds straightforwardly or linearly along lines, for example, of hierarchical standing.

Multidirectionality in socialization is exemplified above as well. Jennie's cultural productions of the ESL student were in part constitutive of the broad-based Local ESL CoP in the high school's ESL program mentioned above. In this respect, Jennie's actions are of interest because she was a comparative apprentice in the Local ESL CoP, while CJ, IwannaFAL, and Computer were all "oldtimers." Keeping in mind the co-presence of these latter three students to the interaction, Jennie's performance in it can be seen not only in terms of her participating in Local ESL community practices but also as an instance of a Local ESL apprentice demonstrating her developing L2 interactional competence and oppositional identity to oldtimer peers. Thus, Jennie's participation in the interaction above, and CJ's as well, not only served to (re)produce the Local ESL CoP but worked as socializing resources for each other, Mr. Day, IwannaFAL, Computer, and any other students who were proximate to it.

Multidirectionality in socialization is also suggested in terms of Mr. Day's actions above. Whereas I have argued that Jennie and CJ ultimately did not accommodate the official cultural productions of the ESL student, Mr. Day arguably accommodated theirs. This is most clearly indicated in Mr. Day's acceptance of Jennie's account in line 21, which he had previously (line 06) rejected. It is also suggested in the aligning interactional features and codeswitches in lines 23–37, which were constitutive of the new "friendly, facilitative teacher/forgetful student" SRP version, a version Mr. Day remained oriented to as the interaction with CJ unfolded.

When considered in the wider context not just of this particular class session, but of the course as a whole, the interaction above signals multidirectionality in socialization of much broader significance. The interaction occurred during a "study hall" session, in which students were to be "working ahead or behind" on coursework that had previously been or would soon be assigned. As increasing numbers of Local ESL students withdrew participation in the predicates attached to the production of the "good student in ESL class" category—for example, by not completing the bookwork, leaving materials "at home," and doing only a minimum of the simplest assignments (cf. the vocabulary quiz and grammar exercise above)—first-year ESL teachers such as Mr. Day made adjustments to their curricula and teaching practice. These adjustments included extending deadlines, reducing the amount of and requirements for assignments, eliminating homework, and adding study hall sessions such as this one (see Talmy, 2005, pp. 534–585; 2008).[16] This had important implications for what was and was not made available for learning in these classes: as the official curriculum slowed down and became increasingly restricted, a space in the formal schooling enterprise opened up, which allowed the development of an "unofficial" curriculum, in part constituted by and constitutive of Local ESL community practices.

ESL as a low-prestige category

The M/CA analysis also warrants arguments I have made (Talmy, 2005, 2008, forthcoming) regarding the (re)production of "ESL student" as a low-prestige identity category. The comparatively few applied linguistics studies that concern K–12 ESL as an institution in North America have overwhelmingly asserted the status of ESL as a "dummy program" (McKay & Wong, 1996, p. 586), with ESL students deemed in various ways to be "candidate[s] for cognitive overhaul and rescue" (p. 590). Much of this research has usefully located the stigma of ESL in broader discourses and social processes, for example, in terms of contemporary language and educational policies that reflect a monolingual English bias, in negative social attitudes toward minority languages and their speakers, in popular discourses concerning the putative "problems" that result from bi- and multilingualism, in linguistic nationalism, linguistic prejudice, and more. However, equally important is seeing how these broader phenomena are or are not (re)produced in the details of everyday life, for example, in classroom interactional conduct.

The analysis above thus complements arguments concerning the stigma of ESL by examining instances of its local occasioning. These include, certainly, the assignment and expectation for completion of the children's bookwork and the vocabulary and grammar worksheets, that is, the "work" around which the interaction between Jennie, CJ, and Mr. Day centered. They also include Jennie's orientation toward the nonproblematicity of her incumbency as a "bad student in ESL class." They include, too, the contrast she made between doing "nothing" in ESL class and doing "work" in "other classes," an activity contrast that suggests a category contrast between "student in ESL class" and "student in other classes." In fact, this category contrast makes relevant what I have characterized as a "mainstream/ESL hierarchy" in evidence at Tradewinds, both in and outside of the ESL program (Talmy, 2005, 2008, forthcoming). "Mainstream student" at Tradewinds, was, as its appellation connotes, indicative of the category's normative status in the social universe of the high school; conversely, "ESL student" was "marked" (Bucholtz & K. Hall, 2004), relationally defined by how it diverged from the "mainstream" norm. As Jennie's turns in line 11 ("Nothing.") and line 18 ("Work.") suggest, "ESL" was located in a hierarchically subordinate position to "mainstream"; in this respect, Jennie oriented to and reproduced this hierarchical relation. Each of these points—the conflict concerning "work," the comparative nonproblematicity of a candidate categorization as a "bad student in ESL class," the category contrast that made reference to wider linguistic prejudice as manifest in the mainstream/ESL hierarchy—illustrates in different ways how the low prestige of ESL was collaboratively achieved in these interactions.

The analysis above has implications beyond the cultural reproduction of the stigma of ESL. An estimated 20% of secondary ESL students have missed at least 2 years of formal schooling, while 27% are acknowledged to be enrolled in grade levels 2 years or more below age/grade-level norms (Fleischman & Hopstock, 1993). In addition, secondary ESL students are among the most likely school-age populations to drop out and/or be "pushed out" from school, with rates ranging from twice the national average for selected groups in the US (Ruiz de Velasco, Fix, & Clewell, 2000) to a staggering 74% of ESL students at one large urban school in Canada (Watt & Roessingh, 2001). Considering that ESL students as a group are far more likely than non-ESL students to come from families living in poverty (by some estimates, as high as 75%; August & Hakuta, 1997), the social reproductive potentiality of the cultural productions of the ESL student at Tradewinds becomes apparent. Although the analysis above is limited in that it considers two interactions in one ESL class at one school only, it does provide some indication why the alarming numbers cited above just might be. As uninvested students such as Jennie, CJ, and other members of the Local ESL CoP in Mr. Day's and other ESL classes subtly disengaged from "official" L2 literacy and academic language learning, even of the restricted kind associated with the bookwork assignments, little official curricular business beyond grammar and vocabulary worksheets came to be done in these classes over the course of a school year. As a result, ESL became precisely the easy, academically inconsequential program that Local ESL students all along claimed to dislike about it. What is more, many of these students remained, in the words of IwannaFAL, "stuck" in the program, even as they undermined it, caught in a cycle of diminishing academic achievement and declining grades; they thus continued to be denied access to language and literacy practices, and subject-area content, that was made available to their "mainstream" peers.

Finally, the analysis above can be seen as a (small) step toward interrupting this social reproductive potentiality, in part because it sheds light on curriculum and classroom processes in a context (high school ESL) and involving a population (Local ESL or generation-1.5 ESL students) that remain notably underrepresented in the research literature. Regarding the former point, Faltis (1999) has cogently argued that a continued lack of empirical attention to secondary ESL will only contribute to the reproduction of an inequitable status quo: when we ignore "what is happening in secondary schools where there are immigrant and bilingual students, the school benefits by our silence" (p. 4). This study is one attempt to break such silence so that the students might "benefit" instead. This leads to the latter point: the M/CA analysis has provided evidence to support the primarily anecdotal reports in the research literature about ways that generation-1.5 ESL students differ from their lower-L2-proficient and newcomer classmates: for example, in terms of their advanced L2 interactional competence, their generally negative representations about ESL, and their evident affiliations with mainstream (and in this instance, Local) communities beyond ESL. In addition to developing researchers' and educators' understandings of these students, the analysis above thus provides an empirical base upon which curricular and pedagogical recommendations for them can be made. Such recommendations might include developing specialized curricula that utilize as a resource what these students bring to school: for example, that make use of their L2 interactional competence for the development of metalinguistic awareness and for their apprenticeship into academic literacies; that centrally address issues implicated by their negative assessments about ESL, about the status of the category "ESL student" in a North American high school, and about linguistic prejudice as a frequently unexamined form of discrimination; in short, curricula that are specifically designed with these students' diverse needs, interests, affiliations, and experiences in mind (see also Harklau et al., 1999). These are, of course, tentative recommendations; much more research concerning this context and population is needed. I hope to have made a case for including in this research endeavor studies (critical and otherwise) that closely examine the details of talk-in-interaction.

Conclusion

In this chapter, I have analyzed categories and sequence to explicate a "motivated" analysis of interaction that occurred between Local ESL (generation-1.5) high school students and their teacher. I have argued that although many critical researchers eschew M/CA as being incompatible with a critical agenda, M/CA can in fact powerfully substantiate and elaborate a critical analysis of discourse. As the analysis of the interaction between Mr. Day, Jennie, and CJ suggests, M/CA can work to ground and expand claims that are made in a critical analysis of discourse, thereby addressing criticisms about analytic accountability and warrantability of assertions in critically-situated empirical research. Attention to sequential organization and membership categorization also expands methodological options for a critical analytic repertoire, yielding rich and novel insights into precisely those matters of most consequence to a critical agenda. Indeed, M/CA can expand the *critical* agenda itself as these approaches provide the analytic frame and methodological means to investigate how racism, sexism, classism, homophobia, heterosexism, and ageism are variously instantiated, resisted, accommodated, reproduced, and/or transformed in the unfolding details of everyday life, that is, how power is interactionally achieved rather than an *a priori* given or foregone conclusion.

Analyses of sequence and categorization do not simply benefit critical discourse studies; sequential and categorization analyses are benefited from being critically situated as well. As many critics of M/CA have argued, such analyses can seem overly "micro," leaving robust, if technical analyses of the structures of talk that add little to understandings of how talk may or may not relate to matters of social justice, inequality, or hegemony as they pertain to race, class, gender, age, and sexuality. In other words, critically situating sequential and categorization analyses expands and enriches the potential for empirically-grounded, theoretically-driven answers to the "why this now" question that guides ethnomethodological research, beyond the so-called "naïve epistemology" of ethnomethodology to, in this instance, a poststructuralist critical theoretical framework. As Kitzinger (2000) argues, critical researchers should not reject CA based solely on prior work that has not addressed issues of inequality and oppression to the extent they believe is necessary. Instead, she challenges them to investigate for themselves its utility in (further) grounding such analyses. In doing so, she joins with Schegloff (1999b, p. 563), who argues, somewhat exasperatedly, that "those committed to analyzing forms of inequality and oppression in interaction might do better to harness [CA]...as a *resource* for their undertaking than to complain of it as an ideological distraction" (emphasis in original). In this respect, and as I hope to have demonstrated in this paper, M/CA can work as a powerful methodological support to critical researchers interested in explicating cultural production and the potentialities of social reproduction in the micropolitics of social interaction.

Acknowledgements
The research reported in this article was supported by the Spencer Foundation and The International Research Foundation (formerly, TESOL International Research Foundation). I am grateful for this support and for comments made on the earlier draft of this paper by the editors and two anonymous reviewers. The views expressed and any remaining errors are my own.

Notes

1 This critique is commonly made of all kinds of critical research, including, and of relevance to this paper, critical ethnography (see, e.g., Hammersley, 2000). It can thus be seen as part of a broader rift between ostensibly "value-free" forms of empirical research and those that are "politically motivated" in some way. This paper should in no way be construed as an argument for the former position.

2 The names of the school and the research participants have been changed; the students chose their own pseudonyms.

3 By "critical/cultural studies," I refer broadly to poststructuralist critical theories common in contemporary cultural studies (see, e.g., S. Hall, 1996a, 1996b; Williams, 1977) and critical applied linguistics (Pennycook, 2001, 2005).

4 "Local" (with a capital "L") is a widely known identity category in Hawai'i, and it refers to Asian/Pacific Islanders who were born and raised in the Islands (see Okamura, 1994). "Local ESL," an analyst's category, signifies those oldtimer ESL students at Tradewinds who displayed cultural knowledge of and affiliation with Local culture, cultural forms, and social practices, and the L2 interactional competence needed to participate in these social practices (see Talmy, 2008).

5 This latter criticism has also been made of CA by scholars in MCA. See Hester and Eglin (1997) and Watson (1997).

6 Note that my 2005 study did not use CA or MCA, nor did it make the arguments of this paper regarding the use of M/CA for critical discourse research.

7 Utterances in Pidgin (Hawai'i Creole), the Local language of Hawai'i, are transcribed using Odo orthography (Sakoda & Siegel, 2003) followed by an italicized English gloss in {curly brackets}.

8 Revealing the duration of this class session could compromise the confidentiality of the site (and participants).

9 Although in line 01 Mr. Day utters only "work," rather than "bookwork," in line 06 he refers to Jennie's "book," implying that to do "work" Jennie needs her "book." Also, as mentioned above, as recently as 5 minutes before this interaction, Mr. Day had

specifically told Jennie, IwannaFAL, CJ, and Computer that they were to be doing "bookwork," just as he iterates to Jennie in line 28 and CJ in line 54.

10 "Good" and "bad" here are meant in terms of moral assessments that indicate "how [participants] might be assessing and thereby specifying the incumbents of the general categories contained in [a 'base'] SRP" of "teacher/student" (Cuff, 1993, p. 53). By "bad student," I do not necessarily mean a student who earns poor grades, but rather, one who does not engage in the CBAs locally bound to the "good student" category. This is a category that can be heard as collecting activities that the latter one would not; that is, incumbents of it would not be accommodating the "official" cultural productions of the ESL student.

11 Although I cannot be sure that Computer is responsible for the utterances in lines 12, 17, and 52, he was sitting nearby; also, the comments in these turns are consistent with those that he often made in class (when he was not asleep).

12 Whereas the intonational contour for yes/no questions in standardized English generally rises, with questions ending on a high pitch, in Pidgin it falls, with questions ending on a low pitch (Sakoda & Siegel, 2003, p. 30).

13 Confirming whether this is a switch to Pidgin is impossible because this feature could be acrolectal Pidgin or standardized English, and neither Jennie nor Mr. Day orient to it either way. However, based on my observations, I believe that this is evidence of Mr. Day's (language) socialization (see below).

14 CJ seems to attempt to exploit the ambiguity of "work" here as Jennie did earlier. By inquiring specifically about "bookwork" (cf. line 06), Mr. Day appears to have oriented both to this referential ambiguity and the attempt to make use of it.

15 By speaking of Mr. Day's role in instantiating the "official" productions of ESL, I do not implicate him personally but consider ways that social structures regulating ESL students, ESL learning, and the Tradewinds ESL program were realized (or not) through his orientations toward them and situated actions as a member and agent of the "ESL teacher" category. Implicating Mr. Day personally would presume a radically individualist perspective on social action, with agents divorced from context and agency synonymous with "free will" (Ahearn, 2001). This would locate the sources and consequences of social action squarely in the teacher, which would not only be unfair to Mr. Day but would reduce any analysis to, for example, finding fault with or valorizing his conduct. Such a theoretically impoverished accounting of these data would deny inquiry into precisely those matters of most concern in a critical analysis.

16 Note that with the exception of the vocabulary quizzes, the list of assignments that Mr. Day mentions in lines 32–37 represents the *full number* of bookwork assignments that had been given in this quarter. At the time of this interaction, neither Jennie nor CJ (nor several other Local ESL students) had done any of them.

References

Ahearn, L. M. (2001). Language and agency. *Annual Review of Anthropology, 30*, 109–137.

August, D., & Hakuta, K. (1997). *Improving schooling for language-minority children: A research agenda.* Washington, DC: National Academy Press.

Baker, C. (2004). Membership categorization and interview accounts. In D. Silverman (Ed.), *Qualitative research: Theory, method, and practice* (2nd ed.), (pp. 162–176). London: Sage.

Barker, C., & Galasiński, D. (2001). *Cultural studies and discourse analysis.* London: Sage.

Billig, M. (1997). From codes to utterances: Cultural studies, discourse, and psychology. In M. Ferguson & P. Golding (Eds.), *Cultural studies in question* (pp. 205–226). London: Sage.

Billig, M. (1999a). Conversation analysis and the claims of naivety. *Discourse & Society, 10*, 572–576.

Billig, M. (1999b). Whose terms? Whose ordinariness? Rhetoric and ideology in conversation analysis. *Discourse & Society, 10*, 543–558.

Blommaert, J. (2005). *Discourse: A critical introduction.* Cambridge, UK: Cambridge University Press.

Bourdieu, P. (1991). *Language and symbolic power* (G. Raymond & M. Adamson, Trans.). Cambridge, MA: Harvard University Press.

Bucholtz, M., & Hall, K. (2004). Language and identity. In A. Duranti (Ed.), *Companion to linguistic anthropology* (pp. 369–394). Malden, MA: Blackwell.

Cameron, D. (2005). Language, gender, and sexuality: Current issues and new directions. *Applied Linguistics, 26*, 482–502.

Carroll, D. (2000). Precision timing in novice-to-novice L2 conversations. *Issues in Applied Linguistics, 11*(1), 67–110.)

Cashman, H. (2005). Identities at play: Language preference and group membership in bilingual talk in interaction. *Journal of Pragmatics, 37*, 301–315.

Celce-Murcia, M., Brinton, D. M., & Goodwin, J. M. (1996). *Teaching pronunciation: A reference for teachers of English to speakers of other languages.* Cambridge, UK: Cambridge University Press.

Coerr, E. (1977). *Sadako and the thousand paper cranes.* New York: Putnam.

Cuff, E. C. (1993). *Problems of versions in everyday situations.* Washington, DC: International Institute for Ethnomethodology & Conversation Analysis/University Press of America.

Davidson, J. (1984). Subsequent versions of invitations, offers, requests, and proposals dealing with potential or actual rejection. In J. M. Atkinson & J. Heritage (Eds.), *Structures of social action: Studies in conversation analysis* (pp. 102–128). Cambridge, UK: Cambridge University Press.

Day, D. (1998). Being ascribed, and resisting, membership of an ethnic group. In C. Antaki & S. Widdicombe (Eds.), *Identities in talk* (pp. 151–190). London: Sage.

Dixon, R. J. (1956). *Regents English workbook, book 2: Intermediate-advanced.* New York: Regents Publishing Company.

Edwards, D. (1998). The relevant thing about her: Social identity categories in use. In C. Antaki & S. Widdicombe (Eds.), *Identities in talk* (pp. 15–33). London: Sage.

Fairclough, N. (1989). *Language and power.* London: Longman.

Faltis, C. J. (1999). Creating a new history. In C. J. Faltis & P. M. Wolfe (Eds.), *So much to say: Adolescents, bilingualism, and ESL in the secondary school* (pp. 1–9). New York: Teachers College Press.

Fleischman, H. L., & Hopstock, P. J. (1993). *Descriptive study of services to limited English proficient students.* Arlington, VA: Development Associates.

Ford, C. E. (2001). At the intersection of turn and sequence: Negation and what comes next. In M. Selting & E. Couper-Kuhlen (Eds.), *Studies in interactional linguistics* (pp. 51–79). Amsterdam: John Benjamins.

Gafaranga, J. (2001). Linguistic identities in talk-in-interaction: Order in bilingual conversation. *Journal of Pragmatics, 33*, 1901–1925.

Gafaranga, J. (2005). Demythologising language alternation studies: Conversational structure vs. social structure in bilingual interaction. *Journal of Pragmatics, 37*, 281–300.

Garrett, P., & Baquedano-López, P. (2002). Language socialization: Reproduction and continuity, transformation and change. *Annual Review of Anthropology, 31*, 339–361.

Grossberg, L., Nelson, C., & Treichler, P. A. (1992). *Cultural studies.* New York: Routledge.

Hall, J. K. (1995). "Aw, man, where you goin'?": Classroom interaction and the development of L2 interactional competence. *Issues in Applied Linguistics, 6*(2), 37–62.

Hall, J. K. (1999). A prosaics of interaction: The development of interactional competence in another language. In E. Hinkel (Ed.), *Culture in second language teaching* (pp. 137–151). Cambridge, UK: Cambridge University Press.

Hall, S. (1996a). Cultural studies and its theoretical legacies. In D. Morley & K. Chen (Eds.), *Stuart Hall: Critical dialogues in cultural studies* (pp. 262–275). London: Routledge.

Hall, S. (1996b). Gramsci's relevance to the study of race and ethnicity. In D. Morley & K. Chen (Eds.), *The Stuart Hall reader: Critical dialogues in cultural studies* (pp. 411–440). London: Routledge.

Hammersley, M. (2000). *Taking sides in social research: Partisanship and bias in social enquiry.* London: Routledge.

Harklau, L., Losey, K. M., & Siegal, M. (Eds.). (1999). *Generation 1.5 meets college composition: Issues in the teaching of writing to US-educated learners of ESL.* Mahwah, NJ: Lawrence Erlbaum Associates.

He, A. W. (2003). Novices and their speech roles in Chinese heritage language classes. In R. Bayley & S. R. Schecter (Eds.), *Language socialization in bilingual and multilingual societies* (pp. 128–146). Clevedon, UK: Multilingual Matters.

Heritage, J. (1984). *Garfinkel & ethnomethodology.* Cambridge, UK: Polity Press.

Heritage, J., & Sorjonen, M. (1994). Constituting and maintaining activities across sequences: And-prefacing as a feature of question design. *Language in Society, 23*, 1–29.

Hester, S. (1998). Describing 'deviance' in school: Recognisably educational psychological problems. In C. Antaki & S. Widdicombe (Eds.), *Identities in talk* (pp. 133–150). London: Sage.

Hester, S., & Eglin, P. (1997). Membership categorization analysis: An introduction. In S. Hester & P. Eglin (Eds.), *Culture in action: Studies in membership categorization analysis* (pp. 1–23). Washington, DC: International Institute for Ethnomethodology and Conversation Analysis & University Press of America.

Kincheloe, J. L., & McLaren, P. (2000). Rethinking critical theory and qualitative research. In N. K. Denzin & Y. S. Lincoln (Eds.), *Handbook of qualitative research* (2nd ed., pp. 279–313). Thousand Oaks, CA: Sage.

Kitzinger, C. (2000). Doing feminist conversation analysis. *Feminism & Psychology, 10*, 163–93.

Kitzinger, C., & Frith, H. (1999). Just say no? The use of conversation analysis in developing a feminist perspective on sexual refusal. *Discourse & Society, 10*, 293–316.

Koshik, I. (2002). A conversation analytic study of yes/no questions which convey reversed polarity assertions. *Journal of Pragmatics, 34*, 1851–1877.

Koshik, I. (2003). *Wh*-questions used as challenges. *Discourse Studies, 5*, 51–77.

Lather, P. (1986). Issues of validity in openly ideological research: Between a rock and a soft place. *Interchange, 17*(4), 63–84.

Lave, J., & Wenger, E. (1991). *Situated learning: Legitimate peripheral participation.* Cambridge, UK: Cambridge University Press.

Levinson, B. A., Foley, D. E., & Holland, D. C. (Eds.). (1996). *The cultural production of the educated person: Critical ethnographies of schooling and local practice.* Albany, NY: State University of New York Press.

McKay, S. L., & Wong, S.-L. C. (1996). Multiple discourses, multiple identities: Investment and agency in second-language learning among Chinese adolescent immigrant students. *Harvard Educational Review, 66*, 577–608.

Moerman, M. (1988). *Talking culture: Ethnography and conversation analysis.* Philadelphia: University of Pennsylvania Press.

Norton, B. (2000). *Identity and language learning: Gender, ethnicity, and educational change.* London: Longman.

Ohara, Y., & Saft, S. (2003). Using conversation analysis to track gender ideologies in social interaction: Toward a feminist analysis of a Japanese phone-in consultation TV program. *Discourse & Society, 14*, 153–172.

Okamura, J. Y. (1994). Why there are no Asian Americans in Hawai'i: The continuing significance of local identity. *Social Process in Hawai'i, 35*, 161–178.

Orfield, G., Losen, D., Wald, J., & Swanson, C. B. (2004). *Losing our future: How minority youth are being left behind by the graduation rate crisis.* Cambridge, MA: The Civil

Rights Project at Harvard University & The Urban Institute. Contributors: Advocates for Children of New York, The Civil Society Institute.

Pennycook, A. (2001). *Critical applied linguistics: A critical introduction*. Mahwah, NJ: Lawrence Erlbaum Associates.

Pennycook, A. (2005). Critical applied linguistics. In A. Davies & C. Elder (Eds.), *The handbook of applied linguistics* (pp. 784–807). Malden, MA: Blackwell.

Pomerantz, A. (1984a). Agreeing and disagreeing with assessments: Some features of preferred/dispreferred turn shapes. In J. M. Atkinson & J. Heritage (Eds.), *Structures of social action: Studies in conversation analysis* (pp. 57–101). Cambridge, UK: Cambridge University Press.

Pomerantz, A. (1984b). Pursuing a response. In J. M. Atkinson & J. Heritage (Eds.), *Structures of social action: Studies in conversation analysis* (pp. 152–163). Cambridge, UK: Cambridge University Press.

Ruiz de Velasco, J., Fix, M., & Clewell, B. C. (2000). *Overlooked and underserved: Immigrant students in US secondary schools*. Washington, DC: The Urban Institute.

Sacks, H. (1992). *Lectures on conversation* (Vol. I). Oxford, UK: Blackwell.

Sakoda, K., & Siegel, J. (2003). *Pidgin grammar: An introduction to the creole language of Hawai'i*. Honolulu, HI: Bess Press.

Schegloff, E. A. (1972). Notes on a conversational practice: Formulating place. In D. Sudnow (Ed.), *Studies in social interaction* (pp. 75–119). New York: Free Press.

Schegloff, E. A. (1999a). Naivete versus sophistication or discipline versus self-indulgence: A rejoinder to Billig. *Discourse & Society, 10*, 577–582.

Schegloff, E. A. (1999b). Schegloff's texts as "Billig's data": A critical reply. *Discourse & Society, 10*, 558–572.

Schieffelin, B. B., & Ochs, E. (1986). Language socialization. *Annual Review of Anthropology, 15*, 163–191.

Speer, S. A. (1999). Feminism and conversation analysis: An oxymoron? *Feminism & Psychology, 9*, 471–478.

Stokoe, E. H., & Smithson, J. (2001). Making gender relevant: Conversation analysis and gender categories in interaction. *Discourse & Society, 12*, 217–244.

Talmy, S. (2005). *Lifers and FOBs, rocks and resistance: Generation 1.5, identity, and the cultural productions of ESL in a high school.* Unpublished doctoral dissertation, University of Hawai'i at Mānoa, Honolulu, HI.

Talmy, S. (2008). The cultural productions of the ESL student at Tradewinds High: Contingency, multidirectionality, and identity in L2 socialization. *Applied Linguistics*, Advance Access published June 9, 2008, doi:10.1093/applin/amn01

Talmy, S. (forthcoming). Forever FOB?: Resisting and reproducing the Other in high school ESL. In A. Reyes & A. Lo (Eds.), *Beyond Yellow English: Toward a linguistic anthropology of Asian Pacific America*. Oxford, UK: Oxford University Press.

ten Have, P. (1999). *Doing conversation analysis: A practical guide*. London: Sage.

ten Have, P. (2001). Applied conversation analysis. In A. McHoul & M. Rapley (Eds.), *How to analyze talk in institutional settings: A casebook of methods* (pp. 3–11). London: Continuum.

van Dijk, T. (1985). Introduction: The role of discourse analysis in society. In T. van Dijk (Ed.), *Handbook of discourse analysis, Volume 4: Discourse analysis in society* (pp. 1–8). London: Academic Press.

Watson, R. (1997). Some general reflections on 'categorization' and 'sequence' in the analysis of conversation. In S. Hester & P. Eglin (Eds.), *Culture in action: Studies in membership categorization analysis* (pp. 49–75). Washington, DC: International Institute for Ethnomethodology and Conversation Analysis & University Press of America.

Watt, D., & Roessingh, H. (2001). The dynamics of ESL drop-out: Plus ça change... *Canadian Modern Language Review, 58*(2), 203–222.

Wenger, E. (1998). *Communities of practice: Learning, meaning, and identity.* Cambridge, UK: Cambridge University Press.

Wetherell, M. (1998). Positioning and interpretative repertoires: Conversation analysis and post-structuralism in dialogue. *Discourse & Society, 9*, 387–412.

Widdicombe, S. (1995). Identity, politics and talk: A case for the mundane and the everyday. In S. Wilkinson & C. Kitzinger (Eds.), *Feminism and discourse: Psychological perspectives* (pp. 106–127). London: Sage.

Williams, R. (1977). *Marxism and literature.* Oxford, UK: Oxford University Press.

Wooffitt, R. (2005). *Conversation analysis and discourse analysis: A comparative and critical introduction.* London: Sage.

Zimmerman, D. (1998). Identity, context, and interaction. In C. Antaki & S. Widdicombe (Eds.), Identities in talk (pp. 87–106). London: Sage.

9 Turn-Taking and Primary Speakership During a Student Discussion

Eric Hauser
The University of Electro-Communications, Tokyo

Introduction

In what has become a foundational work of conversation analysis, Sacks, Schegloff, and Jefferson (1974, 1978) present an analysis of turn-taking in conversation. These authors point out that an important feature of the organization of turn-taking in conversation is that it is a locally managed and "'party-administered' system" (1974, p. 726). This local management and party administration apply also, or perhaps especially, when the organization of turn-taking is temporarily modified, such as in storytelling (Jefferson, 1978). As talk in institutional settings has become one focus of attention within conversation analysis, a fair amount of research has investigated how the turn-taking organization of institutional talk deviates systematically from the turn-taking organization of mundane conversation, as described in Sacks, Schegloff, and Jefferson (1974, 1978; e.g., Clayman & Heritage, 2002; contributions to Boden & Zimmerman, 1991, and to Drew & Heritage, 1992a). This has included research on turn-taking in classrooms, such as language classrooms (e.g., Markee, 2000; Olsher, 2004). For example, one possibility is that certain forms of talk in certain institutional settings involve a degree of turn pre-allocation, which would apparently entail that it is correspondingly less locally managed in nature. However, even when turns appear to be pre-allocated, local management and party administration

Talk-in-interaction: Multilingual perspectives, pp. 215–244, Hanh Nguyen & Gabriele Kasper (Eds.), 2009
Honolulu, HI: University of Hawai'i, National Foreign Language Resource Center

may still be of primary importance to the accomplishment of turn transition at the local level.

The relationship between institutional setting and the organization of turn-taking is neither unilaterally causal nor deterministic. Drew and Heritage (1992b) make the point that talk is both *context shaped* and *context renewing*. While the institutional setting can be viewed as influencing the organization of turn-taking, so that it is context shaped, the way in which participants organize their turn-taking displays an orientation, or lack of orientation, to the institutional setting. Through their turn-taking practices, participants may do being participants in institutional talk, taking on certain institutionally relevant roles, and thus renewing the institutional context, or they may organize their turn-taking differently, and thus treat the institutional setting as not being a relevant part of the local context, at least as far as turn-taking is concerned. For example, Schegloff (1988–1989)[1] analyzes how, through a change in their turn-taking practices, then-Vice President of the US, George Bush, and television news personality Dan Rather move from doing being participants (interviewee and interviewer) in a news interview, a speech-exchange system with its own turn-taking practices, to being engaged in a quarrelsome confrontation. Similarly, in classrooms, through their turn-taking practices, participants may do being participants in a classroom and thus renew the classroom context, or they may organize their turn-taking in such a way as to treat the classroom setting as irrelevant. They may also adjust how they organize their turn-taking as they orient to different classroom-relevant activities (Markee, 2004).

As stated above, a starting point for research on turn-taking in institutional settings is how it differs from turn-taking in mundane conversation. Sacks, Schegloff, and Jefferson (1974, 1978) provide a set of rules for turn-taking in such mundane conversation, rules that can account for the well-coordinated occurrence and recurrence of turn transition readily observable in mundane conversation. To briefly summarize (and oversimplify) these rules, turn transition becomes relevant when a turn reaches a point of possible completion. Such a point may thus be labeled a *transition relevance place* (TRP).[2] When a speaker reaches a TRP, if this speaker has selected a next speaker by, for example, asking him or her a question, then the next turn goes to the selected speaker (rule 1a); if a next speaker has not been selected, then another participant may self-select (rule 1b); and if another participant does not self-select, the current speaker may continue (rule 1c). These rules are ordered so that rule 1b may apply if rule 1a does not and rule 1c may apply if rules 1a and b do not. (Current speakers may of course try to prevent turn transition by rules 1a and b, such as by rushing through a TRP.) As demonstrated below, this rule set can also account for turn-taking organization that appears quite different from that of mundane conversation, once it is understood how participants orient to the rules.

This chapter analyzes the organization of turn-taking during two student discussions in a language classroom. After illustrating how the participants orient to an avoidance of gaps and overlap, a turn-taking relevant orientation also observable in mundane conversation, the analysis turns to two ways in which the organization of turn-taking during these discussions is observably different from that of mundane conversation. These "deviations," while related to the structure of the task in which they are engaged, can be understood as accomplishments of the student participants as they locally manage their turn-taking. They also display how the participants orient to the rules for turn-taking. Finally, these "deviations" show how the participants orient to the institutional context as they do being students engaged in a student discussion and how they construct an intersubjective understanding of what it means to be a student so engaged.

Data

The data for this chapter consist of two student discussions,[3] based on a problem posed in a textbook and teacher-assigned discussion questions, during a single session of a university-level English language class in Japan. It seems not unusual for university language classes in Japan to be rather large and for the students in such classes to be fairly inactive, so this particular class may be atypical because it has only 12 students and much of the class time is devoted to tasks which involve them in using English. The 12 students form three groups, each seated at its own table. The data collection focuses on one group of 4 students, 3 male and 1 female, whom I have given the pseudonyms Ichiro, Jiro, Saburo (male), and Hanako (female). Ichiro and Jiro are seated next to each other on one side of the table, with Hanako and Saburo seated next to each other on the other side (see Figure 1).[4]

The total data set consists of approximately 38 minutes of interaction among these four students. The first student discussion is approximately 14.5 minutes and based on a problem posed in the textbook (Day & Yamanaka, 1998) regarding the best advice for a female fictional character of Japanese nationality who is unsure of whether to marry her non-Japanese boyfriend. The data excerpts from this discussion are labeled "Sachiko," the name of the fictional character. The recording of the second student discussion is incomplete because the tape in the primary video-camera ended while the discussion was in progress. The data for this second discussion consist of approximately 23.5 minutes. The discussion is based on a set of four teacher-assigned questions regarding international relationships. Each student is responsible for asking one of these questions and for taking notes on each student's answer. Data excerpts from this discussion are labeled "Questions." The two other groups are ostensibly engaged in the same tasks, while the teacher circulates, monitors, and occasionally joins briefly the interaction in different groups or addresses talk to the class.

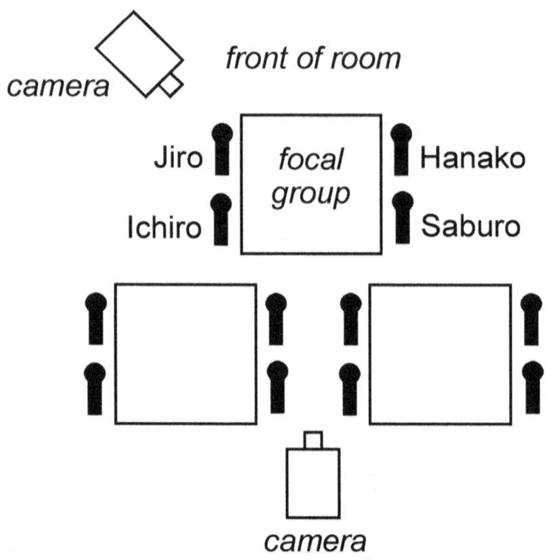

Figure 1. Classroom arrangement.

A first impression likely to be formed by someone listening to these discussions is that the students are not very fluent in their use of English. This can be seen, for example, in Excerpt 1, in contrast to Excerpt 2.[5]

Excerpt 1, Questions (simplified)

```
I: but um (x) eh (.) they can't (0.6) they
   can't understand each other, (0.2)
H: each oth ah:: [:
I:               [uhm .h ((sniff))=
J:               [mm
I: = [(.)  [(if::) they (1.2) eh: they uh:=
H:   [uh::n
J:         [mm mm
I: =broke (.) (the) (0.2) relationship
   (0.3) befor:e (.) they understood.
```

In Excerpt 1, Ichiro produces his turn with a number of disfluencies—five tokens of "uh" or similar nonlexical sounds (two in line 01, one in line 04, two in line 06),[6] elongation ("if::", "eh:", and "uh:", line 06; "befor:e", line 10), word repetition (lines 01–02, line 06), and nine pauses (two in line 01, one in line 02, two in line 06, two in line 09, two in line 10), five of which are longer than a micropause (a pause of less than 0.2 s) and one of which is over 1 s (line 06). In contrast, in Excerpt 2, while the teacher (T) repeats "what about", he produces his turn without any "uh"s or similar nonlexical sounds, without cut-offs, without elongation, and without any pauses.

Of course, disfluencies should not be assumed to be simple, straightforward reflections of limited proficiency in the language nor indexical of being a second language speaker, just as first language speakers should not be assumed to always be "perfect" (see Carroll, 2004). The occurrence of any given disfluency is likely to have a good interactional basis. For example, in Excerpt 2, T first enters into this interaction with the start of his talk in line 01. As he starts to talk, the students in this group are not looking at him or otherwise displaying that they are paying attention to him. As he is completing his utterance of the first two words ("what about"), all four students shift their gaze to him. The teacher then recycles "what about" as he goes on to produce a complete turn. While the repetition of the first two words of his turn is a disfluency, the teacher can be understood as using the first utterance of these two words as a means of entering this interaction and gaining the attention of the students, and then producing a complete turn once he has gained, or is on the verge of gaining, this attention (Goodwin, 1979). Similarly, the 0.2-s pause at the end of line 02 of Excerpt 1, which can be understood as an intraturn pause rather than an interturn gap (see Sacks, Schegloff, & Jefferson, 1974, 1978) given the continuing intonation on the word "other", can also be understood as emerging as Ichiro waits for some indication from another participant that he may continue, which he receives from Hanako in line 03, after which Ichiro indicates that he will continue to talk by saying "uhm" in line 04 (Sacks, 1992). The other disfluencies in Excerpt 1, though, appear to be more resistant to this sort of analysis of their interactional basis. They seem to have more to do with the current speaker searching for, even struggling to find, the words needed to produce his or her talk.

Excerpt 2, Sachiko (simplified)

```
01 T: what about ((all 4 students look towards
02    T)) what about you guys did you say your
03    opinion?
```

Excerpt 1 was chosen as a typical example of how the student participants talk during these two discussions. Disfluencies are abundant and the participants often appear to be struggling. Even so, they show a strong orientation to their responsibility to use English and only rarely switch to Japanese. In the few instances in which Japanese is used, it is not to provide a Japanese replacement for a word or group of words that they are searching for in English.[7] Before looking at turn-taking, then, an overall characterization that can be made of these discussions is that they involve the participants struggling to speak in their second language, but not giving up, even in the face of rather serious difficulties.[8]

Analysis

Orientation to no-gap, no-overlap turn transition

As with mundane conversation and often institutional interaction,[9] an orientation to no-gap no-overlap turn transition and the existence of means to repair violations of this orientation (Sacks, Schegloff, & Jefferson, 1974, 1978) are readily observable in the data. This is so in spite of an abundance of interturn gaps, which may be quite long.

Carroll (2000) and Hosoda and Aline (2005) have found that limited-proficiency second language speakers of English, or as Carroll refers to them, novice L2 speakers, are capable of precision timing of turn transition, that is, of timing the start of a new turn so that it is not in overlap with the prior turn and does not follow a gap between the end of the prior turn and the start of the new turn. While Carroll (2000) found this to be true of Japanese university students, whose proficiency in English may be extremely limited but who also have had several years experience of, at the very least, being physically present during required English classes in secondary school, Hosoda and Aline (2005) also found this to be true for Japanese elementary school students who are just starting to participate in English classes.

The participants in these student discussions are also capable of precision timing in turn transition, as can be seen in Excerpt 3.

Excerpt 3, Sachiko (simplified)

```
01 I: make [more [(0.5) spend (0.3) spend=
02 S:      [(xxxx)
03 H:             [mm:
04→I: =more time.
05→J: spend more ti:me,
06→H: un
```

Precision timing of turn transition can be found in lines 04–05 and 05–06. In line 04, Ichiro reaches a possible completion point, with the completion of the phrase "spend more time," produced with falling intonation. With no gap and no overlap, Jiro then starts his turn in line 05. Then, as Jiro's turn reaches another possible completion point with the full repetition of the phrase "spend more ti:me.", Hanako places her next turn without a gap or overlap.

As Hosoda and Aline (2005) point out, what is important is not merely that second language speakers are capable of precision timing in turn transition but that they show an orientation to the avoidance and minimization of overlaps and gaps at points of transition. This is also true for the participants in these student discussions. Their orientation to no-gap turn transition can be seen in Excerpt 4.

Excerpt 4, Sachiko

```
01 I: ((raises hand))
02 J: yeah
03→I: uhm (0.4) she- (.) she confused (.)
```

Here, a participant can be seen doing work to transform what could become an interturn gap into an intraturn pause (Sacks, Schegloff, & Jefferson, 1974, 1978). Ichiro requests an opportunity to take a turn by raising his hand in line 01, which Jiro recognizes in line 02. With no gap, Ichiro starts his next turn by saying "uhm" and then pausing for 0.4 s (see Sacks, 1992, Lecture 13, Fall 1971). This period of silence is thus produced as an intraturn pause as it does not appear until after Ichiro starts his turn.

In Excepts 5 and 6, a participant works to resolve overlap.

Excerpt 5, Sachiko (simplified)

```
01 S: for example (0.2) we we are (0.5) have-
02    we have known (0.5) uh each other (0.3)
03    with n:igh- (0.4) nine? (0.3) eight
04    [or nine months?]
05→H: [o  h  :  :  : ]:  un
```

Excerpt 6, Sachiko (simplified)

```
01 I: she: love him
02    (0.6)
03 J: [a h :]
04→I: [(it-)] it the: (.) it the important
05    things::.
```

In line 05 of Excerpt 5, Hanako produces a change-of-state token (Heritage, 1984, 2005; Tanaka, 1999) in overlap with Saburo's talk in line 04. She stretches this token so that it ends just slightly after the talk in lines 01–04 reaches possible, and as it turns out, actual, completion in line 04. This allows Hanako's "un" to be produced without any pause between it and the preceding change-of-state token as well as in a position that is free from overlap with Saburo's talk.

In line 04 of Excerpt 6, Ichiro appears to say something in overlap with Jiro's talk in line 03. If he has indeed said "it-" at the start of line 04, then his repetition of this word allows it to be produced in a position that is free from overlap (see Schegloff, 2000).

The participants are capable of no-gap, no-overlap turn transition and do, at least at times, display an orientation to its importance. One thing that makes this possible is the way that turn-shape and upcoming possible completion can be projected (Sacks, Schegloff, & Jefferson, 1974, 1978). One type of evidence that projection is relevant for participants is the collaborative completion of a turn started by another, either preemptive completion (Lerner, 2004) or completion in concert with the one who started the turn (Lerner, 2002). Collaborative completion can be seen in Excerpt 7.

Excerpt 7, Sachiko

```
I:  and he:- (0.5) he- don't (2.2) he
    don't like eh: Japanes::e (0.4)
    Japanes:e [food.
→J:           [food
```

Following a few repetitions of different words and groups of words, Ichiro produces a hearably complete turn as he says "food." with falling intonation in line 03. Jiro collaborates in this completion by saying the terminal item "food" at the same time. In doing this, Jiro displays his understanding of what has been projected by Ichiro's talk up through the production of the second-to-last item, "Japanes:e". Participants may also display their understanding of what has been projected by making an early claim to recognize what a speaker is going to say, as shown in Excerpt 5 above. By starting her change-of-state token where she does, Hanako claims to recognize what has been projected in Saburo's talk up through the word "eight" at the end of line 03 (see Jefferson, 2004).

Overlap during these discussions is actually quite rare. However, in spite of the participants' orientation to no-gap turn transition and their ability to accomplish them, interturn gaps are abundant in the data, as shown in the next section.

Being the primary speaker

Turn-taking organization during these discussions deviates from what is found in mundane conversation in at least two observable and related ways. First, at times during the discussions, different student participants remain in the role of primary speaker for extended periods of time, which involves, for the most part, only this participant taking more than a minimal turn. Second, at points in the discussion, the main interactional work involves the negotiation of a transition of the role of primary speaker. These two features of the organization of turn-taking during the student discussions are obviously related, but for analytic purposes, they are dealt with separately. This section presents analyses of excerpts in which one of the student participants is in the role of primary speaker, with the other student participants acting as more or less active recipients. The next section presents analyses of how the transition of this role is negotiated. The following section then presents analyses of apparent deviations from one student being the primary speaker.

In Excerpt 8,[10] Ichiro is in the role of primary speaker.

Excerpt 8, Sachiko

```
01 I: I think [(0.2) number one is:: the best
02 H:         [mm
03    (1.3)
04 I: a::n:d (1.8) uhm- (1.2) they have (0.5)
05    their own (opinions) [(0.3) ↑but ↓eh:-=
06 J:                      [uh
07 I: =(0.6) ↑he loves (0.4) he- he love her.
08 J: un
09 H: ((nods as J says "un"))
10    (1.2)
11 I: she: love him
12    (0.6)
13 I: [it- it the: (.) it the important=
14 J: [ah
15 H: ((nods as I says "it-" and J says "ah"))
16 I: =things::.
17 H: mm ((nods))
18 J: ((nods as H says "mm"))
19 I: for think (those things).
20 J: mm ((nods))
21 S: mm
22    (1.2)
23 I: becaus:e (1.3) they: sh:ould (0.7)
24    (live together).
25    (0.4)
26 I: they shou:ld (1.0) think (0.5) for a
27    lot of times:
28    (0.7)
29 J: mm
30 I: ((cough)) uh- uh: they decide (their)
31    (0.8) they decide (1.0) (this) this
32    problem.
33    (0.5)
34 I: now what (0.9) what (1.0) what they do.
```

Ichiro's talk in line 01 is a hearably complete unit. However, the other participants do not treat this as a place for turn transition, resulting in a 1.3-s gap before Ichiro starts to produce more talk in line 04.[11] The start of Ichiro's turn, the word "a::n:d", presents what he is going to say next as a continuation of what he has just finished. Ichiro appears to be buying time—he stretches the first word considerably, pauses for 1.8 s, says "uhm-", and then pauses for another 1.2 s before projecting more talk with the words "they have". By doing this, he brings to an end what has emerged as already a fairly long 1.3-s gap in line 03, even while he displays uncertainty as to how to continue.

The sentence that Ichiro starts at the end of line 04 may be hearably complete with the word "opinions", but the limited intelligibility (on the recordings) of this word makes it difficult to tell.[12] Jiro, for his part, treats this as a TRP and takes the next turn, but rather than take a more substantial turn, he produces only a minimal response in line 06. Ichiro continues, reaching a next possible completion point with the word "her." in line 07. In lines 08 and 09, Jiro produces another minimal response, "un", while Hanako nods, actions which can be understood as verbal and nonverbal continuers (Schegloff, 1982), that is, minimal turns that pass the opportunity to say something more substantial. That no new speaker is going to take another turn becomes clear with the emergence of a 1.2-s gap in line 10, after which Ichiro produces more talk, reaching another possible completion point with the word "him". No other participant takes the opportunity provided by this TRP to take a turn, resulting in another gap in line 12 before Ichiro continues. Jiro and Hanako do respond verbally and nonverbally, but after the gap and in overlap with the onset of Ichiro's continuation. At the next possible completion point, Hanako and Jiro again provide verbal and nonverbal continuers in lines 17 and 18. Without any gap, Ichiro continues in line 19. This time, minimal responses are produced by Jiro and Saburo in lines 20 and 21, followed by another long gap. Again, Ichiro is the one who moves to bring this gap to an end as he starts to produce more talk in line 23. Ichiro reaches another possible completion point, at least intonationally, at the end of line 24, but none of the other participants move to take a turn, resulting in another gap before Ichiro continues in line 26. And so on.

The impression one gets from looking at Excerpt 8 is not of opportunities to talk being a scarce resource that participants must compete for and share, but rather something that the participants are unwilling to take and that Ichiro, as the primary speaker, the person who is now giving his opinion about the topic of discussion, has no choice but to take if the discussion is not to come to a complete stop. This sort of situation, far from being unusual, is ubiquitous throughout these two discussions, as can be seen in Excerpts 9, 10, and 11.

Excerpt 9, Questions (simplified)

```
01 J: uh::m (0.2) because (.) uh: (1.3)=
02 I: ((nods as J says "uh::m"))
03 J: =there is no dange (.) uh: for me
04 S: hh ((smiles, nods))
05    (0.4) ((S's non-verbals continue
06    during gap; H and I nod during gap))
07 J: uh:: (3.4) uh uhm about (.) eh: (1.7)
08    (living) (.) my: li- my=
09 S:            ((looks at J, nods starting at
```

```
10       pause))
11 J:  =(living my life)
12 H:  ((nods during J's talk in 11))
13     (1.5) ((S and I nod during gap))
14 J:  uhm (2.0) and (6.9) ↑Japan is: (0.9) ↓the:
15     (0.6) ↑most comfortable (0.4) country.
16     (.) ((S smiles and nods during gap))
17 J:  in the world.
18 H:  hihihihuhuhuhhnnn
19 J:  for me.
20 I:  ((smiles, nods as J says "for me."))
21     (1.3)
22 J:  of course.
```

Excerpt 10, Sachiko

```
01 S:  a:nd (1.4) ↑this is ↓uh::: (.) sh::
02     (0.3) she worried (0.6) uh about it
03 J:                         ((nods during pause))
04     (0.3) ((J nods during gap))
05 S:  alone only
06     (0.6) ((J nods during gap))
07 S:  and (1.8) ↑this problem is (0.4) ↓uh:m
08     (2.6) amee- uh (0.5) Amir (0.3) and=
09 J:                                 ((nods
10     during pause))
11 S:  =(0.4) Sachiko's problem.
12     (0.5) ((J and H nod during gap))
13 S:  uh: and (0.5) ((cough)) (1.0) uh::
14     (0.3) ((cough)) (2.3) they talk about
15     it uh:: (0.4) each other
```

Excerpt 11, Questions (simplified)

```
01 H:  oh okay (0.8) I thought uh:n (2.8) so-
02     (0.2) it's- (0.6) I thought (3.0) uh-
03     (2.4) I ca:n (1.3) enjoy::
04     [(1.0) his country.
05 J:  [mm
06 J:  mm: [:
07 H:      [and understanding culture.
08 J:  mm=
09 H:  =mm .h so (0.3) I: can kn:ow: (0.5) the
10     world is (3.1) ((gesture during pause))
11     buh (xxx) (1.8) ((gesture during pause))
12     very bigu.
13     (0.4)
14 H:  [mm
15 J:  [eh? ah: [big
16 H:           [mm (0.6) I thought uh I th-
17     (0.5) I will think (2.1) many many:
18     (1.1) many culture (.) is (0.5) uh
19     culture (.) exist.
```

In Excerpt 9,[13] Jiro is in the role of primary speaker. He reaches possible completion at the end of line 03, at which point the other three participants produce minimal responses, both verbal and nonverbal. In line 07, Jiro moves to end the emerging gap by saying "uh::," followed by a 3.4-s pause. Eventually, he adds more talk in lines 07–08 and 11. This talk elicits nonverbal minimal responses from Saburo and Ichiro, but as none of the other participants move to take a more substantial turn, a gap emerges in line 13. Again, Jiro moves to end this gap, this time by saying "uhm" in line 14, followed by a 2.0-s pause. Eventually, he produces more talk, which reaches possible completion, both syntactically and intonationally, in line 15. What he has produced is a complete sentence ("Japan is the most comfortable country"), a sentence that he adds to in lines 17, 19, and 22, as the only responses he gets are a nonverbal response from Saburo following the first possible completion point, soft laughter from Hanako following the first addition in line 17, and a nonverbal response from Ichiro in line 20.

In Excerpt 10, Saburo is in the role of primary speaker. After reaching a possible completion point at the end of line 02, the only response is a nod from Jiro. Saburo then continues in line 05, which elicits another nod from Jiro. In line 07, Saburo brings the emerging gap to an end by saying "and", after which he eventually produces more talk in lines 07–08 and 11, where he reaches possible completion at the end of the line. This elicits nonverbal minimal responses from Jiro and Hanako. Once more, Saburo moves in line 13 to end the emerging gap.

Finally, in Excerpt 11, Hanako is in the role of primary speaker. Her first turn in this excerpt reaches a possible completion point at the end of line 04. This elicits a minimal response from Jiro and Hanako continues in line 07. Hanako continues again in lines 09–12, following another minimal response from Jiro. In line 15, Jiro gives something more of a response than is typical while another participant is in the role of primary speaker, at first initiating other-repair, but then immediately aborting it with a change-of-state token and a repetition of the word that the repair initiation had apparently targeted. While it is more than a minimal response, after initiating and aborting the repair, the result is to pass the turn back to Hanako as the primary speaker, who produces more talk in lines 16–19.

Each of Excerpts 8–11 demonstrates what the participants contribute topically to the discussions as primary speakers, which is the delivery of an opinion related to the current discussion topic. This may involve overt marking of what the speaker is going to say or has said as his or her opinion, as in Ichiro's use of "I th<u>in</u>k" in line 01 of Excerpt 8. The participants treat support for their opinions as important. In Excerpt 8, Ichiro's talk in lines 07, 11, 13, 16, and 19 provides a reason to support the opinion he stated in line 01. In Excerpt 9, Jiro is giving a reason for an opinion stated earlier, which is that he would like to live in Japan if he married someone from another country. In Excerpt 10, Saburo's talk in lines 01–02, 05, 07–08, and 11 can be understood as reasons supporting the opinion he states in lines 14–15. In Excerpt 11, Hanako's talk in lines 09–12 and 16–19 can be understood as reasons that enjoying "his country" and "understanding culture" would be positive experiences. As primary speakers, the participants design their talk to deliver not just opinions, but supported opinions.

As these four excerpts (8–11) demonstrate, the role of primary speaker is a role that each of the participants occupies at some point. These four excerpts also demonstrate that this occurred during both discussions. In fact, each of the student participants occupies the role of primary speaker at least once during the first discussion and more than once during the second, longer discussion. A likely basis for this difference is that the first discussion has only one discussion question, while the second discussion has four discussion questions (see discussion below). Of course, in mundane conversation, one can also find cases of a particular participant occupying the role of primary speaker, such as during the telling of a story (Jefferson, 1978). However, the sheer ubiquity of this practice in the data for this chapter renders it an outstanding feature of these two student discussions. While other participants may take minimal turns, for the most part only the primary speaker produces turns much more substantial than a verbal or nonverbal continuer.

Negotiating the transition of primary speakership

I have demonstrated that different participants at different times occupy the role of primary speaker. The question now becomes how they move into and out of this role. As demonstrated in this section, the participants devote a fair amount of interactional work to negotiating the transition of primary speakership. This negotiation typically occurs in a three-part sequence, consisting of (a) a claim to have said enough, which functions as a bid to move out of the role of primary speaker, (b) negotiation regarding who will be the next primary speaker, and (c) acceptance of primary speakership. The description of the negotiation sequence as a three-part sequence should not be taken as entailing that the sequence consists of three turns. In particular, the second part of the sequence, negotiation, is itself composed of one or more turns by different participants.

Excerpts 12–15 illustrate the first part of this sequence, claims to have said enough (or *claims*).

Excerpt 12, Sachiko

```
I: a year- (1.3) mm::: ((nods)) maybe
J: maybe ((nods))
S: ((nods))
H: ((nods, at same time as S))
```

```
05 J: okay
06→I: ((nods once, then moves chair back, looks
07→   up, moves chair forward))
```

Excerpt 13, Sachiko (simplified)

```
01 J: if they: (.) want to:: (0.6) visit (.)
02    (to) their: (2.0) home country, (1.2)
03    they can.
04    (0.6)
05 H: mm mm mm mm ((nods))
06 I: ((nods during H's sounds))
07→J: ((nods once))
08    (0.6)
09→J: mm:: (1.2) >okay. that's all.< ((gestures))
10    [huh huh
11 H: [mm ((nods))
12 I: ((raises hand during J's laughter))
13 J: yeah
14 I: uhm (0.4) she- (.) she confused (.)
```

Excerpt 14, Questions (simplified)

```
01 H: for exampl:e=we- (0.3) we:: (.) I can
02    enjoy: (2.6) the food. in: each
03    country.
04 J: mm ((nods))
05 H: mm:
06→   (4.9) ((H nods once at beginning of gap))
07→H: >that's all.<
08    (0.4)
09 J: that's all hheh heh
10    (2.9) ((during gap, H smiles and nods,
11    I, J, and S nod))
12 J: okay.
13→H: mm ((nods slightly once))
14    (0.7)
```

Excerpt 15, Questions

```
01 S: I (1.6) uh: I:: (1.2) decided her:
02    (1.3) [uh
03 J:       [I decide to live
04    [(0.4) in her country
05 S: [(uhst) yeah ((nods))
06→S: yeah. ((single head nod))
07 J: ah: naruhodo ((I see))
08    (1.3)
09 J: if if sh she want to
10→S: yes: ((single head nod))
11 J: ah: okay,
12 H: mm:
```

```
   (1.7) ((J writing))
J: thanks ((looks at S))
   (0.7)
J: okay? ((gestures towards S))
→S: okay. ((single head nod))
J: that's all?
```

At the start of Excerpt 12, Ichiro is the primary speaker. In lines 06–07, he makes a nonverbal claim. First, he produces a single head nod. The participants in these discussions use nods to perform various actions. For example, prior to this excerpt, Jiro has asked Ichiro a question seeking clarification of one aspect of Ichiro's opinion. He has also provided a candidate answer, "a year." In line 01, Ichiro repeats this candidate answer and then accepts it as a possible answer by saying "maybe" and nodding, looking towards Jiro as he nods. In line 02, Jiro receipts the answer by repeating "maybe" and nodding. In lines 03 and 04, Saburo and Hanako also receipt the answer by nodding. During the nods in lines 02–04, Jiro, Saburo, and Hanako gaze at Ichiro. These nods consist of multiple vertical shakes of the head, though counting the number of shakes is sometimes difficult because this gesture seems to fade in and out, with the start and end of the gesture involving very slight movements. Ichiro's single head nod in line 06 is performed differently. Even though it consists of only a slight movement, it is clearly a single nod, produced by slightly but briskly lowering the head and then returning it to the initial position. Also, as he performs the nod, he is looking down, not at any of the other participants. In these discussions, different participants often use single head nods to index that they have finished saying what they have to say and, thus, to make a claim. Following the nod, Ichiro moves his chair back, looks up, and then moves his chair forward again, a series of moves that can be understood as iconic of movement out of primary speakership (moving back) and then reentering the group (looking up, towards the other participants, and moving forward) as someone who is not the primary speaker.

In Excerpt 13, Jiro, the primary speaker, reaches a TRP with the word "can." in line 03, as his talk is possibly complete both syntactically and intonationally. However, none of the other participants attempts to exploit the opportunity to take a turn, resulting in a 0.6-s gap in line 04 before Hanako and Ichiro respond verbally and nonverbally, without, though, taking very substantial turns. In line 07, Jiro performs a single head nod, similar to the one performed by Ichiro in Excerpt 12, though it is more pronounced and Jiro appears to be gazing towards another participant, Saburo. When no one moves to take a turn, Jiro appears ready at the start of line 09 to continue as the primary speaker, as he says "mm::" and then pauses. Following the pause, though, he makes an overt claim, saying ">okay. that's all.<" while making a gesture with his right hand which consists of lifting the hand from its resting position on his leg to about chest height and then letting it drop back to his leg. In conjunction with his talk, this gesture can be understood as indexing that Jiro has nothing more to add. Jiro then laughs, while simultaneously shifting his attention towards Ichiro, who is raising his hand. Jiro's claim in line 09 can actually be understood as a second, more overt claim, redoing his first in line 07. Because this first claim, made through a single head nod, was followed by a 0.6-s gap, Jiro found it necessary to redo it in a more overt manner. Jiro's laughter in line 10 can be understood as targeting the situation that he has found himself in.

At the start of Excerpt 14, Hanako is the primary speaker. She reaches a possible completion point with the word "food." in line 02 but then adds a bit more before reaching another possible completion point with the word "country." in line 03. Jiro receipts the answer, verbally and nonverbally, in line 04, after which Hanako produces another sound but does not attempt to produce more talk. She then makes an initial, nonverbal claim, a single head nod in line 06. This is more similar to Ichiro's single head nod in Excerpt 12 than is Jiro's in Excerpt 13 as Hanako is looking down and the nod is fairly slight. Having made this claim, Hanako finds herself in the same situation as Jiro's in Excerpt 13 as none of the other participants takes a next turn. She then makes a more overt claim in line 07, saying ">that's all.<". Finally, in line 13, Hanako appears to index that she has finished with another single head nod. However, this particular nod is very slight and almost imperceptible.

In line 01 of Excerpt 15 and prior to this line, Saburo, in the role of primary speaker, appears to be having difficulty formulating what he is trying to say. Jiro provides assistance in lines 03–04, which Saburo accepts in line 06. Saburo also performs a single head nod in line 06, but the work it is doing is ambiguous. Along with Saburo's talk in this line, it could simply be accepting Jiro's formulation. In addition, though, it could be understood as indexing that Saburo has finished, and thus as an initial claim. In lines 09–10, something similar happens, as Jiro adds to his formulation of what Saburo has been trying to say, and Saburo then accepts this with the word "yes:" and another single head nod, which may also be understood as indexing that Saburo is finished and thus as a claim. Whether or not Saburo is finished is ambiguous for Jiro, who receipts Saburo's acceptance of Jiro's additional formulation in line 11, writes down something likely related to Saburo's opinion (jointly formulated by Saburo and Jiro), and thanks Saburo for his opinion in line 14. These actions on Jiro's part indicate that he takes Saburo to be finished and is perhaps treating Saburo's single head nods in lines 06 and 10 as claims. However, Jiro then seeks confirmation that Saburo is indeed finished in line 16. Saburo confirms this by saying "okay." and performing another single head nod in line 17. This confirmation can be understood as another claim.[14]

As can be seen in these four excerpts, the participants use a variety of resources to claim that they have said enough and in doing so, make a bid to move out of the role of primary speaker. The next part of the sequence is negotiation over who should be the next primary speaker. (However, as shown below, claims do not necessarily lead to negotiation.) As illustrated in Excerpts 16–18, this negotiation is generally accomplished nonverbally.

Excerpt 16, Sachiko

```
01 I: ((nods once, then moves chair back, looks
02    up, moves chair forward))
03→J: ((looks at S, gestures towards S))
04→I: ((gestures towards J))
05    (((6.1) from I's last nod to J's laughter))
06 J: huh huh huh huh .h huh=
07→I: ((during J's laughter, gestures towards
08→   S, then back to J))
09→S: ((during J's laughter, gestures towards
10→   J, smiles))
11 H: ((smiles during J's laughter))
12 J: =uh::- (2.0) .hh (0.6) I choo:se (1.8)
13    number two. (2.1)
```

Excerpt 17, Questions

```
01    (0.7)
02→S: ((raises hand, waves it, starts to
03→   lower it but raises it back up, lowers
04→   it; (1.6) total length))
05→J: ((looks at and gestures towards S, after
06→   S  raises hand))
07 S: uh:n (0.4) most fun is (interesting)=
08 H: ((clicks pen on table after S starts
09    saying "uh:n"))
10 S: =thing is uh: (3.5)
```

Excerpt 18, Questions

```
01 J: that's all?
02→  (0.5) ((J looks at I during gap))
03→J: uh [please. ((gestures towards I))
04 I:    [((nods before talking)) ehuh:: I
05    think (0.3) I could.
```

Excerpt 16 continues from the end of Excerpt 12, with lines 01–02 being the same as lines 06–07 in Excerpt 12. Nonverbal negotiation, accompanied by laughter and smiling, occurs in lines 03–10. Jiro starts the negotiation in line 03 by looking at and pointing towards Saburo with a pen or pencil that he has been holding in his right hand. Ichiro, though, appears to ignore this nomination by Jiro of Saburo to be the next primary speaker, as he nominates Jiro in line 04 by gesturing towards him with his right hand, his gaze following the gesture. In lines 07–08, Ichiro then recognizes Jiro's nomination of Saburo by temporarily gesturing and shifting his gaze towards Saburo. At the same time, though, in lines 09–10, Saburo seconds Ichiro's nomination of Jiro by gesturing towards him with his right hand. While Saburo's gesture is still in progress, Ichiro shifts his gaze and gesture back to Jiro, with this gesture containing an extra thrust of his hand towards Jiro. The negotiation over who should be the next primary speaker is nonverbal and multiparty. It is also treated as laughable, as Jiro laughs in line 06 and Saburo and Hanako smile. Finally, the negotiation indexes acceptance of Ichiro's claim to have said enough.

Excerpt 17 continues from the end of Excerpt 14, with the gap in line 01 being the same gap at the end of Excerpt 14. In this excerpt, Saburo begins the negotiation with a fairly long waving gesture with his right hand through which he volunteers to move into the role of primary speaker. After the start of this gesture, Jiro recognizes that Saburo has volunteered by gazing and pointing at him. The other two participants are not very active in this negotiation, which may be one reason for the length of Saburo's waving gesture, as he attempts to elicit some sort of response. As in Excerpt 16, the negotiation is nonverbal and multiparty. It also treats Hanako as having moved out of the role of primary speaker so that the gap in line 01 emerges as not belonging to her.

Excerpt 18 continues from the end of Excerpt 15, with line 01 of Excerpt 18 being the same as line 18 of Excerpt 15. Jiro starts the negotiation by looking at Ichiro in line 02, using his gaze to nominate Ichiro as the next primary speaker. He then makes the nomination more overt by saying "uh please" and gesturing towards Ichiro with his right hand. In this excerpt, what I have been calling negotiation hardly seems to be negotiation at all, as Jiro unilaterally nominates Ichiro for primary speakership and the other participants are not active in the negotiation. Unlike the negotiation in Excerpts 16 and 17, the negotiation in Excerpt 18 is unilateral rather than multiparty and is not accomplished completely nonverbally. As mentioned earlier, during the Questions discussion, each student participant has a question that he or she is responsible for asking the other participants. Each student is also responsible for taking notes regarding the other students' answers. To some extent, the unilateral nature of Jiro's nomination of Ichiro can be explained by the fact that the students are currently discussing Jiro's question, so Jiro has a legitimate reason for taking on responsibility for managing the discussion.

Negotiation is typically multiparty and nonverbal, but it may also be unilateral and/or contain verbal elements. It is sometimes treated as a laughable. Finally, it indexes acceptance by the other participants that the prior primary speaker has said enough and is no longer the primary speaker. As shown in Excerpt 19, though, the participants can move to preempt negotiation and thus reject the primary speaker's claim to have said enough.

Excerpt 19, Sachiko (simplified)

```
01 I: ((raises hand))
02 J: yeah
```

```
I: uhm (0.4) she- (.) she confused (.)
   (xxxx) (0.9) a:::nd (1.2) she:- (2.0)
   she:: (1.3) she thinks and uhm (1.3)
   children (xxxxx)
J: yeah ((nods))
→I: an:d (0.4) what (0.4) eh what (.) do
→  you think about (0.5) about the:
→  children (0.8) problem.=
J: =nationality,
   (0.6)
I: nationality yes::= ((nods))
J: =[of their children
H: =[ah:
I: ((nods))
J: uhm- (1.1) thei:r- (.) nationality (3.0)
   ↓uh: (1.0) is (3.2) America
```

This excerpt continues from the end of Excerpt 13, with lines 01–03 of Excerpt 19 being the same as lines 12–14 of Excerpt 13, in which Jiro made a claim. Ichiro raises his hand in line 01, which Jiro recognizes in line 02. In this brief sequence, we can see Ichiro and Jiro as oriented to Jiro currently being in charge of allocating turns. That Ichiro is not volunteering to take on the role of primary speaker, as Saburo did in Excerpt 17, becomes clear in lines 08–10, as he uses a question to request Jiro to elaborate on one point of his opinion. With this question, Ichiro's talk in lines 03–06 can be understood as background information against which the question should be interpreted, rather than as the start of his own opinion. Jiro treats what Ichiro has said as a request for further elaboration as he first collaboratively confirms what Ichiro is asking, in lines 11–16, and then answers the question in lines 17–18. As he answers the question and elaborates on this aspect of his opinion for several lines of transcript beyond line 18 of Excerpt 19, Jiro continues as the primary speaker. Just as participants in conversation can move out of a closing sequence to continue the conversation (Schegloff & Sacks, 1973), the participants in these discussions can reverse their way out of a negotiation sequence.[15]

When a claim does lead to negotiation, the third part of the sequence is acceptance of the primary speakership by a different participant. This is illustrated in Excerpts 20–22. (These excerpts are the ends of Excerpts 16–18.)

Excerpt 20, Sachiko

```
J: =uh::- (2.0) .hh (0.6) I choo:se (1.8)
   number two. (2.1)
```

Excerpt 21, Questions

```
S: uh:n (0.4) most fun is (interesting)=
H: ((clicks pen on table after S starts
   saying "uh:n"))
S: =thing is uh: (3.5)
```

Excerpt 22, Questions

```
J: uh [please. ((gestures towards I))
I:    [((nods before talking)) ehuh:: I
   think (0.3) I could.
```

In Excerpt 20, immediately following his prior laughter (not shown here), Jiro accepts the role of primary speaker in line 01 with an elongated “uh::-”. After a long pause, an inbreath, and another pause, he then starts formulating his opinion. In Excerpt 21, Saburo does something very similar: he indexes his acceptance of primary speakership by saying “uh:n”, pausing, and then starting to formulate his opinion. For her part, Hanako, who is currently responsible for taking notes, orients to Saburo entering the role of primary speaker by clicking her pen on the table, mechanically setting the pen to be used for writing. In Excerpt 22, Ichiro accepts primary speakership by saying “ehuh::” and then starting to formulate his opinion. As illustrated in these three excerpts, the participants index their acceptance of primary speakership not by immediately starting the formulation of an opinion, but by producing a nonlexical sound, which may be followed by one or more pauses and/or more nonlexical sounds.

Challenging the adequacy of an opinion

Excerpt 19 above illustrates something of a deviation from one student participant being a primary speaker. In requesting elaboration of Jiro’s opinion, Ichiro gives background information and asks a question, thus producing a rather substantial turn of talk, quite unlike the verbal and nonverbal minimal responses in Excerpts 8–11. This request for elaboration can be understood as challenging the adequacy of Jiro’s opinion. Even though Ichiro produces a substantial turn of talk, by challenging the adequacy of Jiro’s opinion, this turn forces Jiro to remain, for the time being, in the role of primary speaker.

This sort of challenge, while not widespread, occurs during both discussions.[16] When one does occur, it seems to be preceded by a claim, on the part of the primary speaker, to have said enough.[17] Excerpt 23 shows another example.

Excerpt 23, Sachiko

```
I:  ((nods once))
    (4.1) ((J raises hand during gap))
→J: uhm (1.4) if they (0.5) have a time (0.3)=
I:  ((looks at J as J says "uhm"))
→J: =for: (1.7) uh (1.3) (thinking then)
I:  yes:
    (1.3)
→J: how long (3.9) should they: (0.4) have a
→   time.
    (0.8)
I:  uhm (.) ↑I thi:nk (.) the best. (0.3) best
```

is ↓uh: (1.3) ↓eh: ↑she- (1.2) eh he and
she decide:d (0.8) decide their- (0.7)
decide the: (1.4) their- (.) hh heh heh
.hh ↑he and she ((smiley voice)) eh:
(2.1) think and uh (5.6) decide thee
answer.

In line 01, Ichiro performs a single head nod. This is actually a second such nod, which follows another performed a few seconds earlier. Both of these come after Ichiro has apparently finished formulating his opinion and can be understood as claims. However, following this claim, Jiro raises his hand and holds it in the air during much of the gap in line 02. Ichiro does not appear to notice this gesture and does not look at Jiro, but he does shift his attention towards Jiro when Jiro says "uhm" in line 03. Jiro then asks a question, in lines 03, 05, and 08–09, which requests elaboration of Ichiro's opinion. As with Jiro in Excerpt 19, Ichiro does not move out of the role of primary speaker and instead attempts to answer the question starting in line 11.[18]

While these challenges may seem to deviate from the general pattern of one participant being the primary speaker, they also illustrate an orientation on the part of the participants to the primary speaker having the responsibility to deliver an adequate opinion. While the primary speaker may attempt to shed this role by claiming to have said enough, the other participants may challenge this claim and force the primary speaker to elaborate his or her opinion. While challenges constitute fairly substantial turns, the participants do not treat them as indicating a change in primary speakership. In addition, in both Excerpts 19 and 23, the participant who makes the challenge first requests permission to take a more substantial turn, or at least to ask a question, by raising his hand, treating the primary speaker as also having rights over turn allocation.

Discussion

It is possible that turn-taking during student discussions in language classrooms often involves students accepting in turn the role of primary speaker or that this is what happens during student discussions in certain types of language classroom and/or with certain types of students and/or with certain tasks. However, the data that I have analyzed are limited to two discussions among the same four student participants during the same class session, so I refrain from making any claims about this being a general feature of student discussions as a particular type of institutional interaction. What I argue is that, in spite of certain appearances, turn-taking during these discussions is locally managed and party administered. In fact, the rule set proposed by Sacks, Schegloff, and Jefferson (1974, 1978) for mundane conversation can account for the organization of turn-taking, once how the participants orient to these rules is understood. In addition, by managing turn-taking as they do, the student participants construct an intersubjective understanding of the nature of the classroom task that they have been assigned and display an orientation to the institutional context.

The four student participants show an orientation to properly having only one primary speaker at any given point in the discussion. The strength of this orientation is evidenced in the prevalence of long gaps, in spite of the fact that the participants are capable of no-gap turn transitions. When a participant is the primary speaker, the other students usually refrain from attempting to take a turn much more substantial than a continuer. In the absence of a claim to have said enough, when the primary speaker has reached a possible completion point, the other participants typically produce at most minimal responses and, perhaps following a gap, the primary speaker continues. Even when other participants produce something more substantial than a minimal response, as Ichiro and Jiro do in Excerpts 19 and 23, such turns may be preceded by the seeking of permission from the primary speaker to ask a question; only seem to occur following a claim to have said enough; function as requests for the primary speaker to elaborate on some aspect of his or her opinion, in a sense challenging its adequacy; and treat the primary speaker as continuing to be responsible for formulating his or her opinion. The emergence of one participant at a time as the primary speaker is a result not just of the actions of the primary speaker but of the orientations and actions of all four participants. Primary speakership is a collaborative local accomplishment.

Primary speakership can also be seen as the outcome of how the participants orient to the rules for turn allocation (Sacks, Schegloff, & Jefferson, 1974, 1978). Techniques for selecting a next speaker can be found during negotiation and when one student challenges the adequacy of an opinion by asking the primary speaker a question, thus selecting the primary speaker as the next speaker. However, primary speakers, when they are also current speakers, generally do not select next speakers, so when the primary speaker reaches a TRP, rule 1a (current speaker selects next) does not apply. Participants who are not currently the primary speaker tend to either refrain from claiming a next turn under rule 1b (next speaker self-selects) or, when they do take a turn, produce only a minimal response, passing the opportunity to take a more substantial turn. When a nonprimary speaker does take a turn to ask the primary speaker a question, this appears to occur only in a specific sequential location, following a claim. As a result, when a TRP has been reached, what most often happens is that either one or more participants take a turn under rule 1b. This turn, though, turns out to be minimal, leaving it to the primary speaker to bring any emergent gap to an end; or, when nobody else has attempted to take any kind of turn, the primary speaker continues under rule 1c.[19]

The participants treat primary speakership as something that each of them must take on at some point during the discussion. Negotiation of this role shows, on the one hand, that they find the transitioning of primary speakership necessary and on the other, that deciding whether the primary speaker has said enough and determining who should be the next primary speaker are problems that the participants must solve. Involving claims to have said enough, nominations and self-nominations of next primary speakers, and acceptance of primary speakership, this negotiation is also a collaborative local accomplishment.

If we move back from individual excerpts and look at each discussion as a whole, a certain pattern emerges from the way primary speakership moves around. In the first discussion, "Sachiko," which has one discussion question, Ichiro is the first student to be the primary speaker. This role is then passed to Jiro, then Hanako, and finally, Saburo. What emerges is that primary speakership gets passed around the table (see Figure 1 above) until each participant has been the primary speaker and delivered his or her opinion as the primary speaker one time. Excerpt 24 shows what happens when Saburo has completed his opinion and is ready to move out of the role of primary speaker.

Excerpt 24, Sachiko

```
01 S: ((nods)) I think so. ((nods once))
02 T: (yeah so) ↑take a couple more=
03 J: ((nods as T says "yeah so"))
04 T: =minutes. (0.2) ↓take a couple more=
05 H: ((nods as T says "minutes." first time))
06 T: =minutes.
07 J: ah::
08→    (9.3)
09→I: I think he: (0.4) ↑she- (0.3) ↓an:d he=
10 J:    ((looks at I as he says "think"))
11 H:    ((looks at I as he says "think"))
12 S:    ((looks at I as he says "think"))
13 I: =(0.4) can talked more.
```

In line 01, Saburo formulates his prior talk as his opinion by saying "I think so." with falling intonation. He also produces a single head nod. Taken together, his verbal and nonverbal actions can be understood as a claim to have said enough. In lines 03 and 05, Jiro and Hanako respond nonverbally, but at the same time, the teacher, addressing the class, indicates that the different groups should bring their discussions to a close. In line 07, Jiro responds once more to what Saburo has said with a change-of-state token. As nobody then moves to open negotiation or to challenge the adequacy of Saburo's opinion or to start talking about something else, a 9.3-s gap emerges in line 08, which is only brought to an end when Ichiro starts to produce more talk in line 09, talk which he designs from the start as his opinion.

Apparently, once each of the student participants has been the primary speaker one time, they no longer require one another to take on this role and do not find it necessary to enter negotiation over who should be the next primary speaker.[20] A student may volunteer to again be the primary speaker, as Ichiro eventually does, but the participants appear to treat their responsibilities as students engaged in a student discussion as at least partially fulfilled once they have each been the primary speaker one time and have each delivered an opinion that the others do not challenge. The pattern is somewhat more complicated in "Questions," and unfortunately, the entire discussion was not recorded. This discussion starts with Jiro asking the question that he has been assigned. He then takes on the role of primary speaker as he gives his opinion related to this question. The other three students then each become the primary speaker in turn. Next, Ichiro asks his question and takes on the role of primary speaker as he delivers his opinion related to this question. Once more, the other three participants then each become the primary speaker in turn. This pattern continues as Saburo and finally Hanako ask their questions.[21] In this discussion, the students treat one another as responsible for being the primary speaker one time for each discussion question and, as the primary speaker, for formulating an opinion related to the question.[22] The participants' understanding of how often each of them is required to be the primary speaker can thus be understood as related to the structure of the tasks that the participants have been assigned. However, while the structure of the task may provide a resource for how the participants handle primary speakership, it is through the collaborative and local accomplishment of primary speakership and its transition that this structure emerges as a concrete, observable object within the interaction.[23]

Some pre-allocation seems to be involved, if not in the allocation of turns, then in the allocation of primary speakership, especially because it appears to move literally around the table, so that this pre-allocation can be understood as related to the physical structure of the classroom environment. That is, if Ichiro is the first primary speaker and Jiro the second, then Hanako, not Saburo, will be third, while if Jiro is first and Ichiro second, then Saburo, not Hanako, will be third. This accounts for a certain difference among instances of negotiation, which is that they are sometimes quite elaborate (as in Excerpt 16), but at other times fairly abbreviated (as in Excerpt 18). The more elaborate negotiations occur when the transition is between the first primary speaker and the second, when what is being negotiated includes not only who will be the next primary speaker, but also the direction in which primary speakership will move around the table. In the more abbreviated cases, who the next primary speaker will be is fairly predictable. However, even when it is predictable, the next primary speaker does not simply move into this role, for example, by stating an opinion (as happens in Excerpt 24), without any negotiation, after the prior primary speaker has moved out of this role. Some interaction dedicated to indicating who will be the next primary speaker is something the participants find necessary, even when this necessity would seem to be very weak.

During these two discussions, the participants construct an intersubjective understanding of what being a student engaged in a student discussion means. It not only means trying to use English, the learning of which is the ostensible purpose of engaging in these discussions in the first place, but also taking the responsibility for delivering an opinion that no students in the group challenge. On the other hand, it does not appear to mean, for these participants, such things as trying to reach a consensus, strongly critiquing one another's opinions, or questioning the validity or relevance of the topics they have been assigned. As these participants do being students engaged in a student discussion, in the process of which they orient to and renew the classroom context, the turn-taking practices that they adopt result in the discussions taking on a fairly monologic character. They are *monologic* in the sense that the students orient to each of them delivering their own opinion, rather than, for example, dialogically developing an opinion they can all agree on or argumentatively forging and defending a position. They are only *fairly* monologic because, aside from the occasional need to elaborate an opinion in response to a challenge, primary speakership is interactively constructed.

Notes

1 See Bogen (1999) for a well-informed critique of conversation analysis constructed through a critique of Schegloff (1988–1989).

2 An anonymous reviewer pointed out that while possible completion points may be TRPs in mundane conversation, this is not necessarily the case in other types of talk, including the talk analyzed in this chapter. However, as will be shown later, in the data for this chapter, when points of possible completion are reached, the recipients often produce minimal responses, while the speakers generally do not continue immediately. I would argue, then, that the participants do treat possible completion points as TRPs.

3 An anonymous reviewer argued that, given the turn-taking organization, the talk that I am analyzing cannot really be categorized as discussions. While I agree that they are perhaps not examples of "good" or typical discussions, they are examples of what is often treated as a discussion in language and other classrooms and perhaps in other settings. I can find no emically derived reason to search for an alternative label.

4 The data were collected using two video-cameras, supplemented by an audio-recorder. Oral consent to record was obtained from all students and the teacher at the start of a prior class session. Oral consent was obtained from the four student participants in the focal group immediately prior to the start of the data collection.

5 To preserve readability, some transcripts have been simplified, involving the removal of information related to nonverbal behavior and/or standardizing the spellings of words that were articulated in a nonnative manner. This simplification has only been applied when the information removed is not necessary for the analysis. Japanese lexical items that appear in the transcripts are in italics. Each is followed by an English gloss, also in italics, enclosed in double parentheses. When elements from the transcripts are quoted in the text, the element is quoted as it appears, including punctuation.

6 Such nonlexical sounds are sometimes called *filled pauses*. However, I would like to avoid such a label to leave open the possibility that such sounds may be used for a variety of different purposes and the possibility that different varieties of so-called filled pauses may be deployed in very different ways. For a related point regarding listener responses, see Gardner (2001).

7 The closest thing to an exception to this is shown in the following excerpt.

Questions

```
01 H: I thought uh I th- (0.5) I will think
02    (2.1) many many: (1.1) many culture
03    (.) is (0.5) uh culture (.) exist.
04    (0.2)
05 J: mm=
06 H: =exist? (.) izu- bih- (.) (igu-) (.)
07    sonzai ((exist)) [(ni)
08 J:                  [yeah yeah
09 H: uhn [sonzai suru. ((to exist)) in uhn.
10 J:     [exist.
11 J: un
```

In this excerpt, Hanako provides the Japanese words *sonzai* and *sonzai suru* as equivalents of the English word *exist*. However, this is not the result of an abandoned word search, as Hanako has already said "exist." in line 03. While this gets a response from Jiro in line 05, it comes a bit late, which may be prompting Hanako to initiate repair in line 06 by repeating "exist?" with rising intonation. After what may be additional attempts to articulate this word, she switches to Japanese in lines 07 and 09. Hanako may be unsure of whether she has the correct English word, or she may suspect that other students do not know the English word she has used, which prompts her to provide a Japanese equivalent. In either case, Jiro confirms that *exist* is the correct translation of *sonzai* in lines 08 and 10. While this comes close to being an exception, it does not actually contradict the observation that the students do not abandon searches for words in English by providing Japanese replacements.

8 An interesting possibility, but one that I will not pursue here, is that the participants' awareness of being observed by the researcher, the recording equipment, and the circulating and monitoring teacher provides one motivation to continue using English (see Foucault, 1977).

9 See, though, McHoul's (1978) analysis of unproblematic gaps during teacher-student interaction.

10 The excerpts in this section (Excerpts 8–11) do not contain arrows to draw the reader's attention to particular points because the analysis focuses on several points in each excerpt.

11 Hanako produces what appears to be a continuer at line 02, at a point that does not seem to be a TRP. Nishizaka (2005) analyzes what he labels *response opportunity places* in Japanese conversation, points where turn transition is not relevant, but some kind of minimal response may nevertheless be offered. An interesting possibility is that Hanako is transferring an interactional practice from Japanese into this discussion in English. However, this is something that I have yet to look at carefully.

12 The 0.3 s of silence from Ichiro has been transcribed as a pause rather than as a shorter gap following Jiro's "uh" in line 06 because of this ambiguity.

13 In the interests of space, the excerpts showing a particular participant in the role of primary speaker do not display all the talk from the point the participant enters this role to the point the participant exits the role. Instead, they show only a portion of this talk. Even so, the excerpts are fairly long.

14 Even though Jiro produces more talk than Saburo at the start of this segment, much of this talk, in lines 03–04 and 09, is produced for or on behalf of Saburo, so Saburo can still be considered the primary speaker at this point. To use terminology from Goffman (1981), Saburo is the principle of what Jiro says, with Jiro as the author and animator.

15 I owe this observation to an anonymous reviewer.

16 I have been able to find three such challenges during Sachiko and two during Questions.

17 Unfortunately, when one of these challenges occurs during the second discussion, it is at a point where noise from another group has rendered some of the recorded talk of the focal group inaudible. In this case, determining whether the challenge follows a claim is therefore not possible.

18 Jiro turns out to not find this initial answer adequate and he pursues a more concrete time formulation. After several turns, Jiro displays satisfaction with Ichiro's answer, and Ichiro again claims to have said enough, with this claim being shown in Excerpt 12.

19 As mentioned in the main text, primary speakers generally do not select a next speaker and thus force the application of rule 1a. They could, but do not, say things such as, "I think they should live in the US. What about you?"

20 Of course, this is complicated by the fact that the teacher addresses the class as Saburo makes his claim to have said enough. The interaction within this group could have developed quite differently if the teacher had not addressed the class at this point.

21 The recording ends while the students are discussing Hanako's question.

22 After each participant has been the primary speaker once for a particular question, they enter negotiation over who should next read his or her assigned question. After reading his or her question, the participant who does so then delivers his or her opinion related to it. In other words, he or she becomes the first primary speaker for his or her question. Thus, negotiation over who should next read his or her assigned question is also negotiation over who should be the next primary speaker.

23 The distinction between task and activity made within sociocultural theory may be relevant here; see Lantolf and Thorne (2006).

References

Boden, D., & Zimmerman, D. H. (Eds.). (1991). *Talk & social structure: Studies in ethnomethodology and conversation analysis.* Berkeley, CA: University of California Press.

Bogen, D. (1999). *Order without rules: Critical theory and the logic of conversation.* Albany, NY: State University of New York Press.

Carroll, D. (2000). Precision timing in novice-to-novice L2 conversations. *Issues in Applied Linguistics, 11*, 67–110.

Carroll, D. (2004). Restarts in novice turn beginnings: Disfluencies or interactional achievements? In R. Gardner & J. Wagner (Eds.), *Second language conversations* (pp. 201–220). London: Continuum.

Clayman, S., & Heritage, J. (2002). *The news interview: Journalists and public figures on the air.* Cambridge, UK: Cambridge University Press.

Day, R. R., & Yamanaka, J. (1998). *Impact issues: 30 key issues to help you express yourself in English.* Hong Kong: Longman Asia ELT.

Drew, P., & Heritage, J. (Eds.). (1992a). *Talk at work: Interaction in institutional settings.* Cambridge, UK: Cambridge University Press.

Drew, P., & Heritage, J. (1992b). Analyzing talk at work: An introduction. In P. Drew & J. Heritage (Eds.), *Talk at work: Interaction in institutional settings* (pp. 3–65). Cambridge, UK: Cambridge University Press.

Foucault, M. (1977). *Discipline and punish: The birth of the prison.* New York: Random House.

Gardner, R. (2001). *When listeners talk.* Amsterdam: John Benjamins.

Goffman, E. (1981). *Forms of talk.* Philadelphia: University of Pennsylvania Press.

Goodwin, C. (1979). The interactive construction of a sentence in natural conversation. In C. Psathas (Ed.), *Everyday language: Studies in ethnomethodology* (pp. 97–121). New York: Irvington Publishers.

Heritage, J. (1984). A change-of-state token and aspects of its sequential placement. In J. M. Atkinson & J. Heritage (Eds.), *Structures of social action: Studies in conversation analysis* (pp. 299–345). Cambridge, UK: Cambridge University Press.

Heritage, J. (2005). Cognition in discourse. In H. te Molder & J. Potter (Eds.), *Conversation and cognition* (pp. 184–202). Cambridge, UK: Cambridge University Press.

Hosoda, Y., & Aline, D. (2005). *Orientation to no-gap transition in an educational setting: English classes in Japanese elementary schools.* Paper presented at Ninth International Pragmatics Conference, Riva del Garda, Italy.

Jefferson, G. (1978). Sequential aspects of storytelling in conversation. In J. Schenkein (Ed.), *Studies in the organization of conversational interaction* (pp. 219–248). New York: Academic Press.

Jefferson, G. (2004). Glossary of transcript symbols with an introduction. In G. H. Lerner (Ed.), *Conversation analysis: Studies from the first generation* (pp. 13–31). Amsterdam: John Benjamins.

Lantolf, J. P., & Thorne, S. L. (2006). *Sociocultural theory and the genesis of second language development.* Oxford, UK: Oxford University Press.

Lerner, G. H. (2002). Turn-sharing: The choral co-production of talk-in-interaction. In C. E. Ford, B. A. Fox, & S. A. Thompson (Eds.), *The language of turn and sequence* (pp. 225–256). Oxford, UK: Oxford University Press.

Lerner, G. H. (2004). Collaborative turn sequences. In G. H. Lerner (Ed.), *Conversation analysis: Studies from the first generation* (pp. 225–256). Amsterdam: John Benjamins.

Markee, N. (2000). *Conversation analysis.* Mahwah, NJ: Lawrence Erlbaum.

Markee, N. (2004). Zones of interactional transition in ESL classes. *The Modern Language Journal, 88*, 583–596.

McHoul, A. (1978). The organization of turns at formal talk in the classroom. *Language in Society, 7*, 183–213.

Nishizaka, A. (2005). Bunsan suru bun: Sougokoui toshite no bunpou. *Gengo, 34*, 40–44.

Olsher, D. (2004). Talk and gesture: The embodied completion of sequential actions in spoken interaction. In R. Gardner & J. Wagner (Eds.), *Second language conversations* (pp. 221–245). London: Continuum.

Sacks, H. (1992). *Lectures on conversation.* Oxford, UK: Blackwell.

Sacks, H., Schegloff, E. A., & Jefferson, G. (1974). A simplest systematics for the organization of turn-taking for conversation. *Language, 50*, 696–735.

Sacks, H., Schegloff, E. A., & Jefferson, G. (1978). A simplest systematics for the organization of turn taking for conversation. In J. Schenkein (Ed.), *Studies in the organization of conversational interaction* (pp. 7–57). New York: Academic Press.

Schegloff, E. A. (1982). Discourse as an interactional achievement: Some uses of 'uh huh' and other things that come between sentences. In D. Tannen (Ed.), *Analyzing discourse: Text and talk* (pp. 71–93). Washington, DC: Georgetown University Press.

Schegloff, E. A. (1988–1989). From interview to confrontation: Observations of the Bush/Rather encounter. *Research on Language and Social Interaction, 22*, 215–240.

Schegloff, E. A. (2000). Overlapping talk and the organization of turn-taking for conversation. *Language in Society, 29*, 1–63.

Schegloff, E. A., & Sacks, H. (1973). Opening up closings. *Semiotica, 8*, 289–327.

Tanaka, H. (1999). *Turn-taking in Japanese conversation: A study in grammar and interaction.* Amsterdam: John Benjamins.

10 Repair Work in a Chinese as a Foreign Language Classroom

John Rylander
Kansai Gaidai University

Introduction

Recently, CA research on classroom discourse has begun to view classroom talk "as a *nexus* of interrelated speech exchange systems rather than as a unified speech exchange system characterized by a single set of practices" (Markee, 2003, p. 4; see also Markee, 2004). As of yet, analysis of the various distinct speech exchange systems and their constitution through interactional organizations within classroom discourse has received little attention. In his 2004 book, *The Interactional Architecture of the Language Classroom: A Conversation Analysis Perspective,* however, Seedhouse argued for analyzing evidence of repair within classroom discourse in light of the "reflexive nature between the pedagogical focus and the organization of repair; as the pedagogical focus varies, so does the organization of repair" (p. 142). This claim links a larger understanding of the pedagogical goals chosen by an instructor within any specific activity to how that instructor uses repair. To further this view—and to highlight the pedagogical relevance underlying instances of instructor repair—Seedhouse categorized types of classroom activities into three contexts: form-and-accuracy, meaning-and-fluency, and task-based. In a form-and-accuracy context, the instructor focuses on a learner's production of specific aspects of the target language explicitly being taught within the activity

Talk-in-interaction: Multilingual perspectives, pp. 245–280, Hanh Nguyen & Gabriele Kasper (Eds.), 2009
Honolulu, HI: University of Hawai'i, National Foreign Language Resource Center

(e.g., the use of the definite vs. indefinite articles or relative clause forms). A meaning-and-fluency context is one in which the instructor encourages learners to produce talk in which the purposeful use of any specific syntactical or lexical item is subservient to conveying meaningful content. In a task-based context, the instructor provides learners, either in pair- or group-work form, with tasks to accomplish without any direct instructor involvement and where task completion is the ultimate goal.[1]

By categorizing classroom contexts in this fashion, Seedhouse proposed the view that "the organization of repair is primarily related to pedagogical focus" (p. 143). In other words, what participants—more precisely, instructors—locate as sources of *trouble*, that is, what constitutes a *repairable item*, is intrinsically bound to the larger pedagogical goal of the classroom context. Excerpt 1 is an example given by Seedhouse of a meaning-and-fluency context in which "the focus is clearly not on linguistic form and accuracy" (p. 150).

Excerpt 1, meaning-and-fluency context[2]

```
T:   could you tell me something about marriage in
     Algeria? who is married here?
L1:  Azo, only Azo.
T:   alright, your opinion about that.
L2:  he will marry.
T:   oh, he is engaged, engaged. tell me something
     about the institution of marriage in Algeria.
     tell me something about it.
L3:  there are several institutions.
T:   you don't have marriage in Algeria. what do you
     have then?
L4:  only women and men.
T:   yes, that's what marriage is.
L1:  the marriage in Algeria isn't like the marriage
     in England.
→T:  what do you mean?
L2:  for get marriage you must pay two thousand.
L5:  yes more expensive than here.
→T:  why do you have to pay money?
L6:  no. it's our religion.
L7:  not religion but our tradition.
L8:  no, religion, religion. in religion we must pay
     women, but not high price, but tradition.
L5:  between women, women does not like to married
     to a low money because it is not, it is (.)
T:   oh, dowry, oh dear.
```

Seedhouse's analysis of the excerpt proposes that (a) within this pedagogically contextualized conversation, the instructor and learners focus on co-constructing information previously unknown to the instructor (displayed by the instructor's "oh" in lines 06 and 26), and (b) the instructor-initiated repairs in lines 16 and 19 are implemented merely to clarify the learners' meaning. The instructor-initiated repair, then, is not implemented to correct learner errors but rather to achieve shared meaning, in the same way that other-initiated repair deals with problems in hearing or understanding in ordinary conversation. As Seedhouse stated, "according to the emic logic of this L2 classroom context, trouble is anything which impedes communication of meaning or content, and any such trouble is repairable" (p. 153). For instance, this logic is revealed in line 17, where instructor-initiated other-repair in the form of overt correction is noticeably absent following the L2 production of "for get marriage."

Focusing on instructor-initiated repair within a similar meaning-and-fluency activity in a Chinese as a foreign language (CFL) classroom, this chapter raises questions regarding Seedhouse's view of the reflexive nature of pedagogy and repair. The evidence shows how, on several occasions, the instructor-initiated repair following learner production of ungrammatical utterances is of a type that may be classified as *overt correction.* Furthermore, contrary to Seedhouse's view that instructor-initiated repair organization is intrinsically bound to a particular pedagogical choice, the overall goal of this chapter is to argue that classifying classroom contexts into rough categories prematurely places restrictions upon researchers using CA methodology to study second language classrooms. Moreover, what I claim is still necessary is the description, not simply classification, of the variety of classroom activities implemented within second language learning environments and the distinct characteristics of repair organizations within each. To do this, researchers must begin by providing descriptions of the nature of each activity from which instances of repair are collected and analyzed.

This chapter, therefore, approaches the analysis of repair in a CFL classroom by (a) detailing the boundedness of a particular "classroom context" (or, rather, classroom speech event) that falls under Seedhouse's category of meaning-and-fluency context and (b) revealing a particular teacher-initiated repair strategy contrary to that proposed by Seedhouse within such a context—the use of instructor-initiated other-repair following trouble sources not hearably hindering communication.

Repair in conversation analysis

In CA research, repair is described as occurring within structurally specific opportunities in talk and is understood as locally organized by participants within the turn-taking system. This organization of repair provides speakers with an ever-relevant mechanism for efficiently signaling, revealing, and resolving sources of trouble, which may occur due to the fact that "any of the systems and contingencies implicated in the production and reception of talk—articulatory, memory, sequential, syntactic, auditory, ambient noise, etc.—can fail" (Schegloff, 1979, p. 269). Repair practices, then, are considered an essential component of talk used by participants as a constantly available resource—whatever the trouble or its cause. Everything speakers say—regardless of how well formed it is syntactically, lexically, or phonologically—is included in the class of "repairables" (Schegloff, Jefferson, & Sacks, 1977).

In contrast to other forms of discourse analysis implemented within the field of second language acquisition (SLA) research with respect to trouble sources in talk, CA does not limit the concept of repair to "error correction," that is, accountable errors, of fact, pronunciation, lexical choice, syntax, pragmatics, etc. These are not conceptualized with instances of correction as a single unit of analysis. The CA framework views trouble sources as anything that participants respond to with repair work, regardless of whether it can be argued to be an "error." What concerns analysts regarding instances of repair is how participants orient to the ongoing talk. The simple existence of an ill-formed lexical item (an "error"), for example, is of no relevance to an analyst if the participants themselves do not hearably or visibly orient to the item as a "repairable." In other words, what stands as paramount to researchers is analyzing "the sequential structure of talk-in-interaction in terms of interlocutors' real-time orientations to the preferential practices that underlie, for participants and consequently also for analysts, the conversational behaviors of turn-taking and repair in different speech exchange systems" (Markee, 2000, p. 25). Because of the omnipresent relevance of repair practices within ongoing talk, their occurrence, the forms they take, and the manner in which participants orient to their presence have been extensively researched in CA (e.g., Drew, 1997; Markee, 2000; Schegloff, 1992, 1995, 1997, 2000; Schegloff et al., 1977; Seedhouse, 2004).

Research has shown that repair practices occur in various forms and locations within the turn-taking structure, with support for a preference in these repair behaviors. Multiple conditions exist under which repair occurs during interaction on a moment-by-moment basis, and such instances are viewed as logically occasioned and bound to the overall turn-taking structure. A summary of the organization of repair is as follows. Within talk, any speaker may initiate repair by targeting a trouble source, thereby designating an element of a previous utterance as a repairable. This repair of sources of trouble may be initiated by either the speaker (self-initiated) or by the hearer (other-initiated). If the speaker initiates and performs repair on his or her own speech (self-initiated self-repair), it can occur within the same turn as the trouble source, either before the turn's completion or within the transition-space between the same turn and the next speaker's. Alternatively, following a repair-initiation from the hearer, the speaker may repair a trouble source in the next relevant space (other-initiated self-repair). However, repair is not the exclusive right of speakers upon their own utterances. Hearers may offer repair in two ways: either by accommodating a speaker's request to the hearer for assistance (self-initiated other-repair) or by the hearer both initiating the repair and repairing the trouble-source (other-initiated other-repair). Regarding these repair practices or trajectories, speakers and hearers display preferences within the turn-taking organization. The assertion that repair is more often realized in one fashion as compared to another out of the set of possible trajectories outlined above is termed "preference" (Pomerantz, 1984; Schegloff et al., 1977); namely, just as there is a preference for a responding *greeting* to follow an initial *greeting* and an *acceptance* to proceed from a *request*, the preference structure for repair within ordinary talk is (self-initiated) self-repair over (other-initiated) other-repair. In this preference structure, both the speaker and the hearer are understood to play integral parts in how repair sequences occur, with *other* allowing for *self* to initiate and repair before offering aid.

This chapter focuses on repair mechanisms not within ordinary conversation but within the language classroom, which research shows contains a divergent preference structure. In general, classroom discourse, as a form of institutional talk, is structured asymmetrically regarding the "distribution of knowledge, access to conversational resources, and to participation in the interaction" (Drew & Heritage, 1992, p. 49). One example of the asymmetry of such talk is that instructors possess rights to "unsanctionable" initiations. That is, learners' opportunities at talk are institutionally more restricted than those of the instructor, to the extent that if learners "talk out of turn," instructors have cause to sanction them. However, learners seldom, if ever, have cause to sanction instructors' initiations or the content of their turns at talk. Furthermore, as a form of institutional talk, classroom interaction is implicitly ordered around institutional tasks or goals that to a large extent control what and how participants talk regarding topics (Sacks, Schegloff & Jefferson, 1974; Schegloff et al., 1977). These broad goals tend to keep participants from straying too far from the business at hand or their institutional roles.

Claims regarding the distinctive nature of classroom discourse are not new. For decades, SLA research on patterns of classroom discourse (see Chaudron, 1988, for a review) has characterized classroom talk as being organized around what is called an initiation, response, and feedback (Sinclair and Coulthard, 1975) turn-taking system in which instructors possess speaking rights of both questioning and evaluating students on subject matter, language use, participation, and behavior. The inherent inequality within institutional talk of this nature (i.e., certain participants "owning" rights to specific turns denied to other participants) led Schegloff (1992) to state that arguments regarding the organization of repair based on the idea of "conversation" cannot immediately be applied to all speech exchange systems due to the fact that "organization of repair is mapped onto a turn-based organization of talk" and that "variation in the setting or context, or anything that can involve some transformation of the turn-taking system by which the talk is organized...may well carry with it differences in the organization of repair" (p. 1337). These differences are such that Macbeth (2004) has referred to instances of classroom repair as "classroom correction." Rather than being subsumed within the larger classification of repair—as has traditionally been the case for correction with the field of CA—classroom correction is an organizational resource used "as an identifying task and achievement of classroom teaching" (p. 705). Classrooms then present their own institutional goals within which corrections occur:

> if knowledge (re)production is the charge of classroom instruction, the production of correct knowledge, and thus correction, unavoidably become a part of the practical and professional organization of the setting, and one of the prevailing orientations of the parties in the room. (p. 721)[3]

Furthermore, Macbeth noted that "there is no reason not to expect production differences across settings and cultures even within 'same' institutions...there may be even less reason to expect continuities across grade levels, and every reason to expect differences" (p. 714). Differing contexts, then, may present CA researchers with differing instances of repair trajectories. With this in mind, let us return to Seedhouse's argument regarding the link between instructor repair and classroom context—that of the *reflexive* nature between pedagogy and repair. Seedhouse wrote, "the principle of reflexivity states that the same set of methods or procedures are responsible for both the production of actions/utterances and their interpretation" (p. 11). Seedhouse continued with an example of how, through the exchange of *greetings*, participants "demonstrate that they are using the documentary method of interpretation, or that they are both orienting to the same schemata." Reflexivity, an element at the heart of the emic perspective, is directly related to the "next turn proof procedure" (Sacks et al., 1974, p. 729) in that the evidence for both participants' and analysts' interpretations of an ongoing interaction lies within the turn-taking system itself. In my view, this notion of reflexivity is misapplied when attempting to explain how an instructor's selection of a pedagogical context (i.e., form-and-accuracy, meaning-and-fluency, or task-oriented) relates directly to instances of instructor-initiated repair. Rather, within various classroom activities, each having their own distinct characteristics, instructors use a range of repair-initiations depending upon the ongoing interaction. Prior research into repair trajectories and institutional discourse suggests that what may first be necessary is the analysis of how both the instructor and learners play parts in talking-into-being a classroom speech event. Once the characteristics of distinct speech events have been revealed, analysts using a CA methodology can focus their attention on how repair mechanisms are used within them.

Methodology

This research was conducted over the course of two semesters in an intermediate CFL classroom. The classes met daily, Monday to Friday, for 50 minutes each. In total, 34 hours of class were audio-recorded: 19 hours from the fall semester and 15 hours from the spring semester. From this database, three classes were chosen at random for transcription and rough analysis. The rough transcriptions provided a macroperspective of class activities, showing the variety of *classroom speech events* present from class to class and the types of instructor-student and student-student interactions. Mitchell, Parkinson, and Johnstone (1981) described a classroom speech event as "a stretch of lesson discourse, having a particular topic, and involving the participants...in a distinctive configuration of roles, linguistic and organizational" (p. 12). Each class began with either a written quiz on textbook vocabulary items or a student presentation followed by a question-answer (Q-A) phase. After this, the class generally covered homework material, either as a whole class or in small groups, with any assignments being collected afterward. For the remainder of the class time, the instructor introduced grammatical points or cultural facets noted in the text, and the learners would form small groups or pairs to work on assigned tasks stemming from that day's lesson. At the end of class, time permitting, the learners made impromptu, whole-class summations of their group-work.

After the initial data analysis, a particular routine speech event was singled out for fine-grained transcription: the student presentation at the start of class, including the whole-class Q-A discussion phase. The rationale for selecting this particular speech event for analysis was that it provided both a good amount of peer-to-peer speaking instances as compared to other speech events and offered an activity in which the students presented information previously unknown to the instructor—an aspect not found within the variety of other class speech events. The transcription process required that the data first be written into *pinyin* and then translated separately into English. Following this, two native speakers of Mandarin reviewed all the written transcripts with the aid of the original audiotapes. Special transcript conventions and symbols were used (see Appendix).

Analysis

An argument for boundedness: Student presentation as speech event

One contention of this chapter is that before analysts can fully understand the role of instructor's repair within various classroom speech events, research first must show how particular events are talked into being by the participants. What follows is an argument for the boundedness of the student presentation as a particular speech event. Through talk co-constructed by the instructor and learners as they participate in this speech event, the presentation is noticeably shaped into a two-part activity composed of an individual learner monologue followed by a whole-class Q-A phase. Through the use of set phrases, the boundedness of this activity is created not simply by the asymmetrical power possessed by the instructor but through the manner in which the learners orient to the instructor's ongoing turns at talk. Also revealed within the following excerpts is how the instructor's use of these set phrases assists in shaping and defining both her role as the instructor and the learner roles as the presenter and audience members throughout the activity. Finally, these five initial excerpts display how the learner presentation and Q-A phase essentially fall into the category of a *meaning-and-fluency context*, as defined by Seedhouse (2004).

The presentation performed routinely near the start of each class is constructed into its two distinct parts through a set of three instructor utterances: (a) an initiation phrase—*ni zhunbei hao le ma?* [are you ready?]—is used to start the monologue phase; (b) a transitional phrase—a variation of *nimen you wenti wenta* [if you have a question ask her/him]—is used to simultaneously close the monologue phase and open the Q-A phase; and (c) a closing phrase—such as *jiu hao le* [that's good]—is used to end the speech activity and transition into the next speech event. Excerpt 2 has *Laoshi*[4] either seated among the audience[5] or in the process of moving from the desk at the head of the class to a seat. L uses this utterance to initiate the monologue phase:

Excerpt 2, initiation phrase (M's presentation)[6]

```
01→L: xia  yi  ge (2.0) ni  %are you ready?% (.) ni
      next one C        you %are you ready?%     you
      next person       you %are you ready?%     are you

02    zhunbei hao  le ma?
      prepare good CRS Q
      ready

03 M: %yeah%
      %yeah%
      %yeah%

04 L: ni  (**) na  yi  ge %menu% ni  meiyou gei  wo
      you (**) that one C  %menu% you N      give me
      you (**) didn't give me that %menu%

05    (ji  le  yi zhang) %you should make a copy% (.)
      (make CRS one C)   %you should make a copy%
      (make a copy)      %you should make a copy%
```

```
06     gei wo
       give me
       and give me
```

In line 01, L states, *ni zhunbei hao le ma?* [are you ready?], which I argue is an initiation phrase used to mark the first part of the speech event, the monologue, and indicates to that day's speaker to proceed to the head of the class and begin his or her prepared speech. Two details are of note within this excerpt: (a) the repetition of this phrase, first in English and then again in Chinese, and (b) L's explanation to M (but assumedly hearable to all members of class) providing specific examples as to what "being prepared" means within this context (lines 04–06). Both of these comments offer us insights as to how participants assemble the roles and responsibilities of various membership categories within the speech event. Clearly hearable is L's orientation to the role of the presenter as coming prepared, which, specific to M, means to bring handouts (which he failed to do). The initiation phrase itself is revealed in the data as not an open invitation to negotiate whether the speaker will give a speech due to his or her preparedness, for though M is clearly not entirely "prepared" in L's view, shortly thereafter, he begins his monologue as a presenter.

Once a presenter has finished the monologue phase, he or she stays at the head of class, with L remaining seated among the audience. The transition from the monologue to the Q-A phase occurs through the use of the second phrase—*nimen you wenti wenta* [if you have any questions, ask him or her]. Excerpt 3 reveals the actions that the participants accomplish by using this phrase.

Excerpt 3, instructor-employed transitional phrase (W's presentation)

```
01 W: %so% xianzai ta  bu zai yaoshi (.5) ta yao
      %so% now     she N  at  if          she want
      %so% now she's not at if            she wants

02    (.5) ta  ta  ~yao~ yanjiu
           she she ~want~ research
           she she ~wants~ research

03 L: zuo yanjiu
      do  research
      to do research

04 W: ta  xihuan [zuo yanjiu   keshi xianzai ta
      she like    do  research but   now     she
      she likes  to do research but now she

05 L:            [zuo yanjiu
                  do  research
                  will do research
```

```
06 W: dang:(.5) yijiaogao de  (.5) eh, zhiwei
      become    transfer  ASSC     eh position
      become    transferred to     eh a position

07    (.5) souyi bu neng yanjiu  (.) ta  (.5) zhi zhi
           so    N  can  research    she      only only
           so she can't do research she'll    only only

08    eh: guangli guan- bangongshi
      eh manage  mana- office
      eh be managing the office

09    (1.5)

10→L: uhm (1.5) hao.  nimen you  wenti    wen ta.
      uhm       good  you   have question ask him
      uhm       good  if you have questions ask him

11    (3.0)

12 L: meiyou?
      N-have
      no

13 X: wo you
      I have
      I have

14 L: meiyou.
      N-have
      no

15 X: you
      have
      have

16    (1.0)

17 X: wo ting bu dong  (2.5) ni   muqin  (.5)
      I  hear N  understand  your mother
      I don't understand     your mother

18    di: yici
      C  first
      the first time
```

In line 08 (of W's presentation), W finishes a description of his mother's job situation. After a 1.5-s pause (line 09), L assesses W's monologue as *hao* [good]. Assessments of this type are implicative of closing down a line of talk or an activity (Goodwin, 1996), which is how *hao* seems to be functioning here. Following this (line 10), L opens the floor to audience participation by asking *nimen you wenti wenta* [if you have any questions ask him]. After a 3.0-s pause in which no one responds, L asks *mei you?* [no?], a truncated repetition of her initial question, to which X responds (line 13) *wo you* [I have]. Not acknowledging X's claim to the floor, L (line 14) repeats *mei you* [no] using falling intonation that signals the end of the Q-A phase. However, X (line 15) repeats his claim to the floor with *you* [I have]. This is followed first by a brief pause of 1.0 s (line 16)—potentially a hesitation for X to confirm or for L to grant rights to the floor—then by the initiation of a question (lines 17, 18).

Excerpts 2 and 3 display how the participants orient to membership categories within the structure of the activity. Seedhouse's original claim provided evidence for the reflexive nature of an instructor's pedagogical choice (e.g., of a classroom context) and that instructor's use of repair within that context. However, within the exchange between L and X, what is clearly seen is the constructed relationship within the ongoing talk of the instructor and learner as they orient to the unfolding context. We see that L orients to the role of the presenter as being responsible for providing a monologue and coming prepared for the task. Excerpt 2 reveals L's orientation to M's failure to bring copies of materials to distribute (at least to her) for his presentation. L also orients to the audience members as being responsible for entering into the Q-A phase by making claims to the floor—specifically, by asking questions of the presenter. Additionally, whether a Q-A phase occurs is decided not solely by L but also by whether individual audience members opt to participate. With no audience member raising a question (line 11), L declares an end to the speech event (line 14). However, X's repeated claim to the floor (line 15) effectively suspends L's move (prematurely, as it turns out) to close down the speech activity, revealing how audience members possess rights to talk into being each part of the activity.

Excerpt 4 (Q's presentation) contains a slightly different take on the phrase *nimen you wenti?* [do you have questions?] and provides a fuller understanding of participant orientation. Q has finished a brief discussion with L regarding whether both male and female residents of a nudist dormitory at Q's previous university went nude.

Excerpt 4, presenter-employed transition phrase (Q's presentation)

```
01 L: hen   hao   wan (1.5) ni   qu (**) shenma dou
      very good fun         you go (**) what   all
      interesting           when you went (**) you

02    meiyou?
      N-have
      didn't wear anything

03 Q: meiyou.
      N-have
      no
```

04 C: ((laughter))

05 Q: hao wan
good fun
interesting

06 L: hen hao wan
very good fun
very interesting

07→Q: mMcalister% daxue (2.5) you wenti ma?
%Macalister% university *have question Q?*
Macalister College *do you have questions?*

08 C: ((laughter))

09→L: you wenti ma?
have question Q
do you have questions

10(): uh::m

11 (2.5)

12 L: meiyou wenti.
N-have questions
no questions

13 (1.5)

14 L: uh.

15 W: uh::: (1.0) %was it% ~Minzhou~? %was that%,
uh *%was it% ~Minnesota~ %was that%*
uh *%was it% ~Minnesota~ %was that%*

In line 07, after repeating *%macalister% daxue* [Macalister College], Q ends his monologue by asking *you wenti ma?* [do you have questions?], a slightly rephrased version of that introduced in Excerpt 3. The class responds (line 08) with laughter but no immediate claims to the floor. L then (line 09) repeats the question *you wenti ma?* [do you have questions?]. An unidentified speaker begins but fails to fully initiate an utterance (line 10). As no successful claims to the floor have been made, L states, *mei you wenti* [no questions] with falling intonation. Again, an audience member uses the turn (line 15) following this potential end to the Q-A phase to claim the floor and initiate a question. Excerpt 4 reveals how presenters may use the instructor's set phrase to begin the process of closing down the first part of the two-part activity. The analysis displays the instrumental role this phrase plays in structuring the student presentation speech event and highlights participants'—both the instructor's and the learners' (as the presenter and audience members)—concerted work in transitioning the speech event.

Yet, during the Q-A phase of Q's presentation, a separate incident occurs where L implements *nimen you wenti wenta* [if you have questions ask him or her] 54 lines after the Q-A phase had "officially" begun. Excerpt 5 reveals how within this context the phrase cannot be categorized as procedurally consequential in terms of being "transitional."

Excerpt 5, next-turn participant prompt (Q's Presentation)

```
01 L: ruguo (.) ruguo (.) wo keyi shuo, (.) wo bu
      if        if        I  can  say       I  N
      if        if        can I say         I don't

02    xiang qu  ne  ge sushe zhu  ma?
      want  go that C  dorm  live Q
      want to live in that dorm

03 Q: uhm?

04 L: ke  bu keyi?
      can N  can
      can I

05 Q: ah (.5) keyi.
      ah      can
      ah      you can

06→L: keyi. (.) hao.  (3.0) nimen you  wenti
      can       good        you   have questions
      I can     okay        if you have questions

07    wen ta
      ask him
      ask him

08 M: ah (.5) qingwen   (.5) ne  ge sushe de:
      ah      excuse me      that C dorm  NOM
      ah      excuse me      what's that dorm's

09    ~dizi~   shi shenma?
      address~ is  what
      ~address~
```

Leading up to where L repeats the phrase *nimen you wenti wenta* [if you have questions ask him or her] (lines 06, 07), Q and L have been working at completing a question (lines 01, 02) initiated by L (i.e., "can people choose to not live in the nudist dorm?"). Q then answers L's question (line 05), saying *ah (.5) keyi* [ah you can]. L then confirms this through repetition (line 06), followed by *nimen you wenti wenta.* This instance requires a re-examination of the role this phrase plays within the activity.

According to Geis (1995), the truth value, or the underlying semantics of an utterance, is indexical; it is "assigned dynamically with respect to the context" in which it occurs (p. 37). In reviewing the above instances where a variation of the phrase *nimen you wenti wenta* [if you have questions ask him or her] occurs, it becomes clear that L uses the phrase as a pre-allocated next-turn signal to prompt audience participation and that when it is produced immediately after the monologue phase, this prompt also serves to transition the activity. L does this by redefining the role of learner-as-audience member to learner-as-(potential)-next-turn-speaker, thereby casting the learners into the role of both paying attention to presenters' monologues and, when prompted, entering into discussion with the presenter by initiating questions. By using this phrase, L effectively redefines the learners' roles from attentive listeners to potential active contributors, determining where speaking rights may be allocated. Likewise, the presenter's role is transformed into that of the recipient of audience questions. This is readily apparent in how the learners orient to L's use of this phrase. Moreover, in choosing this open nomination for next-turn speakership, L defines the activity itself as one in which audience members "willingly" participate; that is, L does not call upon individual audience members to produce spontaneous topic-relevant questions. Applying the notion of reflexivity to this context provides not an opportunity to better understand how L implements a pedagogical choice within the ongoing interaction but to better understand how L, the presenter, and the audience members all orient to the indexical nature of set phrases within the speech event.

In closing the presentation and Q-A phase as a speech event, L did not use a single set phrase as she had when initiating the monologue phase and transitioning into the Q-A phase. Excerpt 6 presents one manner in which this speech event was closed and displays how L conducted a more traditional lock-step type of class activity (one that would potentially fall into Seedhouse's category of a form-and-accuracy context).

Excerpt 6, closing down the speech event (W's presentation)

```
01 L: ta  qu nar   boshi e?
      she go where PhD   eh
      where did she go for her PhD

02 W: boshi (.5) meiyou eh: nei  ge (1.0) ta  de
      PhD        N-have eh  that C        she ASSC
      PhD        no     eh  that          her
```

03 W: daxue meiyou %masters%
university N-have %masters%
university didn't have %masters%

04 L: meiyou %mas[ters%
N-have %masters%
no %masters%

05 W: [zhi you boshi
only have PhD
it only had PhDs

06 L: uh hum

07 W: %did you guys all understand that?%

08→L: wo dong wo dong (1.5) wo dong
I understand I understand I understand
I understand I understand if I understand

09 jiu hao le ((laughs)) you jidian
then good CRS ((laughs)) have time
then it's good ((laughs)) for a while now

10 yao jiang de e (1.0) ta mama lihai (3.5)
want talk ASSC eh his mom strong
he's spoken eh his mom is strong

11 ((writes on board)) wo gaosu nimen e (2.5)
I tell you eh
listen up eh

12 ((writes on board)) zhei ge women xue guo le ba
this C we study ASP ASP BA
we've studied this

13 (6.5) ((writes on board)) xue guo ma?
study ASP Q
did we study this

14 (4.5) ((writes on board)) e? (1.5) mei
eh N
eh we didn't

15 xue guo! (.5) you! (.5) S?
study ASC have S?
study it we did S?

16 S: ((**)) (xue guo)
((**)) (study ASC)
((**)) (we studied it)

17 L: xuewei (1.5) xuewei shi yi ge %degree% %yeah%?
degree degree is one C %degree% %yeah%
degree degree is %degree% %yeah%

```
18    ((writes on board)) xuewei shi %degree% %yeah%
                          degree is  %degree% %yeah%
                          degree is  %degree% %yeah%

19    ((writes on board)) xuewei (0.5) xueshi     shi
                          degree       Bachelor's is
                          a Bachelor's degree is

20    shenme W? (0.5) %bee [ey%
      what   W        %bee ey%
      what   W        %B.A.%

21 W:                   [%bee ey%
                         %bee ey%
                         %B.A.%
```

Excerpt 6 (W's presentation) reveals a distinct transition (line 08) from the Q-A phase (lines 01–07) to a separate though related activity (lines 10–21). Several relevant turns at talk highlight this transformation, beginning with L's receipt "uh hum" (line 06), which registers that W has provided the necessary second pair part of L's earlier question (line 01) regarding W's mother's academic past. W attempts to confirm the comprehension (line 07) of the entire audience in English, to which L responds with *wo dong wo dong (1.5) wo dong jiu hao le* [I understood I understood if I understand then it's good]. Assessments like *jiu hao le* [it's good] commonly signal the conclusion of a comment, question, or sequence of talk and have characteristics that inform participants of an impending closing.

In the remainder of Excerpt 6, we see three features commonly found in more traditional lock-step instructional settings. First, L reassumes her position at the head of the class (evidenced in the numerous references made to her writing on the blackboard in lines 11–14). Second, L directs her "recall" work of materials previously covered in class (i.e., the difference between the terms *xuewei* [degree] and *xueshi* ("B.A."")] by framing her questions in the plural, that is *wo gaosu nimen* [listen up] (line 11) and *zhei ge women xue guo le ba* [we've studied this] (line 12). Third, L overtly selects next-turn speakership (lines 15, 20) as she calls upon S and W to produce answers to display or "previously known" questions. Within this type of context, participant roles reveal a more asymmetrical nature where speaking rights become more constrained.

The excerpts presented above reveal the bounded nature of the student presentations as two-part speech activities in which the presenter and audience members communicate information previously unknown to the instructor and where the primary focus is on meaningful communication rather than "correct" language production. For this reason, I contend that this speech event falls under Seedhouse's category of a meaning-and-fluency context, the pedagogical aim of which is described as maximizing "the opportunities for interaction presented by the classroom environment and the classroom speech community itself" (p. 149).

Through analyzing the manner in which particular classroom speech events are organized, specifically the roles participants play within them, CA of classroom discourse has the potential to enrich SLA research by bringing to the fore a variety of different speech events within the larger series of class activities. Though activities may be classified within the categories set out by Seedhouse, what remains uncertain within classroom language analysis—and which these categories themselves ignore altogether—is the manner in which both the instructor and learners play distinct roles in talking-into-being each activity. Categories that gloss over the importance of how participants participate *in situ* in the ongoing turns at talk fail to provide what I see as a fundamental focus of CA research in the classroom. Given the lack of a larger body of research regarding the nature and variety of activities within the classroom, the question then is whether implementing etically created categories such as meaning-and-fluency context as rough descriptors of what ultimately may become a myriad of distinct speech events benefits future analysis of classroom discourse. Fine-grained analysis of larger stretches of classroom discourse is still essential to fully understand how participants within classroom discourse construct and talk-into-being each speech event. One crucial issue is the unique manner in which learners themselves participate in talking into being the pedagogical contexts instructors provide as the "business at hand" within the classroom as institution. What is clear is that within the student presentation, L oriented to her role as instructor by shaping the presentation into its two parts, while the learners oriented to their institutional roles within the activity by offering a presentation and by posing and answering questions.

Repair mechanisms within the student monologue and Q-A phase

Regardless of the individual characteristics or structure of particular classroom speech events, SLA classroom research (cf. Chaudron, 1988) has placed a great deal of importance on the role of repair and correction within the ongoing turn-taking structure of the language classroom, namely, how instructors orient to learner production of non-target-like forms and subsequently, how learners orient to instructor repair. Classroom repair is a phenomenon distinct from that reported in ordinary conversations in that participants display alternative preferences towards self- and other-repair. For instance, McHoul's (1990) classroom research provides evidence of instructors using other-initiated self-repair strategies—particularly by using partial repetitions or reformulations of elements from learners' turns as ways of highlighting trouble sources. According to Macbeth (2004), the purpose of repair in language classrooms is distinct enough from that found in natural conversations to be termed "correction":

> Correction in classrooms is an identifying task and achievement of classroom teaching. As is true of all discursive practical action, repair is then omnirelevant to it, having to do with the first achievements of common understanding that classroom lessons—and their correction sequences—rely upon and reflexively display. (p. 705)

What follows are several excerpts chosen to reveal repair—or, rather, instructor correction—that both coincide and contrast with Seedhouse's categorization of instructor repair within a meaning-and-fluency context, where "according to the emic logic of this L2 classroom context, trouble is anything which impedes communication of meaning or content" (p. 153). Seedhouse's view is that instructors consciously ignore learners' linguistic "errors" as a way of "establishing mutual understanding and negotiating meaning." The data from the CFL student presentations and Q-A phases reveal that L orients to learner production in a way akin to the Seedhouse database in that as the instructor, L routinely avoids overtly repairing linguistic "errors" but rather focuses on trouble sources that hinder communication. Yet, the data also provide clear examples where L does in fact initiate repair work on aspects of learner production that do not hearably result in miscommunication prior to their repair. The types of other-initiated other-repair shown are aimed at correcting presenter and audience member "errors" at the level of pronunciation and lexical choice.

Instructor's repair within presenter/audience member's turns at talk

First, to better understand how instructors make repairs of the type explained by Seedhouse within a meaning-and-fluency context, let us turn to Excerpt 7, involving Q (the presenter) and M (an audience member). At issue is M's pronunciation of *dongtian* [winter].

Excerpt 7, repairing *dongtian* (Q's presentation)

```
01 M: hum (.) qingwen    (.) nei    ge uhm meiyou
      hum     excuse me      those C   uhm N-have
      hum     excuse me      those people uhm who don't

02→   chuan yifu    de    ren     (.5) tamen ((C laughs))
      wear clothes ASSC people         they  ((C laughs))
      wear clothes those people        they  ((C laughs))

03    ~dongtian~ tamen meiyou chuan yifu?
      ~winter~   they  N-have wear  clothes
      in the ~winter~ they don't wear clothes
```

```
04 Q: bu shi (.2) za::i uh::m (.5) sushe li
      N  is        at    uhm        dorm  inside
      no inside uhm the dorm

05 M: %oh% (.) sushe li
      %oh%     dorm  inside
      %oh%     inside the dorm

06 Q: haishi (1.5) uh::m (2.0) uhm (.5) shenma shuo,
      or           uhm         uhm      what   say
      or           uhm         uhm      what can I say

07    (1.5) zai:: uhm (2.5) uhm-
            at    uhm       uhm
            at    uhm       uhm

08 M: -sushe waibian chuan yifu?
       dorm  outside wear  clothes
       outside the dorm do they wear clothes

09 C: ((laughter))

10 Q: shenma shihou (.5) keshi zai (.5) uhm (.5) uhm
      what   time        but   at       uhm      uhm
      what time          but at         uhm      uhm

11    wanshang youshiyou qu (1.5) tamen xihuan (.) da
      night    sometimes go       they  like        play
      night    sometimes they like to go play

12    %frisbee%
      %frisbee%
      %frisbee%

13 L: mei chuan yifu?
      N   wear  clothes
      they don't wear clothes

14 Q: mei chuan yifu    [dui
      N   wear  clothes  correct
      they don't wear clothes correct

15→M:                   [~dongtian dong- dong-~
                         ~winter   wint- wint-~
                         ~winter   wint- wint-~

16→L: -dongtian
       winter
       winter

17 M: dongtian
      winter
      winter
```

```
18 Q: dongtian (.5) dui      dongtian hen(.5)
      winter        correct winter   very
      in winter     correct in winter its very

19    hen  leng
      very cold
      very cold
```

M states his question (lines 01–03) *qingwen (.) neige uhm meiyou chuan yifu de ren (.5) tamen ~dongtian~ tamen meiyou chuan yifu?* [excuse me those people who don't wear clothes...in the ~winter~ they don't wear clothes?], to which Q, in his proceeding turn, begins to formulate an answer. L's other-initiated repair does not come until 11 lines later (line 16), at a time when M returns to reference *~dongtian~* [winter]. Though L interjects a comment (line 13), the conversation about where and when the nudist dormers go nude and what they like doing is clearly produced entirely by M and Q, with L and other audience members withholding talk.

M produces the repairable item, *dongtian* [winter], first in a question in line 02 and then again in line 15 as a rephrased version aimed at refocusing Q's attention to an unanswered element from his original question. Following M's initial question, Q responds (line 04) that the dormers wear no clothes inside the dorm—an answer that fails to fully provide the second pair part to M's question in that it does not address the issue of the winter. M follows with the change of state token "oh" and confirms Q's response with a repetition (line 05). Attempting to continue his answer, Q uses a conventional display of distress, *shenma shou*? [what to say?], along with numerous other false starts and disfluencies. M redirects Q (line 08) with another question, *sushe waibian chuan yifu?* [outside the dorm do they wear clothes?]. Q not only answers this but also provides an explanation as to what the dormers do while outside—though whether the dormers play Frisbee during the winter months is still unclear. Following a request for confirmation by L (line 13) and Q's response to it, M returns to *dongtian* [winter] with what appears (line 15) to be the start of (what eventually results in) his own confirmation regarding the yet unanswered element of his initial question. However, M falters once again in his pronunciation, producing false starts in the form of repetitions—to which L provides self-initiated other-repair. M orients to L's repair by offering a repetition of the trouble source.

Repair work of the kind produced by M and L in lines 15–17 corresponds to previous findings reported by Hosoda (2000, 2006) regarding instances of verbal distress by speakers prompting other-repair. Hosoda's conversation data between advanced nonnative speakers of Japanese and native-speaking Japanese[7] revealed how the occurrence of other-repair was prompted in some way, either verbally or nonverbally, and that this type of other-repair "may have been a sequence-initiating action that made the repair recipient's acceptance behavior in the next slot relevant" (p. 61). The verbal distress (line 15) M produces initiates L's other-repair in the following turn. This type of repair is similar to that reported by Jefferson (1987) as being "exposed correction," in that this type of repair is intended to somehow make known to the prior speaker an error in his or her utterance, that is, "correcting is now the interactional business of these interchanges" (p. 88). More specifically, "someone who at one point produced one sort of object now produces the alternative to it proffered by a co-participant" (p. 89), a pattern that Jefferson describes as X, Y, Y, in which X represents the initial trouble source, Y signifies the proffered correction, and the final Y then indicates that the speaker of the trouble source has provided a repetition of the correction. This, similarly to Hosoda's findings, subsequently makes relevant M's next-turn acceptance (line 17) in which he offers a repetition of L's other-repair. What is important here is not that the repair-work follows a specific repair trajectory but that it provides Q with enough material to respond with his evaluation of winter (lines 18, 19). Clearly, something within this exposed correction sequence handled the miscommunication problem between M and Q. The repair-work generated by L, therefore, noticeably assisted M and Q in continuing their conversation by aiding Q to understand M's question. Excerpt 7 reveals how the instructor repair done in a timely manner addresses the issue of miscommunication between the presenter and an audience member, even though L is not an active participant within the ongoing interaction.

This type of instructor repair work occurs again later as Q and M attempt to overcome difficulties with the lexical item *dizhi* [address], which M has trouble pronouncing and Q, understanding. However, something quite different occurs with respect to the timing of L's other-repair and how that repair is oriented to in the subsequent turns. This difference calls into question Seedhouse's claim of instructor-initiated repair being solely concerned with addressing issues of miscommunication. The Q-A phase is in progress by the time M asks Q for the address of the nudist dormitory.

Excerpt 8, correcting dizhi (Q's presentation)

```
01 M: ah (1.5) qingwen   (.5) nei  ge  sushe de:
      ah       excuse me      that C   dorm  NOM
      ah       excuse me      what is  that dorm's

02    ~dizi~    shi shenma?
      ~address~ is  what
      ~address~

03→L: dizhi
      address
      address
```

04 C: ((laughter))

05 Q: dizi?
address
address

06 M: ~dizi~
~address~
~address~

07 L: dizhi-
address
address

08 M: -zai zai nar?-
at at where
where is it

09 L: -zai na[r?
at where
where is it

10→M: [dizhi
address
address

11 L: ta xiang qu
he want go
he wants to go

12 C: ((laughter))

13 Q: uhm::

14 C: ((laughter))

15 L: ta xiang qu <u>kan</u> (zhei ge)
he want go see (this C)
he wants to go and see ((this))

16 Q: dizhi zai uh:::m (1.5)
address at uhm
the address is uhm

17 M: kai wanxiao mei guanxi
make joke N problem
just joking forget it

18 C: ((audible laughter))

19 Q: zai uhm (.5) %footba::lls% uh (.5)
at uhm %footballs% uh
it's at uhm the %football% uh

```
20    %stadium% (.5) ah:
      %stadium%  ah
      %stadium%  ah
```

Excerpt 8 (Q's presentation) provides an interesting set of other-initiated other-repair items within this rather strained conversation brought on by M's question to Q regarding the location of the nudist dormitory. Regardless of whether M's intention in posing his question (lines 01, 02) was one of humor (as he openly states is the case in his retraction in line 17), once more we see that Q requires extensive repair work on the part of L and M before providing the second pair part answer. As described above, the underlying interactional organization of the Q-A phase is one in which a question from an audience member limits next-turn speakership to the presenter. Therefore, M's question—*nei ge sushe de: ~dizi~ shi shenma?* [what is the ~address~ of that dorm?]—nominates Q as next-turn speaker. However, unlike what we saw in Excerpt 7, in which Q orients in the immediate next turn to M's question by providing some type of response, here L initiates other-repair on the item *dizhi* [address].[8] No signals of distress are apparent within line 01: no false starts, disfluencies, or delays prior to M's production of *dizi*. Yet, L produces other-repair of the "exposed correction" type. Clearly, the timing of this other-initiated other-repair cannot be explained as handling miscommunication. True, Q does target *dizi* as a repairable (line 05) and, following that, requires a good deal of repair work to attend to the second pair part of M's question, but evidence of Q's misunderstanding is apparent only after L's other-initiation of repair. Q's targeting of *dizi* provides proof that L's exposed correction (line 03) fails to forestall miscommunication between Q and M (though at this point, note that audience members display comprehension by responding with laughter).

What is also of interest is how M fails twice to orient to L's other-repair (lines 03, 07) as items requiring specific "repair work." Instead, M directs his own repairs toward remedying Q's misunderstanding in the form of other-initiated self-repair. Notice that instead of attending to L's other-initiated other-repair (line 06), M offers repair following Q's targeting of *dizi* as a repairable in line 05. Though L once again offers other-initiated other-repair (line 07), M responds instead by rephrasing his question (line 08) to *zai zai nar?* [where is it?], thereby attempting to circumnavigate the trouble source altogether. This prompts L to repeat M's rephrased question. Only then does M offer a correction of the trouble source, a delayed orientation to the other-repair L offers (line 07). (However, this temporary "delay" may simply occur due to the series of overlaps we see in lines 06–09.) However, even after six instances of repair (offered by L and M over lines 03 and 06–10), Q has yet to produce the necessary second pair part to M's question. What we then see happening (lines 11, 15) in L's explanation, *taxiangqu* [he wants to go], is not repair work but follow-up work on M's question in the form of a best guess attempt to interpret M's original question. This results in general class laughter (lines 12, 14) and effectively redirects Q to the task of providing the missing second pair part—which he starts to attend to (line 16). Notice that at this point, both learners have produced accurate pronunciations of the trouble source. Thus, L displays her own role within the ongoing activity not only as a facilitator attending to trouble sources causing miscommunication between the presenter and audience member but also as an instructor focusing on the learners' accurate production of the language of instruction. In respect to this, note that both learners, in their respective roles, reveal their orientation to L's repair work focusing on learner forms by either offering repetition (as was the case with M in line 10) or by appropriately pronouncing the targeted word (as with Q in line 16).

Though the type of instructor-initiated repair work seen in Excerpt 7 supports what Seedhouse explains as "the expression of personal meaning rather than... linguistic forms" (p. 149), the manner in which L provides repair in Excerpt 8 is visibly dissimilar to that reported as occurring within Seedhouse's database and thus presents a distinctly unique instructor role played by L within this speech event—one in which L orients to learner errors of linguistic form using exposed correction. Furthermore, how M is shown to orient to L's other-initiated other-repair also raises the question as to whether exposed correction necessarily makes relevant acceptance behavior (e.g., repetition) in the next turn slot.

Instructor repair and individual learner responses: Presenters and audience members

The data presented above shed light on how L's orientation to the ongoing turns-at-talk between the presenter and an audience member both is consistent with Seedhouse's claims of instructor-initiated repair addressing issues of miscommunication (Excerpt 7) and provides conflicting evidence in the example of instructor repair as exposed correction (Excerpt 8). The CFL data also reveals instances where L produces repairs in two other situations: in response to elements within the presenter's monologue and during the Q-A session. In these situations, L performs repairs of the exposed correction type attending to linguistic forms rather than repairs as treatments of troubles made noticeable by overt miscommunication revealed in participants' turns at talk. As we have seen in the above excerpts, the two main trouble sources to which L directs repairs involve learner mispronunciations and inappropriate lexical choices; this is true of L's orientation to learners' language production also in the excerpts that follow. The first two excerpts focus on the repair mechanism at work between L and the presenter; the last, on repair within a conversation between L and an audience member.

In Excerpt 9, M is still in the monologue phase of his presentation, talking about his prior restaurant work experience, when L initiates repair of the exposed type.

Excerpt 9, M's correcting Liang NianQian and Gongzuo (M's presentation)

```
01→M: %yeah% %so% suoyi wo (2.5) eh: (2.5) ~liang
      %yeah% %so% so    I        eh         ~two
      %yeah% %so% so I eh ~two

02    ge:: nian (.5) duo~
      C    year      more~
      years more~

03→L: liang nian qian
      two   year before
      two years ago

04 M: eh (.) wo zai (1.5) TNR
      eh     I  at        tee en arr
      eh at TNR I

05    ~zhongguo-~
      ~China-~
      ~China-~

 06→L: -gongzuo
       work
       worked

07 M: ni  (.5) wo zai TNR
      you      I  at  tee en arr
      you      I worked at TNR

08    [gongzuo
      work
      worked

09→L: [TNR shi shenma?
       TNR is  what
       what does TNR mean

10 M: Today's Noodle and Rice
```

M begins his turn (lines 01 and 02), stating "%yeah%" and "%so%" before producing two noticeably long pauses of 2.5 s each. These disfluencies occur immediately prior to his inappropriate use of *~liang~ ge:: nian (.5) duo* [~two~ years (.5) more]. Immediately following this, L initiates other-repair, stating *liang nian qian* [two years ago], which M acknowledges with *eh* (line 04) before continuing to attempt a completion of the idea begun in his prior turn. However, M then mispronounces the word *gongzuo* [to work], mistakenly producing its spoonerism version, *zhongguo* [China]. L targets this as a trouble source and offers her second other-initiated other-repair (line 06). In his response, M provides more than an acknowledgement; he produces a full repetition of his prior turn, this time incorporating L's repair within a syntactically appropriate slot. Following these two instances of exposed correction, L initiates self-repair (line 09) by asking what the restaurant initials represent. Note that this is a clear example of L initiating repair aimed specifically at addressing her own possible communication problem, a repair of a type absent of targeting language use for correction. Up to this point, L's initiation of repair has been either at resolving hearable instances of communication problems between learners' interaction (Excerpt 7, line 16) or at providing exposed correction (Excerpt 8, line 03). Here in Excerpt 9, in contrast, L offers exposed correction in response to the presenter within the monologue phase of the speech event. M's production of the above spoonerism is a hearable trouble source for L because within the context, the noun "China" does not make sense. Finally, as was shown in Excerpt 7, M reveals his orientation to L's other-initiated other-repair as assigning elements of his prior utterance as trouble-sources and as being in need of some type of acceptance. This is revealed by M's acknowledgement (at the start of line 04) and by his repetition (at the ends of lines 07 and 08).

Another instance of L orienting to a learner's inappropriate lexical choice occurs during W's presentation. In his monologue phase, W has been speaking about his mother's job following her graduation with a PhD in marine biology.

Excerpt 10, W's correcting Zuo Yanjiu (W's presentation)

```
01 W: %so% xianzai ta  bu zai yaoshi (.5) ta yao
      %so% now     she N  at  if          she want
      %so% now     she's not at if        she wants

02    (.5) ta  ta  ~yao~  yanjiu
           she she ~want~ research
           she she ~wants~ research

03→L: zuo yanjiu
      do  research
      to do research

04 W: ta  xihuan [zuo yanjiu   keshi xianzai ta-
      she like    do  research but   now     she
      she likes  to do research but now she

05→L:            [zuo yanjiu
                  do  research
                  to do research

06 W: dang:   (.5) yijiaogao de   (.5) eh,
      become       transfer  ASSC      eh
      going to become transferred to eh,

07    zhiwei (.5) souyi bu neng yanjiu   (.) ta
      position    so    N  can  research     she
      a position  so she can't do research she'll
```

08 (.5) zhi zhi eh: guangli guan- bangongshi
only only eh manage mana- office
only only be eh managing the office

The kinds of obvious displays of verbal distress we saw occurring in Excerpts 7 and 9 just prior to the production of what L then targets as a trouble-source in the next turn slot occur in lines 01 and 02 of Excerpt 10 (W's presentation). W produces several pauses and false starts before saying *~yao~ yanjiu* [~wants~ research]. Following Hosoda, these displays of distress signal L to offer (line 03) the corrected item *zuo yanjiu* [do research]. Though W does not offer an immediate acknowledgment or repetition, W's next independent use of the repaired verb phrase (a continuation of the larger idea begun in lines 01 and 02) is incorporated appropriately. Notice, as well, how L (line 05) offers additional repair work by repeating *zuo yanjiu* [do research] in overlap as W encounters a grammatically relevant insertion place for the trouble source. Once more, L directs repair following hearable displays of distress in the form of pauses and false starts. And, likewise, the learner—as the presenter—orients to L's other-initiated other-repair as being in need of some type of acceptance. As in Excerpts 7 and 9, W displays his orientation by producing repetition.

Excerpt 11 reveals a similar type of repair organization orienting to a learner's mispronunciation. However, what is different here is that this conversation takes place between L and an audience member—rather than the presenter—in a brief discussion of Chinese restaurants and Chinese food.

Excerpt 11, correcting Zhongguo Cai (M's presentation)

01 L: shei qu guo?
who go ASP
who has gone

02 (2.0)

03 L: ni qu guo? ni qu guo?
you go ASP you go ASP
have you gone have you gone

04→ (1.5)

05 L: %oh% shi ba.
%oh% is BA
%oh% really

06 Y: uh hum

07 L: zenma yang?
how kind
how was it

08 S: (ni keyi qing Laoshi)
(you can treat instructor)
(you can treat the instructor to a meal there)

09 C: ((laughter))

10 L: ni bu yao zheiyang zi ta (.) bu shi
you N want this kind offend him N is
you won't offend him it's not

11 ta de dian eh (.) ni qu de Today's Noodle
he ASSC place eh you go ASSC Today's Noodle
his place when did you go to Today's Noodle

12 and Rice shenma shihou qu guo? chi le shenma?
and Rice what time go ASP eat ASP what
and Rice what did you eat

13 zenma yang?
how type
how was it

14 Y: %oh% (.5) uhm (1.5) yi nian yiqian wo qu guo
%oh% uhm one year before I go ASP
%oh% uhm I went a year ago I

15 (.5) wo (.) wo wang le (1.5) keshi wo bu
I I forget ASP because I N
I forgot because I don't

16 xihuan ~zhong(2)guo(2)~ cai
like ~chinese~ food
like ~Chinese~ food

17→L: zhong(1)guo(2) cai
Chinese food
Chinese food

18 Y: ~zhong(1)guo(2)~ cai
~chinese food~
~Chinese~ food

19 L: zhongguo cai (2.5) ni bu xihuan zhongguo cai?
Chinese food you N like Chinese food
Chinese food you don't like Chinese food

20 (1.5) bu hao
N good
not good

21 C: ((laughter))

22 L: y ni yiding xihuan zhongguo cai
Y you must like Chinese food
Y you must like Chinese food

23 C: ((laughter))

24 (2.0)

25 L: hao.
good
good

After L asks who has gone to M's uncle's restaurant, in the 1.5-s gap (line 04), Y apparently self-selects and responds in some nonlinguistic manner to L's question. What makes Y's self-selection apparent is L's comment (line 05) *oh shi ba* [oh really], to which Y responds with "uh hum." This establishes the two speakers and the topic to follow, with L directing questions to Y, an audience member. In the talk that follows (10 lines later in line 17), L initiates other-repair of Y's pronunciation of *zhongguo* [Chinese], which he produces as *zhong(2) guo(2)*[9]rather than as *zhong(1)guo(2).* In the immediate next turn (line 18), Y repeats L's repair. As with Excerpts 9 and 10, no signs of hearable communication problems are oriented to by the other participants—only the exposed correction provided by L.

Summary

Excerpts 8 through 11 reveal the underlying structure of other-initiated other-repair implemented by L in response to learners' mispronunciations and trouble sources involving lexical choice at the word or phrasal level. These instances of instructor repair occur following the production of a trouble source by either a presenter or an audience participant, revealing how, rather than initiate self-repair, L provides other-repair. The data show that this type of instructor repair may be labeled exposed correction rather than repair work as a result of communication problems. The situations in which there was evidence of repair initiated by L have been shown to be: (a) within a Q-A session involving a presenter and an audience member, (b) within a monologue phase between a presenter and L, and c) within a Q-A session between an audience member and L. The data reveal that the learners do at times, though not always, produce hearable displays of distress immediately prior to producing what L subsequently targets for exposed correction. Whether these instances of linguistic distress result in miscommunication with audience members is not revealed in the data (though this may simply be an artifact of the nature of the speech event, in that within a presentation, audience members may not attend to instances of miscommunication in the same manner as within conversations).

The learners—both as audience members and presenters—have a tendency to provide acceptance of correction by L through acknowledgement tokens, repetition, or incorporating the targeted trouble source repair within the next possible grammatically relevant slot. Finally, instructor-initiated repair of this type—having momentarily suspended a monologue or a Q-A segment—does not reveal itself in the data to hamper learners from attending to yet-to-be-completed ideas in the turns following the instances of repair and acceptance.

Discussion

Macbeth (2004) stated of classrooms that:

> the production of correct knowledge, and thus correction, unavoidably become a part of the practical and professional organization of the setting, and one of the prevailing orientations of the parties in the room. (p. 721)

The data above show how one location for instructor-implemented other-initiated other-repair in response to mispronunciation and issues of lexical choice occurred within the next position relative to a trouble source. This type of repair is of the type described by Macbeth (2004) as *classroom correction*, and it, as revealed in the data, assisted in assembling the situated identity of the instructor—as one whose role is to quickly and efficiently correct learner errors within prior turns—and the identities of the presenter and the audience members, whose roles are to accept such correction through acknowledgement tokens, repetitions, or incorporations. This orientation reveals the participants' common understanding of the institutional goals enacted through the co-construction of a speech event and in particular through correction as being "both a contingent *and* a normative exercise, routinely assigned to teachers and played out in their assessments of students' replies in next turns" (Macbeth, p. 723; emphasis in original).

In receiving the correction, the learners displayed their orientation to the instructor's efforts to make known, at the earliest possible moment, trouble sources within the ongoing turn-taking structure. These early initiations of correction effectively suspended turn constructional units projecting further talk, but they were nonetheless accounted for—and therefore made relevant—through learners' acknowledgements, repetitions, or incorporations prior to completion points and relevant sites of speaker change. L's corrections and the subsequent responses offered by the learners, both as presenters and as audience members, allow for the view that such correction sequences were understood by the participants as sequentially appropriate within the ongoing turns at talk of the speech activity. Such collaborative behavior may in fact be common to all language classroom discourse. According to Schegloff et al. (1977), "it appears that other-correction is not so much an alternative to self-correction in conversation in general, but rather a device for dealing with those who are still learning or being taught to operate with a system which requires, for its routine operation, that they be adequate self-monitors and self-correctors as a condition of competence" (p. 381). By producing repetitions, acknowledgement tokens, or incorporations following instructor-initiated repair, the learners displayed a receptive behavior to the modeling of appropriate language use proffered by the instructor. This is the case as well with how the participant learners used turns at talk to position themselves within the overall organization of the classroom speech event. By responding to how the instructor structured the presentation as a speech event to be talked into being, the learners' turns at talk evinced their roles as "presenters" and "audience members."

Seedhouse's (2004) findings were arrived at initially through an emic analysis of a large database composed of a variety of classroom speech events containing instances of instructor repair. From this, the category of meaning-and-fluency context was then constructed to represent the entirety of excerpts within that database, classified as follows:

> the focus is on the expression of personal meaning rather than on linguistic forms, on fluency rather than on accuracy. The focus of repair in this context is on establishing mutual understanding and negotiating meaning....Moreover, it appears that incorrect linguistic forms and interlanguage forms are frequently ignored, unless they lead to breakdown in communication....Exposed and overt correction of incorrect or inappropriate linguistic forms does occur, but it appears to be used only when there is trouble which prevents the interaction from continuing. (p. 148)

Now that we have discussed the manner in which instructor-initiated repair occurred and the issue of learner preference behavior in the third turn position within the CFL data, let us return briefly to Excerpt 1, reported by Seedhouse. The instructor-initiated repair sequences highlighted in Seedhouse's analysis occur in lines 16 and 19. This repair work reveals that in both instances, the learners whose utterances have been targeted for T's repair work in the second turn (L1, L5) produce no follow-up within the third turn, as we saw in the CFL student presentations; instead, two other learners—L2 and L6—self-select to offer repair in the form of additional information. We see that leading up to T's first repair initiation, L1 states, "the marriage in Algeria isn't like the marriage in England" (lines 14, 15). T then initiates repair on L1's utterance, of the type Seedhouse describes as "a clarification of the message or meaning which [T] is aiming at" (p. 150). Though T has initiated repair upon L1's utterance, L2 self-selects with additional information (line 17), with L1 withholding comment. This type of exchange occurs once more in the lines leading up to and following the second instance of instructor-initiated repair, where we first see L5 make the comment "yes more expensive than here" (line 18) and then see T offering repair to obtain further information regarding L5's comment. L5, though, does not produce a comment in the third turn; L6 does (line 20).

This interaction is therefore framed by T requesting information previously unknown to him or her in the form of questions, assessments, and repairs that allow the learners to not only designate the individual best capable of answering such questions but also to self-select at any moment and assist in providing the necessary clarification required by T's repair initiations. As a result, the preference structure found within naturally occurring conversation—self-initiated (self-repair)—is suspended within this speech event as the participants produce what is effectively quite a different take on other-initiated other-repair, in which the "other"s are in fact two separate participants. As the repair work is constructed over the three-turn sequence, three separate participants produce turns at talk. This repair work, however, does not reveal itself to be problematic for the participants as they fulfill their roles in the "business at hand," that is, "clarification of the message or meaning the teacher is aiming at" (p. 150). This statement, which serves as a form of addendum to Seedhouse's definition of a meaning-and-fluency context, raises an interesting question about what the underlying purpose of such a context is: for learners to produce personal meaning or for learners to produce language geared toward a meaning orchestrated by the instructor. This is a question, too, that may be applied to the CFL data, in terms of how L directs the flow of information within the student-presentation as a speech event. Regardless of to what extent each of these instructors controlled the flow of information within each of these speech events (arguably the job of instructors within classrooms), the manners in which each used repair strategies and the ways in which the learners responded to such instances of repair in the third turn are clearly different.

Findings from the CFL data presented in this chapter have revealed instances of instructor repair that are similar to what Seedhouse observed (Excerpts 7, 9, 10), but other cases are contrary to those of Seedhouse (Excerpts 8, 11). The contrast cases may stem from differences in the classroom speech events examined by Seedhouse and in this chapter. My main contention is that Seedhouse's framework seems to ignore the possibility of more than three manners of instructional discourse being provided by language teachers within classrooms of teachers managing and assisting in assembling learner roles within various classroom speech events in differing ways. Within the data that Seedhouse provides, for instance, nothing comparable is found in regards to how language learners are positioned within the speech event to fulfill roles where they are actively assuming more control of the amount and type of discourse produced within the language classroom. Instead, in Seedhouse's data, one generally finds examples where the teacher is controlling most if not all of the interaction. The kind of questioning of the students to obtain information regarding cultural aspects unknown to the instructor as seen in Excerpt 1 seems to be only a part of a larger activity looked at without its full context. The data from the Chinese language classroom thus represents a single deviant case to Seedhouse's categorization framework and therefore is evidence enough to rethink the scope of the framework. This point confirms Macbeth's point, quoted earlier, in that there is reason to question the assumption that data derived from differing educational contexts, even different levels within the same context, will produce similar repair trajectories. Instructors come to the business of providing repair and correction in various ways, depending potentially on such conditions as educational philosophy, teacher training, learner level, language (culture) of instruction, or particular speech events. Because of this, I believe that it is premature for researchers analyzing classroom discourse using a CA approach to use etic categories to define larger speech events as being directly linked to the mechanism of repair or classroom correction. Instead, I believe that more examination is required to better understand how the variety of speech events within differing second language classroom contexts not only provide examples of the organization of repair but also reveal how each may distinctly be talked into being through the joint participation of the instructors and learners.

Notes

1 Although Seedhouse claimed that these categories were motivated by his emic analysis of data, these categories have an etic origin in second language acquisition research, not to mention that the very act of imposing categories is etic in nature. The data in this paper demonstrate that adopting these etic categories is problematic.

2 Data originally reported in Hasan (1988, pp.258–259).

3 While Hall (2007) recently argued for a distinction between repair and classroom correction, others (including Seedhouse, 2007) have continued to view classroom correction practices as special cases of repair under the particular constraints of the classroom as an institutional setting.

4 *Laoshi,* translated as "instructor," is referred to as L throughout both data transcripts and discussions.

5 "Audience" or "audience member(s)" are terms used to highlight the roles that certain learners play within the presentation, as opposed to the "presenter."

6 Data excerpts come from three presenters, noted within transcripts as M, Q, and W. Various letters of the alphabet indicate all other audience members, with C (i.e., "class") signifying multiple audience members of an indeterminate number responding at once.

7 The use of the categories "nonnative" and "native" speaker follows Hosoda (2000).

8 At issue here is the zh [t§] sound in *dizhi*, which M mispronounces as z [ts].

9 Within the Wade-Gile pinyin orthographic system, parenthetic numbers such as these signify which of the four tones is used to pronounce any individual character.

The word "China" is pronounced as zhōng(1)guó(2), with a first (flat) tone for zhōng(1) and a second (rising) tone for guó(2).

References

Chaudron, C. (1988). *Second language classrooms: Research on teaching and learning.* Cambridge, UK: Cambridge University Press.

Drew, P. (1997). "Open" class repair initiators in response to sequential sources of trouble in conversation. *Journal of Pragmatics, 28*, 69–101.

Drew, P., & Heritage, J. (1992). Analyzing talk at work: An introduction. In P. Drew & J. Heritage (Eds.), *Talk at work: Interaction in institutional settings* (pp. 3–65). Cambridge, UK: Cambridge University Press.

Geis, M. L. (1995). *Speech acts and conversational interaction.* New York: Cambridge University Press.

Goodwin, M. N. (1996). Announcements in their environment: Prosody within a multi-activity work setting. In E. Couper-Kuhlen & M. Selting (Eds.), *Prosody in conversation: Interactional studies* (pp. 436–461). Cambridge, UK: Cambridge University Press.

Hall, J. K. (2007). Redressing the roles of correction and repair in research on second and foreign language learning. *Modern Language Journal, 91*(4), 511–526.

Hasan, A. S. (1988). *Variation in spoken discourse in and beyond the English foreign language classroom: A comparative study.* Unpublished doctoral dissertation, University of Aston, Aston, England.

Heritage, J. (1984). A change-of-state token and aspects of its sequential placement. In J. M. Atkinson & J. Heritage (Eds.), *Structures of social action: Studies in conversation analysis* (pp. 299–345). Cambridge: Cambridge University Press.

Hosoda, Y. (2000). Other-repair in Japanese conversations between nonnative and native speakers. *Issues in Applied Linguistics, 11*(1), 39–63.

Hosoda, Y. (2006). Repair and relevance of differential language expertise in second language conversations. *Applied Linguistics, 27*(1), 25–50.

Jefferson, G. (1987). On exposed and embedded correction in conversation. In G. Button & J. Lee (Eds.), *Talk and social organisation* (pp. 86–100). Clevedon, UK: Multilingual Matters.

Macbeth, D. (2004). The relevance of repair for classroom correction. *Language in Society, 33*, 703–736.

Markee, N. (2000). *Conversation analysis.* Mahwah, NJ: Erlbaum.

Markee, N. P. P. (2003). *Zones of interactional transitions.* Paper presented in the invited colloquium on Classroom Talks at the American Association of Applied Linguistics conference, Arlington, VA.

Markee, N. (2004). Zones of interactional transition in ESL classes. *The Modern Language Journal, 88*, 583–596.

McHoul, A. (1990). The organization of repair in classroom talk. *Language in Society, 19,* 349–377.

Mitchell, R., Parkinson, B., & Johnstone, R. (1981). *The foreign language classroom: An observational study.* Stirling Educational Monographs (No. 9). Stirling, UK: Department of Education, University of Stirling.

Pomerantz, A. (1984). Pursuing a response. In J. M. Atkinson & J. Heritage (Eds.), *Structures of social action* (pp. 152–163). Cambridge, UK: Cambridge University Press.

Sacks, H., Schegloff, E., & Jefferson, G. (1974). A simplest systematics for the organization of turn-taking for conversation. *Language, 53*, 361–382.

Schegloff, E. (1979a). Identification and recognition in telephone conversation openings. In G. Psathas (Ed.), *Everyday language: Studies in ethnomethodology* (pp. 23–78). New York: Irvington.

Schegloff, E. (1979b). The relevance of repair to syntax-for-conversation. In T. Givón (Ed.), *Syntax and semantics, Vol. 12: Discourse and syntax* (pp. 261–288). New York: Academic Press.

Schegloff, E. (1987). Recycled turn beginnings: A precise repair mechanism in conversation's turn taking organization. In G. Button & J. Lee (Eds.), *Talk and social organisation* (pp. 70–85). Clevedon, UK: Multilingual Matters.

Schegloff, E. (1992). Repair after next turn: The last structurally provided defense of intersubjectivity in conversation. *American Journal of Sociology, 98,* 1295–1345.

Schegloff, E. (1995). Parties and joint talk: Two ways in which numbers are significant for Talk-in-Interaction. In P. ten Have & G. Psathas (Eds.), *Situated order: Studies in the social organization of talk and embodied activities* (pp. 31–42). Washington, DC: University Press of America.

Schegloff, E. (1997). Practices and actions: Boundary cases of other-initiated repair. *Discourse Processes, 23,* 499–547.

Schegloff, E. (2000). Overlapping talk and the organization of turn-taking for conversation. *Language in Society, 29,* 1–6.

Schegloff, E., Jefferson, G., & Sacks, H. (1977). The preference for self-correction in the organization of repair in conversation. *Language, 53,* 361–382.

Seedhouse, P. (2004). *The interactional architecture of the language classroom: A conversation analysis perspective.* Oxford, UK: Blackwell.

Seedhouse, P. (2007). On ethnomethodological CA and "linguistic CA": A reply to Hall. *Modern Language Journal, 91*(4), 527–533.

Sinclair, J., & Coulthard, M. (1975). *Toward an analysis of discourse: The English used by teachers and pupils.* Oxford, UK: Oxford University Press.

Appendix: Special transcript symbols and abbreviations

~	encloses lexical items mispronounced and producing other-initiated repair
!	indicates lexical item said abruptly
%	encloses lexical items in English
N	negator
ASP	aspectual marker
CRS	currently relevant state (*le*)
PRT	particle
Q	question marker
C	classifier
ASSC	associative
BA	*ba*
NOM	nominalizer (*de*)
CP	complement
CSC	complex stative construction

11 CA for Computer-Mediated Interaction in the Spanish L2 Classroom

Marta González-Lloret
University of Hawai'i at Mānoa

Introduction

During the past 20 years, starting with the popularization of Internet Relay Chat (IRC) and Web-based chatrooms, a number of studies have been conducted on the use of synchronous[1] computer-mediated communication (SCMC) and its effect on language learning. Most of the early studies focused on quantifiable aspects of SCMC and compared these with oral face-to-face (FtF) interaction (Beauvois, 1998; Kern, 1995; Lee, 1998; Warschauer, 1996).

Since the new century began, the line of research on SCMC has moved from descriptive accounts to the exploration of the uses of and practices in the medium. This research has focused mainly on interactional, social, and cultural aspects of SCMC. Several studies have examined the communication language students used to describe their interactional patterns and negotiation strategies under the assumption that interaction is beneficial for L2 acquisition (Kern, 1995; Kötter, 2003; LeMond, 2004; Ortega, 1997; Smith, 2003; Toyoda & Harrison, 2002; Tudini, 2003; Warschauer, 1996), others have focused on the relationship between the task and the medium (Jonassen & Kwon, 2001; Pellettieri, 1999; Smith, 2001). Most of the recent studies seem to be moving towards finding a more direct link between the use of SCMC and actual learning (Payne & Ross, 2005; Payne & Whitney, 2002; Pellettieri, 2000; Smith, 2004).

Talk-in-interaction: Multilingual perspectives, pp. 281–316, Hanh Nguyen & Gabriele Kasper (Eds.), 2009
Honolulu, HI: University of Hawai'i, National Foreign Language Resource Center

Studies focusing on the social aspects of SCMC are intercultural studies on telecollaboration (usually also incorporating e-mail and FtF components) and involve students of one specific L2 interacting with L1 speakers of that language (Belz, 2003, 2005; Belz & Kinginger, 2002; Furstenberg, 2003; Furstenberg, Levet, English, & Maillet, 2001; Kinginger, 2000; Kramsch & Thorne, 2002; Thorne, 2003; Ware, 2003). In a different line of research are classroom studies that focus on patterns of social participation (Darhower, 2000; Freiermuth, 2002) and issues of identity, gender, and ethnicity (Nguyen & Kellogg, 2005; Warschauer, 2000; Wolfe, 2000).[2]

Although several of the studies mentioned above have investigated interactional patterns of SCMC, they have not done so from a microanalytical perspective. Such an approach to the data can help us discover the more fine-grained details of language learners' interactions, how they respond to the medium, and how their interaction is constructed and maintained. These are important research questions if SCMC is to be incorporated into language classrooms because the more we know about how the interaction is constructed, the more we can help our students socialize into a medium increasingly used in their everyday communication.

Several authors have taken a conversation-analytic (CA) approach to SCMC interaction among speakers (not language learners), investigating the nature of SCMC sequence organization and its turn-taking system and how these compare to the well-established findings of sequence and turn organization in oral communication described by Sacks, Schegloff, and Jefferson (1974), Schegloff (1968, 1996, 1997, 2007), and Schegloff, Jefferson, and Sacks (1977; Garcia & Jacobs, 1999; Herring, 1999; Hutchby, 2001; Murray, 1989). In addition, a few studies have used a CA perspective to study specific sequences in SCMC such as openings (Rintel, Mulholland, & Pittam, 2001), lack of response (Rintel, Pittam, & Mulholland, 2003), repair (Schönfeldt & Golato, 2003), and requests and second assessments (Golato & Taleghani-Nikazm, 2006).

In SLA, there is a growing interest in the analysis of language learners' interactions from a CA perspective (Brouwer, 2003; Carroll, 2000; Hauser, 2005; Kasper, 2006; Kurhila, 2001; Lee, 2004; Mori, 2002; Mori & Hayashi, 2006; Seedhouse, 2004; Wong, 2000; Wong & Olsher, 2000; see also Gardner & Wagner, 2004; Richards & Seedhouse, 2005; and a special issue of *The Modern Language Journal*, Markee, 2004). However, to the best of my knowledge, only a few studies (Kitade, 2000; Negretti, 1999) have investigated the interactional SCMC patterns of language learners from a CA perspective.

Negretti (1999) investigated the dialogue produced by eight NNSs of English (L1 Italian) engaged in SCMC interaction with NSs of English through a cybercafé site. She studied the sequence organization of the chatroom interactions, paying special attention to the organization of turn-taking, openings, closings, and turn design. She also reported on several paralinguistic features found in her data and how NSs and NNSs used them differently. Negretti concluded that her participants (both NSs and NNSs) demonstrated the context relevance of Web chat in their interactions, adapting to the medium as needed. They engaged in complicated interactions, maintained turn-taking sequences that were more disrupted than in oral interaction, performed opening and closing sequences similar to oral interactions, and used speaker selection as the main technique for turn allocation. In addition, the participants in her study used a variety of paralinguistic features to compensate for the lack of visual cues present in oral interaction, mainly, punctuation and uppercase writing. However, the NSs and learners used some paralinguistic features differently. While the NSs used onomatopoeia and emoticons frequently, the learners never used them. Negretti pointed out that this difference was probably due to the learners' lack of familiarity with the technology.

Kitade (2000) studied learner–learner and learner–native speaker interactions in a Japanese Internet chat environment. She presented those features of CMC that are conducive to language learning according to several theories of learning: negotiation of input, modification of output, and cooperative learning in the zone of proximal development (ZPD). Kitade examined the data from a CA perspective and concluded that CMC facilitates collaboration and comprehensible input by providing opportunities for learner-centered interaction.

Given the interactive nature of SCMC and the characteristics that make it so similar to FtF interaction, approaching the study of SCMC from a CA perspective seems a sensible decision, especially because CA has proved a useful approach to the study of talk-in-interaction for 40 years (however, see Murray, 1991, for some criticism of the use of CA to study CMC). In addition, CA may be a useful approach to studying SCMC because it considers the importance of context in shaping the structure of interaction and in shaping participants' roles in meaning creation and the use of strategies that help them make sense through sequences of action that constitute the context itself (Heritage, 2004).

As is obvious from the scant number of microanalytical studies of SCMC to date, research is strongly needed in this area. This study is intended to fill this gap by providing a conversation analysis of SCMC interaction among language learners.

SCMC as a different form of interaction

SCMC discourse has been defined as a hybrid between oral and written communication, with shared characteristics, but different from both (Coolot & Bellmore, 1996; Davis & Brewer, 1997; Ferrara, Brunner, & Whittemore, 1991; Lanham, 1993; Murray, 1995). This hybrid quality is one of the most salient characteristics of this medium, but it is not unique to it. A note on the refrigerator written to a roommate is delivered in the written medium; nevertheless, it may contain linguistic features (e.g., colloquialisms, simplified structures, incomplete sentences, jokes) that are more typical of oral communication. In the case of SCMC, the mode of communication is written (keyboard strokes transmitted via the Internet), but the interactional features of the discourse are similar to an oral conversation. The fact that the medium is an emergent form of communication entails that the participants are helping shape the medium. This study investigates whether the resources learners deploy are similar to those used by native speakers. Methodologically, I consider whether CA is a suitable approach to the study of SCMC and in particular, to the study of L2 learners' SCMC, given the restrictions that the medium and the participants' proficiency may impose on the interaction.

Participants and data

The participants were 25 fourth-semester university students enrolled in a low-intermediate level Spanish conversation class. The interactions took place outside of the classroom, at times negotiated by the students in groups of 3 or 4. For each interaction, the students had to complete an assigned task. The first task was a simple vocabulary game, where one student gave definitions and examples of relevant vocabulary words that the other students needed to guess; the students switched roles by turns. The second activity was designed as a decision-making task. The students were asked to choose the next semester classes for a foreign/exchange student new to their university, selecting the classes that would benefit a foreign freshmen most based on the university's offerings, their experience in the classes, and their ideas on how to socialize and integrate the new student in the state's culture (see Appendix A for the task instructions).

Each group met online in their university Web page chatroom, which was restricted to class members. This chatroom consisted of three windows: On the right side was a window showing the participants who were online. On the left side, the upper window recorded the chat script. A lower smaller window presented a space for typing messages. Messages could be sent to the entire group by pressing enter or to one selected member by pressing the "whisper" button[3] (see Figure 1). The students did not receive special training on the use of this tool because all of them were familiar with it and had used it in the past. Each conversation lasted between 10 and 45 minutes, and at the end, one of the students was responsible for e-mailing the script of the interaction to the researcher (because this chat tool did not have the capacity to save the interactions). Although the students were free to connect through different chat software, only one group used a different program: Yahoo Messenger, a free downloadable program and Internet-based application (available at http://messenger.yahoo.com/).

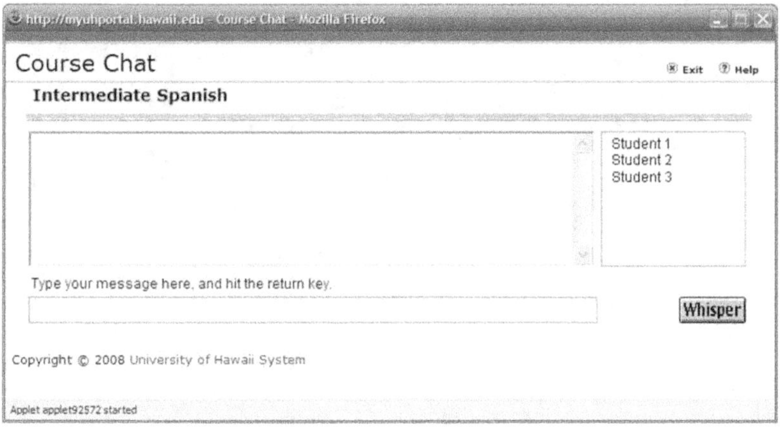

Figure 1. Chatroom screen shot.

Findings

Sequence organization

The sequence organization in SCMC seems chaotic and highly disrupted, without any adjacency (Herring, 1999), mainly due to the fact that the exact timing of message placement cannot be controlled by the interactants. That is, they do not know exactly where in the interaction their messages are going to be placed, and this is even more unpredictable when more participants join the interaction (Schönfeldt & Golato, 2003). All researchers agree that the structure of SCMC is very different from that of oral communication, and although some researchers have claimed that the interaction is not sequential and does not follow the time patterns of adjacency pairs and sequences described for oral interaction by previous CA research (Negretti, 1999), others have maintained that the overall structure of the interaction is different from the individual strands or conversations, which do seem to adhere to the basic rules of sequential organization, especially with respect to adjacency pairs (Schönfeldt & Golato, 2003).

Although the data for this study seemed chaotic at first glimpse, a closer look demonstrated that the students conducted complicated interactions without any apparent problems and that multiple strands of communication are intertwined, forming the macrosequence of the interaction.

Excerpt 1[4]

```
01 A Heidi (10:41:31PM):      Hola chicas!
                              Hello girls!

02 A Heidi (10:41:37PM):      como estan?
                              how are you?

03 A, B John (10:41:46PM):    Buena! Escuchas que carlos
                              va a Hawaii para escuela?
                              Good!  You hear that Carlos
                              is going to Hawai'i for school?

04 A Sheila (10:41:54PM):     hola, bien, y tu
                              hello, good, and you

05 B Heidi (10:41:58PM):      no!
                              no!

06 B John(10:42:03PM):        si es la verdad
                              yes it is true

07 B Sheila (10:42:12PM):     cuando llegara?
                              when will he arrive?

08 A Heidi (10:42:14PM):      bien.
                              good.

09 B John (10:42:45PM):       este verano, pienso en junio
                              this summer, I think in June

10 B Heidi (10:43:08PM):      o perfecto! el puede empezar
                              con el semestre de verano
                              oh perfect! he can start
                              with the summer semester
```

In spoken interaction, some turns that appear next to each other constitute adjacency pairs, which form strongly interrelated sequences.[5] When we observe the turns that appear next to each other in Excerpt 1, we can see that the next turn following a first pair part is not necessarily a second pair part as projected by the preceding turn. However, a closer look shows that interlocutors' messages clearly orient to specific previous turns within the conversation. This phenomenon was observed in chatrooms where all interactants were native speakers and was termed "virtual adjacency" by Schönfeldt and Golato (2003). Excerpt 1 contains several such virtual adjacency pairs, for example, greeting-greeting (lines 1/2–4, 1/2–8, 1/2–3), question-answer (lines 03–05, 07–09), and news announcement-response (lines 03–05).

The data also suggest that students orient to a sequence composed of adjacency pairs, even inside a "disrupted" interaction. Excerpt 2 exemplifies how students orient to the absence of an expected response in a greeting sequence, where the second part of the adjacency pair is missing.

Excerpt 2

```
01 Lee (9:15:25PM):        Hola
                           Hello

02 Pat (9:15:26PM):        hey
                           hey

03 Pat (9:15:28PM):        hola iris
                           hello iris

04 Iris (9:15:30PM)        chicos como estas?
                           guys how are you?

05 Pat (9:15:35PM):        bien, empezamos tnego (err)
                           mucha trabaja
                           good, we start I have (err) a
                           lot of work

06 Lee (9:15:40PM):        si me too
                           yes me too

07 Iris (9:15:50PM):       kristie
                           kristie

08 Iris (9:15:52PM):       !
                           !

09 Pat (9:15:55PM):        Kristie Kristie Kristie Kristie
                           Kristie!!!
                           Kristie Kristie Kristie Kristie
                           Kristie!!!

10 Kristie (9:16:08PM):  si estoy
                         yes I am

11 Iris (9:16:12PM):     finalmente
                         finally

12 Iris (9:16:15PM):     jajajaja
                         hahahaha

13 Lee (9:16:20PM):      es damn tiempo
                         it's damn time

14 Iris (9:16:24PM):     jajajaja
                         Hahahaha

15 Iris (9:16:30PM):     como estas
                         how are you
```

16 Iris (9:16:33PM): ?
?

17 Pat (9:16:38PM): Kristie?
Kristie?

18 Pat (9:16:43PM): alo>
hello>

19 Iris (9:16:55PM): kristie? hola?
kristie? hello?

20 Kristie (9:17:02PM): lo siento
I'm sorry

21 Lee (9:17:10PM): hola, mi nombre es companera de kristie, yo hablo y hablo
hello, my name is Kristie's partner, I talk and talk

Lee, Pat, and Iris greet their classmates when they enter the chatroom. Although Kristie shows as present in the chatroom, she has not answered anybody's greeting. In line 07, Iris summons Kristie unsuccessfully. After this, we see an upgraded turn by Pat in line 09 with multiple uses of her name and a typographic extension, which is usually the equivalent to a phonetic indication of excitement, negative or positive (Danet, Ruedenberg-Wright, & Rosenbaum-Tamari, 1996; Werry, 1996). The missing second pair part to the summons is treated as relevantly absent by the coparticipants. Both Iris in line 11, with *finalmente* [finally] and Lee in line 13, with *es damn tiempo* [it's damn time] hold Kristie accountable for her lack of response when she finally shows up briefly in line 10. Kristie orients to this accountability by apologizing in line 20, entering *lo siento* [I'm sorry] when she reenters the conversation.

Several instances of adjacency pairs and virtual adjacency pairs, especially opening and closing sequences, are present in the data (in agreement with Negretti, 1999). These sequences are very similar to those used by native speakers in SCMC (Rintel, Pittam, & Mulholland, 2003), and both are very similar to those used in FtF or telephone interaction (in addition to the CA literature, see Braun, 1998; Edmondson, 1981).[6] The data also present instances where messages that seem part of a sequence are only placed next to each other by chance (called "phantom agency" by Garcia & Jacobs, 1999), resulting from the participants' lack of control over the placement of their postings. Commitment from the participants is required to distinguish and orient to those messages that are relevant to their conversational strands and disregard those that are not. Language students do not seem to be different from native speakers in this respect.

Turns and the turn-taking system

While in oral conversation the floor usually belongs to one speaker at a time (Sacks et al., 1974), in SCMC, all participants can compose and post messages simultaneously. The sequence in which the messages appear depends on when they are received by the server, which in turn depends on the length of the turn, the composer's typing speed, and the speed of the connection between the participant's computer and the server. Therefore, no competition occurs for the *right* to submit a message (all messages can be submitted at any time), although competition may occur to submit first for a specific turn space (Garcia & Jacobs, 1999; Schönfeldt & Golato, 2003) because the farther a message is placed from its referent, the higher the probability that it be misunderstood or ignored.

SCMC studies highly agree that the turn-taking system in SCMC is quite different from any FtF turn-taking system and that it is highly constrained by the medium (Garcia & Jacobs, 1999; Herring, 1999; Murray, 1989; Negretti, 1999; Schönfeldt & Golato, 2003). In oral conversation, participants indicate to their coparticipants the ends of their turn construction units (TCUs) through vocal and nonvocal behaviors. When the end of a turn can be projected, a turn-transition becomes relevant, at which point the current speaker may select the next speaker, or if this does not happen, a next speaker may self-select, and if the next speaker does not self-select, then the current speaker may continue (Sacks et al., 1974). Because in SCMC, turns appear onscreen as complete units, recipients cannot anticipate transition-relevance places; in fact, each posted message is viewed as a transition-relevance place (Garcia & Jacobs, 1999). Based on this, most authors have claimed that the concept of TCU is irrelevant to SCMC and that chat interactions cannot exhibit overlaps, recycled turn beginnings, collaborative completions, interruptions, continuers, and so forth (Garcia & Jacobs, 1999; Negretti, 1999; Schönfeldt & Golato, 2003).

Although most of the data for this study were gathered using the class' selected chat program, one group used Yahoo Messenger for their interactions, which includes timestamps indicating when a message is posted. Even though the timestamps cannot guarantee that the turns were produced at the same time because Internet connections, server access and speeds, and typing speeds influence the exact order in which a turns appear onscreen, timestamps indicate how overlaps[7] are recorded by the computer, how turns appear onscreen, and when they are made available to the participants (see Excerpt 3).

Excerpt 3

```
26 John (10:46:04PM):    pienso que el debe estudiar
                         historia tambien
                         I think he should study
                         history too
```

27 Sheila (10:46:16PM): si!
yes!

28 John (10:46:19PM): →porque hay muchos cursos de historia en la universidad
because there are a lot of history courses at the university

29 Heidi (10:46:19PM):→carlos va a estar muy ocupado
carlos is going to be very busy

30 John (10:46:27PM): es la verdad!
it is true!

33 Sheila (10:46:56PM): porque todavia el debe sabe algo de historia
because he still needs to know some history

34 John (10:47:00PM): →como la historia de Hawai y otras
like history of Hawai'i and others

35 Heidi (10:47:00PM):→si un poco de la historia
yes some history

((lines omitted))

88 Heidi (10:55:29PM): pero no mucha lectura
but not a lot of reading

89 John (10:55:34PM): →exactamente
exactly

90 Sheila (10:55:34PM):→si
yes

Excerpt 3 shows three instances where students' postings overlap, and although the timestamps cannot guarantee the students' intentions of posting the messages at that exact time, the microanalysis shows that Heidi's statement *Carlos va a estar muy ocupado* [Carlos is going to be very busy] in line 29 is a comment on John's proposal in line 26, *pienso que el debe estudiar historia tambien* [I think he should study history too]. Heidi's comment could be seen as a mild disagreement to John's proposal and Sheila's emphatic agreement (line 27), which happens at the same time that John expands his idea in line 28. Lines 34 and 35 are both tokens of agreement with Sheila's statement in line 33 that are posted at the same time. Similarly, both lines 89 and 90 are tokens of agreement with Heidi's statement in line 88 and they appear simultaneously onscreen.

However, the timestamps are not the best indicators that some overlapping is occurring. Excerpt 4 illustrates that the participants themselves orient to the overlapping messages in SCMC. Mele, in line 26, posts, "we wrote this at the same time," orienting to the overlap of her turn in line 24 and Ana's turn in line 23.

Excerpt 4

22 Mele: diane lane es una actriz que me gusta tambien
diane lane is an actress that I like also

23 Ana: Si. me gusta Ia pelicula "Under the Tuscan Sun"
Yes. I like the movie "Under the Tuscan Sun"

24 Mele: "debajo el tuscan sol" es un video muy bueno
"Under the Tuscan Sun" is a good video

25 Mele: que sorpresa
what a surprise

26 Mele: nosotros escribimos esta al mismo tiempo
we wrote this at the same time

27 Ana: ;)
;)

These data suggest that some type of overlap occurs in SCMC and that it is visible not only in the timestamps (which may be deceiving as an etic measurement) but also in the participants' orientations to the phenomenon.

Turn allocation is highly constrained by the characteristics of the computer as a medium of interaction. The lack of visual and audio clues limits the strategies that the participants can use for turn allocation. Common features for turn allocation in FtF interaction such as gaze, intonation, and gestures (Mori & Hayashi, 2006; Olsher, 2004) are not available. Nevertheless, SCMC participants use a variety of different turn allocation techniques. They select a next speaker, or what Garcia and Jacobs (1999) have termed "next poster," by addressing their postings to a specific participant, especially in multiparty SCMC. Garcia and Jacobs pointed out that this method of turn allocation does not guarantee that a participant's turn selected as next will be posted in the 'next' turn, and therefore, they refer to the selected participant as a "future" poster rather than a 'next' poster. Although nothing guarantees that a selected participant will be the next poster, the participants are motivated to position messages as closely as possible to their referents to increase the chances of being understood. One of the techniques that has been pointed out to select a next speaker in SCMC is to address the next speaker explicitly inside a turn. While previous studies found high use of address terms in SCMC (Herring, 1999; Kitade, 2000; Negretti, 1999; Schönfeldt & Golato, 2003), the students in my data did not show such a phenomenon. Quite likely, because most of the interactions involved only two or three participants, the need for explicit future poster selection was not as great as in public chatrooms where turns are highly displaced by the large numbers of postings from multiple participants.

The following is an example of the use of the 'current speaker selects next' technique. Quite similar to instances of telephone openings, Charles opens the conversation with a summons, which makes a response relevant in the next turn as part of a 'summons-answer sequence' (Schegloff, 1968).

Excerpt 5

```
30 Charles: hola Donde estan mi amigas?
            hello Where are you my friends?

31 Charles: hoy, tengo muchas otras tareas Garamba!
            today, I have a lot of other homework darn!

32 Charles: hola!!
            hello!!

33 Anna:    como esta ?
            how are you ?

34 Rose:    hola
            hello

35 Rose:    bien, gracias
            good, thank you
```

Because Charles's summons (line 30) receives no answer, he continues, upgrading his turn with an expletive and an exclamation mark (line 31). When he still does not obtain a response, he repeats his summons, upgrading it with several exclamation marks (line 32), a common practice in SCMC, usually equivalent to some intonation emphasis in oral conversation.[8]

In oral conversation, the current speaker may decide to hold his or her turn and continue speaking beyond a transition-relevance place. This practice would usually be accompanied by nonfinal pitch (Selting, 1996) and/or nonverbal cues that would prevent a potential next speaker from treating the turn as having reached a transition-relevance place. In SCMC, turn-keeping practices are highly constrained because prosodic and nonverbal cues are limited. One of the techniques that native speakers use to hold the floor is to post shorter messages that can be typed and submitted faster, and if the message is too long, divide it in two or more separate turns (Garcia & Jacobs, 1999). The students' data also show instances of participants trying to maintain the floor. For example, in Excerpt 4 above, Mele breaks her message into two turns (line 25, "what a surprise," and line 26, "we wrote this at the same time"), probably to ensure that at least her turn in line 25, a very short one, is placed before Ana continues the conversation. Although participants seem to have no conventional way to signal that a turn is incomplete beyond a possible completion point, Herring (1999) explained that one of her participants reported agreeing with his partner on the use of "%" at the end of a message to indicate that the poster was not ready to yield the floor. Similarly, in Excerpt 6, one of the students uses an ellipsis to maintain her turn. In line 03, Chrisi announces that she is ready to start the task at hand and negotiates her role as the conductor ("I will start, do you agree?"). Her partner accepts her role in line 04, and a multiturn sequence starts that Chrisi marks with ellipsises to hold the floor for five turns (lines 05–09). Not until she types a period instead of an ellipsis, in line 09, does Moto venture his answer, which seems to imply that Moto orients to the ellipses as a device to hold the floor and to the period in line 09 as indicating a transition-relevance place.

Excerpt 6

01 Chrisi: hola, Moto! Como estas?
hello, Moto! How are you?

02 Moto: Hola Chrisi, estoy lista, y tu?
Hello Chrisi, I am ready, and you?

03 Chrisi: si, estoy lista. Yo empezara, de acuerdo?
yes, I am ready. I will start (err), do you agree?

04 Moto: si
yes

05 Chrisi: OK, esta persona tiene mucho dinero y trabaja con peliculas...
OK, this person has a lot of money and works with movies…

06 Chrisi: tiene coches buenos...
has good cars

07 Chrisi: su trabajo es va a fiestas y paga los actores...
his job is he goes to parties and pays the actors…

08 Chrisi: y director ...
and director…

09 Chrisi: su nombre siempre en poster de la pelicula.
his name is always in movie poster.

10 Moto: es el productor?
is it the producer?

```
11 Chrisi: si, es cierto.
           yes, it is true.
```

This interaction suggests that students adapt conventions from talk to the affordances of the SCMC environment.

Similarities and differences between L1 and L2 discourse in SCMC

In general, the students' data in this study reflect most of the practices that L1 interactants use to compensate for the different sequential structure in SCMC.[9] Their interactions incorporate many paralinguistic features such as typographical extensions (exclamation marks, letter repetition, full uppercase) analogous to phonetic indicators of verbal excitement, and emoticons, which are ASCII elements ordered to form silhouettes (see Appendix B for examples). This is a finding opposite to that of Negretti (1999), who observed that emoticons were used much less by NNSs than NSs, probably due to the reported unfamiliarity of her Italian students with the medium. The students also use punctuation marks very often (consistent with Negretti's and Kitade's data), orienting to the meaning these symbols convey.

Excerpt 7

```
108 John (10:59:55PM):    necesitamos con el sobre las
                          clases optativas también
                          we need with the envelope the
                          optional classes also

109 John (11:00:19PM):    hay mucho, como ceramica,
                          fotografia.....
                          there is a lot, like ceramics,
                          photography.....

110 Heidi (11:00:25PM):   ?
                          ?

111 John (11:00:35PM):    necesitamos HABLAR con el
                          we need TO TALK with him

112 Sheila (11:00:39PM): si
                          Yes

113 Sheila (11:01:09PM): todavia tiene una peticion de
                          ingreso?
                          does he still have an admission
                          petition?
```

In Excerpt 7, Heidi's use of a single question mark (line 110) seems to indicate a lack of understanding and a request for clarification, and John orients to it by repairing his previous turn (line 108) by inserting the missing key word *hablar* [to talk] in line 111, which he capitalizes for emphasis. This is understood and acknowledged by Sheila with an agreement token, "yes," in line 112.

Excerpt 8

```
23 Rose: gracias?
         thank you?

24 Dani: no problema
         no problem

25 Rose: i mean, gracias.
         I mean, thank you.
```

In Excerpt 8, Rose does a third-turn repair (Schegloff, 1997) in line 25 by repeating her turn in 23 without the question mark, suggesting that the symbol carries enough meaning to convey an erroneous message worth repairing, even though Rose had already received a relevant response from Dani.

Another feature, which also coincides with Negretti's data, is the lack of onomatopoeia, a phenomenon quite abundant in NS data. Few instances of onomatopoeia were in the present study's data, most of them representing laughter. Excerpt 9 is an example of an interaction containing two types of onomatopoeia (*aye* in lines 284 and 286 and *jajajjaja* in line 287), and several emoticons (*=/* [a worried face] in line 277, *=(* [a sad face] in line 279, and *=P* [a mouth with a tongue sticking out] in line 287) as part of a sequence containing joking and laughter.

Excerpt 9

```
277 Jane: si esta bien, pero no tengo tiempo =/
          yes it's ok, but I don't have a lot of time =/

278 Dani: no se
          I don't know

279 Jane: =(
          =(

280 Low:  que quiere hacer?
          what do you want to do?

281 Jane: mierda
          shit

282 Dani: I could just get some random person

283 Jane: si esta bien
          yes that's fine
```

284 Low: aye!!!
aye!!!

285 Low: Jane dice un palabra mala!!!!!
Jane says a bad word!!!!!

286 Dani: aye!
aye!

287 Jane: jajajjaja =P
hahahhaha =P

288 Dani: que es mierda?
what is 'mierda'?

In line 284, Low uses the onomatopoeia *aye* as a response to Jane's use of the word *mierda* [shit] in the conversation. In line 286, Dani aligns with Low's reproach, although he does not know what the meaning of the word is. Jane uses an onomatopoeia to laugh, marked by the use of an emoticon that represents joking or mockery (a tongue sticking out a mouth), which mitigates the severity of her previous action.

Two other discrepancies between L1 users of SCMC and the students in this study were the students' nonuse of acronyms[10] (e.g., *LoL* [Laughing out Loud]) to increase the speed and efficiency of communication and of "bracketed actions" such as *((nods))*, *((grinds))*, and *((giggles))* next to textual entries (Murphy & Collins, 1997). A possible explanation for the lack of these forms is that they require a sophisticated knowledge of the target language that the students did not yet posses. When the students occasionally switch to their L1, they then incorporate these features, as in Excerpt 10. Here, both Fred in lines 57 and 60 and Rose in line 61 display familiarity with these conventions, although they do not use them in Spanish.

Excerpt 10

57 Fred: **r u** suppose to ask questions first,
cuz *i'm confused*

58 Cris: Rose, tu tiene una palabra y nos hagamos
preguntas para tu?
Rose, you have a word and he ask (err) each
other for you?

59 Rose: only one person at a time describes, and we
have to guess

60 Fred: **r** we asking yes and no **Qs**

```
61 Rose: u give clues and we have to guess. same as the
         oral test, like what i was doing
```

A final point regarding similarities between L1 and L2 SCMC data is the inclusion of humor in chats. Herring (1999) suggested that the high popularity of CMC, in spite of its lack of sequential coherence, can be explained by its potential for language play and the use of humor. Several other authors also described CMC as an inherently playful medium (Baym, 1995; Danet, 2001; Danet et al., 1996; Rafaeli & Sudweeks, 1998). Students in the present study also use humor and laughter during their interactions. Note that students are actually "laughing in Spanish" because they are using an onomatopoeia that reflects the sound of laughter through Spanish spelling (*jajaja*, instead of the conventional English form *hahaha*). This is exemplified by line 287 in Excerpt 9 above, line 19 in Excerpt 11, and line 98 in Excerpt 12.

Excerpts 11 and 12 are also examples of students joking with each other and playing with language (laughter, onomatopoeia, and the use of emoticons).

Excerpt 11

```
18 Rose: hold mi novio esta en el telefono
         wait my boyfriend is on the phone

19 Dani: jajajajajaja
         hahahahahaha

20 Jane: aye!
         aye!

21 Dani: tiene 26 anos
         he is 26 years (old)

22 Rose: y tu tienes 0 anos
         and you are 0 years (old)

23 Jane: =P
         =P

24 Dani: digas ''hola abuelo'' para mi
         say (err) "hello grandfather" from (err) me

25 Rose: =P
         =P
```

In Excerpt 11, line 22, Rose orients to Dani's comment about her boyfriend's age in line 21 and jokes about Dani being childish by using a parallel language structure (line 22) to Dani's turn in line 21. Jane aligns with Rose against Dani by posting the emoticon in line 23, a mouth with a tongue sticking out, a symbol usually used to state mockery or annoyance towards Dani, which was common among the girls in this group.[11]

Dani jokes again in line 24 about Rose's boyfriend's age by calling him *abuelo* [grandfather], to which Rose repeats Jane's "gesture" in line 25, reinforcing her alliance with Jane against Dani.

Excerpt 12

```
95 Kimo: quien envia esto a la profesora?
         who sends this to the teacher?

96 Fred: necesita ser una mujer, porque los hombre estan
         demasiado inteligente
         it should be a woman, because men are (err)
         too intelligent

97 Mele: voy hacer lo
         I am going to do it

98 Kimo: jaja, un chiste una vez mas
         haha, a joke one more time

99 Melo: harelo?
         I will do it (err)?
```

In Excerpt 12, one of the participants makes an explicit reference to the joking nature of Fred, one of his classmates. Although the laughter token in line 98 (*jaja*) would have been enough recognition of the joke, Kimo adds "a joke one more time," which suggests that Kimo has experienced several of Fred's jokes before.

Orientation to language and task

One main finding from the microanalysis is that in the SCMC, the students are not only concerned with constructing and maintaining the interaction, but they are also orienting to the task they are performing and the language they are using.

The interactions are shaped and characterized by the orientation to the task at hand, as in Excerpt 13, where both students orient to the nature of the task.

Excerpt 13

```
001 Chrisi: hola, Moto! Como estas?
            Hello, Moto! How are you?

002 Moto:   Hola Chris, estoy lista, y tu?
            Hello Chris, I am ready, and you?
```

003 Chrisi: si, estoy lista. Yo empezara, de acuerdo?
yes, I am ready. I will start(err), agree?

004 Moto: si
yes

((lines omitted))

150 Moto: Pues, OK. Buen trabajo. Tengo que hacer mi tarea. Tengo que leer mucho ingles.
Well, OK. Good job. I have to do my homework. I have to read a lot of English.

151 Chrisi: Aye de mi. Buena suerte. Hasta manana.
Poor me (?). Good luck. See you tomorrow

152 Moto: Si, adios, Chrisi!
Yes, good bye, Chrisi!

153 Chrisi: Adios!! =)
Good bye!! =)

In line 03, Chrisi announces that she is going to start the task by posting *Yo empezara (err), de acuerdo?* [I will start, agree?], when Moto in line 02 affirms to be ready ("I am ready, and you?"). They are not talking about starting the conversation because the conversation is already going on; they are co-constructing the transition to the institutionally mandated task-structured activity (see also He, 1995). At the end of the interaction, Moto in line 150 compliments his classmate for a job well done, orienting to the interaction as a classroom activity.

Besides several mentions of the task, the data show different turn-taking patterns when the students are engaged in the task-structured activity rather than in social conversation.

Excerpt 14

330 Low: En este clase, los estudiante aprenderan de la profesora famosa Pele, tambien se llama la dio *de volcanos.*
In this class, students will learn from the famous professor Pele, also called the god (error)of volcanoes.

331 Dani: sounds good

332 Dani: hows everyone doing on their page description of their class

333 Low: 54 palabras de yo
54 words of I

334 Jane: en el curso de ingles ensenaran por billy shakespear, un pariente de william shakespeare. Aprenderan sobre los estilos de escritos differentes como dramatico, theme (err), opinionado, infromativo y mas. Tambien...
In the English coùrse will be taught (err) by Shakespeare, a relative of William Shakespeare. They will learn about different writing styles, such as dramatic, arugemnto, opinion (err), informative and more. Also...

335 Kay: en la asignatura Coro Concierto aprendaria a cantar musica de renacimiento al presente. Tambien aprendaria a cantar con el piano, la guitarra y sin acompanamiento. Ademas cantaria en grupos de varios tamanos.
In the subject Concert Choir would learn (err) to sing Renaissance music to the present. Also they would learn to sing with the piano, guitar, and without an instrument. Also they would sing in several groups of various sizes

336 Low: yo pensaba esto fue mi descripción
I thought that was my description

337 Jane: tambien, escrito creativa y partes de gramatica y composición
also creative writing and parts of grammar and composition

338 Kay: estoy finuto con mi descripción
I am finished with my description

339 Jane: cuales los actividades de sus clases?
which class activities?

340 Jane: yo olvide. Lo siento
I forgot. I am sorry

While sentences are usually short in SCMC interaction, the students use very long, uninterrupted turns when sharing their written passages for their common project (Excerpt 14). This technique is somehow parallel to reading from a passage out loud during spoken interaction.

In addition to orienting to the task, the students orient frequently to the language, which is usually not the case with L1 interactants in SCMC, who also produce misspellings and typing errors. Excerpt 15 illustrates an L1 speaker misspelling the word *graduar* in line 45 without any orientation to it or attempt to self-correct it. Likewise, the L1 speaker in Excerpt 16 produces a morphological error in the auxiliary verb (*ha* instead of *he*) and two misspellings (*mam* for *mamá* and *comencar* for *comenzar*) without any type of repair sequence being initiated.[12]

Excerpt 15

44 May [11:00:39AM]: me duele la cabeza un poco
I have a small headache

45 Sara [11:00:43AM]: hey, te vas a graudar pronto no?
hey, you are going to graduate (err) right?

46 May [11:01:10AM]: si, es verdad
yes, it is true

47 Sara [11:01:15AM]: lo siento que te duele. Muchos estudios huh?
I am sorry it hurts. Lots to study huh?

Excerpt 16

15 Sole [11:07:44AM]: si. Yo ha visitado. muchas veces. Mi mam va a ir. este agosto Yo no puedo porque acabo de comencar un trabajo
yes. I have (err) visited. many times. My mom (misspelled) is going to go this august. I cannot because I have just started (err) a job

16 Sole [11:08:11AM]: si, me gustaria MUCHISIMO si vienes.
Yes, I'd love it A LOT if you come.

17 Ali [11:08:27AM]: a mi tambiem
me too

The students' data, however, contain many self-corrections, especially of spelling and morphological markers (subject-verb agreement, gender and number noun-adjective agreement), which seems to indicate that they saw the activity not simply as a free conversation or leisure activity, but as an activity linked directly to language learning and language practice.

Excerpt 17

27 Ana: ok... umm este grupo filman las peliculas o las espectaculos
ok...umm this group film the movies or the shows

28 Ana: pero las personas no son los actores
but the persons are not actors

29 Ana: *este grupo filma
this group films

30 Charles: el equipo de grabacion
the filming crew

31 Ana: si
yes

Excerpt 18

03 Dani: estaes lista?
are (err) you ready?

04 Rose: eh?
eh?

05 Dani: spelling was wrong

06 Rose: lista....con?
ready... with?

07 Dani: con la ejericio
with the exercise

08 Rose: ok.

09 Rose: no

Excerpt 17 is an example of how a student (Ana) takes an extra turn, in line 29, to repair a morphological error—she had marked the verb ending for plural form *filman* [they film], while the subject is singular: *este grupo* [this group]. She initiates the repair with an asterisk, perhaps to note that this was a repair and not new information, although this error would probably not have had much impact on the meaning of her turns in lines 27 and 28. In Excerpt 18, Dani attempts an other-initiated repair of his turn in line 03 after Rose signals nonunderstanding in line 04. Instead of repairing with a correction, Dani gives a metalinguistic explanation in the L1[13] of his mistake, which is enough for Rose to understand the turn and continue the interaction in line 06. These students' orientations towards their own language production may have a positive impact on their language acquisition (Buckwalter, 2001; Foster & Ohta, 2005; Swain, 2000).

Summary

Although the interaction in SCMC did not allow the students to use the same resources as in oral conversation (e.g., relying on the prior turn as context, accessing a turn as it is being produced to project an upcoming transition-relevance place), the students engaged in meaningful and organized interaction, coping with the lack of nonverbal resources and restrictions of the medium by using new resources, such as splitting messages, using emoticons and diacritic markers, and verbalizing sounds such as laughter, much in the same way that native speakers do.[14] They collaboratively constructed their interactions in spite of several constraints of the medium (Murray, 1989) and successfully accomplished the task at hand while orienting to their language production. The students also engaged in interactional practices such as greetings, topic management, and closings, which are usually not part of their classroom practices but are highly frequent in social interaction and therefore necessary for their development of L2 interactional competence. For this reason and because SCMC is becoming more and more prominent in any student's daily communication, the incorporation of SCMC in the language classroom seems to be a positive complement to any well developed second language curriculum.

CA for L2 SCMC?

From the scant number of studies referred to earlier in this chapter, we can gather that research on L2 computer-mediated interaction is still in the early stages. CA is an excellent approach that allows the researcher to microanalyze data by "attending to the minute details of the interactional conduct" (Kasper, 2004, p. 564). Through CA, we can see that students engaged in SCMC can successfully manage complex interactions, orienting to sequences composed of "virtual" adjacency pairs, allocating turns through principles borrowed from oral interaction and incorporating a variety of resources that define the medium and compensate for a lack of visual clues. In addition, CA reveals that language students can dynamically construct interaction and switch between different types of activities, orienting to their talk not only as mundane conversation, but also as an institutionally bounded classroom activity. In summary, CA allows us to see language learners as competent users of SCMC who interact with others and the medium in a fashion very similar to that of L1 speakers in spite of their limited linguistic abilities.

On the other hand, some researchers have pointed out the multidimensional and nonlinear sequentiality of SCMC, which poses a problem for CA's sequential approach to data (Garcia & Jacobs, 1999). SCMC may well not conform to the turn-taking sequence as proposed by Sacks et al. (1974) because it does not use purely oral conversation, and the sequential principles are tidily related to the medium. Therefore, rather than imposing existing structures on the new medium, we should be looking at how the participants are achieving different sequence types in the medium, much in the same way that telephone conversations have been explored using a CA approach (Schegloff, 1979, 2002; Wong, 2002).

Finally, Garcia and Jacobs (1999) claimed that CA may not be an appropriate tool for the study of SCMC because analysis of only the textual data may not be enough to explain what happens in the process. Garcia and Jacobs used video data of their participants' screens to investigate the composing process before the turns were posted to the chatroom. They concluded that without video, the turn-taking process cannot be seen, and no claims can be made about, for instance, the process of repairs in SCMC because when a turn is posted, whether any self-correction occurred before posting is impossible to know. Although video recording of this type may be imperative for certain areas of study (e.g., institutional use of SCMC, composition processes), it is not necessary for the study of interaction as constructed and viewed by participants. From a CA perspective, what happens before turns are posted is not relevant to the interaction unless the participants demonstrate it explicitly through their interactions or unless it is "brought into being by the actions people produce" (Pomerantz & Fehr, 1997, p. 70). Participants cannot see what is written on the other participants' screens before it is posted or deleted; therefore, it is irrelevant to them and to the interaction. I believe that CA is a solid and useful framework for the study of computer-mediated interaction.

Notes

1 The term 'synchronous' is used here to refer to conversation in a chatroom where all participants are connected at the same time. Some authors prefer to term this type of interaction 'quasi-synchronous,' reserving the term 'synchronous' for oral communication (Garcia & Jacobs, 1999).

2 For an annotated bibliography of some of these studies, see Kern, Ware, and Warschauer (2004).

3 Although anonymity is a characteristic of most chatrooms, this environment was not anonymous: the students' names were displayed in the right window, and the students could not select nicknames. This feature made the interaction even more similar to FtF oral interaction. Although the environment included a "whisper" feature that allowed one student to communicate with another without the rest seeing that interaction, none of the students used this feature.

4 All orthographic and diacritic marks in the transcripts represent the participants' original postings, including typographical errors. The translation was done by the researcher, and efforts were made to reflect the students' utterances as much as possible. Morphological, typographical, and lexical errors, although frequent, are only marked in the translation (as "err") when relevant for the interaction. All names are pseudonyms.

5 Although very common in SCMC, the interruption of adjacency pairs is not exclusive of this medium. Insertion sequences, repairs, and utterances from a

multiparty oral conversation might interrupt an adjacency pair in FtF conversation (Schegloff, 2007).

6 Note that Murray (1998) found opposite results in her data of technical consultations through CMC.

7 Some of the ongoing debate about what constitutes 'overlapping' in SCMC has to do with the definition of overlap. If we take a very general definition, "talk by more than one person at a time in the same conversation" (Schegloff, 2000, p. 2), instances such as the ones in Excerpt 4 could be considered overlapping. However, if we consider Schegloff's provision that overlapping occurs when more than one speaker talks in a conversation, "which is the locus for the 'one-speaker-at-a-time' provision in the first instance" (Schegloff, 2000, p. 5), then SCMC does not seem to be an appropriate environment in which to be discussing overlapping because one of the main intrinsic characteristics of SCMC is the possibility of multiple speakers and multiple conversations occurring at the same time.

8 Note that in oral communication, if a current speaker selects a next speaker, and the other speakers do not take a turn, the resulting absence of a turn (silence) may be part of the format of a dispreferred second pair part. However, the tolerance for the absence of a turn from the recipient of a 'current speaker selects next' technique in SCMC seems to be nonproblematic for the participants (lines 33–35). This is an important area in much need of further research.

9 Note that in this study, the participants are learners of Spanish, while in Negretti's study, the participants were learners of English, and in Kitade's study, they were learners of Japanese. Although the ideal comparison would be between SCM interactions among L1 Spanish speakers on the one hand and learners of Spanish on the other, most of the published studies of SCMC among native speakers included English or German L1 participants. Although this difference in language may somehow affect the interaction (Egbert, 1996), the lack of studies of L1 Spanish speakers engaged in SCMC makes this less ideal comparison a necessary step.

10 The use of acronyms is a general practice in several languages. However, the acronyms themselves are language specific.

11 In this group, Dani often joked and flirted with the girls, who usually agreed that he was a "silly" student.

12 See Appendix C for examples of students orienting to grammatical mistakes.

13 Although not explored in detail in this study, some codeswitching occurs during the interactions where most students shared an L1.

14 This is in comparison to several interactions between L1 Spanish speakers and students of Spanish as a foreign language, collected as part of a future project (data not presented here).

References

Beauvois, M. H. (1998). Conversations in slow motion: Computer-mediated communication in the foreign language classroom. *The Canadian Modern Language Review, 54*, 455–464.

Baym, N. (1995). The emergence of community in computer-mediated community. In S. G. Jones (Ed.), *Cybersociety, computer-mediated communication and community* (pp. 138–163). Thousand Oaks, CA: Sage.

Belz, J. A. (2003). Linguistic perspectives on the development of intercultural competence in telecollaboration. *Language Learning and Technology, 7*, 68–117.

Belz, J. A. (2005). Intercultural questioning, discovery and tension in Internet-mediated language learning partnerships. *Language and Intercultural Communication, 5*, 1–37.

Belz, J. A., & Kinginger, C. (2002). The cross-linguistic development of address form use in telecollaborative language learning: Two case studies. *The Canadian Modern Language Review, 59*, 189–214.

Braun, F. (1998). *Terms of address: Problems of patterns and usage in various languages and cultures*. Berlin, Germany: Mouton de Gruyter.

Brouwer, C. E. (2003). Word searches in NNS-NS interaction: Opportunities for language learning? *The Modern Language Journal, 87*, 534–546.

Buckwalter, P. (2001). Repair sequences in Spanish L2 dyadic discourse: A descriptive study. *The Modern Language Journal, 85*, 380–397.

Carroll, D. (2000). Precision timing in novice-to-novice L2 conversations. *Issues in Applied Linguistics, 11*, 67–110.

Danet, B. (2001). *Cyberpl@y: Communicating online*. Oxford, UK: Berg Publishers.

Danet, B., Ruedenberg-Wright, L., & Rosenbaum-Tamari, Y. (1996). "Hmmm...where's that smoke coming from?" Writing, play and performance on Internet Relay Chat. *Journal of Computer-Mediated Communication, 2*(4). Available at http://www.ascusc.org/jcmc/vol2/issue4/danet.html

Darhower, M. (2000). Interactional features of synchronous computer-mediated communication in the intermediate L2 class: A sociocultural study. *CALICO Journal, 19*, 249–275.

Davis, B. H., & Brewer, J. P. (1997). *Electronic discourse: Linguistic individuals in virtual space*. New York: State University of New York Press.

Edmondson, W. (1981). *Spoken discourse: A model for analysis*. London: Longman.

Ferrara, K., Brunner, H., & Whittemore, G. (1991). Interactive written discourse as an emergent register. *Written Communication, 8*, 8–34.

Foster, P., & Ohta, A. S. (2005). Negotiation for meaning and peer assistance in second language classrooms. *Applied Linguistics, 26*, 402–430.

Freiermuth, M. R. (2002). Online chatting: An alternative approach to simulations. *Simulation & Gaming, 32*, 187–195.

Furstenberg, G. (2003). Reading between the cultural lines. In P. Patrikis (Ed.), *Reading between the lines: Perspectives on foreign language literacy* (pp. 74–98). New Haven, CT: Yale University Press.

Furstenberg, G., Levet, S., English, K., & Maillet, K. (2001). Giving a virtual voice to the silent language of culture: The CULTURA project. *Language Learning and Technology, 5*(1). Available at http://llt.msu.edu/vol5num1/furstenberg/default.html

Garcia, A. C., & Jacobs, J. B. (1999). The eyes of the beholder: Understanding the turn-taking system in quasi-synchronous computer-mediated communication. *Research on Language and Social Interaction, 32*, 337–367.

Gardner, R., & Wagner, J. (Eds.). (2004). *Second language conversations*. London: Continuum.

Golato, A., & Taleghani-Nikazm, C. (2006). Negotiation of face in Web chats. *Multilingua, 25*, 293–322.

Hauser, E. (2005). Coding 'corrective recasts': The maintenance of meaning and more fundamental problems. *Applied Linguistics, 26*, 293–316.

He, A. W. (1995). Co-constructing institutional identities: The case of student counselees. *Research on Language and Social Interaction*, *28*, 213–231.

Heritage, J. (2004). Conversation analysis and institutional talk: Analyzing data. In D. Silverman (Ed.), *Qualitative research* (2nd ed.). (pp. 222–245). London: Sage.

Heritage, J., & Atkinson, J. M. (1984). Introduction. In J. M. Atkinson & J. Heritage (Eds.), *Structures of social action: Studies in conversation analysis* (pp. 1–15). Cambridge, UK: Cambridge University Press.

Herring, S. (1999). Interactional coherence in CMC. *Journal of Computer Mediated Communication, 4*. Available at http://jcmc.indiana.edu/vol4/issue4/herring.html

Hutchby, I. (2001). *Conversation and technology: From the telephone to the Internet.* Cambridge, UK: Polity Press.

Jonassen, D., & Kwon, H. (2001). Communication patterns in computer mediated versus face-to-face group problem solving. *Educational Technology Research and Development, 49*, 35–51.

Kasper, G. (2004). Participant orientations in German conversation-for-learning. *The Modern Language Journal, 88*, 551–567.

Kasper, G. (2006). Beyond repair: Conversation analysis as an approach to SLA. *AILA Review, 19*, 83–99.

Kern, R. (1995). Restructuring classroom interaction with networked computers: Effects on quantity and characteristics of language production. *The Modern Language Journal, 79*(4), 457–476.

Kinginger, C. (Ed.). (2000). *Learning the pragmatics of solidarity in the networked foreign language classroom.* Mahwah, NJ: Lawrence Erlbaum.

Kitade, K. (2000). L2 learners' discourse and SLA theories in CMC: Collaborative interaction in Internet chat. *Computer Assisted Language Learning, 13*, 143–166.

Kötter, M. (2003). Negotiation of meaning and codeswitching in online tandems. *Language Learning and Technology, 7*(2), 145–172. Available at http://llt.msu.edu/vol7num2/kotter/default.html

Kramsch, C., & Thorne, S. (2002). Foreign language learning as global communicative practice. [Electronic version]. In D. Block & D. Cameron (Eds.), *Language learning and teaching in the age of globalization*. London: Routledge.

Kurhila, S. (2001). Correction in talk between native and non-native speaker. *Journal of Pragmatics, 33*, 1083–1110.

Lanham, R. A. (1993). *The electronic word: Democracy, technology, and the arts*. Chicago: University of Chicago Press.

Lee, L. (1998). Going beyond classroom learning: Acquiring cultural knowledge via on-line newspapers and intercultural exchanges via on-line chatrooms. *CALICO Journal, 16*, 101–120.

Lee, Y-A. (2004). The work of examples in classroom instruction. *Linguistics and Education, 15*, 99–120.

LeMond, M. M. (2004). *Synchronous computer-mediated team-based learning in the Spanish foreign language classroom*. Unpublished doctoral dissertation, University of Texas at Austin, TX.

Mori, J. (2002). Task-design, plan and development of talk-in-interaction: An analysis of a small group activity in a Japanese language classroom. *Applied Linguistics, 23*, 323–347.

Mori, J., & Hayashi, M. (2006). The achievement of intersubjectivity through embodied completions: A study of interactions between first and second language speakers. *Applied Linguistics*, *27,* 195–219.

Murphy, K. L., & Collins, M. P. (1997). Communication conventions in instructional electronic chats. *First Monday, 2*(11). Available at http://www.firstmonday.org/issues/issue2002_2011/murphy/index.html

Murray, D. (1989). When the medium determines the truth: Turn-taking in computer conversation. In H. Coleman (Ed.), *Working with language* (pp. 319–337). The Hague, Netherlands: Mouton.

Murray, D. (1991). *Conversation for action: The computer terminal as medium of communication*. Amsterdam: John Benjamins.

Murray, D. (1995). *Knowledge machines: Language and information in a technological society*. London: Longman.

Negretti, R. (1999). Web-based activities and SLA: A conversational analysis approach. *Language Learning and Technology, 3*, 75–87. Available at http://llt.msu.edu/vol3num1/negretti/index.html

Nguyen, H. & Kellogg, G. (2005). Emergent identities in online discussions for second language learning. *The Canadian Modern Language Review, 62*, 111–136.

Olsher, D. (2004). Talk and gesture: The embodied completion of sequential actions in spoken interaction. In R. Gardner & J. Wagner (Eds.), *Second language conversation* (pp. 221–245). London: Continuum.

Ortega, L. (1997). Processes and outcomes in network classroom interaction: Defining the research agenda for L2 computer-assisted classroom discussion. *Language Learning and Technology, 1*, 82–93.

Payne, J. S., & Ross, B. (2005). Working memory, synchronous CMC, and L2 oral proficiency development. *Language Learning and Technology, 9*(3), 35–54.

Payne, S., & Whitney, P. J. (2002). Developing L2 oral proficiency through synchronous CMC: Output, working memory, and interlanguage development. *CALICO Journal, 20*(1), 7–32.

Pellettieri, J. (1999). *Why talk? Investigating the role of task-based interaction through synchronous network-based communication among classroom learners of Spanish.* Unpublished doctoral dissertation, University of California at Davis, CA.

Pellettieri, J. (2000). Negotiation in Cyberspace: The role of chatting in the development of grammatical competence. In M. Warschauer & R. Kern (Eds.), *Network-based language teaching: Concepts and practice* (pp. 59–86). Cambridge, UK: Cambridge University Press.

Pomerantz, A., & Fehr, B. J. (1997). Conversation analysis: An approach to the study of social action and sense-making practices. In T. van Dijk (Ed.), *Discourse as social interaction* (pp. 1–37). Thousand Oaks, CA: Sage.

Rafaeli, S., & Sudweeks, F. (1998). Interactivity on the Nets. In F. Sudweeks, M. McLaughlin, & S. Rafaeli (Eds.), *Network and netplay: Virtual groups on the Internet.* Cambridge, MA: MIT Press.

Richards, K., & Seedhouse, P. (Eds.). (2005). *Applying conversation analysis.* New York: Palgrave Macmillan.

Rintel, E. S., Pittam, J., & Mulholland, J. (2003). Time will tell: Ambiguous non-responses on Internet relay chat. *Communication Institute for Online Scholarship, 13(1).* Available at http://www.cios.org/getfile/rintel_v13n1

Rintel, S., Mulholland, J., & Pittam, J. (2001). First things first: Internet relay chat openings. *Journal of Computer Mediated Communication*, 6. Available at http://jcmc.indiana.edu/vol6/issue3/rintel.html

Sacks, H., Schegloff, E. A., & Jefferson, G. (1974). A simplest systematics for the organization of turn-taking for conversation. *Language, 50*, 696–735.

Schegloff, E. A. (1968). Sequencing in conversational openings. *American Anthropologist, 70*, 1075–1095.

Schegloff, E. (1979). Identification and recognition in telephone conversation openings. In G. Psathas (Ed.), *Everyday language: Studies in ethnomethodology* (pp. 23–78). New York: Irvington Publishers.

Schegloff, E. A. (1996). Turn organization: One intersection of grammar and interaction. In E. Ochs, E. A. Schegloff, & S. Thompson (Eds.), *Interaction and grammar* (pp. 52–133). Cambridge, UK: Cambridge University Press.

Schegloff, E. A. (1997). Third turn repair. In G. R. Guy, C. Feagin, D. Schiffrin & J. Baugh (Eds.), *Towards a social science of language: Papers in honor of William Labov, Vol. 2: Social interaction and discourse structures* (pp. 31–40). Amsterdam: John Benjamins.

Schegloff, E. (2000). Overlapping talk and the organization of turn-taking for conversation. *Language in Society, 29*, 1–63.

Schegloff, E. A. (2002). Beginnings in the telephone. In E. Katz & M. Aakhus (Eds.), *Perpetual contact: Mobile communication, private talk, public performance* (pp. 284–300). Cambridge, UK: Cambridge University Press.

Schegloff, E. A. (2007). *Sequence organization in interaction.* Cambridge, UK: Cambridge University Press.

Schegloff, E. A., Jefferson, G., & Sacks, H. (1977). The preference for self-correction in the organization of repair in conversation. *Language, 53*, 361–382.

Schönfeldt, J., & Golato, A. (2003). Repair in chats: A conversation analytic approach. *Research on Language and Social Interaction, 36*, 241–284.

Seedhouse, P. (2004). *The interactional architecture of the language classroom: A conversation analysis perspective.* Oxford, UK: Blackwell.

Selting, M. (1996). On the interplay of syntax and prosody in the constitution of turn-constructional units and turns in conversation. *Pragmatics, 6*, 357–388.

Smith, B. (2001). *Taking students to task: Task-based computer-mediated communication and negotiated interaction in the ESL classroom.* Unpublished doctoral dissertation, University of Arizona, Tucson, AZ.

Smith, B. (2003). Computer-mediated negotiated interaction: An expanded model. *The Modern Language Journal, 87*, 38–57.

Smith, B. (2004). Computer-mediated negotiated interaction and lexical acquisition. *Studies in Second Language Acquisition, 26*, 365–398.

Swain, M. (2000). The output hypothesis and beyond: Mediating acquisition through collaborative dialogue. In J. P. Lantolf (Ed.), *Sociocultural theory and second language learning* (pp. 97–114). New York: Oxford University Press.

Thorne, S. L. (2003). Artifacts and cultures-of-use in intercultural communication. *Language Learning and Technology, 7*(2), 38–67.

Toyoda, E., & Harrison, R. (2002). Categorization of text chat communication between learners and native speakers of Japanese. *Language Learning and Technology*, 6, 82–99.

Tudini, V. (2003). Using native speakers in chat. *Language Learning and Technology*, 7, 141–159.

Ware, P. (2003). *From involvement to engagement in online communication: Promoting intercultural competence in foreign language education.* Unpublished doctoral dissertation, University of California, Berkeley, CA.

Warschauer, M. (1996). Comparing face-to-face and electronic discussion in the second language classroom. *CALICO Journal, 13*, 7–26.

Warschauer, M. (2000). *Language, identity, and the Internet.* New York: Routledge.

Werry, C. C. (1996). Linguistic and interactional features of internet relay chat. In S. Herring (Ed.), *Computer-mediated communication. Linguistic, social, and cross-cultural perspectives* (pp. 47–63). Amsterdam: John Benjamins.

Wolfe, J. (2000). Gender, ethnicity, and classroom discourse communication patterns of Hispanic and white students in networked classrooms. *Written Communication, 17*, 491–519.

Wong, J. (2000). Delayed next turn repair initiation in native/nonnative speaker English conversation. *Applied Linguistics, 21*, 244–267.

Wong, J. (2002). "Applying conversation analysis" in applied linguistics: Evaluating dialogue in English as a second language textbooks. *International Review of Applied Linguistics in Language Teaching, 40*, 37–60.

Wong, J., & Olsher, D. (2000). Reflections on conversation analysis and nonnative speaker talk: An interview with Emanuel Schegloff. *Issues in Applied Linguistics, 11*, 111–128.

Appendix A: Task instructions

Students received the instructions only in the target language. A translation is offered to help the reader.

Task 1

Juego de vocabulario

En cada grupo uno de los estudiantes va a definir y dar pistas sobre una de las palabras del vocabulario de este capítulo relacionada con el cine y el mundo del entretenimiento. Pueden dar ejemplos y claves, pero no usar la palabra que están definiendo. Cuando alguien adivina la palabra, esa persona define la siguiente palabra. Deberían definir al menos 5 palabras cada uno.
Instrucciones de Yahoo: No olvides poner el "timestampt" cuando empieces la conversación. Al final UNO de los estudiantes necesita copiar (copy & paste) la conversación y enviarla a la profesora por correo electrónico a xxxx@xxxxx.edu

["In each group, one of the students is going to give the definition and give clues for one of the vocabulary words in this chapter, related to the movies and the entertainment world. You can give examples and clues, but you cannot use the word you are defining. When someone guesses the word, it is that person's turn to define another word. You should at least explain 5 words each.
"Yahoo instructions: Don't forget to select the "timestamp" when you start the conversation. At the end, ONE of the students needs to copy (copy and paste) the conversation and send it to the teacher via e-mail to xxxx@xxxxx.edu]

Task 2

Un estudiante de intercambio

Manolo, un estudiante de Costa Rica amigo de un amigo tuyo, va a matricularse para el próximo semestre en nuestra universidad. Te ha pedido consejo porque no sabe mucho sobre las clases del próximo semestre. Entre todos decidid qué clases son más apropiadas para Manolo considerando que su nivel de inglés en bueno, pero no perfecto, y que está interesado en aprender e integrarse en la cultura de Hawai. Podéis conectaros a myuhportal para ver el horario del próximo semestre si necesitáis ideas sobre las clases que se ofrecen.
Instrucciones de Yahoo: No olvides poner el "timestamp" cuando empieces la conversación. UNO de los estudiantes necesita copiar (copy & paste) la conversación y enviarla a la profesora por correo electrónico a xxxx@xxxxx.edu

["Manolo, a student from Costa Rica, a friend of a friend of yours, is going to register for next semester at our university. He has asked for your advice because he doesn't know much about next semester's classes. Among all of you, decide which classes are most appropriate for Manolo, considering that he has a good level of English, although not perfect, and he is interested in learning about and integrating himself into the culture of Hawai'i. You can connect to myuhportal to see next semester's schedule if you need to look at the classes offered.
"Yahoo instructions: Don't forget to select the "timestamp" when you start the conversation. At the end, ONE of the students needs to copy (copy and paste) the conversation and send it to the teacher via e-mail to xxxx@xxxxx.edu]

Appendix B: Paralinguistic features in students' SCMC discourse

UPPERCASE indicates a louder tone of voice.

```
001 H: LO SIENTO MUCHO!! Mil disculpas por llegar tarde!
       I AM SO SORRY!! Thousands of apologies for being
       late!
```

Letter extension is used for emphasis.

```
007 L:   yo bailo mucho
         I dance a lot

008 D:   ahhhhhhhh
         ahhhhhhhh

076 Sh:  uhhhh  no me gusta nadaaaa ese hombre!!!!
         uhhh I don't like at aaallll1 that man!!!!!


090 Sh:  juanito. si??
         juanito. right??

091 J:   si, juanitoooooooooo
         yes, juanitoooooooo
```

Laughter

```
105 Low:  un chiste dani
          a joke dani

106 Jane: jajajajaja
          hahahaha
```

Emoticons

```
331 Low:  pienso que necesitas cerrar su boca.
          I think you need to close your(err) mouth

332 Jane: o_O

333 Low:  jajaja
          hahaha
```

Appendix C: Examples of students orienting to grammatical mistakes

Boldface type indicates the errors.
All other symbols were originally used by the participants.

```
221 J:  puedo hacerlo si no **le gusta**
        I can do it if you (err) don't like

222 J:  *te gusta
        *you like

223 J:  no es importa para **me**
        it doesn't matter to me (err)

224 J:  *mi
        *me

294 J:  es **el mismo** cosa
        it is the same (err) thing

295 J:  jajajajaja
        hahahaha

296 L:  que **un** mala
        that a (err) bad

297 J:  *la misma cosa
        *the same thing

298 L:  una mala*
        a bad*

299 L:  26, 20, lo mismo
        26, 20 the same

35 John: hay dos anuncios?
         are there two commercials

36 John: o solo **un**?
         or only one (err)

37 John: *uno
         *one

38 John: *uno
         *one

94 H:    y no tienes tiempo **a** ir al cine?
         and you don't have time to(err) to to the movies?
```

95 H: *para ir al cine?
to the movies?

57 Anna: este es **una** programa de variedad donde
tambien se hablan con actores famosos
*this is a (err) variety program where
they also talk to famouse actors*

58 Anna: *un programa
**a program*

12 The Korean Discourse Markers *-nuntey and kuntey* in Native-Nonnative Conversation: An Acquisitional Perspective

Younhee Kim
University of Hawai'i at Mānoa

Introduction

Research interest has dramatically increased in the use and acquisition of discourse markers in the past 20 years (G. Andersen, 2001; Fraser, 1990, 1996, 1999; Jucker & Ziv, 1998; Müller, 2004, 2005; Romero Trillo, 2002; Schiffrin, 1987). Because discourse markers often deal with attitudinal and interactional aspects of communication, they are an essential resource for managing successful communication, although they themselves tend to be void of any propositional meaning. This, in turn, is one reason that discourse markers present a challenging task for language learners (Kasper, 1979; Lörscher & Schulze, 1988; Scarcella, 1983).

In this chapter, I examine the use of two Korean discourse markers, *-nuntey* and *kuntey*, by L2 Korean speakers from a conversation analytic perspective and discuss how the findings relate to language acquisition. I begin with a general overview of the definitions and functions of discourse markers and review the literature on the use and acquisition of discourse markers both in L1 and L2 settings. I then continue with an introduction of the target discourse markers, *-nuntey* and *kuntey* before I report on the findings of my study.

Talk-in-interaction: Multilingual perspectives, pp. 317–350, Hanh Nguyen & Gabriele Kasper (Eds.), 2009
Honolulu, HI: University of Hawai'i, National Foreign Language Resource Center

Discourse markers

Discourse markers have been examined from a variety of perspectives, and thus, various terminology has been used to refer to them (Fraser, 1990; Jucker & Ziv, 1998; Schiffrin, 1987): discourse connectives (Blakemore, 1987, 1992), discourse particles (Schorup, 1985), pragmatic connectives (Stubbs, 1983; van Dijk, 1979), pragmatic markers (Fraser, 1996), gambits (Kasper, 1979), and cue phrases (Knott & Dale, 1994). As reflected in the variety of terms used to refer to discourse markers, the types of work that discourse markers achieve are also diverse, ranging from managing textual coherence to marking stance and other interactional work. The heterogeneous nature of the functions of discourse markers makes it hard to create one succinct definition that covers all of their different features. As Schorup (2000) pointed out, different theoretical perspectives differently carve out the analytical object of discourse markers.

Schiffrin (1987) defined discourse markers as "sequentially dependent elements which bracket units of talk" (p. 31) or more succinctly, "contextual coordinates" (p. 312). Jucker and Ziv (1998) observed that discourse markers invoke "instructions on how given utterances are to be processed" (p. 4).[1] The category of discourse markers, however, is distinguished from other pragmatic classes such as pragmatic force modifiers (Nikula, 1996) and epistemic stance markers (Kärkkäinen, 1992) in that discourse markers are characterized by their role of marking the relationship of the current utterance to the larger discourse. In the following section, I review previous studies investigating the use and development of discourse markers by L1 and L2 speakers.

Discourse markers in L1 acquisition

Previous research suggests that a developmental order is present in the use of discourse markers in first language acquisition (E. S. Andersen, Brizuela, DuPuy, & Gonnerman, 1999; Kyratzis & Ervin-Tripp, 1999; Sprott, 1992): from textual to register function, marking the social relationships between interlocutors (Kyratzis & Ervin-Tripp, 1999; Sprott, 1992); from local to global; and from more literal, contextually situated uses to more metaphorical, abstract discursive functions (Montes, 1999).

Jisa (1984–1985; 1987) reported on the fine-tuning process of the functions of the French sentence connector *et pis* (a version of *et puis* [and then]) in the speech of 3-year-old children. Initially, the children used *et pis* as an all-purpose connector but began to narrow its scope of usage as they acquired other forms (such as *alors*).

Montes (1999) traced the development of discourse markers in Spanish by specifically examining interjections in a young child's speech. Montes found that although most of the interjections were present in the first period of observation, the achieved functions of the markers differed developmentally.

Use of discourse markers by L2 speakers

Recently, the volume of research on the use of discourse markers by L2 speakers has dramatically increased. Müller (2005) presented one of the most comprehensive studies available. Based on the Giessen Long Beach Chaplin Corpus, Müller compared the use of four discourse markers (*so*, *well*, *like*, *you know*) between native speakers of English and German speakers of English. Combining qualitative and quantitative methods of analysis, she identified different frequencies and usages in the discourse markers used by the native and nonnative speakers of English. She also investigated whether the use of discourse markers by nonnative speakers is related to such factors as time spent in English-speaking countries, the amount of contact with native speakers, and formal/informal learning contexts.

Romero Trillo (2002) presented a comparison of the use of English discourse markers by adult and child native speakers of English and nonnative speakers of English (L1 Spanish) based on corpus data. He pointed out that overwhelmingly, the native and nonnative children showed a similar pattern in the use of discourse markers but that as they grew up, the nonnative children did not learn how to appropriately use the discourse markers, probably due to the lack of a natural learning environment. Romero Trillo termed this phenomenon "pragmatic fossilization."

Debrock, Flament-Boistrancourt, and Gevaert (1999) showed that the frequent use of the phrase *disons* [let's say] makes French native speakers' speech more indirect and less imposing in comparison to that of Dutch learners of French. Belz and Vyatkina (2005) added another valuable contribution to this inquiry by showing the development of the use of German modal particles in electronically mediated chat data. Along with the German modal particles, the Japanese particle *ne* is one of the most extensively researched markers, as it appears alone or in phrases such as *n desu ne* (Yoshimi, 1999, 2001). Yoshimi found L1 pragmatic transfer in nonnative speakers' use of discourse markers (1999) and showed the beneficial effects of explicit instruction on the use of discourse markers by learners of Japanese as a foreign language (2001).

Another study that concerns nonnative speakers' use of discourse markers but is distinct from the studies reviewed so far is Wong (2000). Whereas Belz and Vyatkina (2005), Müller (2004, 2005), Romero Trillo (2002), and, to some extent, Debrock et al. (1999) are corpus-driven studies, Wong's (2000) study used the detailed microanalytic method of conversation analysis (CA) to analyze the use of *yeah* by nonnative speakers of English. The current study also uses

CA to examine the conversational usage of two Korean discourse markers by L2 Korean speakers.

Kuntey and *-nuntey*

Korean is an agglutinative language and has a fully developed and actively used arsenal of verbal suffixes that mark sentence type, mood, honorifics, tense/aspect, or modality (Sohn, 1999). Due to these structural features, there are two variant forms of a connective that share the same suffix component: a conjunction type and a verbal suffix type. The conjunction type (e.g., *kulentey*) consists of *kuleha* [be so] + a relevant connective suffix (e.g., *-ntey)* and the other (e.g., *-nuntey)* is a suffix itself. The parallel between the two variant forms is illustrated in Figure 1.

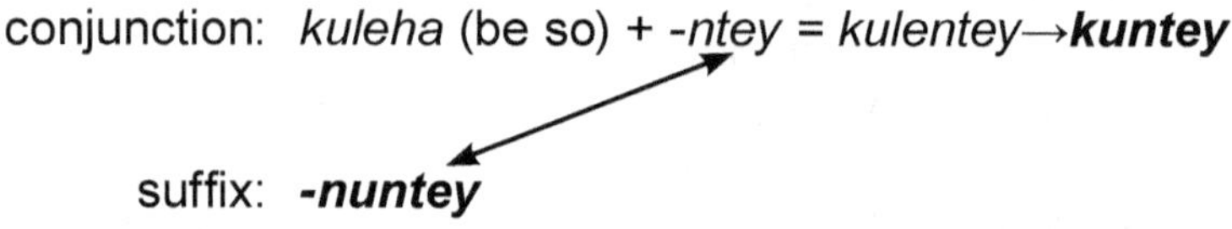

Figure 1. Etymology of *kuntey* and *-nuntey*

As shown in Figure 1, *kuntey* and *-nuntey* are two variant forms of the connective *-nuntey (kuntey* is a reduced form of *kulentey* although it has now gained a few functions that are distinguished from those of *kulentey)* . Because of their grammatical properties, *kuntey* is usually used in sentence-initial position, and *-nuntey* is found in clause-final position, thus showing a complementary syntactic distribution. These two forms were selected as the target markers because they were found to be the most frequently occurring contrastive connectives in Korean conversation and have received good coverage in previous studies (H. Choi, 1965; J. Choi, 1990; H. Lee, 1999; K. Lee, 1980, 1988, 1993; Park, 1997, 1999a, 1999b).

As with its original form, *kulentey, kuntey* has been erroneously translated as "*by the way*" in Korean textbooks. This seems to be the result of overhighlighting its topic shift function. Although both *kulentey* and *kuntey* can be used to index topic shift, they are quite different from the English *by the way*, which has been characterized as a misplacement marker by Schegloff and Sacks (1973). According to Park (1997), the usage of *kuntey* shows a striking resemblance to the use of the English contrastive connective *but* and the Japanese contrastive connective *demo*. Although another word, *kulehciman*, has been regarded as a prototypical contrastive connective in Korean, *kuntey* has been identified as the most frequent contrastive connective in Korean native speaker conversation, covering as much as 95% of the total use of contrastive connectives (Park, 1997).

An English counterpart for the verbal suffix form, *-nuntey*, is difficult to pinpoint. This form is often translated as "but," "and," "so," or "given that." Previous studies (H. Choi, 1965; J. Choi, 1990) have identified two important functions of *-nuntey*. One is that of a background provider, and the other, that of a contrastive marker. Each of these functions is illustrated in the following sentences.

```
(1) pap-ul   mek ko   iss  nuntey cenhwa ka o-ass-ta
    meal-ACC eat CONN PROG CIRCUM phone-NOM come-ANT-DECL
   "I was having my dinner nuntey the phone rang"

(2) (From Park, 1997)
    Ilwel   i  -ntey  an  chwup-ta
    January be CIRCUM NEG cold DECL
   "it's January nuntey it's not cold"
```

Example sentence 1 shows *-nuntey*'s function as a background provider. The first clause, "(I) was having dinner," is presented as simple background for the main event to be described ("the phone rang"). In the second example sentence, while the first clause ("it is January") is presented as background for the second clause ("it is not cold"), it contrasts with the second one, contradicting the assumption that it should be cold in January.

I have briefly explained the grammatical status and meanings of *kuntey* and *-nuntey*. However, this is far from showing the full range of use of *kuntey* and *-nuntey*. Park (1997) presented a comprehensive analysis of the discourse functions of *kuntey* and *-nuntey* in Korean native speaker conversations from a CA perspective. Examining their functions according to their positions in turns, Park (1997) identifies the following sequential environments where *kuntey* and *-nuntey* are used in conversation.

***Turn-initial position* (kuntey)**

Introducing dispreferred responses (e.g., disagreement), topic resumption

***Turn-medial position* (-nuntey)**

Pre-to-main action in a turn (dispreferred action), preliminaries to preliminaries (Schegloff, 1980), dealing with two actions,[2] and speaker return after self-repair

***Turn-final position* (-nuntey)**

Requests, dispreferred responses, self-identification in telephone openings, telling-my-side (Pomerantz, 1980)

Research questions

The present study seeks to examine the use of *-nuntey* and *kuntey* in L2 Korean speakers' conversations and to compare it across different proficiency level groups and against findings from native speaker data. It addresses the following questions.

- In what sequential environments are *-nuntey* or *kuntey* used in L2 Korean speakers' conversations? Is there any difference across proficiency groups?
- What kinds of actions are achieved by the use of *-nuntey* or *kuntey* in L2 Korean speakers' conversations? Is there any difference in the range of types of actions across different proficiency groups?
- Are the sequential environments where the L2 speakers use *kuntey* or *-nuntey* different from those in native speaker conversations?
- In which sequential environments are *-nuntey* or *kuntey* expected but *not* occurring in L2 Korean speakers' data?
- Is there a developmental order in terms of form or function?

Data and methodology

Table 1. Participants' language profiles and conversation lengths

name (sex)	OPI level	first language	length of residence in Korea	total length of recorded conversation (min:s)
Thom (M)	Advanced-mid	English	2 years, 3 months (2000/03–2002/02)	53:00
Liz (F)	Advanced-mid	Turkish	3 years, 4 months (1994/03–1997/06)	87:32
Greg (M)	Intermediate-mid	English	2 years, 0 months (1998/03–2000/02)	177:04
Jean (F)	Intermediate-low	English	4 years, 3 months (1996–2000)	47:27
Mike (M)	Novice-mid	English	1 week	164:45

The dataset for the current study is composed of roughly 9 hours of audio-recorded conversation between Korean native speakers (Kim and Hee) and L2 Korean speakers. All of the five L2 Korean speakers were friends or acquaintances of

Kim or Hee. Thom, Greg, and Mike had been regularly meeting with Kim (for more than 6 months) to improve their Korean and were friends with Kim at the time of the audio recording. Liz and Jean were classmates of Hee, who was a graduate student. Although Liz and Jean were not regularly conversing for the purpose of language learning, they had an interest in improving their Korean and welcomed every opportunity to socialize with their Korean friends. Liz in particular had a keen interest in practicing her Korean because she was teaching undergraduate Korean as a graduate assistant at the university. Table 1 presents a more detailed description of the L2 Korean speakers' language learning profiles and the lengths of the recorded data.

The ACTFL OPI[3] level of each participant was assessed by a certified ACTFL rater after the data collection had been completed. Except for Mike,[4] all of the L2 Korean speakers had some experience living in Korea—although the length of their residence varied from 2 to 4.25 years. All of the participants are nonheritage learners and, at the time of data collection, were in their late 20s or early 30s. Except for Mike, all were graduate students.

For transcribing the Korean data, the Yale Romanization was adopted. For the abbreviations used in morpheme-by-morpheme glossing, see the Appendix.

Findings

Positioning in relation to turns-at-talk was found to provide an effective criterion by which to organize the individual functions of *-nuntey* and *kuntey*; thus, the results of the examination are presented accordingly.

Turn initial position *(kuntey)*

Disagreement

In Korean native speaker conversation, *kuntey* has been shown to mark *disagreement*, especially when delivered without any preface or pause in turn-initial positions (Park, 1997). The use of *kuntey* in similar sequential contexts was also found in the database of the current study, in both the advanced- and intermediate-level speakers' conversations, but not in the conversations with the novice-level speaker. The novice-level speaker used a different connective device in such sequential contexts and did not use *kuntey*. One example from Greg (intermediate level) and one example from Mike (novice level) are presented here.

In Excerpt (1), Greg, Kim, and Hee are talking about whether DNA or the environment determines one's food preferences and ease of digestion. In lines 05–09, 12, and 14–16, Kim states his view that the kind of food people had in their childhood seems to affect their preferences.

Excerpt 1, Greg: 8B114: 5–22

05 K: =elil ttay pwuthe wuywulul an meku::n
young-ATTR time from milk-ACC NEG drink-ATTR
06 salam kathun kyengwunun, nai tulese wuywulul
person like case-TOP age get-CONN milk-ACC
07 mekumun (0.5) selsa hako mak, (0.5)
drink-if diarrhea do-and DM
08 sok-aphu-ko kule- ai kka, (0.7) cincca
have a stomachache-CONN so DM DM seriously
09 (0.6) selsa hakey toycyana. [hwacangsilul
diarrhea have-CONN become-FP toilet-ACC

10 H: [ey::::::::::::

11 G: [um:::::::::

12 K: =cawu kanun ili peleci nuntey,
often go-ATTR occasion-NOM happen-CIRCUM
"As for someone who never had milk when they were young, if (she) drinks milk after (she) gets older, usually she will have diarrhea or a stomachache, seriously (she) gets diarrhea, and has to go to the toilet so often -nuntey"

13 H: ey:=

14 K: =mikwuk salamtul kathun kyengwu, wuywu
American people like case milk
15 mekesstako, (.) mak hwacangsil ttwiekako hanun
drink-REASON DM toilet run-and do-ATTR
16 salamtul eps[cyanha.=
people not exist-FP
"In the case of American people, it does not happen that they have to run to the toilet just because they had milk"

17 H: [ey::::

18→G: =**kuntey**::, mikwuk salam cwungeyse, (0.5) a-
DM American people among a,
19 nem- manhun salam::tulli, (.)ku, wuywu (.)
too many-ATTR people-NOM the, milk
20 mek-ul swu epseyo.
drink-ATTR way not exist-POL
*"**kuntey**, among Americans, many people cannot drink milk"*

21 H: ku:: kulayse ku, wuywu naon ke
the so the milk made-ATTR fact

```
22      anieyyo?   lactaid?
        not-be-POL lactaid
        "isn't that why that milk was made? Lactaid?"
```

To support his view, Kim resorts to the category of American people as an example of those who do not have any problem digesting milk (lines 14–16). Kim's categorization is countered by Greg's disagreement (lines 18–20): that many American people cannot digest milk. Here, Greg's disagreement is prefaced with *kuntey* and delivered immediately after Kim's previous turn. One use of *kuntey* is to mark disagreements, especially when they are delivered without pauses or any other prefacing devices, thus carrying a rather strong tone of directness. This sequential context for *kuntey* is the most salient in native speakers' conversation data. Another point that is noteworthy is that Greg's orientation to his membership in the category of 'American' (Sacks, 1992) seems to affect the formatting of his disagreement. In other words, being American himself, Greg is able to present his disagreement with directness and certainty.

Excerpt 2 presents a very similar sequential environment, although a different contrastive connective is used turn-initially. Mike, Kim, and Hee are talking about rental rates in Michigan, Mike's home state.

Excerpt 2, Mike: 7A 078: 1–14

```
01 K: e: Ann Arbor nun [pissa-tako     ha-tela.
      eh Ann Arbor TOP  expensive-QUOT say-RETRO-INT
      "Well, (they say) that things are expensive in Ann
      Arbor"

02 M:                  [(              )

03 K: tayhak      chon-i-ko   talun ette:n (0.8) key
      university town-be-and other some         thing-NOM
04    eps-napw-a.[(0.5) ku     mwe, (.) mek-ko sa-l
      not exist-seem-IE the DM eat-CONN live-ATTR
      "Since it is a university town and has nothing
      much there, I mean, nothing much to do for a living"

05 H:             [°um:°

06 K: manha-n     kulen [kestul-i    kulayse ku  ccok-ulo
      worth-ATTR such   things-NOM so       the area-LOC
      "so they say it's a little expensive in that area"

07 H:                   [°u::::m°

08 K: (0.6) com        pissa-tako,     Lansing to
            a little expensive-QUOT Lansing also
09    ama::↑[(1.1) pissa-l         ke-ya
      maybe         expensive-ATTR fact-IE
      "probably it must be the same in Lansing, too"
```

10→M: [**kulehciman** like Michigan cwu ey-nun
but like Michigan state in
11 (2.6) manh-un cip like khu:-n [(0.6) cip=
many-ATTR house like big-ATTR house
"**kulehciman**, *in Michigan State, many, uhm, house like, (there are) big houses"*

12 H: [um:

13 M: =iss-eyo. kulayse:, you know, (1.7[) cwu[5]=
exist-POL so you know seven

14 K: [rent?

15 M: =myeng hako kathi sal-ayo. (0.7)
CL with together live-POL
"so, you know, (people) live there with seven *other people, like with seven other people?"*

16 K: yele salamtul hako kathi sal-ayo?
several people with together live-POL
"live together with several other people?"

17 M: yey, yele salam
yeah several people
"yeah, several other people."

Kim submits a claim about rental rates in Ann Arbor and Lansing in lines 01–09, to which Mike responds with a rather direct disagreement by pointing out other aspects of the housing situation in Michigan (i.e., that there are many big houses in Michigan that may be shared by several tenants, and hence, housing is not always expensive). Here, Mike's disagreement in lines 10–16 closely resembles that of the preceding sequence in that it is a rather direct disagreement. First, it is delivered in slight overlap with the previous speaker's turn. Second, the way that membership categorization affects the shape of interaction is similar to that of the preceding sequence. In lines 01–09, Kim's knowledge about rental rates in Michigan is presented as being secondhand, a fact evidenced by the use of the quotative marker, *tako*, and the reporting verb, *ha-* [say] in line 01; the modal auxiliary *na pw-* [seem] in line 04; the quotative marker, *tako*, in line 08; and the adverb *ama* [maybe] in line 09. By using these linguistic devices, Kim displays an affiliation to the category of 'non-Michigander'. Mike, on the other hand, displays an orientation to the category of 'Michigander' by presenting his knowledge more directly and confidently. This is reflected in the temporal delivery and the turn shape of Mike's disagreement. It is delivered in partial overlap with Kim's turn in line 09 and without any prefacing device.

In brief, Mike's disagreement in line 10 is very similar to that of the preceding excerpt except for the contrastive connective that is used in the turn-initial position: *kulehciman* instead of *kuntey*. One of the reasons that the use of *kulehciman* here is noteworthy is that *kuntey* is not found anywhere in Mike's data, and in positions where *kuntey* is expected, he uses *kulehciman*. Excerpt (2) is presented here as one typical example of this phenomenon.

Two observations may be drawn from these parallel sequences as a group: Mike appears not to have acquired *kuntey*, and he uses *kulehciman* to perform the functions of *kuntey*. Several reasons are possible for Mike to use *kulehciman* as a substitute for *kuntey*, or probably, as an all-purpose contrastive connective. One is that *kulehciman* is introduced as a prototypical contrastive connective in many Korean language textbooks (Cho et al., 2001). Its inherent meaning component is explicit, thus marking only a contrastive relationship between utterances. Contrastingly, *kuntey*, having been derived from the basic function of background provider (see the section on *kuntey* and *-nuntey* above and the Discussion), is used to mark a wider variety of relationships including dispreferred responses (as in this case), topic resumption, and interruption of a sequence (Park, 1997). In other words, *kulehciman* may be easier to acquire due to its functional simplicity, whereas *kuntey* may be more difficult to master because of the diversity of its functions. However, Park (1997) reported that *kulehciman* is rarely found in Korean native speakers' conversation and that *kuntey* is the most frequently used contrastive connective.[6]

Compared with *kuntey*, what kinds of different interactional effects does the use of *kulehciman* achieve in this sequential position? If such use is not incorrect, how does it differ from that of *kuntey*? Compared to *kulehciman*, *kuntey* is a more flexible (although still contrastive) connective by which to preface a disagreement in that it marks the upcoming utterance not so much as something directly contrastive to the previous one, but as something to consider against the previous speaker's turn. This difference may be linked to the background marking function of *kuntey*. In this way, although what the current speaker is saying may in fact constitute a disagreement to the previous turn, the speaker does not indicate the disagreement relevance of the to-be-delivered talk in such an overt manner. It is in this sense that the use of *kulehciman* sounds a little bit too formal and too serious compared to that of *kuntey*.

In this section, two similar sequences that feature disagreements were presented and compared. The novice-level learner's nonacquisition of *kuntey* and the use of *kulehciman* as a substitute for it were discussed. In the following section, the use of *kuntey* for another function is examined in the conversations of L2 speakers at different proficiency levels.

Topic resumption sequences

Another major use of *kuntey* identified in Korean native speaker conversation is topic resumption. *Kuntey* has been shown to be used when the speaker returns to a topic of the previous talk that was not fully pursued (Park, 1997). This function of *kuntey* was also found in the L2 Korean speakers' conversations, specifically, in the advanced- and intermediate-level speakers' interactions but not in those of the novice-level speaker. The sequence in Excerpt 3 is from Liz (advanced level). Hee and Liz are talking about how Liz learned Korean.

Excerpt 3, Liz: Red MD 012 12:14

01 H: ani, **kuntey**:: ikkey (2.6) hankwuk mwe:
DM DM like this Korean DM
02 namca chinkwu::ka issta-kena ani, way-,
boy friend-NOM exist-or DM DM(like)
03 mal-u::l (0.8) mal-i nemu cayensulewu-n
language-ACC language-NOM too natural-ATTR
04 ke kath-ayyo::.
fact seem-POL
"well, ***kuntey****, uhm, (2.6) I wonder if you have a Korean boyfriend or, well, I'm just wondering cuz your Korean sounds so natural"*

05 L: uheh heh [heh heh

06 H: [oykwukin thi-ka an na-kwu::,
foreigner tinge-NOM not felt-and
07 mwela kula-yyatoy-na? (.)
what-QUOT say-should-Q
"doesn't sound like a foreigner, how can I say?"

08 L: tsk, e:::::::: namca chinkwu potanun chinkwu::
tsk, eh boy friend rather than friend
09 (0.6) sasil cheum i nyen-u::n ceki
actually first two years-TOP DM
10 ehakta::ng-ul tany-ess[ketun-yo¿
language institute-ACC go-PST-CORREL-POL
"well, rather than a boyfriend, maybe friends, actually for the first two years, I went to the language institute"

11 H: [u::::::m

12 L: mullon ce-nun com theki-eyse
of course I(HUM)-TOP a little Turkey-in
13 payw-ess-ki ttaymun[ey::
learn-PST-NOML because
"of course, I studied (Korean) in Turkey, so"

14 H: [um:::::::

15 (1.2)

16 L: [kekieyse
there
"there"

```
17 H: [thekimal-ilang hankwukmal-ilang pisusha-yyo?
       Turkish-with   Korean-with      similar-POL
       "Is Turkish similar to Korean?"

18 L: eswun-i          pisusha-yyo.
      word order-NOM similar-POL
      "The word order is similar"

19    (0.6)

20 H: a::::::::

21→L: kuntey ku  ttay-nu:n com (1.1) e::: mullon
      DM      the time-TOP  a little  eh   of course
22    hakkyo kongpu-to  manhi hayss-nuntey::
      school study-also a lot do-PST-CIRCUM
23    mal-ul        ku   ttay wenak hato mos ha-yssu-nikka::
      speaking-ACC the time so    too  not do-PST-REASON
      "kuntey, at that time, well of course
      I also did a lot of school work, but
      because my speaking was so bad at that time"

24 H: e::::::

25 L: hankwuk salamtul hako manhi ilehkey (0.5)
      Korean  people   with a lot like this
26    manna-se: com       kulekwu ikhey com      manhi
      meet-and  a little and      DM    a little a lot
27    eccaysstun chinkwutul hako manhi nol-ass[eyo
      anyway      friends    with a lot had fun-PST-POL
      "(I) spent much time with Korean people, and like, a
      lot of, anyway, hung out a lot with friends."

28 H:                                          [e::::
```

In response to Hee's compliment on her Korean, Liz tells the story of how she learned Korean (lines 08–13). In lines 12 and 13, Liz mentions that she learned Korean in Turkey, which triggers Hee's question of whether Turkish is similar to Korean (line 17). This question is launched in overlap with Liz' continuation of her preceding turn (line 16) and wins over it. The side sequence is closed with Liz's answer that the word order is similar (line 18) and Hee's lengthened change-of-state token (Heritage, 1984a), *a::::::::* (line 20). Then, as Liz returns in line 21 to the topic of how she learned Korean, she marks it with *kuntey*. This is an instantiation of the use of *kuntey* for topic resumption.

Excerpt 4 presents an interesting case for comparison. It shows a similar sequential environment of topic resumption, but with a different contrastive connective used. Mike is telling the story of his getting food poisoning the previous night. Because the sequence is long and sometimes difficult to understand due to the learner's phonological and syntactic errors, a brief layout of the overall structural organization of the sequence is presented before the transcript. The excerpt can be divided roughly into four parts.

1. In response to Hee's comment that Mike looks tired, Mike starts to tell a story of what happened to him the previous night. The story starts with Mike having dinner at a restaurant (lines 01–07).
2. Mike, Hee, and Kim try to identify what restaurant Mike is referring to (lines 08–35, not shown in transcript).
3. Mike returns to the main story of what happened the other night, which is sidetracked to Mike's complaint about restaurants in Hawai'i by Kim's question concerning what ethnic food the restaurant served (lines 36–61).
4. Mike comes back to the main story to describe what happened the previous night (lines 62–69).

Excerpt 4, Mike 6A 333:1–66

```
01 H: toykey phikonhay poi-nta, onu::l.
      very   tired     look-FP  today
      "(you) look very tired today"

02    (0.7)

03 M: nu:l?

04 K: phikonhay pointakoyo,       you look, you look tired.
      tired     look-FP-QUOT-POL you look, you look tired
      "she said you look tired. you look, you look tired."

05 M: yeah, well, (0.8) ecey, (0.5) ecey      pam   ey-n,
      yeah, well,       yesterday   yesterday night at-TOP
06    (0.5) kit'n kitchen? (1.1) kit'n kitchen? (.)
            kit'n kitchen        kit'n kitchen
07    uhm siktang    al   ayo?
      uhm restaurant know POL
      "yeah, well, last, last night, Kit'n Kitchen? Kit'n
      Kitchen? uhm, you know the restaurant?"

08    (1.1)
((lines omitted))
32 K:          [ku::, [ani kunkan (.) ku  mwe  nya,=
                the    DM  DM         the what Q
                "the, I mean, uhm, the, what was it?"

33 M:                 [(              )
34    =(0.6) Rainbow Bookstore yeph-ey.
             Rainbow Bookstore beside-at
             "beside the Rainbow Bookstore."

35 H: m::::::
```

```
36 M: i    sitai[7] (1.6) kwuk hako pap (0.6)
      this restaurant    soup and rice
      "this restaurant soup and rice"

37 H: e:::[:::::

38 M:     [siktang
           restaurant
           "restaurant"

39 K: e::::::

40 M: and, na-nun (1.2) black bea:n paste grilled
      and  I-TOP        black bean  paste grilled
41    fish mek-ess-e[yo¿
      fish eat-PST-POL
      "and I had black bean paste grilled fish"

42 H:               [e:::::::

43 K: cwungkwuk cip   ieyyo? Is it Chinese restaurant,
      Chinese   place be-POL Is it Chinese restaurant,
44    or?
      or?
      "Is it a Chinese restaurant? Is it Chinese
      restaurant, or?"

45 M: I have NO:: idea.

46    (1.0)

47 K: hah hah hah [hah hah

48 M:             [Hawai'i cwu   ey-nun (0.5)
                   Hawai'i state in-TOP
49 K: isanghan umsikcem-i    [m(h)a(hh)nh-ayo(h)?
      strange  restaurant-NOM many-POL
      "in Hawai'i (there are) many strange restaurants?"

50 M:                        [yey:::::
                              yeah
                              "yeah"

51 M: [it's like (0.5) cwungkwuk umsi:k (.) hako::=
       it's like       Chinese   food       and
52 H: [pi:::

53 M: =(0.6) hankwuk umsik hako Malaysia umsik,
             Korean  food  and  Malaysia food
54    [(0.7) ]combine ha[mye::n shhhh, yeki isseyo,=
              combine do-if     shhhh  here exist-POL
```

```
        "it's like, (they combine) Chinese food,
         Korean food, and Malaysian food, and bring it to
         your table,

55 H:   [°huhuhu°]           [ccamppong
                              hodgepodge
                              "hodgepodge"

56 M:   =[OK(.) all in all ilako    hayyo,   I don't,=
          OK     all in all be-QUOT say-POL I don't,

57 H:    [huh huh heh

58 M:   =I don't know how they [(                 )] do=
         I don't know how they                        do
59 K:                            [hah hah hah hah ]

60 M:   =it. it's a:ll: different, ta::
         it  it's all   different, all
         "OK it's like all in all. I don't I don't know how
         they (..) do it. it's all different, all"

61       (0.5)

62→M:   kuleh-, yey,  kulehcima::n (0.5) ku  siktang (.)
        kuleh-  yeah  kulehciman          the restaurant
63      ku  siktang-ey::(0.5) mekessko:::,(1.0) musical
        the restaurant-at      eat-PST-CONN      musical
64      tani-ssko::, (0.6) na-nun (0.5) pay-ka       nemu
        go-PST-CONN        I-TOP        stomach-NOM too
65      aph-ass-eyo.
        ache-PST-POL
        "so-, yeah, but, (I) ate at that restaurant, went to
        see a musical, I had a very serious stomachache"

66 H:   way-yo?
        why-POL
        "why?"

67 K:   manhi mek-ese?=
        much  eat-CONN
        "since you had too much?"

68 M:   =yey: umsik poisoning
         yeah food  poisoning
         "yeah food poisoning"

69 H:   .hhh[hha
```

As Kim formulates the location of the restaurant in reference to the bookstore near campus, Hee displays her recognition of the restaurant with a long nasal sound of acknowledgement in line 35. Then, Mike continues his description of what happened the previous night (line 36, 38, 40–41). Mike's turn telling what he ate at the restaurant is met with Kim's question of whether it was a Chinese restaurant in lines 43 and 44. Mike then delivers an answer which claims no knowledge about the restaurant in a volume noticeably louder than the neighboring turns and with great emphasis placed on the word *no*. As foreshadowed by the extraordinarily strong tone of his claim of no knowledge, Mike follows with a complaint about restaurants in the state. Mike's incomplete turn in line 48, thus far only the prepositional phrase *Hawai'i cwu ey nun* [in Hawai'i], is completed by Kim in line 49 ("there are many strange restaurants in Hawai'i") and confirmed by Mike in line 50. Then, Mike elaborates on the complaint by saying that many restaurants in Hawai'i combine different kinds of ethnic food (lines 51, 53–54, 56, 58, 60). After a 0.5-s pause in line 61, Mike returns to the story of what he did the previous night (line 62). Here, after *kuleh-*, the first two syllables of *kulehciman*,[8] and *yey*, Mike begins his turn with a self-repaired *kulehciman*. Note that the transition point from his complaints about restaurants in the state to the main story about the previous night is marked with *kulehciman*. Also notable is that the verb tense marking also changes, with *kulehciman* as a dividing post.

This type of use of *kulehciman* for topic resumption is even more non-target-like than the previous case because the use of *kulehciman* for disagreement in casual conversation is more of a matter of tone or style and still falls within the boundary of usage based on the semantic meaning of *kulehciman*. However, Mike's use of *kulehciman* as a topic resumption marker goes well beyond *kulehciman*'s normal usage. Composed of *kuleh* [be so] + *ci* (committal marker) + *man* (a delimiter) (K. Lee, 1988, 1993; Park, 1999a), *kulehciman* has an explicit semantic meaning that confines its usage to marking a directly contrastive relationship between what comes before and after it.

This section showed that *kuntey* was used in topic resumption sequences by the advanced- and intermediate-level L2 Korean speakers but not by the novice-level L2 Korean speaker. In possible environments for *kuntey*, the novice-level speaker used *kulehciman*, another contrastive connective, to mark topic resumption.

Turn medial position *(-nuntey)*

Pre-to-main action (bridging pro forma agreement)

Among the four functions of *-nuntey* in turn-medial position, the most frequent is to mark the pre-to-main dispreferred action. This section examines how the L2 speakers use *-nuntey* for this function. CA findings have revealed normatively organized constraints on the design of actions and that some of the designs orient to maintaining social solidarity (Heritage, 1984b). One of those design features is the *presequence* in dispreferred action such as *pro forma* agreement before a main action of disagreement or a token praise before a complaint. Korean native speaker conversations (Park, 1997, 1999b) show that these are typical sequential environments for *-nuntey*. The L2 Korean speakers also use *-nuntey* in those sequential environments. As in the case of *kuntey*, however, the novice-level speaker did not use *-nuntey* in this manner. Instead, this speaker used *kulehciman*, the same contrastive connective that he used in place of *kuntey* as shown in the previous section.

Excerpts 5 and 6 show the use of *-nuntey* in pre-to-main dispreferred action—complaint and disagreement, respectively. The first one comes from the data of Liz, an advanced-level speaker, and the second from those of Jean, an intermediate-level speaker. In the talk prior to Excerpt 5, Hee was talking about her experience in a summer institute in linguistics. In response to this, Liz formulates a delicate display of her dissatisfaction with her current program of study.

Excerpt 5, Liz 3B 053:16–27

```
16 (0.8)

17 L: nanun (2.6) kulssey solcikhi (1.2) acwu
     I-TOP       well     honestly       very
18   cohahayyo, yekise kongpuhanun kesto      acwu
     like-POL   here   study-ATTR  thing-also very
19→  cohahanuntey
     like-CIRCUM
     "for me, well, honestly, I like it very much, I like
     studying here very much, too -nuntey"

20 H: yey::::
      yeah
      "yeah"

21 L: ku  ke    enehak, (.) com      kulen
      the thing linguistics a little so-ATTR
22    kes ey tayhayse  com      pucokhan
      thing regarding a little not enough-ATTR
23    nukkimi, (0.6) mullon    nato   com (.)
      feeling-NOM    of course I-also a little
24    mwelako    halkka, (1.0) manhun    swuepul
      what-QUOT say-ATTR-Q    many-ATTR class-ACC
25    patul     swu eps       ki ttaymuney=
      take-ATTR way not exist because of
      "(I) have a feeling that I'm not getting enough
      linguistics, well, maybe, that's also because I
      can't take many courses"

26 H: =ey::::=
       yeah
       "yeah"
```

27→L: =kulenun ke**ntey**, nas-, han il nyenu:n (1.0)
so-ATTR thing-CIRCUM I- around one year-TOP
28 ilnyen cinayko nase, han, pyello
one year pass-CONN after around particularly
29 mikwukeyse kongpuhantanun nukkim an
America-in study-ATTR-IND-ATTR feeling not
30 tulesseyo, waynyamyen kyeysok hankwukelo
got-POL because constantly Korean-in
31 hanikka, swuep [u(h)::::l(h), hah hah hah
do-REASON class-ACC
"that's why **-nuntey** *during the first year, I mean, after I spent one year here, I couldn't have a feeling that I am studying in the U.S., because we use Korean in class all the time"*

32 H: [a:::::::::::::::::::

In this talk, Hee's contribution is minimal, only providing a continuer for Liz in lines 20 and 26 and an acknowledgement token in line 32. In other words, Liz's multiple turn-construction-unit turn constitutes the whole sequence. A careful analysis of this sequence shows a typical pre-to-main action sequence. In lines 17–19, Liz displays positive affect toward her program. She accomplishes this in part by her repeated use of the verb *cohahayyo* [like] in lines 18 and 19 and by using the intensifier *acwu* [very much] in lines 17 and 18. However, this initial utterance is conjoined with the subsequent turn construction units by *-nuntey*. Importantly, the material following *-nuntey* delivers a different aspect of her feelings toward the current program—"not getting enough linguistic stuff."

As has been pointed out by Sacks (1992), complaining and applauding are closely related, and this affinity has been observed in mundane interactions in English with immense regularity. In other words, 'a piece of praise plus a complaint component' is a turn structure that is recurrently observed in mundane interactions. What this turn structure centrally delivers is the complaint, not the applause. That is, the applause component is a pre-to-main action that signals the upcoming action of complaining. Sometimes, the complaint component cannot be recognized as an actual complaint without this pre-to-main action (i.e., applause).

Excerpt (5) shows the same pattern of complaining as the main action. Liz's display of positive affect toward the program constitutes the pre-to-main action and signals the upcoming complaint ("not getting enough linguistic stuff"). Note that these two parts are connected by *-nuntey*. Importantly, the second component of the sequence (complaint) is what the turn centrally delivers—even though the first component of the sequence is formatted in a stronger and more explicit tone (through, e.g., repetition of the verb *cohahayyo* [like] and the use of an intensifier, *acwu* [very much]) than the second part (which seems to be designed in a more hesitant way—note that the verb is not even provided), line 23).

Furthermore, the utterance from *mullon* [of course] in line 23 to *kulenun kentey* [that's why *-nuntey*] in line 27 constitutes another pre-to-main action sequence, although it is slightly ambiguous as to whether it is a hedge relating to the immediately preceding complaint or to the upcoming complaint (i.e., that she could not have the feeling that she was studying in America). This second hedge presents another type of pre-to-main action for a complaint. This is because a complaint always involves some kind of dissatisfaction about other people or things, and thus a potential counterargument to the complaint is to bring up the speaker's responsibility, such as "you don't have any responsibility for that?" By stating that she admits her part in the dissatisfaction, this pre-to-main action effectively preempts any counterargument and justifies the upcoming complaint. Here, again, *-nuntey* is used to deliver the pre-to-main action before the speaker presents her main action, a complaint.

Another example from an intermediate-level speaker can be seen in Excerpt 6. Hee and Jean are talking about living with a roommate.

Excerpt 6, Jean: 4A 313: 14–34

```
14 H: na-nun kuntey, kulemye::n toykey co-, kunkka,
      I-TOP  DM        then        very  lik-  DM
15    (1.1) ikkey roommate nu::n (.)chinha-nikka
               DM    roommate TOP      close-REASON
16    ohilye te    mwe-la-kwula-yya toy-na?
      rather more what-QUOT-say     so-should-Q
      "for me, well, in that case, very, like,
      cuz a roommate is close,
      rather more, how can I say this?"

17 J: yey::::
      yeah
      "yeah"

18 H: kunkka com, (0.6) ku (0.6) com      melli hako
      DM     a little    the       a little far   do-and
19    siph-ul   ttay ka  iss-tela-kwu-yo.   waynyahamye:n
      wish-ATTR time NOM exist-RTR-QUOT-POL because
20    e:,(.) pang-eyse hangsang manna-key toyisskwu,
      eh     room-in   always   see-CONN  be supposed to-and
21    cip-eyse:: (.) kum  hakkyo eyse lato     com
      home-at          then school at    at least a little
22    an  manna-ya-toy-nuntey, yekise-to maynnal
      not see-should-CIRCUM    here-also everyday
23    manna-kwu yekise-to manna-myen cohu-l    ttay-n
      see-and   here-also see-if     good-ATTR time-TOP
24    coh-untey,
      good-CIRCUM
      "well, I mean, sometimes (I) feel like (I) want to
      keep a distance with (a roommate) cuz (you)'re
      supposed to see her always in the room, at home,
      then, (you) should be able to be away (from her) at
```

least at school, but (if you) see her here everyday
and see her here everyday, then when it's good, it's
good but"

25 J: yey=
yeah
"yeah"

26 H: =manyakey yakkan trouble sayngki-mye:::n com
if at all trouble come about-if a little
27 himtul canh ayo::=
difficult-FP POL
"if you get to have any trouble (with her), it gets
a little tough, you know?"

28→J: =yey, cokum=
yeah a little
"yeah, a little"

29 H: =ey:::::=

30→J: =cokum-un (.) himtu:**ntey,** [na-nun (.) pothong=
a little-TOP difficult-CIRCUM I-TOP usually

31 H: [ey:

32 J: =(0.5) il manhi:: hayse::
work much do-so
"(it) is hard a little bit, ***-nuntey*** *usually I*
work a lot, so"

33 H: e:::::

34 J: cip-eyse nemu nuckey::[wa-ssko: Eri hako (0.6)
home-at too late come-PST-and Eri with
"(I) came home too late and with Eri"

35 H: [e::::::, e:::

36 H: cip-eyse [kathi iss-ci [ankwuna::::
home-at together be-NOML not-UNASSIM
"(you) don't spend (much) time at home"

37 J: [yey::: [kathi: yey::::
yeah together yeah
"yeah, together, yeah"

38 H: a::::::

39 J: kulayse, cokum [°kwaynchanh-ayo.°
so a little okay-POL
"so, it's okay"

In the interaction prior to the beginning of Excerpt 6, Jean tells Hee that she was taking three classes together with her roommate this semester. In response to this, Hee raises her concern, in question form, that it could be a little bit tough to share too much with a roommate. All the hedging devices (repetition of connectives such as *kuntey* [but], *kulemye::n* [then], *kunkka* [that is to say], and *mwe-la-kwula-yya toy-na* [how do I say this?]) in Hee's turn in lines 14–16 display hesitancy on Hee's part. However, Hee's question has an agreement-seeking format, as can be seen in the use of a sentence-final particle, *-canh-* in line 27. This particle has been characterized as marking an epistemic stance that the speaker has a high degree of expectation that the addressee will agree with what the current speaker says (Kawanishi, 1994; Kawanishi & Sohn, 1993). Jean first gives a weak agreement, *yey* [yeah], followed by a hedging adverb, *cokum* [a little]. After Hee's latched agreement token (line 29), however, Jean's full answer ensues from line 30, which shows the design features typical of weak disagreement, that is, *pro forma* agreement plus weak disagreement (Pomerantz, 1984). Note that the presequence part, the *pro forma* agreement, is connected to the main action of disagreement by *-nuntey*.

Excerpt 7 is from one of Mike's conversations. It shows a sequential environment parallel to that seen in Excerpts 5 and 6 in the sense that a presequence occurs before a dispreferred action is delivered. Mike, Hee, and Kim are talking about how Mike, who is a soldier, got assigned to Hawai'i.

Excerpt 7, the Middle East and Hawai'i

```
01 K: cwungtong    kal      ppen    ha-yss-eyo,
      middle east go-ATTR almost do-PST-POL
02    ku-cy-o?     kulem ipen-ey       cal   hamyenun↑(1.0)
      so-COMM-POL then  this time-at well do-if
03    Aphkhanisthan kal     swu-to   iss-ess-keyss
      Afghanistan   go-ATTR way-also exist-PST-DCTRE
04    ney yo? if you choose Arabic, you can,(.)
      FR-POL  if you choose Arabic,  you can,
05    [you might be go to=
      "(you) almost went to the Middle East, right? you
      might have been sent to Afghanistan this time,
      yeah? if you choose Arabic,  you can, you might be
      go to"

06 M: [um::

07→M: =ney,  ama,     maybe, mwe.[(.)kulehciman
       yeah  perhaps maybe  well     but
       "yeah, maybe, maybe, well… but"

08 H:                            [cwungtong   pota-n
                                  middle east than-TOP
```

```
09      Hawaii ka  nas-ney-yo.
        Hawaii NOM better-FR-POL
        "(I guess) Hawai'i is better than the Middle East,
        yeah?"

10      (0.7)

11→M: ney.[(.) Hawaii cwu   coh-ayo. kulehciman, uhm,=
      yeah     Hawaii state good-POL but         uhm

12 H:     [heh heh

13 M: =(1.4) cwungtong   ka, kaum, (.)kamyen↑
             middle east go, go-??    go-if
      "yeah, Hawai`i is good, but uhm, if you go, go, go
      to the Middle East"

14 K: uh-huh

15    (0.7)

16 M: seykum (1.5) nay:ci,[(1.0) nayci    haci    an ayo¿
      tax          pay-NOML      pay-NOML do-NOML not-POL
      "you don't have to pay taxes"

17 H:                     [a:::::::::
```

Prior to this excerpt, Mike told Kim and Hee that he had a choice between Arabic and Korean for his language study in the army and that Korean meant being assigned to Hawai'i and Arabic, to the Middle East. While Kim is playfully entertaining the hypothetic possibility that Mike could have been assigned to Afghanistan (lines 01–05) and continuously seeking Mike's response, as is witnessed by the tag question *kucyo* [isn't it?] in line 02 and the factual realization marker *ney* in line 04,[9] Hee presents her opinion that Hawai'i is better than the Middle East (lines 08–09; also marked with *ney*). This is done in overlap with Mike's previous turn, and as a result, Mike temporarily aborts his turn (line 07). Mike's response (lines 11, 13, 16) to Hee's comment after a 0.7-s pause embodies a typical weak disagreement design: weak agreement ("yeah, Hawai'i is good") plus weak disagreement ("but, if you go to the Middle East, you don't have to pay taxes").

However, consistent to our observations so far, Mike uses *kulehciman* instead of *-nuntey* to connect the presequence to the main action (line 11). Based on what has been presented so far, Mike may be assumed not to have *-nuntey* in his repertoire and to be using *kulehciman* for functions that are normally associated with *-nuntey*.

So far, the difference in the use of the contrastive markers seems to lie only between the novice-level speaker on the one hand and the intermediate- and advanced-level speakers on the other. In terms of the turn-initial use of *kuntey* and turn-medial use of *-nuntey*, the advanced- and intermediate-level participants of this study have not shown much difference. However, the turn-final use of *-nuntey* turns out to discriminate between the advanced- and intermediate-level speakers.

Turn-final use (-nuntey)

From a syntactic point of view, *-nuntey* is a verbal connective, and thus, a main clause is expected to come after *-nuntey*. However, according to recent studies, *-nuntey* clauses are observed frequently without following main clauses (H. Kim, 1992; Park, 1997, 1999b). In L1 conversation, *-nuntey* clauses without subsequent main clauses have been shown to account for 60% of the total use of *-nuntey* (Park, 1999b, p. 196).

Park's (1997; 1999b) analysis of the use of *-nuntey* from a CA perspective revealed an interesting function in turn-final position. Drawing on *-nuntey*'s function as a background provider, *-nuntey* clauses without main clauses index that inferences are due; that is, they invite the interlocutor to infer what might be in the unrealized main clause by providing only the background information. Describing this turn-final use of *-nuntey* as setting up an "accountability relevance point" (Park, 1999b, p. 197), Park observed that this function has to do with the practice of Korean speakers to "oversuppose, undertell."

What is noteworthy is that in the conversations examined for the current study, the L2 speakers' turn-final use of *-nuntey* occurs not only with much less frequency than in the L1 Korean conversation but is limited to the advanced-level speakers. Even in their speech, not many instances were found.

Excerpt 8 is one example of how Thom, an advanced-level L2 speaker, uses *-nuntey* in turn-final position. The extract comes almost at the end of a 1-hour conversation between Hee and Thom in a student cafeteria on campus. They are talking about Thom's plans to visit Korea.

Excerpt 8, learning Japanese

```
01 H: kulem enceynka-nun tto   hankwuk-ey tasi  kasi
      then  sometime-TOP again Korea-to   again go-HON
02    keyss-ney-yo?
      DCTRE-FR-POL
      "then maybe you would visit Korea again sometime in
      the future"

03    (1.3)

04 T: kuleh-ki-l  pala-yyo, encey ka-l-ci (0.6)
      so-NOML-ACC hope-POL  when  go-ATTR-NOML
05    hwaksilhi molu-keyss-eyo.    ipen (0.8) ipen
      centainly not know-DCTRE-POL this       this
06    yelum-ey::: (1.1) ilpon-ey kako    siph-eyo.
      summer-in         Japan-to go-CONN wish-POL
```

```
        "(I) hope so, though I'm not sure when I can visit
        Korea. This, this summer, I'd like to go to Japan"

07 H:   e::[::
        oh
        "oh"

08→T:      [mwe ilpone: (.) payweya   toynuntey,
            DM  Japanese     learn-NECE become-CIRCUM
            "Well, I should learn Japanese nuntey"

09 H:   a::::, ilpone  com          ha-se-yyo?
        ah     Japanese a little bit speak-HON-POL
        "oh, so you speak Japanese a little bit?"

10      (0.7)

11 T:   cokkum       al-ayo.
        a little bit know-POL
        "I know just a little bit"

12 H:   [e:::::

13 T:   [yey:: ipen cikum, (1.4) one o two (0.4)
         yeah  this now          one oh two
         "yeah, this, now, 102"
```

Asked about his plans to visit Korea (lines 01–02), Thom, while expressing his wish for such plans to be realized (line 04), brings up his more immediate plans to visit Japan that summer (lines 05–06). In partial overlap with Hee's news-receipt token, *e::::* (line 07), Thom brings up the new subtopic that he should learn Japanese (line 08), marking it with *-nuntey*. This use of *-nuntey* is effective in that it achieves an effect of leaving the utterance to be taken up by the interlocutor. Placed almost at the end of the conversation, Thom's turn in line 08 ("I should learn Japanese *-nuntey*"), packaged with *-nuntey*, can be heard as presenting his utterance as a sort of postscript to what he had said before and thus avoids sounding like a proposal of a new topic for conversation while still presenting the possibility to be taken up as such by the interlocutor. This is made possible by the interactional import of the clause-final use of *-nuntey*, that is, inviting the interlocutor's attention, but at the same time, leaving it to the interlocutor.

Discussion

The findings of the current study can be summarized as follows. The examination of the use of *-nuntey/kuntey* in L2 Korean speaker's conversation has revealed a graded distribution of the different functions of *-nuntey/kuntey* according to the speakers' proficiency level. This distribution is summarized in Table 2.

Table 2. L2 Korean speakers' proficiency level and distribution of *-nuntey/kuntey* use

OPI level	turn-initial use	turn-medial use	turn-final use
Advanced	*kuntey*	*-nuntey*	*-nuntey*
Intermediate	*kuntey*	*-nuntey*	
Novice	*kulehciman*	*kulehciman*	

As shown in Table 2, the advanced-level speakers used *-nuntey/kuntey* for a range of functions identified in all three turn positions, whereas the intermediate-level speakers used *-nuntey/kuntey* only in turn-initial and turn-medial positions. This observation suggests that the intermediate-level speakers in this study had not yet acquired *-nuntey*'s turn-final use. Neither *-nuntey* nor *kuntey* was used by the novice-level speaker. In the possible environments for these markers, the novice-level speaker used a different contrastive connective, *kulehciman*.

From the perspective of second language acquisition, two findings of this study are noteworthy. (a) The novice-level speaker used *kulehciman* in environments where more proficient speakers use *-nuntey* or *kuntey*. (b) The individual functions of the focal discourse markers appear in a developmental order; that is, the turn-final use of *-nuntey* seems to be acquired later than the other functions.

The first observation seems to be due to the far more diverse patterns of usage of *-nuntey/kuntey* compared to those of *kulehciman*. A language item with one clear meaning is easier to learn than an item with several different functions. Beginning learners tend to resort to one clear invariant form for one function (R. Andersen, 1984; S. W. Andersen & Shirai, 1996; Pienemann, 2002; Shirai & Andersen, 1995) which explains the pattern observed in Mike's language use profile: the tendency to resort to *kulehciman*. The multifunctionality and colloquial nature of *-nuntey/kuntey* seem to make it difficult to find exact English equivalents of either one. In addition, as has been discussed before, *-nuntey*'s turn-final use and *kuntey* are distinctive features of conversational discourse. Therefore, for Mike, who had relatively little contact with native speakers of Korean (as indicated by the length of his residence in Korea), exposure to the usage in the input might have been limited. Because *kulehciman* is typically introduced as the equivalent of *but* in many Korean language textbooks for foreigners (Cho, Schulz, Lee, & Sohn, 2001), *kulehciman* is not surprisingly an all-purpose contrastive connective in the still-limited Korean repertoire of the novice-level speaker.

The second observation leads to a significant implication for second language acquisition because it suggests a parallel between the diachronic grammaticalization process and acquisition order. A brief account of the grammaticalization process of *-nuntey* is due here. Work on the Korean language by functional linguists provides a detailed account of the grammaticalization process of *-nuntey* (for a full analysis, see H. Lee, 1999). Here, I touch upon only two stages that are relevant to the discussion. In the first stage, *-nuntey* gains its function as a contrastive marker from its original function as a background provider. This process can be better understood with reference to Figure 2.

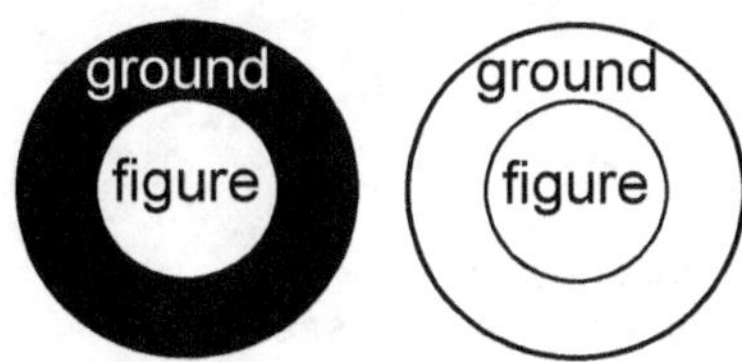

Figure 2. Figure-ground relationship.

As can be seen in Figure 2, the saliency of the figure is enhanced when the ground is contrastive to the figure. For this reason, when a figure is introduced against its ground, often, the figure part is in a contrastive relationship to the ground part. The repeated use of *-nuntey* to connect a contrastive background to a figure seems to have caused *-nuntey* to gain the function of a contrastive connective. At the same time, *-nuntey* still retains its basic function as a background provider. Hence, the function of *-nuntey* is best understood as being on a continuum. At one end of this continuum lies the background provider function of *-nuntey* (without any connotation of contrast), and at the other end lies its solely contrastive function (with no function as a background provider). The following two sentences show examples of each.

(9) pap -ul mek ko iss nuntey cenhwa ka o -ass-ta.
meal-ACC eat CONN PROG CIRCUM phone- NOM come-ANT-DECL
"I was having my dinner ***nuntey*** *the phone rang."*

(10) hyeng un khi ka cak **-untey** tongsayng
(older-brother TOP height NOM short CIRCUM younger-brother
un khuta.
TOP tall)
"The older one is short, ***untey*** *the younger one is tall."*

The next stage of the grammaticalization of *-nuntey* has to do with the pervasive phenomenon of main clause ellipsis in conversation in Korean. This frequent ellipsis is well documented (H. Kim, 1994; Park, 1999b; H.-m. Sohn, 1986). The function of *-nuntey* of indicating contrast takes a more interactional role when the figure part (the main clause) is left unrealized. The original function of *-nuntey* as a background provider and clausal connective suffix makes the interlocutor search for the unrealized main clause (figure) and infer what the unrealized but relevant figure is. This achieves the effect of inviting some inference work from the interlocutor, which in turn achieves the effect of being indirect.

A diagrammed summary of the grammaticalization stages of *-nuntey* is represented in Table 3, modified from H. Lee (1999).

Table 3. Grammaticalization stages of *-nuntey* (modified from H. Lee, 1999)

Stage 1	**figure-ground** <background provider>
Stage 2	**figure-ground** <contrast in textual relation> figure-ground relation is suppressed
Stage 2-1	**figure-ground** <contrast in contextual relation> continuum between contrast and figure-ground
Stage 3	**(figure)-ground** <interactional marker> figure left unrealized: invite inference and signal incompatibility/discrepancy

What is noteworthy is the parallel found between the grammaticalization stages of *-nuntey* and the developmental order of the different uses of *-nuntey* that emerged across speakers of different proficiency levels. The turn-final use of *-nuntey*, which seems to evolve at the last stage of grammaticalization, was found to be the last to be acquired by L2 Korean speakers. This suggests the possibility that a process similar to the way in which *-nuntey* has gained its turn-final use as an interactional marker through repeated use in discourse might be going on within individual learners' language use. In other words, individual learners' processes of acquiring *-nuntey*'s functions mirror that of diachronic grammaticalization.

The parallel nature of diachronic grammaticalization and acquisitional grammaticalization has been a longstanding topic in the study of first language acquisition (Slobin, 1977) and has also been taken up by second language acquisition (SLA) researchers (Dittmar, 1992; Giacalone Ramat, 1992; Pfaff, 1992; Skiba & Dittmar, 1992). In their proposal to explain some SLA processes as grammaticalization, they showed that learners start with lexical items and gradually move toward morphological devices. In her study of the early second language acquisition of Turkish and German children, Pfaff (1992) showed parallels of diachronic grammaticalization with those found in early second language acquisition, for example, pronominal use preceding the definite article use of *der*, *die*, and *das*, and main verb use preceding the auxiliary use of *sein* [be] and *haben* [have]. In other words, the acquisition of individual functions of plurifunctional items proceeded in a manner that parallels the diachronic grammaticalization sequence.

Semantic-pragmatic aspects of grammaticalization that are actively discussed in the grammaticalization literature (Traugott, 1982, 1989, 2003) might provide valuable insight to broaden our understanding of second language learners' development of pragmatic competence. Whether and how much grammaticalization research can shed light on our understanding of SLA processes is still to be seen, but it seems to present a fruitful direction for research efforts.

Conclusion

In this chapter, based on the examination of approximately 9 hours of L2 Korean speakers' conversation, I have shown that there is a developmental order among individual functions of *-nuntey/kuntey*. Examining the data from a conversation-analytic perspective, in particular, the positions of the markers in the turn structure (turn-initial vs. turn-medial vs. turn-final) revealed the distribution of the different functions of *-nuntey/kuntey* according to the L2 speakers' proficiency levels. The developmental order was found to be mapped onto the grammaticalization stages of *-nuntey*, which in turn suggests a parallel relationship between diachronic grammaticalization and acquisitional grammaticalization. One caveat is that the findings regarding the acquisition order should be regarded as preliminary because the number of speakers in the database is small. Further studies are needed to put these findings on firmer empirical footing.

The current study contributes to the research agenda of grammaticalization in SLA, which is still a new territory. In addition, this study shows the potential of CA to contribute to SLA research by exploring fruitful contact points between these two fields of research.

Notes

1 Jucker and Ziv (1998) presented the categorization of the functions of discourse markers as follows.

1. text-structuring devices (marking openings or closings of discourse units or transitions between them)
2. modality or attitudinal indicators
3. markers of speaker-hearer intentions and relationships
4. instructions on how given utterances are to be processed (p. 4, numbers added).

2 This refers to the use of *-nuntey* to connect two contrastive responses when the speaker has to address two different actions in the prior turn, especially when

there is a cross-cutting preference between an action as a linguistic vehicle (e.g., question) and an interactional one.(e.g., offer).

3 For more information on the ACTFL OPI, refer to their website: http://www.actfl.org/public/arrticles/details.cfm?id=17

4 Mike had the lowest level of proficiency in the group and had been to Korea only for a week-long business trip.

5 This is an error; it should be *chil* (seven).

6 Park (1997) reported that the form *kulehciman* did not occur in her data. It only appeared in the form of *(ha)ciman*, with 1.6% in turn-initial position, 3.3% in turn-medial position, and 1.3% in turn-final position. *Kuntey* has been identified as the most frequently used contrastive connective (87.0% in turn-initial position, 96.6% in turn-medial position).

7 This is a mispronunciation of *siktang* ('restaurant').

8 The *kuleh-* could also be the first two syllables of *kulentey* or *kulena*.

9 See Kim (2004) for *ney*'s interactional function of inviting the hearer's attention.

References

Andersen, E. S., Brizuela, M., DuPuy, B., & Gonnerman, L. (1999). Cross-linguistic evidence for the early acquisition of discourse markers as register variables. *Journal of Pragmatics, 31*, 1339–1351.

Andersen, G. (2001). *Pragmatic markers and sociolinguistic variation.* Philadelphia: John Benjamins

Andersen, R. (1984). The one to one principle of interlanguage construction. *Language Learning, 34*(4), 77–95.

Andersen, R. W., & Shirai, Y. (1996). The primacy of aspect in first and second language acquisition: The pidgin-creole connection. In W. C. Ritchie & T. K. Bhatia (Eds.), *Handbook of Second Language Acquisition* (pp. 527–570). San Diego, CA: Academic Press.

Belz, J. A., & Vyatkina, N. (2005). Learner corpus analysis and the development of L2 pragmatic competence in networked intercultural language study: The case of German modal particles. *The Canadian Modern Language Review, 62*(1), 17–48.

Blakemore, D. (1987). *Semantic constraints on relevance.* Oxford, UK: Blackwell.

Blakemore, D. (1992). *Understanding utterances.* Oxford, UK: Blackwell.

Cho, Y. M., Schulz, C., Lee, H., & Sohn, S. (2001). *Integrated Korean: Intermediate 1.* Honolulu, HI: University of Hawai'i Press.

Choi, H. (1965). *Wuli malpon* [Korean Grammar]. Seoul, Korea: Ceng'umsa.

Choi, J. (1990). *Kwukeui cepsokmwun kwuseng yenkwu* [Studies on the structure of Korean connectives]. Seoul, Korea: Thap chwulphansa.

Debrock, M., Flament-Boistrancourt, D., & Gevaert, R. (1999). Le manque de “naturel” des interactions verbales du non-francophone en français. Analyse de quelques aspects à partir du corpus LANCOM [The absence of naturalness in the French verbal interactions of nonnative speakers. An analysis of certain aspects from the LANCOM corpus]. *Faits de Langues, 13*, 46–56.

Dittmar, N. (1992). Grammaticalization in second language acquisition. *Studies in Second Language Acquisition, 14*(3), 249–257.

Fraser, B. (1990). An approach to discourse markers. *Journal of Pragmatics, 14*, 383–395.

Fraser, B. (1996). Pragmatic markers. *Pragmatics, 6*(2), 167–190.

Fraser, B. (1999). What are discourse markers? *Journal of Pragmatics, 31*, 931–952.

Giacalone Ramat, A. (1992). Grammaticalization process in the area of temporal and modal relations. *Studies in Second Language Acquisition, 14*, 297–322.

Heritage, J. (1984a). A change-of-state token and aspects of its sequential placement. In J. M. Atkinson & J. Heritage (Eds.), *Structures of social action* (pp. 299–345). Cambridge, UK: Cambridge University Press.

Heritage, J. (1984b). *Garfinkel and ethnomethodology.* Cambridge, UK: Polity Press.

Jisa, H. (1984–1985). French preschoolers' use of et pis ('and then'). *First Language, 5*, 169–184.

Jisa, H. (1987). Sentence connectors in French children's monologue performance. *Journal of Pragmatics, 11*, 607–621.

Jucker, A. H., & Ziv, Y. (1998). *Discourse markers: Descriptions and theory.* Philadelphia: John Benjamins.

Kärkkäinen, E. (1992). Modality as a strategy in interaction: Epistemic modality in the language of native and non-native speakers of English. In L. F. Bouton & Y. Kachru (Eds.), *Pragmatics and language learning monograph series Vol. 3* (pp. 197–216). Urbana, IL: Division of English as an International Language, University of Illinois, Urbana-Champaign.

Kasper, G. (1979). Errors in speech act realization and use of gambits. *The Canadian Modern Language Review, 35*, 395–406.

Kim, H. (1992). *Clause combining in discourse and grammar: An analysis of some Korean clausal connectives in discourse.* University of Hawai'i at Mānoa, Honolulu.

Kim, H. (1994). 'Speech act' adverbial clauses in Korean. In Y.-K. Kim-Renaud (Ed.), *Theoretical Issues in Korean Linguistics* (pp. 495–516). Stanford, CA: CSLI.

Kim, K. (2004). A conversation analysis of Korean sentence-ending modal suffixes -ney, -kwun(a) and -ta: Noticing as a social action *The Sociolinguistic Journal of Korea, 12*(1), 1–35.

Knott, A., & Dale, R. (1994). Using linguistic phenomena to motivate a set of coherence relations. *Discourse processes, 18*(1), 35–62.

Kyratzis, A., & Ervin-Tripp, S. (1999). The development of discourse markers in peer interaction. *Journal of Pragmatics, 31*, 1321–1338.

Lee, H. (1999). *Discourse-pragmatics of the Korean connective -nûnte/(û)nte: A case of grammaticalization of figure-ground relation.* Unpublished manuscript, Potsdam.

Lee, K. (1980). The pragmatic function of the connective *nûnte*. *Ene* [Language], *5*(1), 119–135.

Lee, K. (1988). Verbal connectives of contrast. In E.-J. Baek (Ed.), *Papers from the Sixth International Conference on Korean Linguistics* (pp. 403–415). Seoul, Korea: Hanshin.

Lee, K. (1993). *A Korean grammar on semantic pragmatic principles.* Seoul, Korea: Hankwukmwunwhasa.

Lörscher, W., & Schulze, R. (1988). On polite speaking and foreign language classroom discourse. *International Review of Applied Linguistics in Language Teaching, 26*, 183–199.

Montes, R. G. (1999). The development of discourse markers in Spanish: Interjection. *Journal of Pragmatics, 31*, 1289–1319.

Müller, S. (2004). '*Well you know that type of person*': Functions of *well* in the speech of American and German students. *Journal of Pragmatics, 36*, 1157–1182.

Müller, S. (2005). *Discourse markers in native and non-native English discourse.* Philadelphia: John Benjamins Publishing Company.

Nikula, T. (1996). *Pragmatic force modifiers: A study in interlanguage pragmatics.* Unpublished doctoral dissertation, University of Jyväskylä, Jyväskylä, Finland.

Park, Y.-Y. (1997). *A cross-linguistic study of the use of contrastive connectives in English, Korean, and Japanese conversation.* University of California at Los Angeles, Los Angeles, CA.

Park, Y.-Y. (1999a). *Incorporating discourse into classroom activities and teaching grammar in pragmatics: Teaching the connectives kulentey and kulehciman.* Paper presented at the 4th AATK conference proceedings.

Park, Y.-Y. (1999b). The Korean connective *nuntey* in conversational discourse. *Journal of Pragmatics, 31*, 191–218.

Pfaff, C. W. (1992). The issue of grammaticalization in early German second language. *Studies in Second Language Acquisition, 14*, 273–296.

Pienemann, M. (2002). Issues in second language acquisition and language processing. *Second Language Research, 18*, 189–192.

Pomerantz, A. (1980). Telling my side: "Limited access" as a fishing device. *Sociological Inquiry, 50*, 186–198.

Pomerantz, A. (1984). Agreeing and disagreeing with assessments: Some features of preferred/dispreferred turn shapes. In M. Atkinson & J. Heritage (Eds.), *Structures of social action* (pp. 57–101). New York: Cambridge University Press.

Romero Trillo, J. (2002). The pragmatic fossilization of discourse markers in non-native speakers of English. *Journal of Pragmatics, 34*, 769–784.

Sacks, H. (1992). *Lectures on conversation.* Malden, MA: Blackwell.

Scarcella, R. (1983). Discourse accent in second language performance In S. M. Gass & L. Selinker (Eds.), *Language transfer in language learning* (pp. 306–326). Rowley, MA: Newbury House.

Schegloff, E. A. (1980). Preliminaries to preliminaries: "Can I ask you a question?" *Sociological Inquiry, 50*, 104–152.

Schegloff, E. A., & Sacks, H. (1973). Opening up closings. *Semiotics, 8*, 289–327.
Schiffrin, D. (1987). *Discourse markers*. New York: Cambridge University Press.
Schorup, L. C. (1985). *Common discourse particles in English conversation: Like, well, y'know*. New York: Garland.
Schorup, L. C. (2000). Rethinking *well*. *Journal of Pragmatics, 33*, 1025–1060.
Shirai, Y., & Andersen, R. (1995). The acquisition of tense-aspect morphology: A prototype account. *Language, 71*, 743–762.
Skiba, R., & Dittmar, N. (1992). Pragmatic, semantic, and syntactic constraints and grammaticalization. *Studies in Second Language Acquisition, 14*, 323–349.
Slobin, D. I. (1977). Language change in childhood and history. In J. Macnamara (Ed.), *Language learning and thought* (pp. 185–221). New York: Academic Press.
Sohn, H.-m. (1986). *Linguistic expeditions*. Seoul, Korea: Hanshin.
Sohn, H.-m. (1999). *The Korean language*. Cambridge, UK: Cambridge University Press.
Sprott, R. (1992). Children's use of discourse markers in disputes: Form-function relations and discourse in child language. *Discourse Processes, 15*, 423–439.
Stubbs, M. (1983). *Discourse analysis*. Chicago: The University of Chicago Press.
Traugott, E. C. (1982). From propositional to textual and expressive meanings: Some semantic-pragmatic aspects of grammaticalization. In W. P. Lehmann & Y. Malkiel (Eds.), *Perspectives on historical linguistics* (pp. 245–271). Amsterdam: Benjamins.
Traugott, E. C. (1989). On the rise of epistemic meanings in English: An example of subjectification in semantic change. *Language, 57*, 33–65.
Traugott, E. C. (2003). From subjectification to intersubjectification. In R. Hickey (Ed.), *Motives for language change* (pp. 124–139). Cambridge, UK: Cambridge University Press.
van Dijk, T. A. (1979). *Macrostructures: An interdisciplinary study of global structures in discourse, interaction, and cognition*. Hillsdale, NJ: Erlbaum Associates.
Wong, J. (2000). The token 'yeah' in nonnative speaker English conversation. *Research on Language and Social Interaction, 33*, 39–67.
Yoshimi, D. R. (1999). L1 language socialization as a variable in the use of *ne* by L2 learners of Japanese. *Journal of Pragmatics, 31*, 1513–1525.
Yoshimi, D. R. (2001). Explicit instruction and JFL learners' use of interactional discourse markers. In K. R. Rose & G. Kasper (Eds.), *Pragmatics in language teaching* (pp. 223–244). New York: Cambridge University Press.

Appendix: Abbreviations in transcripts

For morpheme-by-morpheme glossing, the following abbreviations are used:

ACC	accusative
ATTR	attributive
CIRCUM	circumstantial
CL	classifier
COMM	committal
CONN	connective
CORREL	correlative
DCTRE	deductive reasoning
DM	discourse marker
FP	sentence-final particle
FR	factual realization
HON	honorific
HUM	humble
IE	informal ending
IND	indicative
LOC	locative
NECE	necessitative
NEG	negative
NOM	nominative
NOML	nominalizer
POL	polite
PST	past
Q	question marker
QUOT	quotative marker
REASON	reason
RTR	retrospective
TOP	topic
UNASSIM	unassimilated

13 Development of Interactional Competence: Changes in the Use of *ne* in L2 Japanese During Study Abroad

Midori Ishida
University of Hawai'i at Mānoa

Introduction

This chapter investigates the development of the use of the Japanese particle *ne* by a second language (L2) learner of Japanese during a 9-month study abroad. The particle *ne*, which is normally called a sentence-final particle, does not have a functional or semantic equivalent in English, although it is sometimes compared to *isn't it* in a tag question and the discourse marker *you know.* Linguists have tried to identify its central meaning and social functions but have not been able to come to a consensus on a single description that can cover its versatile use. However, this very versatility makes this particle a highly useful linguistic resource for participating in social interaction. Therefore, L2 learners of Japanese must learn how to use *ne* as they develop their interactional competence (Hall, 1995; He & Young, 1998; Young, 1999), or the knowledge and ability to participate in social interactions through the use of linguistic and other semiotic resources. The development of knowledge about how to use a language in socially appropriate ways and how to formulate grammatically acceptable sentences has been claimed to be important for a few decades, but L2 researchers have only recently begun to pay attention to the development of interactional competence as a necessary part of becoming a competent speaker of a language (e.g., Firth & Wagner, 1997; Nguyen, 2004;

Talk-in-interaction: Multilingual perspectives, pp. 351–385, Hanh Nguyen & Gabriele Kasper (Eds.), 2009
Honolulu, HI: University of Hawai'i, National Foreign Language Resource Center

Young & Miller, 2004). No study has yet examined in a longitudinal perspective how an L2 learner's interactional competence develops through the use of a particular linguistic resource. In an effort to fill this gap, this chapter focuses on how one learner of Japanese used the Japanese particle *ne* in interaction during a 9-month study abroad.

Application of CA to the analysis of *ne*

To understand the focal L2 learner's competence in his use of *ne* at different times during his study abroad, I examine the interactional functions of *ne* in his conversations by using conversation analysis (CA). In CA, two of the major threads of analysis are how people construct social activities on a turn-by-turn basis (e.g., telephone openings, Schegloff, 1979) and how an action is accomplished through the sequential placement of particular turns (e.g., agreeing and disagreeing, Pomerantz, 1984). Another central concern, and one that is of special interest to linguistics, is how a linguistic form is deployed in the organization of ongoing talk-in-interaction (e.g., *oh*, Heritage, 1984a, 2002). The interactional functions of a linguistic form at a moment in talk-in-interaction can be understood through the turn-by-turn analysis of participants' understanding of what is going on at that moment, which is displayed in their verbal and nonverbal actions.

CA has contributed to the development of interactional linguistics (Selting & Couper-Kuhlen, 2001) and research on grammar and interaction (Ochs, Schegloff, & Thompson, 1996). While sentence grammar may be used by an individual to construct syntactically possible sentences, interactional grammar, or how linguistic forms function at a given moment in interaction, is co-constructed and shared by the participants in social interaction. For instance, Ford and Mori's (1994) analysis of conversations showed how the connective *but* is used in agreeing and disagreeing, and Koshik's (2002) analysis of a writing conference showed how a teacher used yes-no questions to help a student solve the problems that the teacher found in a written text. Such an approach has also been taken in studies of Japanese, as exemplified by Mori's (1999) study of the contrastive connectives *kedo* [but, although] and *demo* [but, however] that are used for negotiating agreement and disagreement.

Research on the Japanese particle *ne* also benefits from the use of CA, as I discuss later (Morita, 2003; Tanaka, 2000). However, earlier theories and empirical studies of the use of *ne* that are not CA-oriented are still relevant to the present paper and are reviewed here. The particle *ne* is sentence-final and has been characterized as an index (Cook, 1992) with which a speaker expresses his or her epistemic stance (e.g., Kamio, 1990, 1997; Masuoka, 1991) and affective stance (e.g., Cook, 1992; Maynard, 1993) and produces communicative effects such as politeness. Kamio (1990, 1997), who regarded *ne* primarily as an evidential marker, argued that using *ne* is obligatory when the knowledge conveyed in the proposition is equally or more deeply embedded in the hearer's than in the speaker's territory of information. However, he acknowledged that *ne* can also be used as an index of affective stance, arguing that *ne* can "suggest[s] camaraderie between the speaker and the hearer" when used in nonobligatory contexts (Kamio, 1997, p. 153). While Kamio's theory centers on the use of *ne* as an index of epistemic stance, Maynard (1993) and Cook (1992) proposed that *ne* serves primarily as an index of affective stance. Based on an examination of mother-child conversations, Cook argued that *ne* directly indexes "affective common ground" (p. 510) and indirectly indexes various social acts, including requesting confirmation, introducing new topics, and mitigating face-threatening acts.

Provided that *ne* can convey such a wide range of indexical meanings as these researchers suggest, a participant in social interaction must understand which particular meaning is being indexed using the particle and make informed decisions about what kind of action he or she can take in response. With its focus on the participants' perspective, CA is thus quite suitable for identifying the workings of *ne* in social interaction. For example, Tanaka's (2000) CA study of *ne* cast new light on one of the functions of *ne* that most studies have identified as soliciting confirmation and agreement (e.g., Cook, 1992; Masuoka, 1991; McGloin, 1990; Morita, 2003; Nittono, 2003; Uyeno, 1971). Similar to *isn't it*, used in English tag questions (e.g., McGloin, 1990; Nittono, 2003; Tanaka, 2000), such use of *ne* makes an affiliative action (Tanaka, 2000) or an aligning action (Morita, 2003) relevant as a next-turn response. According to McGloin (1990), who explained this use of *ne* as that of an epistemic stance marker, the speaker can use *ne* in such a manner when he or she believes that the information is located in the hearer's territory and seeks confirmation from the hearer because the sharedness of knowledge is in question. Meanwhile, when the information conveyed is based on experience shared by the speaker and hearer, the use of *ne* projects agreement (McGloin, 1990), or "approval or concurrence" (Uyeno, 1971, p. 118). However, such an explanation based on the speaker's assessment of information status does not apply well to a request such as *Naisho ne* [Keep this a secret, okay?]. Using this example, Tanaka's (2000) analysis provides evidence for how a particular use of *ne* can invite an affiliative action. When the speaker in her study said *Naisho ne* and the addressee laughed without providing any immediate affiliative response such as *un* [okay], the speaker then repeated the word *naisho* [secret] with an added copula, *da*, and interactional particle, *yo*: *Naisho da yo* [It's a secret, you understand?], which is more forcible than the use of *ne* in inviting an affiliative response. Through an analysis of subsequent actions, Tanaka (2000) identified one type of interactional work that *ne* accomplishes in social interaction.

Morita (2003) also demonstrated that CA is useful for analyzing the interactional functions of *ne*. Her analysis shows in detail how *ne* segments a long narrative into smaller chunks and allows non-turn-grabbing responses from the hearer. This use of *ne* in both intrasentential and sentence-final positions within a long stretch of talk has been studied by Maynard (1993). Based on the finding that more than 50% of occurrences of *ne* in casual conversations receive listener responses, Maynard (1993) claimed that one of the functions of *ne* is to encourage a "listener back-channel response" as a "conversation management device[s]" (p. 211). However, her quantitative analysis does not show the exact mechanism of how *ne* serves that function. In contrast, Morita (2003) presented a detailed analysis of turn-taking to argue that this use of *ne* "foreground[s] a certain stretch of talk as an 'interactionally relevant unit' to be operated on—whether that unit is itself a whole utterance or merely one particular component of that utterance" (p. 126). The particle operates as a turn management device so that the hearer has an opportunity to show his or her involvement in the speaker's talk by producing backchanneling acknowledgment tokens (*aizuchi*) upon hearing *ne*. Morita's and Tanaka's CA analyses thus further our understanding of those interactional functions of *ne*, which cannot be explained as indexing stances.

Following Tanaka and Morita, I examine the interactional functions of *ne* used by a learner of Japanese by analyzing the sequential placements of *ne* and the interlocutor's subsequent actions.

L1 and L2 development in the use of *ne*

While L2 learners of Japanese have difficulty developing their competence with respect to the versatile use of the particle *ne*, children who speak Japanese as their first language (L1) seem to start using it at a very early stage of their language development. Clancy's (1986) study on the L1 acquisition of Japanese revealed that *ne* emerges at 1.5–2 years of age, which is about the same time as the earliest two-word utterances. The earliest production of *ne* is found in a response to an adult's utterance that ends with *ne*. When an adult points to some flowers and says *Koko ni mo aru ne* [There are some here too, aren't there], the child repeats part of the utterance and adds *ne*: *Koko aru ne* [There are some here, aren't there] (p. 429). After beginning to use *ne* when agreeing with another person, children start using *ne* in expressing opinions or making comments, for example, about a very large boat in a picture, saying *Ookii ne* [It's big, isn't it?]. Other uses include those that solicit agreement and those that present information that is not available to the hearer. Clancy concludes that "from its earliest occurrences, *ne* is used appropriately in different types of speech acts" (p. 430).

The early development in the use of *ne* by L1 children contrasts with that by adult L2 learners of Japanese. While L1 children start to use *ne* at the two-word stage, L2 learners' development in the use of *ne* lags behind the development of general vocabulary and grammatical particles, as Sawyer (1992) found in his study of L2 learners who were studying abroad in Japan. Although L2 learners start to use *ne* earlier than other sentence-final particles such as *yo* and *no* (Haijikano, 1994; Mine, 1995; Mine et al., 2002), a large proportion of its use is found in a formulaic expression, *soo desu ne* (["That's right]; Sawyer, 1992; Yoshimi, 1999). In Ohta's (2001) longitudinal study of first-year classroom learners of Japanese, *soo desu ne* and other aligning expressions such as *ii desu ne* [That sounds good] appeared in L2 learners' speech after a stage where the learners used an acknowledgement expression, *soo desu ka* [Is that right?/ Really?], in response to a speaker telling new information. When the phrase *soo desu ne* began to be used in response turns, it was often inappropriately used. While the appropriateness of this phrase was not examined in Sawyer's (1992) study, Yoshimi (1999) also found that it tended to be used in inappropriate contexts. L2 learners seemed to use *soo desu ne* in response turns to show alignment, indicating that they are with the current speaker, but many of its uses were inappropriate in terms of the epistemic stance that the expression indicates. This problem of inappropriate use should be investigated by paying closer attention to the sequential placement of the phrase.

L2 learners use *ne* also in "contributory" turns, in which the speaker is talking about his or her "own experience or ideas, or in the assessment of or commenting on the experiences or ideas of others" (Yoshimi, 1999, p. 1517). According to Shibahara (2002), who examined the use of *ne* by intermediate and advanced L2 learners of Japanese in oral proficiency interviews twice during their 9-month stays in Japan, "facilitating" *ne*, which is used when the speaker assumes a shared perspective and invites an agreement, was used most frequently. She also found that "softening" *ne*, which is used in imparting nonshared information, was used less frequently and often inappropriately. The pervasiveness of inappropriate use of "softening" *ne* was also pointed out in Mine's (1995) 8-month study of learners from beginning to advanced levels.

To sum up, previous research indicates that although L2 learners' rate of development is slower than that of L1 children, they have been found to begin using *ne* in response turns as early as their first year in L2 classrooms. The formulaic expression *soo desu ne* may be readily used but appropriateness seems to be difficult at first. In contributory turns, learners use *ne* frequently and appropriately when they state information that is assumed to be shared, while its use in imparting nonshared information is often inappropriate initially.

Although L2 research on the use of *ne* during the past 15 years has given us an outline of development in terms of the order of emergence and frequency and appropriateness of use, how learners can use the linguistic resource *ne* in social interaction is not clear yet, except for acknowledgment and alignment in response turns (Ohta, 2001). In most of the previous studies, the functions of *ne* were coded according to predetermined categories to count the frequencies. Additionally, because those studies only provide the sentences that include *ne* in their reports, we cannot tell how *ne* in those instances can be "facilitating" (Shibahara, 2002) the flow of a conversation. With the aim of understanding how a learner of Japanese develops interactional competence with respect to the use of *ne* during a study abroad, this chapter analyzes in detail how *ne* functions in the sequential organization of talk-in-interaction.

Study

Data

The data for the present study comprises eight conversations (chronologically ordered from FR1 through FR8) that a learner of Japanese video-recorded during his stay in Japan. The learner, Fred,[1] is an American college student who studied Japanese for 2 years in high school and another 2 years at a university. After completing the second-year courses, he participated in a study-abroad program in Japan for two semesters from September 2004 to May 2005. I asked Fred to record 30-minute conversations once a month with people whom he regularly interacted with. He chose to record interactions with his host family (FR1, 2), his Japanese tutor and friend (FR3, 4), his American friend and his host mother (FR5), a friend of his Japanese tutor (FR6), his American friend and his Japanese girlfriend (FR7), and the Japanese person who participated in FR7 (FR8).

The data were given a "comprehensive data treatment" (ten Have, 2007) with regard to Fred's use of *ne* in the eight sessions (FR1–8). Single case analyses of each occurrence of *ne* in the data were done using CA (e.g., Heritage, 1984b; Hutchby & Wooffitt, 1998). Although applying CA methodology to talk-in-interaction involving L2 speakers involves some difficulties, previous research has shown that it is a fruitful enterprise (Gardner & Wagner, 2004; Schegloff, Koshik, Jacoby, & Olsher, 2002; Wong & Olsher, 2000). As Heritage (1984b) stated, "[c]onversation analysis...is concerned with the analysis of the *competences* which underlie ordinary social activities" (p. 241). The competences of L2 speakers can also be understood by refraining from prescribing the regularities found in native speakers' interactions as the norm. By analyzing how responses to *ne*-ending turns are oriented to by others, we can understand the interactional functions that *ne* plays as a linguistic resource and the participants' interactional competence. After analyzing all of Fred's uses of *ne*, I compared his use of this particle across conversation sessions.

Analysis of Fred's use of *ne*

After transcribing all eight conversations that Fred recorded, I found that he did not use *ne* at all in the first two conversations (FR1, 2). His initial uses of *ne* were twice in FR3, once in FR4, and once in FR5. While the use of *ne* was restricted to these few occasions in FR3–5, Fred's use of *ne* greatly increased from FR6: It was used 10 times in FR6, 22 times in FR7, and 13 times in FR8. Therefore, I first analyze Fred's initial uses in FR3 through FR5 in chronological order and then present the analysis of its uses in the rest of the conversations (FR6–8) according to the sequential placement of *ne* in relation to the previous turns. I discuss Fred's development later in the discussion section.

Fred's initial uses of ne

Presenting a possible new topic after the previous topic ceased to develop further. Fred used *ne* twice in FR3, including the segment presented in Excerpt 1.

Excerpt 1, final exam (FR3, 12/7/2004, 3'58")

Maho (MH) is Fred's (FR) friend and tutor whom he meets every week. After the previous topic comes to an end by Fred saying "*soo soo soo*" [right, right, right]" and Maho saying "*soo soo soo*" [right, right, right]" Fred initiates a new topic (line 1).

```
01 FR: kimatsu      shiken ga ar:imasu     ne,
       end of term test   SB exist-polite ne
       "There are final exams, aren't they?"

02     (1.1)

03 MH: un.  aru. (.)    tada   anmashi nai.
       yeah exist-plain except much    not exist
       "Yeah, there are. But not many."

04     (0.3)

05 FR: anmashi (nai) (0.2) un.
       much    (not exist) yeah
       "You don't have many. Yeah."

06     (0.4)

07 FR: watashi wa: shinpai
       I        TP  worried
       "I am worried."
```

In response to Fred's *ne*-ending statement about the final exams, Maho says *un* and produces a partial repetition of his utterance (*aru* [exist-plain], which corresponds with *arimasu* [exist-polite]), confirming that Fred's statement is correct (line 03). However, this is not a wholehearted confirmation as indicated by the 1.1-s pause before the response and also by a qualification, or an utterance that restricts the applicability of the prior statement, which Maho provides using *tada* [except]. This sequence of an affirmative response followed by a qualification is very similar to the partial agreement that Pomerantz (1984) found in second assessments, in which the hearer of the first assessment agrees with *yes* and then presents a weak disagreement with *but*. This suggests that Fred's turn that ends with *ne* invites an affirmative response as a preferred one. Then, in line 05, Fred repeats the last two words of Maho's qualification and says *un* [Yeah] after a 0.2-s pause, showing his acknowledgment of her response. Such a response indicates that Fred is taking the role of a hearer and that he regards Maho as the main speaker who contributes to the development of the topic that he initiated. However, Maho does not continue her story. After a 0.4-s pause, Fred in line 07 picks up the topic of the final exam and starts telling his own story with the use of the topic marker *wa* in comparison to Maho's story. In this way, Fred not only initiates a topic with the use of *ne* but also contributes to the development of the topic when his interlocutor does not contribute to it.

The correspondence of a *ne*-ending statement and an affirmative response, *un*, was also observed in another segment in the same conversation (transcript not presented here) when Fred initiated a topic at the beginning of the conversation. Following a 1.9-s pause after Fred greeted Maho, he introduced the topic of the recent weather, saying, *samuku narimas ne* [It gets cold, doesn't it?]. Maho said *hai* [yes] after five lines of negotiating the tense and aspect of this utterance, which suggests her orientation to the absence of an affirmative response after Fred's *ne*-ending turn. In this instance, Maho's delayed response, *hai*, reflexively indicates that Fred's *ne*-ending turn makes an agreement the relevant next turn and that the five lines of negotiation were inserted between the pair of utterances. With the use of *ne* in this interactional structure, Fred invited an agreement to his view of the recent weather and introduced a new topic, which unfortunately faded out with a long pause after Maho's utterance, *hai* [yes].

In these instances in FR3, *ne* was used to make a next turn agreement or confirmation relevant as a preferred response. With this use of *ne*, Fred provided his interlocutor an interactional space to display her understanding of the matter (whether it is about the recent weather or test schedule). Such use of *ne* to introduce a topic was also observed twice in FR7.

Stating an opinion within Fred's own telling. While the ne-ending statements which Fred used in FR3 made relevant confirmation or agreement in the next turn, the particle used once in FR4 does not have such a function.

Excerpt 2, Fred's impression of people in Tokyo (FR4, 1/18/2005, 1'56")

```
Fred (FR) and Maho (MH) both live in the Kansai area. Fred
is talking to Maho about his recent trip to Tokyo.
```

01 FR: tookyoo jin wa::. (0.8) ano: (0.4)
Tokyo people TP well
02 hakkiri itte::. (0.3) h. ((sniffs))
frankly say-and
03 aa:. (0.2) chotto:: shitsurei
mm a little rude
04 to(h) o(h)mo(h)imas **ne,**
QT think ne
"Tokyo people are, well, frankly speaking, mm, a bit rude, I think"

05 (0.5)
06 MH: aa a[a.
ah ah
"Ah, ah."

0 7FR: [doite:. doite:. doite:.
move away move away move away
08 *((performing 'elbowing one's way out'))*
"Move away, move away, move away."

After characterizing Tokyo as a metropolitan city, Fred in line 01 begins making a negative assessment about people in Tokyo (*shitsurei* [rude]). This action is a dispreferred one, as projected with the adverbial phrase, *hakkiri itte* [frankly speaking], and as indicated with several features of his turn: delaying the assessment with the use of sniffs and *aa* [mm], mitigating the criticism with *chotto* [a bit], and adding a modal expression *to omoimasu* [I think that] with chuckles. At a first glance, the utterance-final *ne* in this assessment turn appears to be "soften[ing] the declarative nature of the sentence. [Its] use, therefore, gives the effect of humbling the speaker and being polite to the addressee" (Uyeno, 1971, p. 131). However, even though some politeness is communicated in this utterance, we cannot be certain that the particle *ne* produces this effect because *ne* is used together with other means of softening the utterance. What we can do here is analyze the turns after the occurrence of *ne*. When Maho acknowledges Fred's opinion by saying *aa aa* [Ah, ah] (line 06), Fred in line 07 continues his turn without explicitly demanding an agreement to his view. Fred's continued telling suggests that the *ne*-ending turn does not put the hearer in a position to agree with his statement. As Morita (2003) argued in her analysis of *ne*, a teller can chunk his telling into interactionally relevant segments and provide interactional space for the hearer to respond without pushing for any specific type of response. This example has shown that Fred was capable of using the particle *ne* to mark interactional chunking when stating an opinion. This use of *ne* was also seen in his later conversations, FR7 and FR8, in addition to FR4.

Emphasizing confirmation in response to a prior turn that ends with deshoo. While Fred's use of *ne* was seen as part of his opinion statement in FR4, the only instance of Fred's use of *ne* found in FR5 was part of the formulaic phrase *soo desu ne* [That's right], which emphasizes a prior confirmation he has made in response to a turn that ends with *deshoo* [I suppose; Isn't it so?].

Excerpt 3, Fred's host sister (FR5, 3/3/2005, 2'11")

Fred (FR) and his friend, Gordon, are in Gordon's host mother's (GM) house. Gordon's host mother is talking about Fred's host brother and sisters based on what she has heard from Fred's host mother. After talking about Fred's host brother, she begins to talk about one of Fred's host sisters (line 1).

01 GM: oneesan wa suisu ka dokka ni
older sister TP Switzerland or somewhere in
02 iru deshoo.
live I suppose
"The older sister is in Switzerland or somewhere, isn't she?"

03 (0.7)

04 FR: [un n,
yeah
"Yeah."

05 GM: [°musume-san°
daughter
"The daughter of your host mother."

06 (0.4)

07 FR: **soo desu ne**[2]
right CP ne
"That's right"

08 GM: hnn,
mm
"Mm."

09 (0.8)

10 FR: shitte iru
know
"I know that."

Gordon's host mother states her knowledge about Fred's host sister in lines 01 and 02, followed by a 0.7-s pause. Fred confirms the information by saying *un* [yeah], but this is overlapped with her clarification that the person she is referring to as *oneesan* [older sister] is the *musume-san* [daughter] of his host mother. This clarification reflexively indicates that the information presented with the modal expression *deshoo* [I suppose] in her first turn requires confirmation. Evidence for this is the 0.7-s pause (line 3) and the host mother's attempt to make sure that Fred understood her message by clarifying the referent. Fred's utterance in line 07, *soo desu ne* [That's right], displays his understanding of the referent and also reaffirms, as an addition to his first response, *un*, that the information about the referent is correct. It is important to emphasize the confirmation because *un* can be taken either as a sign of confirmation or a sign of indecisiveness, especially here because of the subtle prosody in which *un* was uttered and the delay in its utterance. Fred further adds *shitte iru* [I know that] in line 10 and further claims his knowledge by providing information about the sister three lines after that. This example suggests that Fred was capable of using the formula *soo desu ne* to emphasize his confirmation, in response to the interactional demand of the turn sequence.

Fred's use of *ne* after his interlocutor's use of *deshoo* was also seen twice in FR8. Interestingly, in both instances, the uses of *ne*—once in the form of *soo desu ne* and the other with a partial repetition of the *deshoo*-ending statement—were seen not immediately after the minimal responses, *aa* and *un*, but after his interlocutor concluded her telling with an assessment, *kara meccha urayamashii* [so, I am really envious of you] and *Dakara sugoku omoshirokatta* [So, it was very interesting]. Fred used these *ne*-ending utterances, not only to emphasize confirmation, such as in Excerpt 3, but also as a way to mark the end of his interlocutor's previous telling before initiating a related telling.

As we have seen so far, in his initial uses of *ne*, Fred demonstrated his interactional competence in the use of this particle from his third through fifth conversations, although its frequency was very low. Using *ne* in different sequential environments, Fred was able to introduce topics, signal segments of his telling for his interlocutor to come in with some responses, and emphasize confirmation as a way to proceed with the topic at hand. These uses of *ne* are seen not only in the earlier conversations but also in Fred's later conversations, which indicates that Fred used *ne* early in his study abroad not simply by chance.

Expanded use of* ne *in FR6–8

While Fred's use of *ne* in FR3–5 was very limited in frequency and did not show any patterns in terms of its interactional functions, his use of *ne* clearly increased in FR6. I present my analysis here according to the sequential placement of *ne*. When similar uses of *ne* appeared in multiple conversations, I chose an excerpt from the earliest conversation.

In response to the interlocutor's ne-ending statement. While Fred retrospectively used *soo desu ne* and partial repetition after his interlocutor's *deshoo*-ending statements, he also used these responses immediately after *hai* [yes] or *un* [yeah] in response to his interlocutor's *ne*-ending statements. Such use of *ne* after Fred's interlocutor's use of *ne* was seen four times in FR7 and once in FR8. Excerpt 4 presents one of these instances.

Excerpt 4, American Standard English (FR7, 4/8/2005, 30'45")

Fred (FR), Derek (DR) and Maki (MK) are talking about regional varieties of American English. When Derek says "*nansee no eego wa* [English spoken in the Southwest is]" "*hyoojun-go* [the standard language]," Fred agrees with him by saying "*un. soo to omoimasu* [Yeah, I think so]." He then begins to state his opinion in line 1, using the word "Hollywood," which Derek provided.

01 FR: hariudd, (0.2) no eego wa:. (0.3)
Hollywood LK English TP
02 hyoo-go: (0.2) hyoogen-go?
language expression-language
"The English spoken in Hollywood is st- language, stand- language?"

03 (0.4)

04 DR: hy[oojun-go
standard-language
"Standard language."

05 MK: [hyoojun-go,=
standard-language
"Standard language."

06 FR: =hyoojun-[go
standard-language
"Standard language."

07 DR: [to: iema:su ne:. (.)
QT say-can-Polite ne
08 to [iwareteima[s ne:,
QT say-PASSIVE-PROG-Polite ne
"We can say so. It is being said that way."

09 FR: [un. [un.
yeah yeah
"Yeah, yeah."

10 (0.2)

11 FR: hai. (.) **soo desu ne,**
yes right CP ne
"Yes, that's right."

12 DR: °u:n.°
yeah
"Yeah."

In lines 01 and 02, Fred tries to say that the English spoken in Hollywood is the Standard English in the USA, using the same sentence structure that Derek used earlier. When Fred indicates difficulty in pronouncing the word *hyoojungo* [standard language] by using a rising intonation in line 02, Derek and Maki model the pronunciation. Before Fred finishes repeating their models, Derek in line 07 completes the sentence initiated by Fred in line 01, building on the word that he modeled in line 04. Fred responds to Derek's *ne*-ending statement (line 07) with *un* [Yeah] in line 09, but it is overlapped with Derek's restatement (line 08). Although Fred says *un* again when Derek's restatement reaches the end of a sentence (the *masu* form of a verb), he further responds to Derek when he completes his restatement with *ne*. This time, Fred in line 11 says, *hai. soo desu ne* [Yes, that's right] instead of a short token *un*, specifically in response to Derek's second *ne*-ending statement.

The use of *un* (the first *un* in line 09) seems to be sufficient to show agreement with Derek's first *ne*-ending statement (line 07) because the statement was originally initiated by Fred in line 01. However, Derek's overlapping *ne*-ending restatement makes a renewed agreeing response relevant in the next turn. We have seen in this excerpt that Fred used the phrase *soo desu ne* to respond to the immediate need for a renewed display of agreement to his interlocutor's *ne*-ending statement.

In response to the interlocutor's statement that aligns with Fred's earlier telling. In the previous example, Fred used *un soo desu ne* to agree with Derek's *ne*-ending statement. However, his use of this phrase was not limited to responding to a statement that ends with *ne*. As shown in Excerpt 5, Fred used *soo desu ne* even when his interlocutor did not use *ne*.

Excerpt 5, scary ride on a roller coaster (FR6, 3/8/2005, 6'32")

Fred (FR) is telling Yuko (YK), whom he met for the first time, about a ride at an amusement park. After Yuko says that she was scared when she rode on a roller coaster, Fred starts telling her about how his host sister expressed her fear and hesitation before riding with him.

```
01 FR: sore ato   de:. (0.7) ((imitating host sister))
       that after in
02     aa::. (.) daijoobu:. kowanakatta(h). hh=
       ah        alright    scary-Neg-past
       "After that, she said, 'Ah, I'm okay. It was
       not scary'."

03 YK: =ah hah hah: .hh (0.3) kowag[atteru     dake
                                scary-pretending only
       "She was just pretending to be scared."
```

```
04 FR:                                          [soo   desu ne:.
                                                 right CP   ne
                                                 "That's right."

05      eh heh heh heh heh

06      (0.5)

07 YK:  heh heh

08      (0.2)

09 FR:  heh heh

10      (0.4)
11 FR:  hosuto oneesan      wa (0.4)
        host   older sister TP
12      ano (1.0)totemo tanoshii hito.
        um        very   funny    person.
        "My host sister is, um, a very funny person"
```

After Fred imitates his host sister's expression of relief in line 02, Yuko in line 03 laughs along with him and expresses her interpretation that Fred's host sister might have been merely pretending to be scared. Fred overlaps with Yuko's interpretive comment with the phrase *soo desu ne* and laughs in line 04. Considering the timing of the overlap, Fred's use of *soo desu ne* cannot be said to show agreement with Yuko's interpretation. However, the syllables *kowa-(i)* [afraid, scary] are enough to show that the content of Yuko's utterance is about Fred's host sister's emotional state. With the anticipation that Yuko is aligning with his story, Fred in line 04 is acknowledging Yuko's ongoing turn. His later assessment of his host sister (lines 11, 12) and his subsequent story about her suggests that his story about the roller coaster ride is completed when the alignment with Yuko is achieved.

This example shows that when Fred's interlocutor displayed her understanding of Fred's telling by making an aligning comment, Fred used the phrase *soo desu ne* to acknowledge her contribution before continuing his telling. Fred's competent use of *soo desu ne* in this sequential environment was seen in FR8 as well as in FR6.

In response to an interlocutor's telling that does not align with Fred's earlier telling. While Fred's use of the phrase *soo desu ne* alone served well to acknowledge his interlocutor's aligning turn as seen in Excerpts 4 and 5, its use seemed to require some explication when the prior interlocutor's turn presented a view that contrasted with Fred's telling, as shown in Excerpt 6.

Excerpt 6, making friends with apartment neighbors (FR6, 3/8/2005, 11'43")

```
In response to Yuko's (YK) question of where he used to
live in Hawai'i, Fred (FR) tells her that he used to live
```

in a dorm [*ryoo*] and adds "*gakusee no apaato* [apartment for students]." He explains that living in a dorm was cheaper than living in a regular apartment.

01 YK: huu:[n:
       um hum
       "Um hum."

02 FR: [iroirona: (.) iroirona tomodachi: (0.4) aa:
            various   various   friend   um
03   (0.3) ga: (0.4) tsukatta:. (0.3) tsuka:u?
                 SB   use-past   use-present
       "I used (=made) various, various friends. Use?"

04   (0.5)

05 YK: apaato   ni sundetemo:, (0.2)
       apartment in live-even if
       "Even if (we) live in an apartment,"

06 FR: un   un un.=
       yeah
       "Yeah, yeah, yeah."

07 YK: u::[:n.
       uhm
       "uhm,"

08 FR: [hai.
           yes
           "Yes."

09   (0.9)

10 YK: nihon de wa: apaato   ni: sundetemo:. (0.5)
       Japan in TP apartment in live-even if
11   tonari   dooshi   anmari nakayoku [(wa nare-)[3]
       next door each other much   befriend   TP become-can
       "in Japan, even if (we) live in an apartment, (we) can't make friends with the neighbors that much."

12 FR: [aa aa.
                                                     ah ah
13   **soo** [**desu ne:**.
       right CP   ne
       "Ah, ah. That's right."

14 YK: [u::n.
             yeah
             "Yeah."

15   (0.8)

```
16 FR: aa. apaato    ni sundeimasu ka?
       uhm apartment in live        Q
       "Uhm, do you live in an apartment?"
```

After Fred tells that he made (*tsukatta* [used] for *tsukutta* [made]) many friends (lines 02, 03), Yuko in line 05 begins presenting an opposing view about interpersonal relationships in apartments. Although her utterance in line 05 is incomplete as a sentence, the connective *-temo* [even if] shows a contrast with Fred's telling. After receiving Fred's encouragement to continue with her telling in lines 06 and 08, Yuko repeats her previous statement following a qualification (*nihon de wa* [in Japan]), which enables her to not have to contradict Fred's argument about the situation in Hawai'i. Before she finishes talking, Fred in lines 12 and 13 begins saying *aa, soo desu ne* [Oh, that's right]. This overlap indicates that he has already understood her argument and can anticipate how her telling will proceed without hearing it. Yuko halts her telling just after Fred's overlapping utterance starts, and says *u:n*, with which she acknowledges Fred's display of understanding. When Fred asks a question after a 0.8-s pause (line 16), the difference brought up by Yuko is left up in the air.

Fred's response *aa soo desu ne* in this excerpt requires some discussion. Although his use of the phrase indicates at least that he understands Yuko's argument and possibly that he agrees with the statement, Fred's subsequent turn (line 16) does not help us understand what he is doing exactly with the phrase. If he is only indicating his understanding, he should have said *aa. soo desu ka* [Oh, is that right?]. Otherwise, because he has never lived in an apartment in Japan, he could have used a secondhand evidential *rashii* [according to what I have heard], as in *soo rashii desu ne* before eliciting a firsthand story about apartment life in Japan (line 16). In addition to the problem with the choice of linguistic resources, this response consequently prevents Yuko from continuing her telling. Although Fred elicits more telling from Yuko, the question seems to be brought up abruptly. To relate this question to Yuko's argument, Fred could have used a different form, *sunde iru n desu ka*?, which regards *sunde iru* [living in an apartment herself] as the supporting evidence for her argument.

This example shows that the phrase *soo desu ne* cannot be readily used as the sole response when Fred's interlocutor's previous turn is not in alignment with Fred's earlier telling. The epistemic marking of the phrase might need some adjustment, and coherence with subsequent turns should be established with the use of other linguistic resources. In another instance found in FR6, Fred used *soo desu ne* and supported this response with a "second story" (Sacks, 1995, p. 257). As an answer to Fred's question, his interlocutor, Yuko, told him that she wanted to improve her English, at least before trying to learn other languages. Following a 0.8-s pause after he said *un un.* (.) *soo desu ne:*, Fred began talking about his experience learning Spanish as a second language by saying *boku ni totte:* [For me]. Although what Fred was doing with the phrase was not clear at the time of its utterance, his "second story" reflexively indicates that he was aligning with Yuko as a foreign language learner. With a second story, a listener of a narrative can present another story in alignment with the first speaker's story. Although the use of *mo* [also] after *boku ni totte* [for me] would have made it clearer that he was aligning with Yuko, the meaning of *soo desu ne* in this instance is clearer than the one in Excerpt 6 due to the telling of a second story.

In contrast to the two examples I have just described, Excerpt 7 shows that Fred made a clearer alignment with the interlocutor's previous turn.

Excerpt 7, cold classrooms in summer (FR8, 5/6/2005, 2'04")

Maki (MK) is telling Fred (FR) about air conditioned classrooms at a private high school that her friend attended. According to her friend, during the summer, the classrooms were freezing cold because of the excessive air conditioning.

```
01 MK: reeboo           samusugiru  tte yut[te::.
       air conditioner too cold    QT  say-and
       "She says the air conditioner is too cold and"

02 FR:                                          [huun:,
                                                 oh, is that so
                                                 "Oh, is that so?"

03     (0.3)

04 MK: jugyoo[chuu  ni seetaa  kiteru [toka yut(h)]te(h)=
       during class in sweater wear     like say-and
       "says like 'I wear a sweater in class' and"

05 FR:       [soo    desu ne:.        [soo    desu ne:.]
              right  CP   ne           right  CP   ne
              "That's right. That's right."

06 MK: =h[::

07 FR:   [aa jaketto wa: ki[ru  ne,]
          ah jacket  TP  put on ne
          "Ah, they wear jackets, don't they?"

08 MK:                     [ryoohoo] soo soo:.=
                            both     right
                            "Both of them. That's right."

09 FR: =u:n.
        yeah
       "Yeah."
```

```
10      (0.2)

11 MK: hunde (n)an(ka) kooritsu no kookoo      no
       so      like      public   LK high school at
12     hito    wa[::. sugoku urayamashigatteta:.=
       people TP      very    envied
       "So, like, we at a public high school were very envious."

13 FR:          [un
                 yeah
                 "Yeah."

14 FR: =aa   hawai    mo:   ano:: onaji (.) ano
        uhm Hawai'i also well   same      well
       "Uhm, it's the same in Hawai'i. Well,"

((Fred continues to say that he would put on a jacket
in the classroom during the summer but feels hot
when he goes outside.))
```

While Fred's initial response to Maki's telling, *huun* [Oh, is that so?] (line 02), indicates that the telling has provided some information new to him (cf. Mori, 2006, on the use of a similar expression, *hee* [oh, I didn't know that]), he says *soo desu ne* [That's right] a little later (line 05). Fred's use of these contrastive responses can be interpreted in two ways. Considering his earlier response, *huun*, Fred could have misused the final particle *ne* in the phrase *soo desu ne*: that is, Fred should have used the phrase *soo desu ka* [Is that right?] in line 02 to acknowledge the new information. However, taking into consideration Fred's subsequent turns, it is more probable that, after acknowledging Maki's telling of her friend's experience, he realizes that the experience of being in a cold classroom is, actually, not unfamiliar to him. He first shows alignment with Maki's story by using the phrase *soo desu ne* in line 05, then displays his understanding of how an air-conditioned room can get too cold (line 07). His second story introduced in line 14 clarifies the ground on which he said *soo desu ne* in line 05: He also has experienced such cold classrooms in Hawai'i. I submit that what Fred proceeds to tell from line 14 onward is a second story to Maki's story. Although he clearly aligns his upcoming story with Maki's story by using the particle *mo* [also] and the lexical item *onaji* [same] (line 14), this second story about his experience in cold classrooms is not simply a reiteration of Maki's telling of envious feelings that she and her friends at a public school had toward students in private schools (lines 11, 12). In this light, the *ne*-ending comment in line 07 serves both as a supporting statement for the agreement made with *soo desu ne* and also as a preliminary to his second story.

In this excerpt, we have seen that Fred aligns with the previous telling with the use of the phrase *soo desu ne*, a *ne*-ending statement, and a second story. Compared to Excerpt 5, where the previous speaker is already in alignment with

Fred, the phrase *soo desu ne* by itself does not seem to be enough to show alignment. While the interactional function of *soo desu ne* is left ambiguous in Excerpt 6, Fred's subsequent turns make it clear in Excerpt 7. With regard to the aligning comment to which the particle *ne* is attached (line 07, Excerpt 7), Maki agrees to it by saying *ryoohoo* [both jackets and sweaters] and *soo soo* [That's right], which is uttered immediately after Fred says *ne*. Because Fred's *ne*-ending comment is showing alignment with Maki's story, an agreement in the next turn seems to be projected. Such projection of an agreement was also observed in three instances in FR7 where Fred used a *ne*-ending comment that aligns with the previous telling.

However, not all of Fred's *ne*-ending statements are in alignment with the interlocutor's earlier telling, as shown in Excerpt 8.

Excerpt 8, scenery in Arizona (FR7, 4/8/2005, 1'06")

Fred (FR), Derek (DR) and MK (Maki) are talking about the State of Arizona, where Derek is from. After Fred asks Derek what Arizona is famous for, Derek tells him that it is famous for its cactuses and hot weather, and continues his telling with the connective *kedo* [but].

01 DR: keshiki: ga (.) utsukushii.
scenery SB beautiful
"Its scenery is beautiful."

02 (0.3)

03 FR: soo,
right
"Is that so?"

04 (0.4)

05 DR: °un:.°
yeah
"Yeah."

06 (0.9)

07 FR: demo keshiki wa:: (0.2) ((sniff)) (1.0)
but scenery TP
08 nanimo arimasen **ne?**
nothing not exist ne
"But speaking of the scenery, there's nothing, right?"

09 (0.4)

```
10 DR: [ee::.
        yeah
        "Yeah."

11 MK: [uh hh [hh hh

12 FR:        [eh he he he he [he he he heh

13 DR:                        [(-zen)
                               (not at all)
14      sonna koto  na:i
        such  thing not exist
        "That's quite wrong."
```

After Derek positively comments on Arizona's scenery, Fred in line 03 utters a word, *soo* [right, correct], with a slightly rising tone, which sounds like saying, "Is that so?/Really?" Then, in lines 07 and 08, he presents an opposing view of Arizona's scenery by starting out with the contrastive connective *demo* [but] and ending with *ne*. Because this statement presents an opposite view to Derek's previous statement, Derek may make an upfront disagreement. However, he negates Fred's statement in line 14 only after saying *ee* [Yeah] 0.4 s after Fred's *ne*. Derek's response, *ee*, seems to convey two meanings. Produced with a falling tone, it can be a formal form of *yes*; yet being lengthened, it may indicate hesitation. In its sequential context, this utterance delays Derek's disagreement. Such a delayed response suggests that Fred's *ne*-ending evaluative comment in lines 07 and 08 projects an agreement as its preferred response, as seen in the structure of partial agreement after an assessment (Pomerantz, 1984).

Fred's use of *ne* with an oppositional statement, which is initiated with the connective *demo* [but], is also seen once in FR7 and once in FR8. In both of these instances, his interlocutors immediately responded with an affirmative response token (*ee*, *un*, and *soo soo*) before making disagreeing comments. This suggests the coerciveness of *ne* in this sequential position.

As we have analyzed so far, even though Fred seems to have been using *ne* to mark alignment with his interlocutor's previous telling because of its placement in aligning turns, he also used the particle to project upcoming alignment. Although his interlocutors could have chosen not to agree with his *ne*-ending statement, they used affirmative response tokens to delay their disagreements.

With an assessment about new information provided. As seen in Excerpt 8, Fred used *ne* when assessing an object that was found in the previous turn. Fred's use of a *ne*-ending assessment is also observed in response to a single word utterance with which his interlocutor provided new information without indicating his or her viewpoint. Excerpt 9 shows Fred's use of *ne* in such a sequential environment.

Excerpt 9, Shiga Prefecture (FR6, 3/8/2005, 0'48")

After talking about where he lives, Fred (FR) asks Yuko (YK) where she lives (line 1).

```
01 FR: docchi ni sundeimasu ka?
       which  in live        Q
       "Where do you live?"

02     (0.4)

03 YK: eeto: shiga-ken.=
       well  Shiga prefecture
       "Well, in Shiga prefecture."

04 FR: =shig[a-ken.
        Shiga  prefecture
       "Shiga prefecture"

05 YK:      [shiga-ken      [(tte)
             Shiga prefecture QT
             "A prefecture called Shiga."

06 FR:                      [aa:. tooii desu ne, (0.2)
                             oh   far   CP   ne
                             "Oh, it's far, isn't it?"

07 YK: ha:[i.=
       yes
       "Yes."

08 FR:    [(sugoi    oto   dashi-)[4] (0.3)
            horrible sound emit
       kyoo (1.2)
       today
09     ima wa: nanka tazunete imasu ka?
       now TP  like  visit-PROG     Q
       "It's a horrible sound. Today, are you, like,
       visiting now?"
```

In response to Fred's question in line 01, Yuko answers that she lives in Shiga prefecture. After repeating her answer without a pause (line 04), Fred makes an assessment about the information given (line 06) by attending to the distance between the prefecture and the place where they are having this conversation. Although Yuko in line 05 repeats her answer as if she is trying to check Fred's understanding, she discontinues her utterance when Fred claims his understanding by saying *aa* [oh]. Then, she agrees with Fred's *ne*-ending assessment by saying *hai* [yes]. Building on the agreement on the distance he brought up, Fred asks whether she is visiting the town on that day (lines 08, 09).

In this excerpt, Fred, with the use of a *ne*-ending assessment, gave a new meaning to the information that his interlocutor provided as an answer to his question and developed the conversation based on the perspective that they mutually agreed on in lines 04 and 07. Three more instances of such use of *ne* together with assessments were found: one in FR6 and two in FR7.

The use of *ne*-marked assessments after hearing new information is similar to what was reported in Ohta's (1999) study. In the initiation-response-follow-up sequence found in typical foreign language classrooms, teachers of Japanese use *ne* as in *ii desu ne* [Your answer is good] to evaluate the correctness of students' answers to display questions. In contrast, when teachers ask real questions about students' lives, such as places they go on weekends, their feedback to the answers are acknowledgments (e.g., *aa soo desu ka* [Oh, is that right?]) or assessments such as *omoshiroi desu ne* [That's interesting] and *ii desu ne*: [That's nice]. Ohta (1999, 2001) found that students in Japanese as a foreign language classrooms used a greater variety of utterances in the follow-up turn. In addition to the use of *ii desu ne*, which teachers would use to evaluate students' answers, Ohta found an increasing use of *ne*-ending assessments in the students' follow-up responses. However, one of the four students who participated in Ohta's study was found to misuse the phrase *soo desu ne* [That's right] in the follow-up turn. Fred also misused the phrase in FR6, as shown in Excerpt 10.

Excerpt 10, trip to America (FR6, 3/8/2005, 3'34")

```
After Fred (FR) tells a story about an old lady who went
to many foreign countries, he asks Yuko (YK) a question
(line 1).

01 FR: amerika itta koto  ga arimasu  ka?=
       America went thing SB there is Q
       "Have you been to America?"

02 YK: =a (.) arimasu
        uh    there is
       "Uh, I have."

03     (0.2)

04 FR: arimasu  k(a)=
       there is Q
       "You have."

05 YK: =a etto::. [losanzerus  to:[:.
        let me see Los Angeles and
       "Let me see, I've been to Los Angeles and"
```

```
06 FR:               [hai,            [aa. so- (.) desu ne:.
                      yes              oh  right   CP   ne
                      "Yes. Oh, that's right."

07 YK: rasu begasu.
       Las  Vegas
       "Las Vegas."

08 FR: ras begasu: ya  na:. (.)
       Las Vegas   CP  IP
09     ras begasu: wa doo datta?
       Las Vegas   TP how CP-PAST
       "I see, Las Vegas.  How was Las Vegas?"
```

In response to Fred's question of whether she has been to the United States, Yuko answers positively (line 02). In the follow-up turn, Fred acknowledges her answer by repeating *arimasu* [there is] and ending with a question marker *ka*, which indicates the receipt of new information in a falling tone. This acknowledgment serves as a continuer as Yuko' immediate elaboration of her answer in line 05 indicates. Fred also encourages the continuation of Yuko's answer by saying *hai* [yes] after she says *etto:* [umm, let me see]. After Yuko mentions the first city, Fred acknowledges the information by saying *aa* and adds *soo desu ne* [That's right]. As projected through the use of the connecting particle *to* [and] in line 05, Yuko in line 07 continues naming another city she has visited, thus treating Fred's response in line 06 as a continuer.

While we have analyzed the use of *soo desu ne* in a turn that aligns with the interlocutor's previous telling, the previous turn in this excerpt (line 05) presents new information that is ill-suited to be aligned with "that's right." The information could be acknowledged by saying *Aa, soo desu ka* [Oh, is that right?] or by adding *ka* after the repetition of the new information (Los Angeles *desu ka* [Oh, you've been to Los Angeles], as he did in line 04. If he wanted to show recognition of Los Angeles as a familiar place, he could have said *Aa, LA desu ne* [Oh, LA] instead of using *soo* [right].

The analysis of this excerpt suggests that providing an acknowledgment or an assessment in the follow-up turn requires the right choice of linguistic resources and the skill to anticipate the projected trajectory of the current speaker's turn to find the right moment to respond. The next excerpt shows that the timing of an assessment and the choice of linguistic resources are consequential for the interlocutor's treatment of the turn.

Excerpt 11, Maki's summer plan (FR8, 5/6/2005, 10'12")

In response to Fred's (FR) question about her summer plan, Maki (MK) says that she will be going on a trip to England. After Fred says *un* [yeah], she elaborates her answer by saying she will be going there together (line 1) with her friend if the friend can save enough money for the trip.

```
01 MK: isshoni  iku to omou.
       together go  QT think
       "I think we will go there together."

02     (0.4)

03 FR: °un.°
        yeah
       "Yeah."

04     (0.4)

05 MK: da[kara:]
       therefore
       "So,"

06 FR:   [°tano]shis[oo°
           sound-fun
           "That sounds fun."

07 MK:                  [moo sorosoro (.) keekaku-suru
                         soon soon        plan
                         "we will make a plan soon."

08     (0.2)

09 FR: un::. tanoshimi       ne:,=
       yeah  looking forward ne
       "Yeah. It's exciting, isn't it?"

10 MK: =u[n.
        yeah
       "Yeah."

11 FR:   [n heh heh.

12     (0.2)

13 MK: sugoi tanoshimi
       very  looking forward
       "I'm looking forward to it very much."
```

After Maki's elaborated answer about her summer plan comes to a short halt at the end of a turn constructional unit (TCU) in line 01, Fred says *un* in line 03. This token is taken as a continuer, as Maki's resumed telling in line 05 indicates. Meanwhile, as reflexively indicated by Fred's assessment that overlaps with Maki's utterance (line 06), *un* for Fred is not a continuer but an acknowledgement that has to come before making an assessment. Failing to make his assessment taken up as such, Fred in line 09 makes another assessment after saying *un*.

While his first assessment *tanoshisoo* [That sounds fun] is not responded to by Maki, who has already resumed her telling with *dakara* [therefore], his second assessment after *un* uttered at the end of a TCU (line 07) is responded with *un* by Maki and even upgraded in line 13.

Both of the two instances of Fred's assessment after *un* occurred at the end of a TCU (lines 01, 07), but only the second assessment was responded to and taken up as such by Fred's interlocutor. A question arises as to what the differences are between the two instances. The most noticeable difference is the presence of a 0.4-s pause (line 02) after the first acknowledgment token *un*, while the second instance has no pause. Second, the token *un* itself in the first instance is short (lasting 0.2 s) and uttered in a soft voice, while the second *un* (line 09) is much longer (lasting 0.4 s) and produced at regular speech volume. Although the verb form at the end of Maki's utterance in line 01 indicates the completion of a TCU and suggests a transition-relevance place, Fred's soft and short uttering of *un* followed by a short pause seems to indicate that he will not grab a turn for a further response. In addition, Fred utters the overlapped assessment (*tanoshisoo* [That sounds fun]) also in a soft voice, thus failing to claim it as a legitimate turn to be responded to. In contrast, Fred utters "*un::. tanoshimi ne:* [Yeah, it's exciting, isn't it?] in a normal voice quality and volume (line 09) at a transition-relevance place, making a legitimate acknowledgment and an assessment to be responded to. Because the word *tanoshimi* [looking forward] indicates Maki's state of mind, this assessment requires a confirmation from Maki that Fred's guess of her emotional state about the trip was right. Thus, Fred uses *ne* after *tanoshimi* as a linguistic resource that makes an upcoming confirmation relevant. The analysis of Excerpt 11 suggests that the timing, voice quality, choice of lexical item, and the use of *ne* all contribute to how an assessment gets acknowledged and responded to as such.

The particle *ne* is a useful linguistic resource to be used with an assessment in the follow-up turn because the speaker can project an upcoming alignment in the subsequent turn. As I have analyzed in this subsection, Fred in FR6 began to use *ne* in such a way (Excerpt 9). The analyses of Excerpts 10 and 11 have suggested that precise placement of the follow-up utterance and the choice of linguistic resources, including the use of *ne*, are important for successfully providing acknowledgments and assessments.

Within a longer telling. While previous subsections have analyzed Fred's use of *ne* immediately after his interlocutor's previous turns, his use of *ne* was also seen in longer tellings that present his viewpoint without being in direct response to his interlocutors' previous turns. Excerpt 12 is one of those instances.

Excerpt 12, speaking different varieties of English (FR7, 4/8/2005, 31'53")

```
Fred (FR), Derek (DR) and Maki (MK) are talking about
different varieties of English. Fred states that
```

because American people expect foreigners to speak American Standard English, if people used Australian English and British English, it would be strange.

01 FR: ano chotto okashii: (0.4) °to omou.°
um a little strange QT think-plain
"Um, it's a little strange, I think."

02 (0.2)

03 °to: omo[(imasu)°
QT think-polite
"I think so."

04 DR: [hyo- hyoogen.
expression
"Expression."

((4 lines omitted. Fred and Derek talk about the word "hyoogen." Then, there is a 0.9-s pause.))

09 FR: a nihon-jin wa: oosutoraria no yoo ni:.
um Japanese people TP Australia LK way in
10 hanashite imasu kedo aa. (.) hanas (0.6)
speak-PROG but uh speak-
11 hanas:seba:.
speak-if
"Um, Japanese people are speaking like Australians do but, uh, if they spea- speak that way,"

12 MK: °un.°
yeah
"Yeah."

13 DR: °un.°
yeah
"Yeah."

14 (0.8)

15 FR: chotto okashii **ne**,
a little strange ne
"it's a little strange, isn't it?"

16 (0.4)

17 MK: huu:n
uh-huh
"Uh huh."

18 (0.7)

```
19 DR: nan[ka
       like
       "Like,"

20 FR:     [a  amerika-jin    no  baai      wa.
           um America person LK  situation TP
           "Um, for Americans."

21     (0.3)

22 MK: u:n=
       humm
       "Humm."

23 FR: =un.
        yeah
       "Yeah."

24     (1.3)

25 DR: demo iro:nna (.) sekai: de:. (.) sekaijuu     de
       but  various     world  in        world-around in
26     ironna  nihongo  ga a- (.) aru   kara shikatanai
       various Japanese SB        exist so   nothing to do
       "But there're various Japanese in various places in
       the world, all over the world. So they must be allowed."
```

In this excerpt, Fred says *chotto okashii* [a little strange] twice (lines 01, 15). When he makes this statement for the first time, he adds *to omou* [I think that] in the plain form after a 0.4-s pause. Then in line 03, he again expresses the same epistemic stance by using the same verb but this time in the polite form (*to omoimasu*) after a 0.2-s pause. Receiving no response to his opinion statement from the hearers at each of these pauses, Fred seems to be extending the TCU until one of the hearers joins with a response. Although Derek eventually joins to say *hyoogen* [expression], this utterance does not show his position toward Fred's opinion.[5] Fred repeats the opinion statement ending with *ne* in line 15, after specifying the situation to which his opinion pertains (lines 09–11). Although he receives responses from both Maki and Derek, they are both delayed and not in agreement with Fred's opinion. Maki's delayed unenthusiastic response *huun* [uh-huh], which is produced in a monotone, acknowledges Fred's opinion without clarifying what she thinks about it (line 17). Derek, who starts telling something by saying *nanka* [like] in line 19, discontinues this turn when Fred starts adding a qualification to his earlier opinion (line 20) and restarts his telling with the contrastive connective *demo* [but] (lines 25, 26). Hearing Maki's rather indifferent response and Derek's incipient disagreement in lines 17 and 19, Fred in line 20 adds a qualification that limits the effect of his earlier statement. Although the use of a qualification does not elicit any clear agreement, such fine-tuning of his turn to Maki's and Derek's responses suggests that he is anticipating an agreement to his opinion when he repeats the opinion statement *chotto okashii* in line 15. Thus, Fred used *ne* in line 15 as a resource for pursuing an agreement, along with the use of the epistemic expression *to omou* [I think that], specification of the situation, repetition of the opinion statement, and a qualification.

In this excerpt, we have seen Fred's use of *ne* as a resource for pursuing an agreement from his listeners. This use of *ne* in a longer telling was observed five times in FR7.

Discussion: The development of Fred's use of *ne* as part of his interactional competence

As the analysis of Fred's use of *ne* in the previous section has shown, Fred used *ne* in a variety of sequential positions and with various interactional functions. Although his initial uses of *ne* in FR3–5 were very limited in frequency, a sudden expansion of its use was observed in FR6. The increase of the frequency in the use of *ne* during learners' stays in Japan has also been found in earlier L2 studies of *ne* (e.g., Shibahara, 2002).

Although the developmental path that Fred took is difficult to compare with the findings from other studies, its characteristics are worth discussing here. A large proportion of Fred's use of *ne* was found as part of the formulaic expression *soo desu ne*, which is consistent with the findings in Sawyer's (1992) and Yoshimi's (1999) studies. Note that Fred began using the phrase rather late, only from FR5, and that some of his early uses of *soo desu ne* were found in inappropriate contexts (FR6), as seen in Excerpt 10. Fred's relatively late start in using the phrase and his occasional misuse are consistent with the findings by Ohta (2001) and Yoshimi (1999): The formulaic expression is rarely used by beginning learners, and when they start to use it, its uses are often inappropriate. Although Sawyer (1992) concluded that "the acquisition of *ne* began with the formulaic expression *soo desu ne*" (p. 104), without examining the sequential contexts in which the phrase was used, we cannot rely on frequency counts to investigate "acquisition."

With regard to other uses of *ne*, the findings of the present study have a similarity with those of Shibahara (2002) and Mine (1995). Many of Fred's *ne*-ending turns are immediately responded to with an affirmative response *un* [yeah] or *hai* [yes] (e.g., Excerpts 1, 7–9, 11) even when the interlocutor disagrees later (Excerpt 8). Also, even when Fred's interlocutor does not agree with him, he is observed to use *ne* as a resource to pursue agreement (Excerpt 12). Shibahara (2002) also found that the use of *ne* that was responded to with agreement was most frequent, and Mine (1995) found that this use had a low percentage of misuse. On the other hand, they found that the use of *ne* in reporting turns, which can be exemplified by the one instance found in Excerpt 2, was observed less frequently (Shibahara) and with a high percentage of misuse (Mine). Although some learners may overuse *ne* in reporting turns as found in Mine's study, Fred's use of *ne* in his longer telling was selective and showed sensitivity to the sequential context.

While the findings of the present study have some similarities to those from earlier research, the comparison is based on a rough estimate of frequencies of different uses of *ne*, and such an approach does not deepen our understanding of the interactional competence that learners develop by using *ne* as a linguistic resource. Therefore, the excerpts we have analyzed in the previous section must be reviewed in their own right. The analysis of *ne* as used by Fred is shown in Table 1 in chronological order.

Table 1. Summary of Fred's uses of *ne*

session	initial instance of Fred's use of *ne*	excerpt
FR1	(not found)	
FR2	(not found)	
FR3	in introducing a topic, makes an aligning response as the relevant next turn	1
FR4	with an opinion statement, provides a space for the interlocutor to respond	2
FR5	*soo desu ne*: emphasizes confirmation that is made relevant with *deshoo*	3
FR6	*soo desu ne*: acknowledges the interlocutor's aligning comment	5
	soo desu ne: displays understanding; alignment is not clearly indicated	6
	soo desu ne: acknowledges information provided; misuses *soo* or *ne*	10
	with an assessment in response to a short answer, invites agreement	9
FR7	*soo desu ne*: shows agreement to a *ne*-ending statement	4
	with a contrasting statement, projects agreement as the preferred response	8
FR8	*soo desu ne*: shows alignment; alignment is made clear in subsequent turns	7
	with an assessment, makes an alignment in the next turn relevant	11
	with an opinion statement, pursues agreement	12

First, Fred began using *ne* in turns where he could take control over the trajectory of talk-in-interaction. In FR3, Fred used *ne* as a linguistic resource for achieving intersubjective understanding of the topic he introduced. In FR4, *ne* was used at the end of a TCU, which allowed his interlocutor to join in with a response in the middle of his narrative.

While Fred's earliest uses of *ne* were found in turns that did not require him to fine-tune his use of *ne* as an immediate response to the previous speaker's turn, the use of *ne* in a response turn was first found in FR5. In the form of *soo desu ne*, Fred in FR5 emphasized the confirmation that his interlocutor projected with the use of *deshoo* [I suppose, isn't it true?] (Excerpt 3). Fred later used *soo desu ne* also in response to the previous speaker's *ne*-ending turn, which made next turn agreement a relevant response (FR7, Excerpt 4). His uses of *soo desu ne* in these confirmation or agreement turns demonstrate his competence in using an appropriate phrase in the second part of an adjacency pair. Moreover, Fred was found to take the opportunity to elaborate on the information (FR5, Excerpt 3) and his opinion (FR7, Excerpt 4) after saying *soo desu ne.*

In FR6, Fred began using *ne*-ending responses not only in turns where aligning responses were made relevant but also in other sequential environments. For example, Fred used *soo desu ne* after his interlocutor made an aligning comment about Fred's narrative (Excerpt 5) and made a *ne*-ending assessment about the information his interlocutor provided as an answer to Fred's question (Excerpt 9). In some cases, his use of the phrase *soo desu ne* did not seem to fit the sequential environment (e.g., Excerpts 6, 10). Although previous studies (Ohta, 2001; Yoshimi, 1999) have also pointed out learners' inappropriate use of *soo desu ne*, the source of the inappropriateness may not be the use of *ne* per se. In Excerpts 6 and 10, the source of the problem might be the combination of linguistic resources such as *soo*, *ka,* and *ne* and the choice of epistemic stance markers. Moreover, when alignment had not been established in the preceding turns, the use of *soo desu ne* as the sole response did not seem to be enough for the current topic to develop further. Although the function of *soo desu ne* could be made clear through the actions in the subsequent turns (e.g., FR8, Excerpt 7), Fred was not capable of linguistically marking alignment in FR6.

In the final two conversations (FR7–8), the function of the phrase *soo desu ne* was made clear by Fred's subsequent turns. He began using *ne*-ending statements not only in turns where he had already displayed alignment (FR8, Excerpt 7) but also when presenting a view that contrasted with his interlocutor's previous statement (FR7, Excerpt 8). As we observed in Excerpt 12, he also began using *ne* as a resource to pursue agreeing responses to his opinion statements. His active pursuit of a mutually aligning view on a certain matter is also seen in his *ne*-ending assessment about his interlocutor's narrative (FR8, Excerpt 11). As these instances suggest, in later conversations, Fred was able to use *ne* not only to build his talk on the alignment already established in previous turns but also, by presenting his view with ne attached, to actively pursue alignment when it was absent.

As we have seen, Fred was found to use *ne* in a wider range of sequential contexts and take more active roles in developing a conversation through its use in his later conversations. While Fred's development of interactional competence can be thus understood through the comparison of his various uses of *ne* used in the longitudinally collected conversational data, I make some notes on the interpretation of the present findings. First, the situational set-up of the particular conversation affects the interactional roles that one can take, although interactional roles can also be negotiated locally. For example, the role of introducing topics was more or less assigned to Fred in FR3. Before the formal beginning of the conversation in Japanese started, his interlocutor, Maho, asked him in English, "Anything particular that you wanna talk about?" He replied, "Yeah. I'll bring it up." This exchange seems to have helped increase the opportunity for Fred to use *ne* in introducing topics. Because the interactional roles that Fred was able to play varied from conversation to conversation, the comparison of Fred's interactional competence in different conversations is constrained to a certain degree. However, by focusing on how Fred used the particle rather than relying on frequency counts, we were able to see how its interactional work expanded over time when Fred was engaged in different conversations.

While the opportunity to take a certain interactional role in a conversation was affected by the situational set-up and the relationship among the participants that they brought to the conversation, when we compared the actions that Fred accomplished in certain sequential positions, we were able to register a developmental change. For example, when we compare Excerpts 6 (FR6) and 7 (FR8) with regard to his use of *soo desu ne* as an aligning response to his interlocutor's previous telling, we find that in FR8 he was more competent in clarifying his aligning stance through the use of an additional statement and linguistic marking of his second story. Moreover, with regard to his competence in providing assessments, although Fred's first *ne*-ending assessment was found no earlier than in FR6 (Excerpt 9), he had already begun to provide assessments in FR3 without the use of *ne*. In FR3, at a possible completion of his interlocutor's narrative, Fred said *omoshiroi* [interesting], and after a 0.7-s pause, he said *soo soo soo* [right]. Compared to Excerpt 11 (FR8), in which Fred successfully gets a *ne*-marked assessment taken up as a legitimate assessment at a second attempt, his action after making an assessment in FR3 suggests that he was not capable of using *ne* as an interactional resource to mark an assessment.

Note that although the use of *ne* as a linguistic resource helped Fred become interactionally competent, its use itself does not determine his interactional competence. Rather, Fred's interactional competence is co-constructed in the ongoing interaction, as shown by Maho's subsequent action in the example given in the previous paragraph (FR3). Fred at first appears to be incompetent in providing an effective assessment because his assessment, *omoshiroi*, was not taken up as such in the next turn. However, his interlocutor, Maho, did take up Fred's assessment 0.3 s after he said *soo soo soo.* Her delayed response and weak agreement (*Omoshiroi kedo:. demo* [It's interesting but. But]) indicate that his use of *soo soo soo* was taken as emphasizing his assessment and thus as a pursuit of an agreement. Despite his rudimentary use of linguistic resources, Fred made an assessment and did get it taken up as such. Because collaborative work is involved in achieving an activity of making assessments (cf. Goodwin & Goodwin, 1987), a learner's interactional competence should be understood through careful analysis of each participant's contribution within the sequential unfolding of talk-in-interaction. The present study has investigated the development of Fred's interactional competence based on an analysis of how Fred contributed to the collaborative achievement of activities by using the particle *ne*.

Conclusion

Although *ne* is a versatile linguistic resource for engaging in conversations, previous L2 studies of this particle have not investigated how the use of *ne* enables learners to participate in social interaction more competently over time, except for Ohta's (2001) study. The present study has shown an expansion of the interactional work that one learner was able to engage in through the use of *ne* during his 9-month study abroad. The learner, who initially used the particle only in turns that do not require fine-tuning toward the previous speaker's turn, came to use it as an immediate response to the previous speaker's turn and became more active in pursuing aligning responses through its use. We saw in his later conversations how he used *ne* to state opinions that did not align with his interlocutor's previous telling and how his use of *ne* in assessments helped achieve mutual alignment with his interlocutors. Moreover, while his initial use of the phrase *soo desu ne* did not fit as a response to his interlocutor's previous turn at times, he became capable of adding comments to clarify what he was doing with the phrase and further developing his own telling to show alignment with his interlocutor's previous telling.

The present chapter has shown one way of investigating the development of an L2 learners' interactional competence by using CA. While this study comprehensively treated all the instances in which the focal learner used the particle *ne*, aggregated data analysis could also focus on a certain activity, such as the activity of making an assessment, as a unit of analysis. As shown in the discussion section, comparison of what the learner is doing with and without using the particle *ne* is another way of investigating how the use of this resource develops over time. However, by focusing on the learner's use of *ne*, this study showed how the learner became more competent in engaging in conversation by taking a variety of interactional roles.

Acknowledgements

I express my appreciation to the anonymous reviewers and the editors of this volume for their insightful comments and suggestions.

Notes

1 All participant names in this chapter are pseudonyms.

2 Although the use of *ne* here is not unnatural in itself, the utterance would sound more natural if an evidential marker *mitai* (seems) were added, as in *soo mitai desu ne* ('that's right, according to what I heard').

3 A negative form of a verb (*narenai* [cannot become]) is expected here because the adverb *anmari* requires *nai* [not] to mean "not so much."

4 The music in the jazz café where this conversation was recorded was very loud, especially at this moment of the conversation. It is thus highly plausible that Fred in line 8 is referring to the loud music.

5 By saying *hyoogen* [expression], Derek might have meant to say that expressions are different among different varieties of English. However, he could have mispronounced *hoogen* [dialect], a Japanese word that he could have provided for Fred to refer to different varieties of a language.

References

Clancy, P. M. (1986). The acquisition of Japanese. In D. Slobin (Ed.), *The cross-linguistic study of language acquisition* (pp. 373–524). Hillsdale, NJ: Erlbaum.

Cook, H. M. (1992). Meaning of non-referential indexes: A case study of the Japanese sentence-final particle *ne*. *Text, 12*, 495–522.

Firth, A., & Wagner, J. (1997). On discourse, communication, and (some) fundamental concepts in SLA research. *Modern Language Journal, 81*(3), 285–300.

Ford, C. E., & Mori, J. (1994). Causal markers in Japanese and English conversations: A cross-linguistic study of interactional grammar. *Pragmatics, 4*(1), 31–61.

Gardner, R., & Wagner, J. (Eds.). (2004). *Second language conversations: Studies of communication in everyday settings.* London: Continuum.

Goodwin, C., & Goodwin, M. (1987). Concurrent operations on talk: Notes on the interactive organization of assessments. *IPrA Papers in Pragmatics, 1*(1), 1–54.

Hall, J. K. (1995). "Aw, man, where you goin'?": Classroom interaction and the development of L2 interactional competence. *Issues in Applied Linguistics, 6*(2), 37–62.

He, A. W., & Young, R. (1998). Language proficiency interviews: Discourse approach. In R. Young & A. W. He (Eds.), *Talking and testing: Discourse approaches to the assessment of oral proficiency* (pp. 1–24). Philadelphia: John Benjamins.

Heritage, J. (1984a). A change-of-state token and aspects of its sequential placement. In M. Atkinson & J. Heritage (Eds.), *Structures of social action: Studies in conversation analysis* (pp. 299–345). Cambridge, UK: Cambridge University Press.

Heritage, J. (1984b). *Garfinkel and ethnomethodology.* Cambridge, UK: Polity Press.

Heritage, J. (2002). Oh-prefaced responses to assessments: A method of modifying agreement/disagreement. In C. E. Ford, B. A. Fox & S. A. Thompson (Eds.), *The language of turn and sequence* (pp. 196-224). Oxford: Oxford University Press.

Hutchby, J., & Wooffitt, R. (1998). *Conversation analysis: Principles, practices and applications*. Malden, MA: Blackwell.

Kamio, A. (1990). *Joohoo no nawabari riron: Gengo no kinooteki bunseki* [Theory of territory of information: Functional analysis of language]. Tokyo: Taishuukan.

Kamio, A. (1997). *Territory of information*. Amsterdam: John Benjamins.

Koshik, I. (2002). A conversation analytic study of yes/no questions which convey reversed polarity assertions. *Journal of Pragmatics, 34*, 1851–1877.

Masuoka, T. (1991). *Modariti no bunpoo* [Modal grammar]. Tokyo: Kuroshio.

Maynard, S. K. (1993). *Discourse modality: Subjectivity, emotion and voice in the Japanese linguistics.* Philadelphia: John Benjamins.

McGloin, N. H. (1990). Sex difference and sentence-final particles. In S. Ide & N. H. McGloin (Eds.), *Aspects of Japanese women's language* (pp. 23–41). Tokyo: Kuroshio.

Mine, F. (1995). Nihongo gakushuusha no kaiwa ni okeru bunmatsu hyoogen no shuutoku katei ni kansuru kenkyuu [Language acquisition: How learners acquire sentence endings]. *Nihongo Kyoiku, 86*, 65–80.

Mine, F., Takahashi, K., Kurotaki, M., & Ooshima, Y. (2002). Nihongo bunmatsu gyoogen no shuutoku ni kansuru ichi koosatsu: Shizen shuutoku-sha to kyooshitsu gakushuu-sha no jirei o moto ni [Acquisition of Japanese sentence final expressions: Cases of natural acquisition and classroom learning]. In *Dai-ni gengo to shite no nihongo no shizen-shuutoku no kanoosei to genkai* [Second language acquisition in natural settings] (pp. 64–85). Tokyo: Ochanomizu joshi daigaku daigakuin nihongo kyooiku koosu [Ochanomizu Women's University Graduate School Japanese Education course].

Mori, J. (1999). Well I may be exaggerating but.: Self-qualifying clauses in negotiation of opinions among Japanese speakers. *Human Studies, 22*, 447–473.

Mori, J. (2006). The workings of the Japanese token *hee* in informing sequences: An analysis of sequential context, turn shape, and prosody. *Journal of Pragmatics, 38*, 1175–1205.

Morita, E. (2003). *The Japanese interactional particles* ne *and* sa*: An analysis of their conditional relevance for conversation.* Unpublished doctoral dissertation, University of California, Los Angeles, CA.

Nguyen, H. T. (2004). *The development of communication skills in the practice of patient consultation among pharmacy students.* Unpublished doctoral dissertation, University of Wisconsin, Madison, WI.

Nittono, M. (2003). *Japanese hedging in friend-friend discourse.* Unpublished doctoral dissertation, Teachers College, Columbia University, NY.

Ochs, E., Schegloff, E. A., & Thompson, S. A. (Eds.). (1996). *Interaction and grammar.* New York: Cambridge University Press.

Ohta, A. S. (1999). Interactional routines and the socialization of interactional style in adult learners of Japanese. *Journal of Pragmatics, 31*, 1493–1512.

Ohta, A. S. (2001). *Second language acquisition process in the classroom: Learning Japanese.* Mahwah, NJ: Lawrence Erlbaum.

Pomerantz, A. (1984). Agreeing and disagreeing with assessments: Some features of preferred/dispreferred turn shapes. In M. Atkinson & J. Heritage (Eds.), *Structures of social action: Studies in conversation analysis* (pp. 57–101). Cambridge, UK: Cambridge University Press.

Sacks, H. (1995). *Lectures on conversation* (Vols. I and II). Oxford, UK: Blackwell.

Sawyer, M. (1992). The development of pragmatics in Japanese: The sentence-final particle *ne*. In G. Kasper (Ed.), *Pragmatics of Japanese as native and target language* (pp. 83–109). Honolulu, HI: Second Language Teaching & Curriculum Center, University of Hawai'i at Mānoa.

Schegloff, E. A. (1979). Identification and recognition in telephone conversation openings. In G. Psathas (Ed.), *Everyday language studies in ethnomethodology* (pp. 23–78). New York: Irvington.

Schegloff, E. A., Koshik, I., Jacoby, S., & Olsher, D. (2002). Conversational analysis and applied linguistics. *Annual Review of Applied Linguistics, 22*, 3–31.

Selting, M., & Couper-Kuhlen, E. (Eds.). (2001). *Studies in interactional linguistics.* Amsterdam: John Benjamins.

Shibahara, T. (2002). "Ne" no shuutoku: 2000/2001 chooki kenshuu OPI deeta no bunseki [Acquisition of "ne": Analysis of the OPI data during the 2000–2001 long-term training]. *Nihongo Kokusai Sentaa Kiyoo, 12*, 19–34.

Tanaka, H. (2000). The particle *ne* as a turn-management device in Japanese conversation. *Journal of Pragmatics, 32*, 1135–1176.

Uyeno, T. Y. (1971). *Study of Japanese modality: A performative analysis of sentence particles.* Unpublished doctoral dissertation, University of Michigan, Ann Arbor, MI.

Wong, J., & Olsher, D. (2000). Reflections on conversation analysis and nonnative speaker talk: An interview with Emanuel A. Schegloff. *Issues in Applied Linguistics, 11*(1), 111–128.

Yoshimi, D. R. (1999). L2 language socialization as a variable in the use of *ne* by L2 learners of Japanese. *Journal of Pragmatics, 31*, 1513–1525.

Young, R. (1999). Sociolinguistic approaches to SLA. *Annual Review of Applied Linguistics, 19*, 105–132.

Young, R. F., & Miller, E. R. (2004). Learning as changing participation: Discourse roles in ESL writing conferences. *Modern Language Journal, 88*(5), 519–535.

Index

A

B

C

D

J

K

M

N

O

P

Q

R

S

T

V

W

NATIONAL FOREIGN LANGUAGE RESOURCE CENTER
University of Hawai'i at Mānoa

Pragmatics & Language Learning

Gabriele Kasper, series editor

Pragmatics & Language Learning ("PLL"), a refereed series sponsored by the National Foreign Language Resource Center, publishes selected papers from the biannual International Pragmatics & Language Learning conference under the editorship of the conference hosts and the series editor. Check the NFLRC website for upcoming PLL conferences and PLL volumes.

PRAGMATICS AND LANGUAGE LEARNING VOLUME 11

KATHLEEN BARDOVI-HARLIG, CÉSAR FÉLIX-BRASDEFER, & ALWIYA S. OMAR (EDITORS), 2006

This volume features cutting-edge theoretical and empirical research on pragmatics and language learning among a wide-variety of learners in diverse learning contexts from a variety of language backgrounds (English, German, Japanese, Persian, and Spanish) and target languages (English, German, Japanese, Kiswahili, and Spanish). This collection of papers from researchers around the world includes critical appraisals on the role of formulas in interlanguage pragmatics and speech-act research from a conversation-analytic perspective. Empirical studies examine learner data using innovative methods of analysis and investigate issues in pragmatic development and the instruction of pragmatics.

430 pp., ISBN(10): 0-8248-3137-3, ISBN(13): 978-0-8248-3137-0 $30.

NFLRC Monographs

Richard Schmidt, series editor

Monographs of the National Foreign Language Resource Center present the findings of recent work in applied linguistics that is of relevance to language teaching and learning (with a focus on the less commonly-taught languages of Asia and the Pacific) and are of particular interest to foreign language educators, applied linguists, and researchers. Prior to 2006, these monographs were published as "SLTCC Technical Reports."

ordering information at nflrc.hawaii.edu

CASE STUDIES IN FOREIGN LANGUAGE PLACEMENT: PRACTICES AND POSSIBILITIES

THOM HUDSON & MARTYN CLARK (EDITORS), 2008

Although most language programs make placement decisions on the basis of placement tests, there is surprisingly little published about different contexts and systems of placement testing. The present volume contains case studies of placement programs in foreign language programs at the tertiary level across the United States. The different programs span the spectrum from large programs servicing hundreds of students annually to small language programs with very few students. The contributions to this volume address such issues as how the size of the program, presence or absence of heritage learners, and population changes affect language placement decisions.

201pp., ISBN 0-9800459-0-8 $40.

CHINESE AS A HERITAGE LANGUAGE: FOSTERING ROOTED WORLD CITIZENRY

AGNES WEIYUN HE & YUN XIAO (EDITORS), 2008

Thirty-two scholars examine the socio-cultural, cognitive-linguistic, and educational-institutional trajectories along which Chinese as a Heritage Language may be acquired, maintained and developed. They draw upon developmental psychology, functional linguistics, linguistic and cultural anthropology, discourse analysis, orthography analysis, reading research, second language acquisition, and bilingualism. This volume aims to lay a foundation for theories, models, and master scripts to be discussed, debated, and developed, and to stimulate research and enhance teaching both within and beyond Chinese language education.

280pp., ISBN 978-0-8248-3286-5 $40.

PERSPECTIVES ON TEACHING CONNECTED SPEECH TO SECOND LANGUAGE SPEAKERS

JAMES DEAN BROWN & KIMI KONDO-BROWN (EDITORS), 2006

This book is a collection of fourteen articles on connected speech of interest to teachers, researchers, and materials developers in both ESL/EFL (ten chapters focus on connected speech in English) and Japanese (four chapters focus on Japanese connected speech). The fourteen chapters are divided up into five sections:

- What do we know so far about teaching connected speech?
- Does connected speech instruction work?
- How should connected speech be taught in English?
- How should connected speech be taught in Japanese?
- How should connected speech be tested?

290 pp., ISBN(10) 0-8248-3136-5, ISBN(13) 978-0-8248-3136-3 $38.

CORPUS LINGUISTICS FOR KOREAN LANGUAGE LEARNING AND TEACHING

ROBERT BLEY-VROMAN & HYUNSOOK KO (EDITORS), 2006

Dramatic advances in personal-computer technology have given language teachers access to vast quantities of machine-readable text, which can be analyzed with a view toward improving the basis of language instruction. Corpus linguistics provides analytic techniques and practical tools for studying language in use. This volume provides both an introductory framework for the use of corpus linguistics for language teaching and examples of its application for Korean teaching and learning. The collected papers cover topics in Korean syntax, lexicon, and discourse, and second language acquisition research, always with a focus on application in the classroom. An overview of Korean corpus linguistics tools and available Korean corpora are also included.

265 pp., ISBN 0-8248-3062-8 $25.

NEW TECHNOLOGIES AND LANGUAGE LEARNING: CASES IN THE LESS COMMONLY TAUGHT LANGUAGES

Carol Anne Spreen (Editor), 2002

In recent years, the National Security Education Program (NSEP) has supported an increasing number of programs for teaching languages using different technological media. This compilation of case study initiatives funded through the NSEP Institutional Grants Program presents a range of technology-based options for language programming that will help universities make more informed decisions about teaching less commonly taught languages. The eight chapters describe how different types of technologies are used to support language programs (i.e., Web, ITV, and audio- or video-based materials), discuss identifiable trends in elanguage learning, and explore how technology addresses issues of equity, diversity, and opportunity. This book offers many lessons learned and decisions made as technology changes and learning needs become more complex.

188 pp., ISBN 0-8248-2634-5 $25.

AN INVESTIGATION OF SECOND LANGUAGE TASK-BASED PERFORMANCE ASSESSMENTS

James Dean Brown, Thom Hudson, John M. Norris, & William Bonk, 2002

This volume describes the creation of performance assessment instruments and their validation (based on work started in a previous monograph). It begins by explaining the test and rating scale development processes and the administration of the resulting three seven-task tests to 90 university level EFL and ESL students. The results are examined in terms of (a) the effects of test revision; (b) comparisons among the task-dependent, task-independent, and self-rating scales; and (c) reliability and validity issues.

240 pp., ISBN 0-8248-2633-7 $25.

MOTIVATION AND SECOND LANGUAGE ACQUISITION

Zoltán Dörnyei & Richard Schmidt (Editors), 2001

This volume—the second in this series concerned with motivation and foreign language learning—includes papers presented in a state-of-the-art colloquium on L2 motivation at the American Association for Applied Linguistics (Vancouver, 2000) and a number of specially commissioned studies. The 20 chapters, written by some of the best known researchers in the field, cover a wide range of theoretical and research methodological issues, and also offer empirical results (both qualitative and quantitative) concerning the learning of many different languages (Arabic, Chinese, English, Filipino, French, German, Hindi, Italian, Japanese, Russian, and Spanish) in a broad range of learning contexts (Bahrain, Brazil, Canada, Egypt, Finland, Hungary, Ireland, Israel, Japan, Spain, and the US).

520 pp., ISBN 0-8248-2458-X $25.

A FOCUS ON LANGUAGE TEST DEVELOPMENT: EXPANDING THE LANGUAGE PROFICIENCY CONSTRUCT ACROSS A VARIETY OF TESTS

THOM HUDSON & JAMES DEAN BROWN (EDITORS), 2001

This volume presents eight research studies that introduce a variety of novel, non-traditional forms of second and foreign language assessment. To the extent possible, the studies also show the entire test development process, warts and all. These language testing projects not only demonstrate many of the types of problems that test developers run into in the real world but also afford the reader unique insights into the language test development process.

230 pp., ISBN 0-8248-2351-6 $20.

STUDIES ON KOREAN IN COMMUNITY SCHOOLS

DONG-JAE LEE, SOOKEUN CHO, MISEON LEE, MINSUN SONG, & WILLIAM O'GRADY (EDITORS), 2000

The papers in this volume focus on language teaching and learning in Korean community schools. Drawing on innovative experimental work and research in linguistics, education, and psychology, the contributors address issues of importance to teachers, administrators, and parents. Topics covered include childhood bilingualism, Korean grammar, language acquisition, children's literature, and language teaching methodology. [in Korean]

256 pp., ISBN 0-8248-2352-4 $20.

A COMMUNICATIVE FRAMEWORK FOR INTRODUCTORY JAPANESE LANGUAGE CURRICULA

WASHINGTON STATE JAPANESE LANGUAGE CURRICULUM GUIDELINES COMMITTEE, 2000

In recent years the number of schools offering Japanese nationwide has increased dramatically. Because of the tremendous popularity of the Japanese language and the shortage of teachers, quite a few untrained, non-native and native teachers are in the classrooms and are expected to teach several levels of Japanese. These guidelines are intended to assist individual teachers and professional associations throughout the United States in designing Japanese language curricula. They are meant to serve as a framework from which language teaching can be expanded and are intended to allow teachers to enhance and strengthen the quality of Japanese language instruction.

168 pp., ISBN 0-8248-2350-8 $20.

FOREIGN LANGUAGE TEACHING & MINORITY LANGUAGE EDUCATION

KATHRYN A. DAVIS (EDITOR), 1999

This volume seeks to examine the potential for building relationships among foreign language, bilingual, and ESL programs towards fostering bilingualism. Part I of the volume examines the sociopolitical contexts for language partnerships, including:

- obstacles to developing bilingualism
- implications of acculturation, identity, and language issues for linguistic minorities.
- the potential for developing partnerships across primary, secondary, and tertiary institutions

Part II of the volume provides research findings on the Foreign language partnership project designed to capitalize on the resources of immigrant students to enhance foreign language learning.

152 pp., ISBN 0-8248-2067-3 $20.

DESIGNING SECOND LANGUAGE PERFORMANCE ASSESSMENTS

John M. Norris, James Dean Brown, Thom Hudson, & Jim Yoshioka, 1998, 2000

This technical report focuses on the decision-making potential provided by second language performance assessments. The authors first situate performance assessment within a broader discussion of alternatives in language assessment and in educational assessment in general. They then discuss issues in performance assessment design, implementation, reliability, and validity. Finally, they present a prototype framework for second language performance assessment based on the integration of theoretical underpinnings and research findings from the task-based language teaching literature, the language testing literature, and the educational measurement literature. The authors outline test and item specifications, and they present numerous examples of prototypical language tasks. They also propose a research agenda focusing on the operationalization of second language performance assessments.

248 pp., ISBN 0-8248-2109-2 $20.

SECOND LANGUAGE DEVELOPMENT IN WRITING: MEASURES OF FLUENCY, ACCURACY, & COMPLEXITY

Kate Wolfe-Quintero, Shunji Inagaki, & Hae-Young Kim, 1998, 2002

In this book, the authors analyze and compare the ways that fluency, accuracy, grammatical complexity, and lexical complexity have been measured in studies of language development in second language writing. More than 100 developmental measures are examined, with detailed comparisons of the results across the studies that have used each measure. The authors discuss the theoretical foundations for each type of developmental measure, and they consider the relationship between developmental measures and various types of proficiency measures. They also examine criteria for determining which developmental measures are the most successful and suggest which measures are the most promising for continuing work on language development.

208 pp., ISBN 0-8248-2069-X $20.

THE DEVELOPMENT OF A LEXICAL TONE PHONOLOGY IN AMERICAN ADULT LEARNERS OF STANDARD MANDARIN CHINESE

Sylvia Henel Sun, 1998

The study reported is based on an assessment of three decades of research on the SLA of Mandarin tone. It investigates whether differences in learners' tone perception and production are related to differences in the effects of certain linguistic, task, and learner factors. The learners of focus are American students of Mandarin in Beijing, China. Their performances on two perception and three production tasks are analyzed through a host of variables and methods of quantification.

328 pp., ISBN 0-8248-2068-1 $20.

NEW TRENDS & ISSUES IN TEACHING JAPANESE LANGUAGE & CULTURE

HARUKO M. COOK, KYOKO HIJIRIDA, & MILDRED TAHARA (EDITORS), 1997

In recent years, Japanese has become the fourth most commonly taught foreign language at the college level in the United States. As the number of students who study Japanese has increased, the teaching of Japanese as a foreign language has been established as an important academic field of study. This technical report includes nine contributions to the advancement of this field, encompassing the following five important issues:

- Literature and literature teaching
- Technology in the language classroom
- Orthography
- Testing
- Grammatical versus pragmatic approaches to language teaching

164 pp., ISBN 0-8248-2067-3 $20.

SIX MEASURES OF JSL PRAGMATICS

SAYOKO OKADA YAMASHITA, 1996

This book investigates differences among tests that can be used to measure the cross-cultural pragmatic ability of English-speaking learners of Japanese. Building on the work of Hudson, Detmer, and Brown (Technical Reports #2 and #7 in this series), the author modified six test types that she used to gather data from North American learners of Japanese. She found numerous problems with the multiple-choice discourse completion test but reported that the other five tests all proved highly reliable and reasonably valid. Practical issues involved in creating and using such language tests are discussed from a variety of perspectives.

213 pp., ISBN 0-8248-1914-4 $15.

LANGUAGE LEARNING STRATEGIES AROUND THE WORLD: CROSS-CULTURAL PERSPECTIVES

REBECCA L. OXFORD (EDITOR), 1996, 1997, 2002

Language learning strategies are the specific steps students take to improve their progress in learning a second or foreign language. Optimizing learning strategies improves language performance. This groundbreaking book presents new information about cultural influences on the use of language learning strategies. It also shows innovative ways to assess students' strategy use and remarkable techniques for helping students improve their choice of strategies, with the goal of peak language learning.

166 pp., ISBN 0-8248-1910-1 $20.

TELECOLLABORATION IN FOREIGN LANGUAGE LEARNING: PROCEEDINGS OF THE HAWAI'I SYMPOSIUM

MARK WARSCHAUER (EDITOR), 1996

The Symposium on Local & Global Electronic Networking in Foreign Language Learning & Research, part of the National Foreign Language Resource Center's 1995 Summer Institute on Technology & the Human Factor in Foreign Language Education, included presentations of papers and hands-on workshops conducted by Symposium participants to facilitate the sharing of resources, ideas, and information about all aspects of electronic networking for foreign language teaching and research, including electronic discussion and conferencing, international cultural exchanges, real-time communication and simulations, research and resource retrieval via the Internet, and research using networks. This collection presents a sampling of those presentations.

252 pp., ISBN 0–8248–1867–9 $20.

LANGUAGE LEARNING MOTIVATION: PATHWAYS TO THE NEW CENTURY

Rebecca L. Oxford (Editor), 1996

This volume chronicles a revolution in our thinking about what makes students want to learn languages and what causes them to persist in that difficult and rewarding adventure. Topics in this book include the internal structures of and external connections with foreign language motivation; exploring adult language learning motivation, self-efficacy, and anxiety; comparing the motivations and learning strategies of students of Japanese and Spanish; and enhancing the theory of language learning motivation from many psychological and social perspectives.

218 pp., ISBN 0–8248–1849–0 $20.

LINGUISTICS & LANGUAGE TEACHING: PROCEEDINGS OF THE SIXTH JOINT LSH-HATESL CONFERENCE

Cynthia Reves, Caroline Steele, & Cathy S. P. Wong (Editors), 1996

Technical Report #10 contains 18 articles revolving around the following three topics:

- Linguistic issues–These six papers discuss various linguistic issues: ideophones, syllabic nasals, linguistic areas, computation, tonal melody classification, and wh-words.
- Sociolinguistics–Sociolinguistic phenomena in Swahili, signing, Hawaiian, and Japanese are discussed in four of the papers.
- Language teaching and learning–These eight papers cover prosodic modification, note taking, planning in oral production, oral testing, language policy, L2 essay organization, access to dative alternation rules, and child noun phrase structure development.

364 pp., ISBN 0–8248–1851–2 $20.

ATTENTION & AWARENESS IN FOREIGN LANGUAGE LEARNING

Richard Schmidt (Editor), 1996

Issues related to the role of attention and awareness in learning lie at the heart of many theoretical and practical controversies in the foreign language field. This collection of papers presents research into the learning of Spanish, Japanese, Finnish, Hawaiian, and English as a second language (with additional comments and examples from French, German, and miniature artificial languages) that bear on these crucial questions for foreign language pedagogy.

394 pp., ISBN 0–8248–1794–X $20.

VIRTUAL CONNECTIONS: ONLINE ACTIVITIES & PROJECTS FOR NETWORKING LANGUAGE LEARNERS

Mark Warschauer (Editor), 1995, 1996

Computer networking has created dramatic new possibilities for connecting language learners in a single classroom or across the globe. This collection of activities and projects makes use of email, the internet, computer conferencing, and other forms of computer-mediated communication for the foreign and second language classroom at any level of instruction. Teachers from around the world submitted the activities compiled in this volume—activities that they have used successfully in their own classrooms.

417 pp., ISBN 0-8248-1793-1 $30.

DEVELOPING PROTOTYPIC MEASURES OF CROSS-CULTURAL PRAGMATICS

THOM HUDSON, EMILY DETMER, & J. D. BROWN, 1995

Although the study of cross-cultural pragmatics has gained importance in applied linguistics, there are no standard forms of assessment that might make research comparable across studies and languages. The present volume describes the process through which six forms of cross-cultural assessment were developed for second language learners of English. The models may be used for second language learners of other languages. The six forms of assessment involve two forms each of indirect discourse completion tests, oral language production, and self-assessment. The procedures involve the assessment of requests, apologies, and refusals.

198 pp., ISBN 0-8248-1763-X $15.

THE ROLE OF PHONOLOGICAL CODING IN READING KANJI

SACHIKO MATSUNAGA, 1995

In this technical report, the author reports the results of a study that she conducted on phonological coding in reading kanji using an eye-movement monitor and draws some pedagogical implications. In addition, she reviews current literature on the different schools of thought regarding instruction in reading kanji and its role in the teaching of non-alphabetic written languages like Japanese.

64 pp., ISBN 0-8248-1734-6 $10.

PRAGMATICS OF CHINESE AS NATIVE & TARGET LANGUAGE

GABRIELE KASPER (EDITOR), 1995

This technical report includes six contributions to the study of the pragmatics of Mandarin Chinese:

- A report of an interview study conducted with nonnative speakers of Chinese; and
- Five data-based studies on the performance of different speech acts by native speakers of Mandarin—requesting, refusing, complaining, giving bad news, disagreeing, and complimenting.

312 pp., ISBN 0-8248-1733-8 $15.

A BIBLIOGRAPHY OF PEDAGOGY & RESEARCH IN INTERPRETATION & TRANSLATION

ETILVIA ARJONA, 1993

This technical report includes four types of bibliographic information on translation and interpretation studies:

- Research efforts across disciplinary boundaries—cognitive psychology, neurolinguistics, psycholinguistics, sociolinguistics, computational linguistics, measurement, aptitude testing, language policy, decision-making, theses,

dissertations;
- Training information covering program design, curriculum studies, instruction, school administration;
- Instruction information detailing course syllabi, methodology, models, available textbooks; and
- Testing information about aptitude, selection, diagnostic tests.

115 pp., ISBN 0-8248-1572-6 $10.

PRAGMATICS OF JAPANESE AS NATIVE & TARGET LANGUAGE

GABRIELE KASPER (EDITOR), 1992, 1996

This technical report includes three contributions to the study of the pragmatics of Japanese:

- A bibliography on speech act performance, discourse management, and other pragmatic and sociolinguistic features of Japanese;
- A study on introspective methods in examining Japanese learners' performance of refusals; and
- A longitudinal investigation of the acquisition of the particle ne by nonnative speakers of Japanese.

125 pp., ISBN 0-8248-1462-2 $10.

A FRAMEWORK FOR TESTING CROSS-CULTURAL PRAGMATICS

THOM HUDSON, EMILY DETMER, & J. D. BROWN, 1992

This technical report presents a framework for developing methods that assess cross-cultural pragmatic ability. Although the framework has been designed for Japanese and American cross-cultural contrasts, it can serve as a generic approach that can be applied to other language contrasts. The focus is on the variables of social distance, relative power, and the degree of imposition within the speech acts of requests, refusals, and apologies. Evaluation of performance is based on recognition of the speech act, amount of speech, forms or formulæ used, directness, formality, and politeness.

51 pp., ISBN 0-8248-1463-0 $10.

RESEARCH METHODS IN INTERLANGUAGE PRAGMATICS

GABRIELE KASPER & MERETE DAHL, 1991

This technical report reviews the methods of data collection employed in 39 studies of interlanguage pragmatics, defined narrowly as the investigation of nonnative speakers' comprehension and production of speech acts, and the acquisition of L2-related speech act knowledge. Data collection instruments are distinguished according to the degree to which they constrain informants' responses, and whether they tap speech act perception/comprehension or production. A main focus of discussion is the validity of different types of data, in particular their adequacy to approximate authentic performance of linguistic action.

51 pp., ISBN 0-8248-1419-3 $10.